The Batsford
Companion to
MEDIEVAL
ENGLAND

The Batsford
Companion to
MEDIEVAL
ENGLAND

NIGEL SAUL

Batsford Academic and Educational Ltd
London

Typeset by Deltatype, Ellesmere Port, South Wirral
and printed in Great Britain by
Butler & Tanner Ltd,
Frome, Somerset
for the publishers
Batsford Academic and Educational Ltd
4 Fitzhardinge Street
London W1H 0AH

British Library Cataloguing in Publication Data

Saul, Nigel
  The Batsford companion to medieval England.
  1. Great Britain—History—Medieval period—
  1066–1485
  I. Title
  942   DA175

ISBN 0 7134 1345 x

List of Plates

1 Durham Cathedral: interior of the nave, 1099–1128 (*A. F. Kersting*).

2 Canterbury Cathedral: interior of the choir, 1175–84, designed by William of Sens and completed by William the Englishman.

3 Wells Cathedral: south transept looking into the nave, c. 1175–80. Note the carvings of the man with toothache and the man removing a thorn from his foot among the foliage capitals at the top of the right-hand pillar.

4 Westminster Abbey: the choir, 1245–60. Gothic of the Ile-de-France style interpreted by Henry III's masons in an English idiom (*A. F. Kersting*).

5 Gloucester Cathedral: the choir, c. 1337–67. The earliest surviving large-scale work in Perpendicular (*Edwin Smith Collection*).

6 King's College Chapel, Cambridge: begun in 1443 and not completed until the following century (*A. F. Kersting*).

7 a) Stewkley, Bucks: a vaulted Norman chancel.
  b) Dinton, Bucks: Early English lancets.
  c) Elsing, Norfolk. Reticulated Tracery, c. 1340.

8 a) Cruck cottage at Didbrook, Gloucs.
  b) Interior of the Guildhall, Leicester, c. 1347. The trusses are of cruck construction (*Dixon Scott Collection, Public Record Office*).

9 Manor-house of 'upper-hall' design at Bosham, Sussex, as depicted on the Bayeux Tapestry. Harold and his retinue are having dinner before setting out on the journey that was to take them to William's court in Normandy (*Mansell Collection*).

10 a) Stokesay Castle, Salop: the hall range, begun c. 1285.
  b) Little Wenham, Suffolk: built c. 1270–80. On the left is the hall, on the right the chapel with solar above (*A. F. Kersting*).

11 Brass of Sir Robert de Bures, engraved c. 1320, Acton, Suffolk.

12 Brasses of Sir Reginald de Malyns and his two wives, 1385, Chinnor, Oxon: London style 'B' (*British Museum*).

13 a) Brasses of Sir Hugh Halsham and his wife, 1441, West Grinstead, Sussex: London style 'B'.
  b) Brasses of Sir William Etchingham and his wife and son, 1444, Etchingham, Sussex: London style 'B'. Note how similar these two brasses are (*Victoria and Albert Museum*).

14 Brass of Sir Thomas Brounflete, 1430, Wymington, Bedfordshire: London Style 'D'.

15 Brasses of Robert Ingleton and his three wives, 1472, Thornton, Bucks: one of the most lavish products of London style 'D'.

16 Brasses of William and Marion Grevel, 1401, Chipping Campden, Gloucs: London style 'B' (*The National Monuments Record*).

17 a) Silver penny of William the Conqueror, 1066–87 (*British Museum*).
   b) Silver penny of Edward I, 1272–1307: 'long-cross' issue (*British Museum*).
   c) Gold noble of Edward III, 1344 (*British Museum*).
   d) Gold sovereign of Henry VII, 1485–1509 (*British Museum*).

18 Foundation charter of New Minster, Winchester, showing King Edgar, 959–75, offering the charter to Our Lord (*British Library*, MS Vespasian A. VIII).

19 Initial 'B' from the Psalms in the Winchester Bible, *c.* 1160–70, showing Christ driving out the evil spirits (above) and rescuing souls from Hell (below). (*The Dean and Chapter of Winchester*).

20 Scenes from the Book of Genesis, from a Bible picture leaf by W. de Brailes, *c.* 1230–50 (*Reproduced by permission of The Syndics of the Fitzwilliam Museum, Cambridge*).

21 St Omer Psalter, the Beatus page, executed *c.* 1325 for members of the St Omer family of Mulbarton, Norfolk, whose portraits appear in the row of medallions at the foot (*British Library* Add. MS 39810).

22 The Luttrell Psalter, *c.* 1340: Sir Geoffrey Luttrell of Irnham, Lincs., being armed by his wife and daughter (*British Library* Add. MS 45130).

23 The Wilton Diptych, *c.* 1380–90 (*Reproduced by courtesy of the Trustees, The National Gallery, London*).

24 Sherborne Abbey Missal, *c.* 1400: detail from the border (*Collection of the duke of Northumberland*). *Photo: George Skipper*.

25 The Lovel Lectionary, *c.* 1400: the artist, John Sifrewast, presenting his book to John, Lord Lovel (*British Library*, Harley MS 7026).

26 Tinted drawing of John Lydgate presenting his poem *The Pilgrim* to Thomas Montacute, earl of Salisbury (*British Library*, Harley MS 4826).

27 a) The south door of Kilpeck Church, Heref., *c.* 1140–5.
   b) Details from the arch of the south door at Kilpeck.

28 The font at Castle Frome, Heref., *c.* 1170. On the left is the Baptism of Christ. Then come a pair of doves. On the right is the Bull of St Luke, the first of a series of the signs of the Four Evangelists which fills up the remaining space.

29 The Bellfounders Window, York Minster, *c.* 1320–30, given by Richard Tunnoc, who is shown in the lower central panel kneeling before St William of York. The scene on his right shows bell-casting, and on his left probably tuning (*The National Monuments Record*).

30 St Peter Mancroft, Norwich, *c.* 1430–55, the chancel and east window (*A. F. Kersting*).

31 Lady Howard, *c.* 1485, one of a row of benefactors in the windows of the north aisle of Long Melford Church, Suffolk.

32 The Shambles at York, a view taken early this century.

List of Figures

1 The site of the Battle of Bannockburn, 1314. *31*

2 a) Pleshey, Essex: a typical motte-and-bailey castle. *55*
  b) *Lewes, Sussex: an unusual variation combining two mottes with a single bailey.* *56*

3 How Edward I recruited labour for the building of his castles in North Wales after the 2nd Welsh War, 1282–3 *(by permission of the Controller of Her Majesty's Stationery Office).* *58*

4 Beaumaris, Anglesey, 1295–c. 1330, where the concentric plan attained perfection *(Public Record Office).* *59*

5 St Mary's Abbey, Sherborne: ground plan of a Benedictine monastery. *179*

6 Fountains Abbey: the Cistercian plan. The long range on the west side of the cloister contains the cellarium below and the lay brothers' dormitory above. *180*

7 Diagram showing the main English roads in the mid-fourteenth century, derived from the Gough map in the Bodleian Library (Cambridge University Press, *A New Historical Geography of England,* ed. H. C. Darby, 1973). *Photo: Bodleian Library.* *222*

8 European Trade routes in the 1470s. *260*

Appendixes

I Kings of England 1066–1485. *280*
II Archbishops of Canterbury 1070–1500. *280*

Tables

I William the Conqueror and his Children. *281*
II Henry II and his Descendants. *282*
III Edward II and his Descendants. *283*

Acknowledgements

The author and publishers would like to thank the museums, libraries and copyright holders listed on pp. 5–7 for permission to reproduce individual illustrations. They would also like to thank the President and Council of the Royal Historical Society and Professor E. B. Fryde for permission to reproduce the lists of archbishops of Canterbury (Appendix II) from the *Handbook of British Chronology*, ed. F. M. Powicke & E. B. Fryde, 2nd edition 1961.

Preface

Until about a generation ago it used to be possible for a teacher of
medieval history to acquaint himself with near enough all of the
literature written in his field. Art history and literature could be left to
the experts in their separate fields, but certainly the main currents of
social and political development could be mastered. With the seemingly
inexorable increase in the flow of publications, however, it has become
more and more difficult for a single person to cover the whole field;
and if a specialist finds it difficult to keep up, how much more so must
the interested outsider.

We need to have the fruits of modern research made available if we are
to piece together a picture of the past that makes sense to our own age.
But we should resist the temptation to bury ourselves in our own little
corner of the field and to write as if we were writing only for other
scholars. Society at large supports a now considerable army of
professional historians because of the widespread popular interest taken
in history. And a very healthy interest it is too. Each generation asks
its own questions about the past, and its understanding of the past is a
part of its coming to terms with the present. The professional
historian, therefore, has a responsibility to offer the fruits of his own
research in an intelligible way to society, and if he does not he is failing
in his task.

It is considerations of this nature that I have borne in mind while
writing this book. My purpose has been to produce a reference work to
which a non-specialist, though not just a non-specialist, may turn with
profit and with pleasure. I have aimed to bring together articles
discussing a wide range of aspects of medieval society and its legacy
with us today. Inevitably decisions about selection have had to be made
to prevent the book from becoming too unwieldy. Some subjects have
lent themselves to fairly brief treatment – definitions of technical
terms, for example. Others on more general themes have merited
lengthier discussion – art and architecture, and government and
literature, for example. Still, much has had to be left out. Readers,
particularly those with some knowledge of the middle ages already,

may find that their own speciality has been omitted, or if included, then treated no more than cursorily. I can only plead in mitigation that I had to draw the line somewhere.

Again in the interests of brevity I have had to keep bibliographical references to a minimum. For the shorter entries they are omitted altogether. For the longer articles they are intended to do no more than indicate a book or article which can serve as the point of departure for further enquiry.

In the course of writing a book as comprehensive in its scope as this one, I have myself learned much that I did not know before. My own professional interests lie in the political and social history of the late middle ages. When I venture outside that area, therefore, I become more than usually dependent on the advice and guidance of others. In particular I would like to single out for thanks Dr M. F. Wakelin, Professor J. S. C. Riley-Smith, Mr D. Hiley, Dr C. B. Lucas, Professor M. L. Samuels and Mr John Harvey. But along the way I have incurred many debts, more no doubt than I can now consciously recognize. I hope that those whose teaching has influenced me over the years will find their reward in the wider dissemination of history for which I have pleaded. For if this book serves to encourage its readers to ask more questions about the medieval past and to explore more widely in search of answers, then it will have served its purpose.

Royal Holloway College,   *Nigel Saul*
University of London
January 1982

ADVOWSON The right of a patron to fill a vacant benefice was known as the right of advowson. English law regarded an advowson as a piece of property which, like any other property, could be bought or sold or inherited. If a lord had built a church on his estates, it followed that he and his descendants should enjoy the right of nominating the parson. By the twelfth century, however, the canon lawyers had arrived at a different view. They claimed that a church belonged to the saint to whom it was dedicated, and that cases of disputed patronage should, in the words of Pope Alexander III, 'only be decided by judgement of the Church and settled before an ecclesiastical judge'. In England Henry II (q.v.) rejected this novel interpretation, and in the Constitutions of Clarendon restated the older view that disputes over advowsons should be heard in the royal courts. Neither side was ever formally to abandon its position. But in the late 1170s, after Becket's (q.v.) murder, Henry issued a writ prohibiting the hearing in church courts of pleas relating to advowsons, and thereafter the clergy seem tacitly to have accepted that they could do little to stop the king dealing with such cases if he insisted. The Church was less successful in recovering jurisdiction over the filling of benefices in England than it was in other parts of Europe.

AGINCOURT Agincourt was one of those battles, characteristic of the Hundred Years War, that the English succeeded in winning against all odds. In pursuit of his claim to the crown of France, Henry V (q.v.) had landed at the mouth of the Seine in August 1415, and besieged the port of Harfleur. But what he had hoped would prove an easy triumph turned into a lengthy and dispiriting affair. There was an outbreak of dysentery, and when the town finally surrendered on 22 September, it was a much depleted English force that was left wondering what to do next. Henry decided to make a dash for Calais — a bold decision, but one justified by the knowledge that France was bitterly divided between the Burgundian and Armagnac factions. He hoped they would never unite to challenge him. In the event, however, they did, and near Agincourt on 25 October they forced him to offer battle. The French fielded an army of perhaps 40,000 men, against Henry's 6,000. But their overwhelming numerical superiority availed them little because they were confined by the surrounding woods to advancing along a narrow front, and then only at a speed that left them an easy prey for the English archers. Agincourt was perhaps the greatest English victory of the Hundred Years War (q.v.); yet strategically it was insignificant. It enabled Henry to return in triumph; but it brought him no nearer to winning the French crown. To do that he had to embark on the systematic conquest of Normandy (q.v.) two years later.

AGRICULTURE Medieval England was a predominantly agrarian society. Most of its people lived in the countryside and derived their living from the soil. Patterns of settlement varied of course from one part of the country to another. The densely settled lowlands of the Midlands and south were characterized by the compact nucleated vill, the hills and moors of the north and west by dispersed homesteads and farms. It was the classic nucleated vill of the Midland Plain which lay at the centre of the well-known 'open-field' system of cultivation. Information casting any light on the early history of the open fields is so sparse as to leave the question of their origins not only unanswered but probably unanswerable. Suffice it here to say that charter evidence suggests that the main characteristics of the 'open-field' system were in existence in some parts of England as early as the tenth century. Just what were these characteristics?

The arable land of the village would be divided into two or three large fields, on which a scheme of crop rotation would be operated. One field would be given over to winter-sown crops, a second to spring-sown crops, and the third left uncultivated, to allow it to recover fertility in time for next year's sowing. Each of the fields would be divided into furlongs, and each of the furlongs into strips known as selions. Within each field some of the strips would be held by the tenants of the village and some held 'in demesne' (q.v.) by the manorial lord. Whether the demesne lands would usually be scattered indiscriminately throughout the fields or concentrated in one locality is hard to say in the absence of any number of early maps or surveys. At Cuxham (Oxon), however, a policy of purchase and exchange had succeeded in bringing the demesne arable together into two compact blocks of land. The system of co-operative agriculture that applied to the crop-growing fields applied also to the meadowland, which would similar-ly be divided into strips.

Like all such generalizations, this picture of open-field agriculture is subject to all manner of qualifications. To start with, as we have seen, it applies largely to Midland England. Secondly, the number of fields varied from village to village and from one part of the country to another. There is reason to believe that, under pressure of growing population, in many villages there was a movement from a two- to a three-field system in the thirteenth century, the point being that only a third and not a half of the available arable would then be left fallow each year. Finally, and again possibly as a response to the growing population pressure, we find additional fields being created and brought under cultivation on the edge of the village. These were known as the 'outfields', as opposed to the 'infields' or long-established arable fields nearer the centre of the settlement. We should not imagine that the outfields came necessarily to form a permanent feature of the scene. On the contrary, we would do better to visualize a shifting line of cultivation at the margin, as land was brought under the plough whenever it was needed.

What sort of crops were grown on the fields of a medieval village? It used to be thought that the three-field organization of the arable necessarily implied a three-course rotation of crops. Of course, in many cases it did. Thus one field would be sown in winter with wheat. Another would be sown in spring with rye or barley; and (assuming there were three fields) the third would be left fallow. But a three-course rotation could be practised on a two-field system, and similarly a four-course one on a three-field system. Cropping schemes could be based on the unit of the furlong rather than that of the field, allowing, for example, winter wheat to be sown in one field and a combination of legumes and barley in the next. By the procedure known as 'inhoking' legumes could also be planted in the field that under previous arrangements would be left fallow. Schemes of crop rotation could therefore become quite complex. Indeed, they had to be, if the village was to grow all the crops it needed — wheat for sale on the open market, barley for brewing, oats for fodder and so on. But what were crop yields like in the middle ages? By comparison with modern expectations they were very low. For wheat a likely yield was eight or nine bushels an acre, or little more than a quarter of the expected yield today. Medieval agriculture simply did not have the manures, the technical resources, available to the modern farmer to raise productivity, and the soil became exhausted as a result.

The century which best illustrates the system we have just described is the thirteenth. This was the age of 'high farming'. The high prices and low wages encouraged by the steady rise in population were an inducement to landlords to run their demesnes at full capacity. After the Black Death, however, conditions changed. The labour shortage led to a rise in wages. And in the 1370s prices began to fall. The movement of prices and wages, in other words, spelled the end of large-scale demesne husbandry as it had been known in the thirteenth century. Lords who had once been active entrepreneurs now preferred to lease their demesnes, usually in parcels to the tenants of the village.

The implications for agrarian society were far-reaching. In the late middle ages the market was supplied not by big producers like the Benedictine monasteries but by smaller proprietors who added to their holdings by acquiring parcels of the demesne. By running smaller estates than those of the great landlords they were able to cut overheads, and by preventing their estates from becoming too big they were able to economize on labour. These were the days when the yeoman farmer was starting to make his mark on the scene.

Land use was probably becoming more varied in the late middle ages too. Now that cereal prices were lower than they had been a century earlier, landowners began to look for other ways of making a profit. Many of them turned to livestock. John Brome of Baddesley Clinton (Warks) specialized in fattening cattle for sale to local butchers and on occasion to London dealers as well. If Brome made his money supplying the meat trade, other landowners made theirs supplying principally the wool and cloth merchants. They turned their lands over to sheep. They did so less because they envisaged large profits — the price of wool was by and large depressed in the late middle ages — than because sheep grazing carried fewer hazards than cereal growing. In particular, it was economical on labour at a time when labour was in short supply.

So sheep, as contemporaries complained, took the place of people. Whole villages disappeared. If any one part of England suffered worse than the others from the effects of depopulation in the early sixteenth century, it seems to have been the East Midlands. At Charwelton and Fawsley in Northamptonshire, for example, the existence of a former settlement is testified by the sight of the parish church standing alone in the fields. Striking though the transformation in parts of the Midland landscape may have been, the hardship it caused scarcely justified the complaint that the sheep were eating up the people. The villages that disappeared were ones that were already on the wane. Depopulation was an act of desperation, not of oppression, on the part of landlords.

Studies of Field Systems in the British Isles, ed. A. R. H. Baker & R. Butlin, Cambridge, 1973.
A New Historical Geography of England, ed. H. C. Darby, Cambridge,1973.

AILRED OF RIEVAULX   The coming of the first Cistercian monks (q.v.) opened a new chapter in the history of northern England. Their simplicity and austerity, their uncompromising rejection of the values of material life, found an ideal setting in the rugged contours of northern society. Among those who responded to their appeal was Ailred, a young man of about 25 when in 1134 he was sent by the king of Scotland on an embassy to Archbishop Thurstan of York. On his way back he stayed at Helmsley, to see the community of monks recently established by Walter l'Espec on a site in the Rye valley later to become famous as Rievaulx. The next day Ailred passed Rievaulx again. This time he went no further. He chose instead to join the monks in their life of solitude.

The new recruit had spent his younger years at the Scottish court, where he became a life-long friend of King David I (q.v. Scotland). In 1143 he was appointed abbot of Revesby (Lincs), a dependent cell of Rievaulx, but four years later he was recalled to become abbot of the mother house itself. He remained in that office until his death on 11 January 1167. Ailred's saintly personality left its mark on the life of the community at Rievaulx. As Dom David Knowles once wrote,

gentleness, radiance of affection and wide sympathy are not the qualities we normally associate with the early Cistercians, but they are the ones that Ailred possessed to the full. He has been described as the St Bernard of the North. Like Bernard he was the intimate friend of kings and princes. But unlike Bernard he was never a controversialist. He was an active writer, indeed a prolific one when we remember the busy life he led and the physical pain he suffered during his later years. But the strength of his compositions lies in their warmth and sincerity, not in the compelling force of their arguments. Ailred lived by setting an example. That he did not labour in vain is evidenced by the loving tribute paid by the monk Walter Daniel in his biographical *Life of Ailred of Rievaulx*.

Walter Daniel's Life of Ailred Abbot of Rievaulx, ed. F. M. Powicke, Nelson's Medieval Classics, 1950.

AMERCEMENT   In the middle ages a fine incurred in a court was known as an amercement, because an offender had to purchase the mercy of the lord whose peace he had broken. By the twelfth century an unsuccessful litigant in the courts would also be amerced for bringing what turned out to be a false plea (q.v. JUSTICE).

ANSELM   Justly regarded as one of the most saintly men ever to have occupied the see of Canterbury, Anselm was first and foremost a thinker and only on the insistence of others an ecclesiastical administrator.

He was born at the Alpine town of Aosta in 1033, the son of genteel parents who had rather come down in the world. In 1056, after the death of his mother, he abandoned the town of his birth in favour of the life of a wandering scholar. Why he chose to go to France rather than south into Italy we cannot say. Was it the fame of the great Lanfranc (q.v.) at Bec that attracted him? All we can say is that it was to the abbey of Bec that he was admitted as a monk in 1060. He succeeded Lanfranc as prior three years later, and became abbot in 1078. Intellectually he owed a lot to Lanfranc, with whom he continued to correspond after his departure to England in 1070 on appointment as Archbishop of Canterbury. Indeed, after Lanfranc's death in 1089 he was regarded in some quarters as the natural successor in the chair of St Augustine. King William Rufus (q.v.), however, was hardly interested in making a quick appointment so long as he could himself enjoy the revenues of Canterbury during the vacancy, and it was not until 1093 that he was brought to accept Anselm's election.

But Rufus was not the only man who viewed the prospect with dismay. Anselm himself did. He was a child in the world of high politics. And Rufus was the very last man to appreciate the qualities of a saintly and unworldly archbishop. 'You are yoking an untamed bull and a weak old sheep', was the way Anselm described their relationship. How right he was. One dispute cropped up after another. By 1097 Anselm had had enough. He went into exile.

After Rufus's death in 1100, he returned to England. From then on the dispute took a rather different course. The new king, Henry I (q.v.), asked Anselm to do homage for the lands which he held as a tenant-in-chief. Anselm refused, because at the Easter Council he had attended at Rome in 1099 the clergy were forbidden by the pope both to do homage for ecclesiastical honors (q.v. Feudalism) and to accept investiture from laymen. These were the measures of independence for which the Church was fighting in what was to become known in Europe as the 'Investiture Contest'. But Anselm was hardly interested in arguing the merits of the case. For him it was a matter of obedience to the pope. Accordingly he resumed his exile. Messengers went to and fro, and embassies were sent to Rome, but not until 1105 was there any sign of movement. Frightened by the excommunication of some bishops who had received investiture from his hands, Henry went to meet Anselm at Laigle in Normandy. Rather surprisingly, agreement was reached. The king was to retain homage, but to forego investiture. It may not have been a settlement to Anselm's liking, but once it had received the pope's blessing, there was little he could do but accept. He returned to England in September 1106.

Though he was able to devote the last few years of his life (he died on 21 April 1109) to tackling abuses that he found in the English Church, he was not a practical reformer in the mould of Lanfranc. He had made his reputation as a philosopher and theologian. His first two important works were the *Monologion* and *Proslogion*, written in 1077 and 1078 respectively. It is in the latter work that he gives his famous argument for the existence of God. He begins by defining God as a being than whom no greater can exist. According to the fool in the Psalms (13, 1) however, there is no God. But in order to say that, the fool must have an idea in his own mind of what God is. Now, for a Platonist like Anselm it was impossible to conceive of something in one's mind if it did not exist in reality. Therefore a being than whom no greater can exist must exist. In that case we could think of a being greater than God. That would be logically impossible. Therefore God must exist. It is a tribute to the power of Anselm's argument that philosophers can still argue about his proof to this day.

R. W. Southern, *St Anselm and his Biographer*, Cambridge, 1963.

APPEAL Until the fifteenth century the common law offered two main ways of bringing a malefactor to justice – appeal or indictment by jury. Appeal was the older procedure, requiring the appellant to pursue his charge against the appellee by personal appearance in the county court, and to justify it if need be by judicial combat. However, so many procedural pitfalls lay in the path of the unsuspecting appellant that few appeals terminated in resort to arms.

The process of appeal was also employed to bring charges of treason in parliament. It was used apparently for the first time in the Good Parliament of 1376 by Sir John Annesley. It was taken up again in 1388 when Richard II's (q.v.) opponents were seeking a way to indict the king's favourites after the judges had declared in the previous year that the newly-forged weapon of impeachment (q.v.) could not be used against ministers without royal permission. The 'Appellant' lords therefore brought appeals of treason against de Vere and the other favourites which were heard in the Merciless Parliament of 1388, regardless of the absence of four of the accused.

APPROPRIATION An ecclesiastical benefice was said to have been appropriated when it passed into the ownership of a community such as a monastery, which became the corporate rector and entrusted the cure of souls to a stipendiary known as a vicar (q.v. TITHES).

ARCHITECTURE, ECCLESIASTICAL The great cathedrals and churches of northern Europe are the most outstanding monuments the middle ages have passed down to us. In some of our smaller cities we can still visualize how a vast cathedral must have dominated the lives of those who lived under its shadow; even so, a secular age such as our own can hardly begin to understand the instincts of piety which led to such enormous enterprises. We can only share with our medieval forbears the feeling of awe experienced on entering somewhere of the enduring greatness of Durham or York Minster.

When the Normans landed in England in 1066, the prevailing architectural style was Romanesque. Churches were solid and their interiors only dimly lit by the sunshine that penetrated the small, round-headed windows. Though it was a style common to all of Europe, local variations of Romanesque were developed in different parts of Europe, not least in the duchy of Normandy where Jumièges Abbey (consecrated in 1067) provided the inspiration for the churches that were to be built in England after the Conquest. Like the Roman invaders before them (but unlike the Anglo-Saxons) the Normans were builders on a grand scale. The newly appointed Norman bishops, like Walkelin at Winchester, demolished the episcopal churches of their Saxon predecessors, and replaced them with buildings monumental in scale, bigger even than those they had known at home. What above all characterized these cathedrals of the first century after the Conquest was the emphasis on length. At Peterborough Abbey, for example, the nave was ten bays long, at Ely and St Alban's 13, and at Norwich no less than 14. The sensation of length we experience on looking at these naves is emphasized by the strongly horizontal division of the interior elevation. Above the main arcade which separates the nave from the aisles on each side is the triforium (or tribune) and above it in turn, the clerestory. Thus a view eastwards along the nave of Ely Cathedral conveys an impression of slow and regular rhythm, arch upon arch, until finally the eye reaches the Octagon, a towering creation of the fourteenth century, where the upward thrust of Gothic suddenly takes over.

The juxtaposition of styles that is so characteristic of the English cathedrals, and nowhere more than at Ely, teaches us an important lesson. If it is a horizontal movement which distinguishes Norman architecture, it is vertical movement which marks Gothic. Paradoxically, though, most of the elements which went to make up Gothic were present well before their time in the greatest Romanesque cathedral ever built in Europe – Durham (plate 1). Between 1093 and 1130 the masons at Durham erected a church which was without equal in its day for dignity, nobility and architectural sophistication. For the interior elevation the architect employed pairs of bays, in which a pillar of multiple shafts alternates with a mighty cylinder ornamented with patterns. The proportions of Durham are also more satisfying than those of most Norman cathedrals. The triforium is smaller, and for once the horizontal emphasis yields to the verti-

cal in a way that foreshadows the Gothic age. Where Durham most strikingly anticipates the later builders, however, is in its conception of a stone rib-vault, using the pointed arch, to cover the central aisle of the church.

Yet, much as it suggested the shape of things to come, the example of Durham was not followed. It remained an isolated masterpiece. When we come to consider the origins of Gothic architecture in England, we have to look not northwards to the river Wear but across the Channel to France. It was there that the earliest truly Gothic buildings were erected. They were characterized of course by their use of the pointed arch, an architectural form brought to Europe from the Islamic East at the time of the First Crusade (1096–99). Among the first to take it up were the Burgundian Cistercians, yet without any indication that they were aware of the revolutionary implications of what they were doing. The earliest churches to produce a new synthesis based on the pointed arch and the high-level stone rib vault were therefore not those of the early Cistercians but Sens Cathedral (begun c. 1135) and the abbey of St Denis (c. 1135–44) in the Ile de France.

It was this French interpretation of early Gothic which the mason, William of Sens, brought to England in 1174 when he was commissioned to design a new choir for Canterbury Cathedral (plate 2). This is a free adaptation of the style with which William was already familiar at Sens. Its direct influence was to be confined to the retrochoir at Chichester (1187–99) and St Hugh's Choir at Lincoln (1192–1200). But in its extensive use of Purbeck marble shafts set against a light coloured stone it set a fashion which was to be immensely popular in England in the thirteenth century.

Perhaps the Canterbury choir was too strongly influenced by French ideas to gain wide acceptance in England. For meanwhile in the Severn Valley, an area always apt to go its own way architecturally, a quite separate approach to Gothic was being made, and one that in the long run was to prove more significant for the future. In about 1175 the western bays of the nave of Worcester Cathedral were rebuilt to a design which, curiously mongrel though it is, anticipates English Gothic more strongly than the Canterbury choir had done. For example, the round pillars of Canterbury had been discarded in favour of the 'clustered' or multi-shafted piers that English architects were to prefer. The ideas tried out at Worcester were taken up and developed further in the transepts and nave at Wells Cathedral, begun in 1192 and the first purely English Gothic design. Adam Lock, the master mason, brought together the clustered pier, pointed arch and high-level stone vault in an aesthetically satisfying combination enriched by the liveliest set of capitals to be found in any of our cathedrals (q.v. SCULPTURE) (plate 3). Then in about 1230 Wells was given its superb west front, the nearest we can come in England to the great sculpture galleries which adorn the French cathedral fronts.

The work at Wells overlapped with the rebuilding of Salisbury Cathedral on an entirely new site in the valley of the Wiltshire Avon. Salisbury is the classic cathedral of the Early English style – the term by which we know the phase of Gothic that lasted from c. 1180 to c. 1260. The earliest parts – in particular the Lady Chapel – are astonishingly slender for their date, and make profuse use of Purbeck marble. The cathedral was lit by the standard lancet windows of the period, arranged in groups of two or three. It was built to an agreed design throughout in less than forty years, which was quick for the middle ages (1220–58); but before it had reached completion, England was exposed once again to a wave of French influence in the form this time of the newly-rebuilt Westminster Abbey. Inspired by his devotion to the cult of St Edward the Confessor, and seeking to give the English kings a coronation church which could match that of the French Kings at Rheims, Henry III (q.v.) began replacing the Confessor's original church in 1245 with a building consciously modelled on the latest French designs of the day. For example, his master mason, Henry de Reynes (who may or may not have been a Frenchman) rejected the traditional English square east end in favour of the semi-circular or 'apsidal' scheme. Moreover, the heavy use he made of flying buttresses externally and the strong vertical emphasis internally were both French characteristics found in few English churches of the day (plate 4).

How did the design of Henry's Westminster Abbey influence English architecture? As with the equally revolutionary choir at Canterbury three-quarters of a century earlier, its more enduring legacy lay in details rather than in overall design. The apsidal lay-out at the east end was never favoured by English masons, who preferred the square-ended plan for the opportunity it gave to insert an enormous east window. On the other hand, the striking triangular windows in the aisles of the Abbey were adopted at Hereford and Lichfield Cathedrals, and the beautiful angels high up in the transepts may well have provided the inspiration for the celebrated Angel Choir at Lincoln (1256–80). Equally important was the introduction from France, or from Rheims to be precise, of the latest style of window tracery. In a word, Westminster saw the replacement of plate tracery with bar tracery. By plate tracery we mean the grouping of a couple of lancets together with an aperture above, all carved as if they were separate openings in the wall. At Westminster, however, the windows consisted of two lancets surmounted by a circular light so arranged that they all form a single window (plate 4). The stone separating the two lancets was reduced to a mere bar known as a mullion, and the circular foil in the head marks the point of departure for the elaborate forms of tracery we meet in the 'Decorated' period (c. 1280–c. 1350) of Gothic (plate 7c).

By the time the Angel Choir at Lincoln was being built, English architecture had in fact already passed into 'Decorated'. It was characterized by a desire 'to do everything to break up, or rather dissolve, the lines of a composition'.* Several devices were called upon to achieve this end. In the West Country the masons were fond of 'ball-flower' ornament. This was a small rose bud form of decoration used with profusion on the central tower of Hereford and around the windows of Leominster Priory. Another form favoured by English sculptors in this period was the ogee arch, the double curved arch which was employed in wood on choir stalls and in stone on window tracery and wall niches. In the Lady Chapel of Ely in the 1330s the creative ability of the sculptors reached new heights with the invention of the 'nodding ogee': in this the double curved ogee arches which form an arcade

round the wall reach outwards as well as upwards, so as to give a lovely wavy effect to the composition. If the Lady Chapel is the most luxuriant artistic creation of the Decorated period, the Octagon at Ely must rank as the most adventurous. When the central tower collapsed in 1322, it was decided to cover the crossing not with another conventional tower but with an octagonal lantern, thus giving Ely a silhouette unique in English cathedral architecture. It has been said that seen from afar the long outline of Ely, with its tall western tower at one end and the Octagon in the middle resembles nothing so much as a ship in full sail on the seas.

Sooner or later there was bound to be a reaction against all this richness and frivolity. It came in the 1340s and 1350s, when Decorated gave way to Perpendicular (c. 1350–c. 1500). The traditional English liking for linear effect reasserted itself to produce buildings marked by a simple emphasis on the straight line. For the earliest surviving large-scale work in the new style we must go to Gloucester Cathedral, where the choir and transepts were reconstructed between 1331 and 1367. The result was revolutionary. The masons did not rebuild the old Norman choir; they remodelled it, paring down the stone surface and covering it with a network of transoms and mullions to produce a simple grid design (plate 5). The strong vertical emphasis which characterizes Perpendicular was present therefore right at the beginning. So too was another essential element of the new style – a feeling for spatial unity. In the choir of Gloucester the traditional plan which conceived of a church as divided into three parallel aisles was abandoned in favour of altogether excluding the aisles from sight behind the stone

* G. Webb, *Architecture in Britain: The Middle Ages*, p. 124.

19

panelling. Thus the interior of Gloucester strikingly anticipates King's College Chapel, Cambridge, where spatial unity was attained within the structure of a single aisleless hall (plate 6).

Where did the builders of Gloucester derive their inspiration from? Though the south transept at Gloucester is the earliest surviving example of the new style, certain of is features were anticipated in buildings which have since been destroyed. Of these the most important was St Stephen's Chapel, Westminster, which sadly, except for the crypt, was consumed with the rest of the Palace of Westminster in the fire of 1834. St Stephen's was begun in 1292, and not finished until three-quarters of a century later. From old illustrations we know that its upper chapel was an aisleless hall illuminated on each side by tall windows. Between the window heads the stonework was decorated with the kind of panelling later taken up at Gloucester and elsewhere. Gloucester Perpendicular was therefore a court style exported to the provinces. And unlike Early English and Decorated, it was to remain a distinctively English style that found no counterpart across the Channel. France moved on to the aptly-named Flamboyant style, exuberant and over-florid. England opted instead for an art of line. Perpendicular is as good a name for it as any.

By the time the finishing touches were being put on the alterations at Gloucester, two other large-scale works were under way – the naves of Winchester (1360–c. 1450) and Canterbury (1379–1405), both of which rank among the great achievements of English architecture. By the middle of the fifteenth century, when Winchester was finished, most of our major churches had been completed, and there was little

more to be done. York minster, for example, was reconsecrated in 1472 after building activities begun in 1290 which many of the city's inhabitants could be forgiven for thinking would never come to an end. Some of the best Perpendicular architecture, therefore, is to be found not in the cathedrals, to which we have devoted most of our attention so far, but in royal chapels like King's College, Cambridge, St George's, Windsor, and of course in the parish churches. During the fifteenth century few of our churches escaped rebuilding or enlargement. Clothiers in East Anglia, wool merchants in the Cotswolds, burgesses in the towns, captains returning enriched from the battlefields of France – one and all stored up treasure in heaven by improving God's houses on earth.

The parish churches of fifteenth century England have certain features in common. The old cruciform ground plan disappeared in favour of the simpler one of chancel, nave and tall west tower. But that apart, there was plenty of scope for regional variation, and we can find local schools of masons operating in localities like Yorkshire, the Cotswolds and East Anglia (plate 38). The churches of Chipping Campden, Northleach, Chipping Norton and Cirencester are the work of a school of masons who may well have relied for patronage on the great abbeys of the Severn Valley. Their style differed markedly, for example, from that of the masons of Devon and Cornwall, whose churches had three aisles of equal height, dispensing with the traditional clerestory altogether.

With the onset of the Reformation in the 1530s church building in England all but ceased. We must of course remember that although our churches and cathedrals had assumed the architectural form we see today, internally they presented a very different appearance. A medieval church was a blaze of colour. Its windows were filled with stained glass (q.v.) – and stained glass far more satisfying to the eye than the dreadful Victorian substitute that fills places like Ely today. But a modern eye would take far less kindly to the painted decoration which, as far as we can judge, filled every available inch of the walls. The large blank spaces were covered with scenes from the lives of patron saints, which like the windows served to instruct the faithful. But smaller spaces were painted as well, in vivid whites and reds, and sculptured details were picked out in gold. All this today we would regard as vulgar, but it satisfied the delight which medieval people found in bright and contrasting colours, whether in painting (q.v.), embroidery or jewellery.

See also, BUILDING; WYNFORD, WILLIAM; YEVELE, HENRY.

G. F. Webb, *Architecture in Britain: the Middle Ages* (Pelican History of Art), Harmondsworth, 1956; J. Harvey, *English Cathedrals*, Batsford, 1950.

ARCHITECTURE, VERNACULAR

Medieval domestic architecture is a house in which there are many mansions. Even if we exclude castles (q.v.) on the grounds that they were designed to serve military as well as domestic needs, we are still left with a wide range of house-types, extending from the manor-houses of the gentry to the cottages of the peasantry, all of which can be described as vernacular in the sense that they are traditional forms of dwelling sharing certain common architectural characteristics. Moreover, at the end of the middle ages we can identify local vernacular types, such as the distinctive Wealden houses erected by the prosperous yeomen of Kent and Sussex.

Architectural styles in whatever society we choose to study are influenced by the building materials available for use. So it was in the case of medieval peasant housing. On the eve of the Conquest, and for several centuries after, in lowland England the peasant house would have consisted of a light timber frame cut from the local woodlands, filled with clay or wattle and daub and roofed with thatch. In highland England, on sites such as those excavated at Hound Tor and Hutholes in Devon, stone took the place of the timber frame. What evidence there is, mainly collected from deserted village sites, suggests that the insubstantial timber dwelling would have needed rebuilding every generation or so. It was this consideration perhaps, rather than an improved standard of living, that led to peasant houses in many parts of the country being rebuilt in the thirteenth century. The kind of dwelling that has been uncovered in excavations is known from its shape as the 'long-house'. Extending to anything up to 100′ from end to end, it incorporated under a single roof the peasant's living area, a storage room and a byre for the livestock. The stone-built long-house survived to enjoy a long post-medieval history in the north and west of England, and good examples from the sixteeenth and seventeenth centuries are still to be seen in the Pennines and parts of Devon. Down in the south-east, however, a region with ample supplies of timber, a very different sort of house was making its appearance by the fifteenth century. In the late middle ages the rise in wages and fall in prices that followed from the fourteenth century plagues favoured the advancement of small yeomen proprietors who could run a small estate of 100 acres or more with a minimum of overheads. These were the sort of men for whom the lovely Wealden houses of Kent and Sussex were built. In ground plan the timber-framed Wealden house did no more than follow the long-established pattern of gentry manor-houses. In the centre lay a lofty, open hall, flanked at each end by a two-storied service wing, the upper floor jettied, and the whole dwelling under a single hipped roof. The Pilgrim's Rest Cafe at Battle is a good example of this style.

In the Midlands during the same period and earlier, the cruck cottage became a common form of construction (plates 8a and b). The crucks were two big end-timbers, inclined towards each other so as to meet at the crown of the roof. In other words, it was they which supported the roof, as opposed to the lateral walls in any other kind of house. Noakes's Court at Defford (Worcs) is an example of a house of such construction which, to judge from its name, must have been built for a lord of the manor. By the mid-fifteenth century, however, yeomen and gentlemen were building houses that offered more commodious accommodation, and cruck cottages became associated with their dependent tenantry.

Our discussion of the Wealden houses has already served as an introduction to the internal lay-out that had long been common in knightly dwellings. From early Anglo-Saxon days its centrepiece had been the hall. The seventh-century Northumbrian royal palace at Yeavering had consisted quite simply of one enormous timber hall. Both in Saxon and later times the hall had served not only as a banqueting chamber for the lord and his tenants but

also as a meeting place for the manorial court or, in Norman times, the honorial court. Some of the servants might even have slept there. But by the thirteenth century it was no longer a room that was 'lived in'. In that case, where did the lord and his family retire to after dinner? The arrangement of the other rooms in the house was subject, as we might expect, to a fair measure of variation, but two main schemes stand out.

First, there was the type known as the 'upper hall house'. This is the kind of mansion depicted in the Bayeux Tapestry in the famous scene showing Harold and his retainers dining on the eve of the voyage that took them in due course to Normandy (plate 9). The hall is on the first floor, approached by an outside stair, and beneath it is a vaulted sub-structure. The best surviving example of this kind of house is the old manor house at Boothby Pagnell (Lincs), which dates from the end of the twelfth century. On each floor are two chambers, placed end to end. The larger one upstairs, which contained the only fireplace in the building, was the hall, and the smaller one the solar, or 'sun-lit room', which was the private chamber of the lord and his lady. On the ground floor there were again two rooms, corresponding to the plan upstairs. They may have been used for storage, though the greater architectural elaboration of the chamber under the hall suggests that it could have served as a guest room.

By the thirteenth century the 'upper hall' was giving way to the 'end hall' plan. Its dominating feature was a hall running the full height of the house, at right angles to which at one end lay a two-storied block, separately roofed, containing the solar and other rooms. The result was to create an L-shaped building, as at Little Wenham (Suffolk), *c.* 1270–80 (plate 10b). What is remarkable about some of the houses of this plan is the physical separation effected between the hall and the other apartments. At Stokesay (*c.* 1285), for example, there was no internal communication between the hall and the solar, and access could only be obtained by leaving the hall and going up an outside stairway! In many manor houses of this type — Old Soar Kent), for example — the upstairs room next to, and leading out of, the solar was the chapel. Once again there would have been a couple of rooms on the ground floor providing cellarage and storage space for valuables, clothing and food, not to mention salted meat to last out the winter.

Few medieval furnishings have survived to indicate what comforts might have softened the rigours of life in Stokesay or Old Soar. The walls now are bare. But in their time they would have been decorated with wall-paintings, like those commissioned at Longthorpe by Robert de Thorpe, steward of Peterborough Abbey, or hung with tapestries, suspended from mounts a few inches off the wall so as to prevent damage from the damp. Sanitation by modern standards was of course primitive, but not as primitive as it was to be in a great Tudor house like Hardwick, where chamber pots were used and had to be carried down the main stairs to be emptied. The solar at thirteenth century Old Soar had a gardrobe or latrine, which emptied into a pit. One imagines that it would have been difficult to prevent the smells from returning up the shaft into the room. If that was the case, they would have been grateful for all the ample ventilation they could get from the unglazed windows. At Stokesay in the 1280s Laurence de Ludlow was able to afford glass for the upper lights of the tall windows in the hall, but the lower lights were merely shuttered. The windows of the solar might well have been glazed too. As for heating, the only source of warmth in eleventh and twelfth century manor houses, to judge from Boothby Pagnell, was the fireplace in the hall. In many large halls, even that built as late as 1340 by Sir John de Pulteney at Penshurst, the fire took the form of a central hearth from which the smoke would escape through a vent or louvre in the roof. At one time cooking might well have been done at such a hearth, but later on it became usual to erect a kitchen at the opposite end of the hall from the solar block.

In the towns domestic housing took on its own characteristics. The late medieval street scene, which we can recapture by walking along The Shambles (plate 32) or Petergate at York, owed what we would now regard as its picturesqueness to the limitations imposed by urban geography. Space was limited. So the plan of a house followed that of the tenement plot on which it was built. In other words, it combined a narrow frontage with a depth of anything up to 400' back from the front. As often as not the owner would conduct his business from the house, in which case the ground floor would probably serve as a shop. The main living rooms would be upstairs, and the servants' or employees' accommodation right at the top. The constraints of space meant that expansion had to be upwards. Each time a new storey was added to a standard timber-framed building, it would be 'jettied', or projected forwards, to obtain a few more square feet of floor space, until in due course a person leaning forward from the top window on one side of the street could shake hands with someone leaning out of the top window opposite. How the medieval urban working class lived we can hardly say, as their buildings have not survived the passage of time; but we can guess that their surroundings would have been neither spacious nor salubrious.

E. Mercer, *English Vernacular Houses*, London, H.M.S.O., 1975.

ARMOUR The development of armour was a response to the development of weapons of attack. The more lethal these became, the most sophisticated armour needed to be. For long the armourers managed successfully to protect their clients against all manner of assault, but in the end they were defeated by the superior science of the gunsmiths. All the same, they were able to flourish for another century or more by making elaborate suits of armour for use in the tournament (q.v.) lists.

For the period before the fourteenth century from which no actual armour survives we have to rely for our knowledge on indirect sources like manuscripts, tombs and brasses. Of these the earliest and most valuable for our purposes is the Bayeux Tapestry (q.v.). One of the first things we notice in this famous narrative of the Norman Conquest is that the English and Normans wore identical defences, and to tell the two sides apart we need to remember that the former fought on foot and the latter on horseback. The Norman knight wore a long mail shirt called the hauberk, stretching from the head down to the knees. To prevent it from chafing the skin, a coat known as the gambeson was worn underneath. The hauberk was to be the point of departure for all later developments in the history of armour, and although it was eventually to disappear under a welter of plate defences, it was never dispensed with altogether.

In the middle of the twelfth century the familiar flowing surcoat of the knight arrived on the scene. Just what purpose it was intended to serve we cannot be sure. Perhaps to display the wearer's coat-of-arms. Or perhaps to deflect the rays of the sun. If anything, the latter is the more likely explanation, bearing in mind that the surcoat made its appearance at about the time that the knights of Christian Europe were going eastwards on crusade (q.v.) to do battle under the hostile Palestinian sun.

By the later thirteenth century new measures were being taken to defend the more vulnerable parts of the body. First to receive attention were the legs. The thighs were protected by quilted 'cuisses', which have been likened by one recent writer to a pair of waders. To the bottom of the cuisses were attached the poleyns, small plates of metal or boiled leather which defended the knee-caps. Parallel developments were taking place on the arms. Over the elbows were worn disc-shaped pieces known as 'couters', shown for the first time on the tomb in Salisbury Cathedral of the younger William Longespee, earl of Salisbury, dated *c.* 1260. In due course the arms were to receive additional defences in the form of 'vambraces' over the fore-arms, 'rerebraces' over the upper-arms, and small circular 'besagues' over the shoulders. The surcoat becomes shorter, and by the second quarter of the fourteenth century is cut away in front to reveal underneath the coat of plates, a garment of cloth or leather lined with metal plates.

The hauberk, surcoat and poleyns can be seen on the brass of Sir Robert de Bures (d. 1331) at Acton in Suffolk (plate 11). Brasses (q.v.) and monuments are an invaluable source for the history of armour, and never more so than when illustrating the transition from mail to plate in the early fourteenth century. But there are problems of interpretation. Most of the earliest brasses of armoured knights once thought to date from the late thirteenth century have now been redated for one reason or another to the fourteenth. Consequently we must allow for plate defences to have taken rather longer to be adopted than we once believed. The process was not yet over when the Hundred Years War began in 1337. However, by the time of Poitiers (q.v.) nearly twenty years later, a new style had emerged which was to last for the rest of the century. Its main characteristic was the supersession of the linen surcoat by the leather jupon, a close-fitting garment which covered the chest and stomach. Sometimes, as we can see on the Black Prince's tomb at Canterbury (q.v.), the jupon was used to display the wearer's coat-of-arms. To judge from the pigeon-chested appearance of some of the knightly effigies of this period, like that of Sir John Thornbury at Little Munden (Herts) for example, a rather bulbous breastplate must have been forced in between the jupon and the mail hauberk. The arms were encased in plate, and the legs in leather or plate. The head was protected by a pointed helmet or 'bascinet', and the feet by 'sollerets' of laminated plates. Across the hips was slung the baldric or belt from which hung on one side the sword and on the other the misericord dagger — the latter so called because it was used to put an end to the misery of an opponent mortally wounded. These features (except the misericord) are illustrated on the brass of Sir Reginald de Malyns (plate 12).

The one substantial piece of mail still exposed to view was the aventail, which hung from the bascinet and protected the shoulders. It survived until the early fifteenth century, when it was replaced by the steel gorget. At the same time a number of other changes occurred. The jupon gave way to a steel breastplate over the chest and a 'fauld', or skirt of steel hoops, over the lower stomach; and the sword belt was now slung diagonally across the body (plate 14). These features were introduced by the Italian armourers, notably the Missaglia family of Milan, whose workshop was perhaps the most renowned of its day. But even before the end of the fourteenth century they had rivals north of the Alps. The chronicler Froissart tells us that in preparing for their celebrated but abortive duel of 1397 Henry Bolingbroke sent to Italy for his armour and Thomas Mowbray, duke of Norfolk, to Germany for his. The main German armouries of the fifteenth century were at Augsburg, where the workshop of the Helmschmied family produced some superb suits or 'harnesses', to use the technical term, for the Emperor Maximilian in the 1490s. In England the Italian style was beautifully depicted on the brasses (q.v.) produced by the workshop known for lack of a better term as series 'D'. That of Sir Thomas Brounflete is a good example (plate 14). The armour is characterized by symmetry and simplicity. By the middle of the century, however, exaggeration becomes noticeable. Gunpowder was making armour obsolete. The place of the mounted knight was in the tournament lists now, not on the battlefield. Armour no longer had to be so utilitarian. The elaborations to which this departure from reality led in the later fifteenth century can be seen on such brasses as those of Robert Ingleton (plate 15). The fauld is shortened to allow a pair of plates called 'tassets' to be hung from it; the couters become much bigger, and massive pauldrons protect the shoulders.

By this time, as the middle ages draw to a close, we have enough surviving armour to allow us to consider the problem of how much a complete harness would have weighed. The evidence is less startling than we might have expected. A complete Italian armour of about 1450, now preserved in Glasgow Museum, weighs just over four stones. One of the heaviest harnesses, a jousting suit made at Augsburg in about 1500, weighs six stones. That, however, was exceptional. For practical purposes we can reject as exaggerated the later stories of knights having to be lifted onto the backs of their horses by cranes.

But if a knight was unlikely to be borne down by the weight, was he instead going to be borne down by the cost, of his suit of armour? Once again, the answer is probably no. In the 1370s the merchant house of Datini were acting as agents for the sale of Italian armour in Spain and France. For a complete harness of bascinet, aventail, hauberk, breastplate, fauld and leg armour they were charging roughly 45 livres, or £10-£12 in English money of the time. Bearing in mind that a knight would enjoy a minimum income of £40 *p.a.*, and most knights very much more, this was not exorbitant. We must remember too that the price quoted was for a complete harness. An esquire or hard-up knight who did not propose to see more than a season or two's active service could settle if he wanted for just hauberk and bascinet. Armour, moreover, unlike modern motor-cars, did not suffer from built-in obsolescence. It could be passed on from father to son. Only the wealthiest knight would trouble to turn up on the battlefield (or more likely in the lists) sporting an up-to-date Milanese suit. The further down the social scale we go, the simpler and cheaper, and no doubt the less uniform, armour would become. Henry II's (q.v.) Assize of Arms (1181) laid down that the holder of a knight's fee should wear a mail shirt, helmet, shield and lance, and a burgess or freeman a quilted jacket, iron cap and lance. That quilted jacket worn by the infantryman can still be seen in manuscript illustrations of three centuries later. Infantry attire was slow to change. In fact, the only thing worn by the footman that assumed a novel and distinctive form of its own was the kettle-hat, or 'chapeau de fer' to give it its contemporary title, a wide-brimmed head-piece remarkably similar to the tin-hats issued in the two World Wars. Although most commonly associated with the foot-soldiers, it was sometimes worn by members of the nobility, like Aymer de St Amand, who is shown sporting one on the brass of Sir Hugh Hastings at Elsing (Norfolk).

C. Blair, *European Armour*, Batsford, 1958.

ARTHURIAN LEGENDS For the prominent position which Arthur came to occupy in the field of historical romance we have to thank Geoffrey of Monmouth (q.v.), who made this hitherto obscure British King the hero of his *History of the Kings of Britain*. Most of this so-called history, completed in about 1138 is pure fantasy; but the existence back in the fifth or sixth century of someone called Arthur is attested by a ninth century writer called Nennius, who credits him with defeating the Saxons in a series of battles culminating in Mount Badon. When we remember that this victory was attributed by Gildas, an earlier writer, not to Arthur at all but to a leader by the name of Ambrosius Aurelianus, we have some idea of just how insecure his position was in the annals of historical literature before the 1130s. What Geoffrey of Monmouth did was take this shadowy chieftain, and use all his considerable powers of artistry to transform him into a hero figure, a patriot king. Arthur, he says, was the son of Uther Pendragon and Ygerna, duchess of Cornwall. Crowned King of Britain at Silchester at the age of fifteen, he defeated the Saxons at Lincoln and Bath, and then crossed the Channel to subdue France. He was about to set out for Rome, when news reached him that his nephew, Mordred, had seized the crown. Returning to Britain, he defeated Mordred at the battle of Camblan, but was himself mortally wounded and had to be carried away to Avalon. That is the last we hear of him and the crown passed in 542 to his cousin, Constantine.

Such, in its barest outline, is the account of Arthur's career given by Geoffrey. There was enough there to appeal to the imagination — the mysterious nature of his death, for example, and the exploits of the four knights, Cador, Gawain, Bedevere and Kay and enough, too, for later writers to build on. For example, in the *Mort Artu*, part of a thirteenth-century Arthurian cycle, the story of the king's death was worked up to a truly romantic climax. After a fierce battle, we are told, both Arthur and Mordred were mortally wounded, and Arthur ordered Gifflet to hurl the sword Excalibur into the lake. A hand rose from the waters, and grasped the weapon. A boat then drifted along, carrying Morgan and her ladies, who took Arthur on board and sailed off again into the distance.

Although the *History* was criticized a generation later by the chronicler William of Newburgh, Geoffrey's Arthurian yarns were quickly taken up by other writers, both here and in France. Indeed, the popularization of Arthur in the twelfth and thirteenth centuries owed less to English than to French poets, not least among them Chretien de Troyes, who between 1160 and 1180 wrote at least five romances with an Arthurian setting. In England Arthur made an appearance in Layamon's alliterative English *Brut* of c. 1200–20 and in later *Brut* chronicles. But from the literary point of view the two most accomplished treatments of the Arthurian legend in English in the middle ages were the anonymous *Sir Gawain and the Green Knight* of 1360–70 and of course Malory's (q.v.) *Morte d'Arthur*, written in 1469 and printed by Caxton (q.v.) sixteen years later.

The literary Arthur quickly became a European figure, the common property of aristocracies in countries as far apart as England and Cyprus. He became the object of an international cult. The English kings from Stephen to Henry III (q.v.), like their peers elsewhere, subscribed to that cult, but it was Edward I (q.v.) at the end of the thirteenth century who first seized on the political advantages to be derived from identifying the English crown more closely with the memory of the early British King. He and Queen Eleanor were present at Glastonbury in Easter 1278 when the reputed remains of Arthur and Guinevere were transferred to a magnificent new tomb of black marble. Round Tables — a kind of festive tournament — were celebrated on at least three occasions in his reign, at Kenilworth in 1279, Nefyn in Wales in 1284 and at Falkirk in 1302. The advantage to be derived from setting up the English king as Arthur's heir and successor was not lost, either, on

Edward's successors. Edward III (q.v.) evidently had in mind founding a chivalric order on the Arthurian model, before settling instead for the Garter, because he had a circular house built at Windsor Castle suitable for holding a Round Table — very likely the one, dating from about the 1330s, that now hangs on the wall of Winchester Castle. Henry VIII took the trouble of taking the Emperor Charles V to Winchester to see this table on the occasion of his visit to England in 1522. Arthurianism was always good propaganda.

Geoffrey of Monmouth, *The History of the Kings of Britain*, ed. L. Thorpe. Harmondsworth, 1966; R. S. Loomis, 'Edward I, Arthurian Enthusiast', *Speculum*, xxviii (1953).

ASSARTING The process of re-claiming land from the wild was known as assarting (Latin, *ex*, out, *sarrire*, to hoe). As population grew in the course of the middle ages, so it became necessary to extend the margin of cultivation into areas of marsh and moorland that had lain waste. The pace of assarting varied from one part of the country to another. In some areas, like the Felden of south Warwickshire, the limits of cultivation had been reached by the time Domesday Book was compiled in 1086. In other, more inhospitable localities, like the Fens, the frontier was still being pushed back in the thirteenth century. The Fenland included much potentially good farmland, but the bare expanses of moorland known to have been assarted in the same century were too poor to have repaid anything but the most intermittent husbandry, and were abandoned again in the fourteenth century.

ATTAINDER In the early fourteenth century the verb 'to attaint' could describe any process by which judgement was given and the accused found guilty. A century-and-a-half later attainder had become the most solemn penalty known to the common law, incurred usually on conviction for treason, and entailing forfeiture of all possessions and the corruption of blood passing to all direct descendants. During the Wars of the Roses (q.v.), when governments came and went with un-nerving rapidity, Acts of Attainder were regularly used by one side to liquidate the other. But in fact their effects were not as bad as the simple figures would suggest: out of the 397 people attainted between 1453 and 1504 no fewer than 256 had the good fortune to see their sentences reversed.

AUGUSTINIAN CANONS The rapid success of the Augustinian Canons illustrates the ability of the medieval Church to accommodate itself to new spiritual impulses and to new approaches to organized religious life. What was the difference between a canon and a monk? Principally, the nature of the Rule that he obeyed. The monks, Benedictines, Cistercians or whatever, all claimed in one way or another to follow the Rule originally composed by St Benedict. The Regular Canons, on the other hand, followed a much looser Rule, associated with the name of St Augustine of Hippo (354–430). He had been asked by a house of religious women in his diocese to give them advice on how best to live their lives in common. Following a decree of the Lateran Council of 1059, many communities of canons were persuaded for their own benefit to adopt an amplified and updated version of the letter of instructions he wrote, and it was this which became the basis of the Augustinian 'Rule'.

Oddly enough, the secret of the Augustinians' success was the very flexibility of their way of life. Unlike the monks, who were confined to the cloister, they were allowed to go out into the world. They were permitted, for example, to perform pastoral tasks in local communities, something which commended them to the fervour of founders and patrons. As Pope Paschal II put it when writing to the canons of St Botolph's, Colchester, in 1116, 'The dispensation of the Word of God, the offices of preaching, baptizing and reconciling penitents have always been a function of your Order.' Often the houses of the Augustinians were located in the towns, where they ran hospitals and schools, provided help for the poor and sang soul-masses for the rich. Another reason for their popularity was that, being small communities usually, they were cheap to endow. And the greater part of their revenues, it has been pointed out, came not from land, but from appropriated churches bestowed by laymen bowing to papal pressure to divest themselves of ecclesiastical sources of income.

By 1350 there were over 200 Augustinian houses in England. Many were very humble establishments, living on a shoe-string budget, and the number had declined slightly by the Reformation. But some were substantially endowed, and whatever the original intentions of the canonical way of life, had become for all intents and purposes indistinguishable from regular monastic foundations. The Augustinians were never pre-eminent for their way of life or for the intellectual activity of their number, but they produced some men of note, like John Mirk of Lilleshall, a sermon-writer and author of tracts for parish priests.

The surviving buildings of the Augustinians offer as much variety as we would expect in an Order where there was so much disparity between the largest and the smallest foundations. From the earliest days of the canons in England there survive the roofless nave of St Botolph's, Colchester, and the choir of St Bartholomew's Smithfield, and from the reign of Henry II the impressive late Romanesque work at St Frideswide's, Oxford (now Christ Church Cathedral). Of the conventual buildings of the Augustinians, which conformed to the normal monastic plan, those at Lilleshall (Salop) and Christ Church, Oxford, provide the best examples.

See also, MONASTERIES, SERMONS.

J. C. Dickinson, *The Origin of the Austin Canons and their Introduction into England*, London, 1950.

AULNAGE First imposed in 1353, the aulnage was a tax levied on all cloths that were intended for sale, whether at home or abroad. Its administration lay in the hands of officials known as aulnagers who were appointed by the Crown not only to collect the tax but to inspect the cloths for size and quality. From the fifteenth century there is ample evidence to show that they were succumbing to the corrupt practices that proved an irresistible temptation to all but the most scrupulous medieval officials. For example, they would seize a cloth under some pretext, and then sell it themselves for private gain. As a cover they rendered spurious accounts to the Exchequer. For all the notoriety that the aulnage returns have earned, there is, however, little reason to doubt that the earlier accounts, surviving from the fourteenth century, give a reasonably accurate picture of cloth sales for their time.

B

BACON, ROGER Of the English scientific writers of the middle ages Bacon is the most well-known, though not necessarily the most important. A member of an East Anglian knightly family, he studied at Oxford under the great Robert Grosseteste (q.v.), and then lectured at Paris, before returning to Oxford in about 1247 to resume his theological studies. Some ten years later he joined the Franciscans (q.v.) By this time he had given himself over almost wholly to scientific investigations, which he was to write up in the *Opus Maius*, the *Opus Minor* and the *Opus Tertium*. Whether for the alleged 'suspected novelties' his work contained or, more likely, for the hostility aroused by his relentless criticism of many of the greatest Churchmen of his day, he found himself placed in confinement by 1278. When he was released we do not know. All we can say is that he was at large again in Oxford shortly before his death in 1292.

Bacon's modern reputation should not hide from us the fact that as a thinker he stood firmly within the time-honoured Augustinian tradition that saw intellectual illumination as coming only from God. It was quite understandable of him, therefore, to say that 'theology is the mistress of all the other sciences', and to believe that the purpose of studying science was to attain a deeper knowledge of the truths of theology. As a pupil of Grosseteste Bacon favoured the study of mathematics as the best way of demonstrating connections between events. Mathematics, he wrote, is 'the door and the key' 'of the sciences and things of this world'. But, as we know, he was not one to accept blindly the increasing separation between pure thought and experience that was to prove the fatal flaw in medieval scholasticism. He was a great believer in the value of experimenting. In this he was not new. He was merely following the lead given by the Frenchman, Peter de Mauricourt, who had worked on magnetism. But he does seem to have been possessed of an inventive and speculative mind. He dabbled in alchemy, astronomy, astrology and optics. All the same, his importance lay not so much in his own discoveries and achievements as in the experimental method by which he reached them. One phenomenon, for example, that he like Grosseteste sought to explain was the rainbow. He tells us how he had examined prisms, crystals and the spray thrown up by mill-wheels to collect instances of colours similar to those seen in the rainbow, so that he could relate the latter to the general phenomenon of spectral colours. Why these advances in experimental method nevertheless failed to emancipate medieval science from its aristotelian framework raises questions that are better dealt with in a more general discussion of medieval science (q.v.)

D. Knowles, *The Evolution of Medieval Thought*, London, 1962.

BANNOCKBURN When Robert Bruce destroyed Edward II's army at Bannockburn, he ended for the next generation any possibility that Scotland (q.v.) might be conquered by the English. The battle was the outcome of Edward's attempt to relieve the English garrison beleaguered in Stirling Castle. Led by the king himself, the English army reached the Bannock burn, a

couple of miles south of Stirling, on 23 June 1314. Though numbering as many as 15-20,000, compared with a Scots force of 6-10,000, they were ill-led and ill-coordinated. Any reconstruction of the battle is bound to be speculative, because historians cannot agree about its exact site. However, so far as we can tell, Bruce arranged his men in four 'schiltroms', or well-armed brigades of infantry, against which, when battle was joined on 24 June, the English cavalry could make little headway (Fig. 1). Too late Edward thought of deploying the archers. Bruce replied by throwing in his cavalry, and the English broke up in disorderly retreat. Among the noble casualties on the English side was the earl of Gloucester, and among the prisoners were the earl of Hereford,

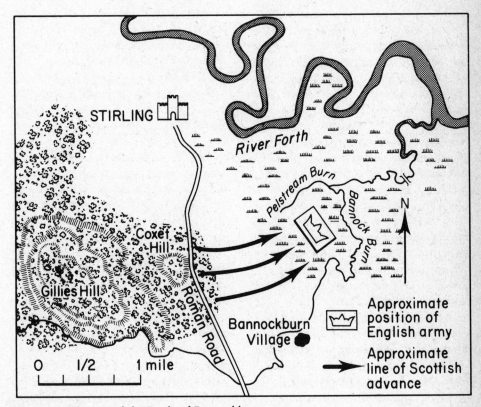

Figure 1   The site of the Battle of Bannockburn, 1314.

Sir Maurice de Berkeley and Sir Anthony de Lucy. For Edward II the political consequences were as serious as the military. Deprived as he was of any standing, any moral authority in the country, he had no alternative but to comply with those like Thomas, earl of Lancaster, who had been demanding that he enforce the Ordinances (q.v.), the programme of reforms imposed on him three years before.

BASTARD FEUDALISM Inelegant though it may be, the term 'bastard feudalism' is the one still generally used to describe the system of ties between lords and retainers in England in the late middle ages. The phrase implies that it was a debased form of feudalism (q.v.). So indeed it was, in the sense that the tenurial link of pure feudalism between lord and vassal gave way to a monetary one between lord and man. But lords were to be searching among the gentry for clients, and the gentry among the lords for patrons for as long as landed society lasted. Arguably, all that changed between the twelfth century and the fifteenth was the way that the relationship of dependence was expressed. In the age of pure feudalism it centred on the oath of homage. In the age of bastard feudalism it centred on the indenture of retinue. This stated the terms of service agreed between the two contracting parties. A good example is provided by the indenture John of Gaunt, duke of Lancaster (q.v.) made with Sir Maurice de Berkeley of Uley in 1391. Maurice was retained to stay with the duke for life in peace and war. When summoned, he would attend the duke, from whom he would receive food and drink in common with the other knights of his rank. In return he would receive annually a retaining fee of £20 assigned on Gaunt's lordship of Monmouth, the first instalment to be paid at Easter, the second at Michaelmas.

The origins of retaining by indenture are probably to be found in the later thirteenth century, when the inadequacy of the feudal levies obliged lords to seek other means of raising men to serve in the king's army. The feudal host had of course long been supplemented by hired mercenaries, whose pay and conditions would have been agreed orally with the king. What was new in Henry III's reign was that these terms were written down. For example, the future Edward I had it recorded, when he went on crusade (q.v.) in 1720, that Adam de Jesmond had contracted to accompany him with four knights for a year. In the course of the next two decades, during the wars in Wales (q.v.) and Scotland (q.v.), it became common to supplement the feudal host in this way with contingents indentured to serve for the duration of a campaign.

Now, if the king could raise a force by making such indentures, so too could his captains in their turn; and if he and they could use them for short-term contracts of military service, so too could they for contracts for life in peace and war. Thus it is significant that the earliest surviving indentures of retinue *for life service* come within a year of the first Welsh War: in 1278 we find William de Swinburne, a Northumberland lord, retaining William de Kellawe and John de Lisle on 13 March and 19 May respectively. By the fourteenth century the indenture had passed into common use; and if the example of John of Gaunt is anything to go by, it was employed to retain not only knights and esquires but also estate and household officials. When historians use the term 'bastard feudalism', however, they are generally referring not to the affinity in its broadest sense but to the nexus of ties linking a lord with the local gentlemen — in other words, with the knights and esquires who would reside on their own estates and attend their lord when summoned to do so.

Ever since the term was coined in the nineteenth century, bastard feudalism has had a bad press from historians, and efforts in the last thirty years to improve the picture have been no more than partially successful. For example, it is still the habit of those who condemn bastard feudalism to blame it for the collapse of public order in the mid-fifteenth century. The proliferation of retaining, it is argued, led to the build-up of large gangs of baronial hangers-on, who provided the mainstay of the armies that fought the Wars of the Roses (q.v.). Yet at the same time, and quite inconsistently, historians have pointed to the shifting and unstable nature of the ties between lord and retainer, one consequence of which was that bastard feudalism could not be such a cohesive force as pure feudalism had been in the twelfth. If in fact a lord could not rely on the loyalty of his feed men, how on earth could he count on them to follow him into battle? Be that as it may, we can certainly admit that there were elements of instability in late medieval bastard feudalism. For example, the tie between lord and vassal in pure feudalism was hereditary, and that between lord and man in the bastard version was not. Late medieval indentures of retainer were generally contracted for life, but by the fifteenth century there is evidence that lords were granting fees for shorter periods, of a year at a time for example, to men who strictly speaking we should call annuitants. These people were much less easily disciplined by their lord than permanent retainers,

and it is perhaps they whom we should blame for the undoubted abuses of the system that we hear about in the age of the Pastons (q.v.). Long before that, however, there had been noisy complaints from the Commons in parliament which had resulted in the first comprehensive legislation on retaining, the so-called Statute of Livery and Maintenance, 1390, which was never actually enforced. It aimed to limit the distribution of fees by forbidding any but lords to retain, and any but esquires and above to be retained. But if great lords chose to give fees to whomsoever they wished, there was nothing the courts could do in practice to stop them. Though the legislation was strengthened in 1468 by Edward IV (q.v.) and in 1504 by Henry VII, there is little to indicate that it was much of a deterrent, and when the great baronial affinities melted away in a much later age, it was for social reasons and not for fear of government legislation.

By concentrating unduly on its malign aspects, we can easily come away with a distorted picture of bastard feudalism. A magnate did not assemble a retinue either solely or primarily with a view to having a contingent ready to serve either in or against the king's army. He did so rather to secure a following that would signal his importance in society and would strengthen his links with the local gentry. Despite the pressures on the nobility in a society which valued extravagant display so highly, there is no evidence to support the suggestion that they bankrupted themselves by competing in the distribution of fees to retainers. Undoubtedly there was intense rivalry among knights and esquires for a place in the retinue, but lords were willing to say no if their rent rolls prevented them from accommodating any more hangers-on.

For that reason it is wrong to think of fourteenth and fifteenth England as filled with rival armies of retainers brushing shoulders with one another. Far from it. There were many who were unattached, and it is their complaints that have provided historians with such ample copy for the abuses of bastard feudalism that they lack for the earlier age of pure feudalism.

K. B. McFarlane, 'Bastard Feudalism', *Bull. Inst. Hist. Res.*, xx (1945).

BAYEUX TAPESTRY This celebrated piece of needlework, so called from the cathedral city in France where it has been preserved at least since the fifteenth century, is a contemporary visual record of the Norman Conquest of England. It is in fact less a 'tapestry' than a strip cartoon, 20″ high and 230′ in length, tracing the story of Duke William's great exploit in over 70 consecutive scenes.

The tale is told, of course, from the Norman point of view. The object is to present a moral case by tracing the fall of a man, King Harold, who had dared to break a solemn oath. In the early scenes of the Tapestry we see Harold, earl of Wessex, as he then was, leaving England to make a journey across the Channel, the purpose of which is not stated (plate 9). On landing on the French coast, he was taken prisoner by Guy, count of Ponthieu, from whose custody he was transferred to that of William, duke of Normandy. He was privileged to accompany William on a campaign in Brittany in the course of which he entered into a relationship of feudal dependence on the duke. And on his return to Bayeux he is shown swearing that famous oath to William, the terms of which, we are told by the Norman chroniclers, were to uphold William's succession to the English throne. Ignoring his commitment, however, Harold seized the crown for himself when Edward died on 5 January 1066. The dire consequences that God was to lay in store for the perjurer are indicated in the Tapestry by the appearance after the coronation of Halley's Comet interpreted, as such events were in the middle ages, as a bad omen. The scene then switches back to Normandy, where we see the duke's men building the ships that were to carry them across the Channel to Pevensey beach. After disembarking, they march to Hastings, where we are shown a simple motte-and-bailey castle (q.v.) being thrown up. A messenger brings news of the approach of Harold's army, and after a pep talk from their leader, the Normans get ready for battle. The remaining scenes then portray with great vigour the events of 14 October 1066 that led to Harold's death and William's victory.

As a source of historical evidence the Tapestry is obviously open to serious criticism. It is an ex parte account which sets forward the Norman version of what happened between about 1064 and 1066. The captions are brief, and sometimes cryptic in the extreme. Take Harold's oath, for example. The Tapestry says it was sworn at Bayeux, and the chronicler William of Poitiers at Bonneville-sur-Touques. And just what did Harold swear? The Tapestry does not say, and we have to go to other sources. On the other hand, the account of the Conquest is unlikely to be pure fiction. It was completed at the latest within a couple of decades of the events it portrayed, and if so dramatic a celebration of the Norman invasion were in fact a tissue of lies, then surely we would have heard some contemporary complaining to that effect.

Our understanding of the Tapestry would be enhanced immeasurably if we could discover a little more about its provenance. It has long been thought that it was made in England, an assumption now converted into reasonable probability by the stylistic links which Francis Wormald demonstrated between the Tapestry and late Anglo-Saxon manuscript illumination. He suggested that it may have been embroidered at Canterbury. But in that case who commissioned it? If anyone occupies a position of such prominence in the Tapestry as to suggest that he may have been involved in its making, that person is Odo, bishop of Bayeux, half brother of Duke William. He says grace before dinner at Hastings. In the heat of the battle it is he who rallies the troops. And it is with his cathedral city of Bayeux that the Tapestry has always been associated. Significantly, at one point where the Tapestry is at variance with other sources — the place where Harold swore his oath to Duke William — its authority is to the advantage of Bayeux. But how are we to reconcile these strong indications that the Tapestry was commissioned by a Norman with the equally compelling evidence that it was embroidered in England, perhaps at Canterbury? Odo, we must remember, was not only bishop of Bayeux. As a reward for his services at Hastings, immortalized in the Tapestry, he was given the English earldom of Kent, the chief town of which was Canterbury. In that case we are probably justified in dating the Tapestry's completion to before 1082, when Odo fell from favour and lost Kent.

The overall design of the Tapestry was probably the work of a single artist, and one moreover who was familiar with the world of manuscript illumination. The needlework was then executed, in wool on a linen background, by a group of embroiderers who presumably operated in a single workshop How exactly they went about the job we do not know, but close examination of the Tapestry shows that they made it in eight separate pieces of uneven length which were then joined together. Bearing in mind its antiquity and the vicissitudes through which it has passed, the Tapestry is in remarkably good condition. Twice during the French Revolution it had to be saved from destruction. Yet it has come down to us complete, apart from the loss of a few feet at the end. If it survived the threats of the revolutionaries, the Tapestry did not escape the attention of nineteenth century restorers who rewove several parts which were faded. The work was in fact accomplished very well, but it does mean that one or two of the most famous scenes — the death of King Harold for example — are largely modern restorations.

The tapestry is a unique source for the history of the Norman Conquest; and as a work of art it has no parallel in the Dark Ages. Within the limits set by the stylized form of portrayal with which he was familiar, the designer proved himself to be a genius. His horses, one ventures to say, are better than those of Stubbs. He could portray vividly the rough and tumble of the battlefield. We would like to know his name; but it is unlikely we ever will.

The Bayeux Tapestry, ed. C. Gibbs-Smith, Phaidon, 1973.

BEAUFORT, HENRY The Beauforts were the illegitimate offspring of John of Gaunt, duke of Lancaster (q.v.) by Catherine Swynford, his mistress and later his third wife. Their high birth, not to mention their kinship to the ruling house after Gaunt's son seized power in 1399 as Henry IV, guaranteed them a position of eminence in the governing councils of the kingdom in the fifteenth century. Not the least important of these three brothers was Henry, the clerical member of the family. Born in about 1376 at the castle of Beaufort, whence the family derived their surname, he was educated at Aachen and Queen's College, Oxford. Ecclesiastical preferment soon followed. In 1398 he became bishop of Lincoln, and in 1404, when still only in his 20s, was translated to Winchester, the richest diocese in England.

On the accession of Henry V (q.v.) in 1413 Beaufort was appointed Chancellor, but his ambitions were by no means confined to his native land. He had been influential in healing the Great Schism in the Church by promoting the election of Martin V as pope. When Martin offered him the gift (or perhaps one should say reward) of a cardinal's hat in 1417, he eagerly accepted. One thing he overlooked, however. He had not obtained the king's prior permission. And Henry V was not a man to take such presumption lightly. Beaufort was prevented from taking the red hat, and it was not until 1426 in the reign of the infant Henry VI (q.v.) that he was able to accept the honour denied him nine years before.

It was in fact during the long minority of Henry VI that Beaufort exercised his greatest influence over the direction of English affairs. But his advice did not pass unchallenged. For a quarter of a century the Council was to be divided, though not necessarily paralysed, by the quarrel between Beaufort and his nephew, Humphrey, duke of Gloucester (q.v.). Duke Humphrey

advocated vigorous prosecution of the war against France. Beaufort, on the other hand, realized that it was a war which England could never win and that negotiations would have to be opened. In the next generation Humphrey's arguments were to be taken up by the duke of York, and Beaufort's by his relative the duke of Somerset. To that extent the divisions of the 1430s anticipate the line-up of forces we find later on in the Wars of the Roses (q.v.).

If Beaufort had any advantage over his opponents, it was an advantage conferred by money. His name, it has been observed, became a by-word for immense wealth. Where it all came from we do not know. What he did with it, we do. He lent it to the Crown. His dealings were not usurious, because it was not then the practice to pay interest (even concealed) on public loans. But his position as the Crown's biggest creditor gave him leverage he might not otherwise have enjoyed. The scene at his deathbed in 1447, which made its way into Shakespeare's *Henry VI, pt. ii*, suggests that he felt remorse as he looked back over his career. But however humbly he faced his Maker, the magnificent tomb and chantry chapel he commissioned in Winchester Cathedral suggest that humility was never among the qualities with which he had faced his fellow men.

G. L. Harriss, 'Cardinal Beaufort — Patriot or Usurer?', *Trans. Roy. Hist. Soc.*, 5th series, 20 (1970).

BECKET, THOMAS The quarrel between Henry II (q.v.) and Becket, involving a clash of both personality and principle, has never lost its appeal for artists, dramatists and in modern times film-makers. The archbishop's murder shocked Europe so deeply that it resulted in his canonization less than three years later. But in fact, until it reached its dramatic climax, the dispute can be said neither to have inconvenienced King Henry greatly nor to have preoccupied his attention to the exclusion of all else.

Where Henry II misjudged Becket was in supposing that relations beween them would remain unchanged after the latter's appointment as archbishop of Canterbury. For until then they had been close friends. Becket (born 1118) was the son of Norman parents who had settled in London. He was educated at Merton Priory, and then joined the household of Archbishop Theobald, where he was soon marked out for rapid preferment. In 1154 he was appointed archdeacon of Canterbury, and later in the same year, on Theobald's recommendation, Chancellor of England. During the eight years that he served as Chancellor, he conducted himself, whether at home or abroad, with a panache that was hardly suggestive of the change that was to come after his move to Canterbury; but at the same time he resisted the temptations of the flesh, and there is no evidence that his extravagance in public life was ever matched by immorality in private.

It was this inner streak of private asceticism which came to the fore when he succeeded Theobald at Canterbury in 1162. Gone were the days of high living. He even severed his links with secular government by resigning as Chancellor, an act calculated to annoy Henry, who had favoured his appointment precisely in order to reach a personal solution to those often difficult questions of Church and State. As a part of his general plan in the 1160s to combat the upsurge in lawlessness to which clerks no less than laymen had contributed,

Henry proposed at Westminster in October 1163 that criminous clerks found guilty in church courts should be handed over to the secular authorities for punishment. Swayed by Becket, the bishops refused, and when Henry followed up this initial proposal with the demand that they should swear to uphold the ancient customs of the kingdom, they annoyed him still further by agreeing only if the words 'saving their order' were added. Had Henry continued to use the gentle arts of persuasion, he might yet have obtained verbal agreement to his proposals, but at the next meeting held at Clarendon in January 1164 he committed the mistake of codifying them in a written document known as the Constitutions of Clarendon. The bishops felt that they could not possibly set their seals to such a document, but as soon as they had become firm in their resolve, Becket caved in. He gave his consent, and urged them to do likewise. Whatever the pressure that had led him to capitulate in the council chamber, once he left Clarendon he repented of his oath, and twice unsuccessfully attempted to leave the country. By now Henry was bent on the final destruction of his archbishop. The chance came in October 1164 at Northampton, when John FitzGilbert, marshal of the royal household, appealed to the king over a case he had lost in the archbishop's court. Becket had failed to attend an earlier meeting at Westminster, enabling Henry to accuse him of contempt of court. But that was not all, for Henry now went on to accuse him of embezzlement while Chancellor. On the final day (12 October) king and archbishop met in different rooms, with intermediaries passing between them. The bishops told Henry that Becket had appealed to the pope against the judgement they had passed on him in the FitzGilbert case — a clear breach of the Constitutions of Clarendon. When they agreed among themselves to appeal to Rome against Becket, Henry released them from the obligation of sentencing him in the embezzlement case. That pleasure was now left for the barons. But as they descended to the lower room, where the clergy were assembled, Becket stormed out. A few days later he left the country.

His destination was Sens, where Pope Alexander III was living in exile under French protection. With a characteristic sense of the theatrical he threw himself at the pope's feet. For the next six years he lived at Pontigny Abbey, waging a war of words that went largely unheeded by Henry II and his advisers. They knew perfectly well that Becket could do little without the authority of Alexander III, and that Alexander would do nothing for fear of driving Henry into the obedience of his rival, the anti-pope Paschal III, who was sponsored by Frederick Barbarossa.

Despite several attempts at mediation by the French king, the dispute showed no signs of coming to a conclusion, until a crisis was provoked by the coronation of Henry's son and heir on 14 June 1170. The crowning of a ruler's heir during his father's lifetime was an Angevin practice, and the right of performing this, as of all coronation ceremonies, lay with the archbishop of Canterbury. Since Becket was abroad, Henry asked the archbishop of York. In so doing, he fully realized that nothing was better calculated to fill Becket with rage, and remarkably, he anticipated the dire consequences that were likely to follow by offering to meet his adversary and make peace. Thus negotiations between the two sides were reopened, and resulted on 22 July 1170 at Freteval in an agreement for Becket's return. The

reason for this rapid and perhaps unexpected breakthrough was quite simply that the great issues in question — appeals, criminous clerks and so on — were ignored. It was agreed that Becket should come back, and that the property of the see of Canterbury should be restored, that was all.

This settlement was much too superficial to assuage the bitter feelings that had been aroused over the previous six years, and when Becket landed at Sandwich on 1 December he was given a hostile reception by Gervase de Cornhill, sheriff of Kent, and other well-known supporters of the king. On his side, Becket hardly helped matters by excommunicating the archbishop of York and the bishops of London and Salisbury. When news of these events reached Henry in Normandy, he flew into a rage so terrible, that four of his knights taking, as they saw it, the hint, made their way to Canterbury. On 29 December Becket was murdered in his cathedral. His cult spread rapidly throughout Europe, and on 21 February 1173 he was canonized.

So what, if anything, was at stake in this quarrel? The compromise Henry II made with the pope at Avranches in May 1172 ignored several of the main issues that had divided him from his archbishop. That was why Becket's most devoted supporters claimed he had died in vain. But they were overstating their case. Even if he did not explicitly say so in the Avranches settlement, Henry in practice abandoned the claim to try criminous clerks in the royal courts. The dispute therefore established the principle of 'benefit of clergy' which entitled an indicted clerk to trial in the court Christian. What the quarrel between king and archbishop highlighted was the problem of reconciling the jurisdiction of the reformed

Church, as expressed in canon law, with the jurisdiction of the secular monarchy, as expressed in the ancient customs of the realm written down at Clarendon. In different times, and with different men, these issues might have been resolved in less dramatic fashion. But Henry and Becket found their respective lines of thought becoming increasingly divergent. As Prof Knowles has written, it was only when he became archbishop that Becket's personality, hitherto concealed under a veil of worldliness, stood revealed. He had found a cause to fight for. He was neither a scholar nor a philosopher; and unlike Anselm (q.v.) or Francis of Assisi, he was not by nature a saint. But he did have the makings of a martyr.

D. Knowles, *Thomas Becket*, A. & C. Black, 1970, and *The Historian and Character*, Cambridge, 1963.

BENEDICTINES The story of monastic life in the West begins with the Rule St Benedict composed in Italy in about 526. Elegant in its simplicity, it provided for the day to be divided into four hours prayer, four hours reading and six hours labour, and for the affairs of the community to be looked after by an abbot and subordinate officials. As monasticism (q.v.) grew ever more popular in the early middle ages, so knowledge of Benedict's code spread throughout Europe. It was first introduced into England by the keen Romanist, St Wilfrid (d. 709). But if the Rule was popular, it was not universally binding. Each monastery, though nominally Benedictine, was independent and autonomous. The first attempt to introduce some measure of uniformity in England came in about 970, when a code known as the Regu-

laris Concordia was adopted. Its association with the fallen Wessex monarchy ensured that it would be consigned to oblivion after the Norman Conquest in 1066. To take its place Lanfranc (q.v.), the new Norman archbishop, issued his own set of Monastic Constitutions, addressed solely to the monks of his own cathedral of Canterbury (q.v.) but widely imitated all the same in other houses. Until this time, as we have seen, all monks regarded themselves as Benedictine. But within a generation or two of the Norman Conquest this Benedictine monopoly was shattered by the rise of the new Orders, the Cluniacs (q.v.), Cistercians (q.v.) and so on. One effect of this was to make the Black Monks (as they were known from the colour of their habit) organise themselves more formally than they had done hitherto. The fourth Lateran Council in 1215 created a legislative body for the Order in the form of the General Chapter. And later in the thirteenth century the system of episcopal visitation from which the Benedictines had previously been exempt, was introduced to correct abuses and maintain standards of religious life.

The Benedictines numbered among their houses some of the oldest and most distinguished foundations in England — Glastonbury, Bury St Edmund's, Peterborough and the cathedral priories of Canterbury (q.v.), Winchester, Worcester and Ely. After the Conquest they were joined by others like Selby and Tewkesbury. Unlike the Cistercians, the Benedictine houses were fully integrated into the fabric of feudal society. Most of their abbots held as tenants-in-chief of the Crown, and were responsible for the provision of a quota of knights in the feudal host.

As landowners on a big scale, the Benedictines did much to shape the economic and social life of medieval England. They were usually conservative proprietors. In the thirteenth century, the age of 'high farming', when their manors were organized for production for the market, they made extensive use of the labour services of their villeins (q.v.) to cultivate the demesnes (q.v.), and after the Black Death (q.v.) in the following century tried continuing to enforce these services when more flexible lords were opting to give up demesne cultivation altogether. Where they did not want the labour services for their own sake, they used them to extract higher money rents and to exploit the financial aspects of villeinage. It was this economic conservatism that made Benedictine monasteries like St Alban's the objects of vehement hostility in the Peasants Revolt (q.v.) of 1381.

Within the cloister the life of the Black Monks was governed, of course, by the Rule of St Benedict as amended and reinterpreted over the centuries. The house would be ruled by an abbot, or in the case of a priory by a prior. Beneath him the officials known as 'obedientiaries' looked after the administration and handled the money. The manner of recruitment to the cloister varied over the centuries. According to the Rule admission could be by 'oblation' as a child or by free choice as an adult. One such child recruit in Norman England was the future chronicler, Orderic Vitalis, who tells us that at the age of ten he was given by his father to a monk who was charged with admitting him to a monastery overseas. The young Orderic was received into the house of St Evroult in Normandy, and there he was to spend the rest of his days. Towards the end of the twelfth century, however, childhood oblation came to be regarded with disapproval. It was no longer felt that a child should be committed to a life in the cloister by a decision not of its making. The steady flow of mature recruits in the twelfth century no doubt enabled this change of policy to be accomplished without any diminution in the numbers admitted. But in the late middle ages, when a wider range of careers opened up, in administration, in the universities, in magnate service, the numbers in the houses of the Benedictines as of the other Orders began to decline.

D. Knowles, *The Monastic Order in England*, 2nd ed. Cambridge, 1966, and *The Religious Orders in England*, Cambridge, 3 vols., 1948–59.

BLACK DEATH

To our great grief the plague carried off so vast a multitude of people of both sexes that nobody could be found who would bear the corpses to the graveyard. Men and women carried their own children on their shoulders to the church and threw them into the common pit. From these pits such an appalling stench was given off that scarcely anyone dared even to walk beside the cemetaries.[*]

The scene described here by William de Dene, a monk of Rochester, would have been an unpleasantly common one in England and western Europe in 1348 and 1349. According to the traditional account, the Black Death arrived in this country in early June 1348 when two ships from Gascony unloaded at Melcombe Regis in Dorset. From there it spread in no time to every corner of England. Its symptoms are best described in the words of the Italian poet Boccaccio:

[*] P. Ziegler, *The Black Death*, Pelican, 1971, pp. 168.

In men and women alike it first betrayed itself by the emergence of certain tumours in the groin or the arm-pits, some of which grew as large as an apple ... which the common folk call gavocciolo. From the two said parts of the body this deadly gavocciolo soon began to propagate itself in all directions ... after which the form of the malady began to change, black spots making their appearance in many cases on the arm or the thigh ... And as the gavocciolo had been and still was an infallible token of approaching death, so also were these spots on whomsoever they showed themselves.*

What Boccaccio was describing was the symptoms of bubonic plague. The virus was carried by a flea which lived on mice and rats. In the crowded and unhygienic conditions of mid-fourteenth century England it was impossible to stop it spreading. That the effects of the plague were devastating can hardly be doubted, though just how devastating is more difficult to say. The most recent estimates suggest that between 30 and 45% of the population were carried off. That of course is an overall figure, and the incidence of mortality may have varied between one social class and another. The clergy saw their ranks decimated because the nature of their work brought them into daily contact with the afflicted. The gentry and the nobility, on the other hand, suffered much less. The more hygienic surroundings in which they lived presumably enabled them to escape affliction.

The Black Death was all the more devastating for being the first outbreak of plague in England. It was not to be the last. A second outbreak occurred in 1361. This time the overall death rate was lower, but interestingly the upper-classes suffered comparatively worse. Was it a different virus? Pneumonic plague perhaps rather than bubonic? A suggestion that ought to be considered certainly, except that if it was a totally different disease contemporaries would surely have noted the fact. What we can say is that this outbreak and the many that occurred in the fifteenth century and later were of sufficient virulence to prevent population (q.v.) from recovering quickly to its earlier levels.

BOSWORTH The controversy about the battle of Bosworth, like that surrounding the career of the king who met his death there, is notable for having generated more heat than light. Richard III (q.v.) was in Nottinghamshire when news reached him that Henry Tudor had landed near Milford Haven on 7 August 1485. To Richard's surprise he had marched unopposed through Wales, and it was finally in the Midlands at Market Bosworth (Leics.) that the opposing armies met on 22 August, Henry's numbering about 5,000 and the king's about 8,000. It used to be held that Richard's fate was determined less by those who did than by those who did not fight that day, but in his recent account of the battle Professor Ross shows that the earl of Northumberland's failure to use his men on Richard's behalf was due not to treachery but to problems of geography. Richard had chosen a dominant position on Ambien Hill. But the advantage this gave him in surveying the surrounding landscape was outweighed by the disadvantage of shortage of space, which prevented him from deploying his men along a wide front. Instead he had to draw them up in a column, one division behind another. Northumberland, who was in the rear, failed to engage, there-

* Ibid., pp. 18–19.

fore, not because he did not want to, but because he couldn't. It was the duke of Norfolk's men at the front who bore the brunt of the struggle. Seeing the difficulties they were facing, Richard launched a charge himself, but in the heat of the battle was cut down. Henry Tudor emerged victorious, and Richard III acquired the unenviable distinction of being the only king since the Norman Conquest to die on an English battlefield.

C. D. Ross, *Richard III*, Eyre Methuen, 1981.

BRACTON, HENRY The most important legal treatise to have come down to us from medieval England is the one commonly known as Bracton's *De legibus et consuetidinibus Anglie* (*The Laws and Customs of England*). A large work, this is the first comprehensive exposition of English law, written apparently in the mid-thirteenth century by a judge drawing on many years experience on the bench. He had at his disposal the court rolls of his predecessors from which he extracted cases to compile the other volume perpetuating his name, known as *Bracton's Note Book* (ed. F. W. Maitland, 3 vols., 1887). Of Bracton himself relatively little can be uncovered. Bratton Fleming or Bratton Clovelly in Devon both claim him as one of their sons. By the 1230s he was a clerk in the service of the king's justice, William de Ralegh, and from 1244 was himself a justice in eyre (q.v.) He died in 1268, and was probably buried in Exeter Cathedral, of which he had been appointed Chancellor in May 1264, a reminder that until the reign of Edward I the king's judges were drawn mainly from the ranks of the clergy.

The famous treatise on the laws of England has long been associated with Henry Bracton because it is his name which occurs at the front of the manuscript which is the archtype of all our manuscripts of the work. But, as Prof Thorne has shown in the introduction to his new edition, its textual history is more complicated than we might suppose. A prototype *De legibus* had been written before 1236 by someone connected with Martin de Pateshull, a distinguished judge of Henry III's early years. It was then subjected to a number of revisions, one of them by a clerk of William de Ralegh who may or may not have been Henry Bracton. Over the next twenty years it was subjected to further revisions, in the course of which the name of the original author was lost and that of Bracton substituted. Soon after 1256 another editor reduced this, by now, swollen text into the archtype of our own *De legibus*. If this reconstruction is correct, then the treatise probably reflects the thinking more of Ralegh or Pateshull than of the man whose name it now bears.

See also, JUSTICE.

Bracton on the Laws and Customs of England, ed. G. E. Woodbine, trans. S. E. Thorne (Selden Soc., 1977).

BRASSES A brass is a flat metal plate, engraved with a figure or inscription or both, and laid down in a church as a memorial.

The origins of brass engraving are to be found in the Low Countries in the twelfth and thirteenth centuries. It was seen that some advantage lay in engraving a figure on a marble slab set in the floor rather than in taking up a lot of space with a tomb chest surmounted by an effigy. These memorials, which survive in large numbers in northern France and Flanders, are known as incised slabs. Their disadvantages were that they lacked durability and that they were visually monotonous. Why not vary the surface, then, by adding an inlay of a different colour? By the 1240s, or perhaps earlier, we find masons in the Tournai area doing just that by inserting marble to depict the face or hands of the commemorated. By the end of the century brass had become the most popular form of inlay.

The earliest surviving figure brass in Europe is at Verden (West Germany) and commemorates Bishop Yso von Wilpe (d. 1231). It shows the bishop in mass vestments, holding a church in each hand, and surrounding the whole design is a marginal inscription. The idea of small brass inlays has been abandoned in favour of engraving the whole memorial on a single rectangular plate of brass. Where von Wilpe's brass was made we cannot be sure. But the most important centre of manufacture in the fourteenth century was Tournai on the river Scheldt in Flanders. The one contract known to us which can be connected with a recorded brass of Continental origin gives the name of a Tournai engraver called Lotars Hanette. This contract was made in 1345. Fifteen years before Lotars is known to have been in partnership with a stonemason called Jean d'Escamaing. Would we be justified in supposing that D'Escamaing specialized in incised slabs and his colleague in brasses?

These Flemish brasses of the fourteenth century were very large, very elaborate and no doubt very expensive too. Some were exported to England, as we can see today at St Alban's, Newark and St Margaret's, King's Lynn. But by the beginning of the fourteenth century workshops had been set up in this country, using metal imported from the Continent. The brasses from this period fall into two main groups. First, there are the great full-length figures, like those of Sir John d'Abernon (?d. 1277) at Stoke d'Abernon (Surrey) and Sir Robert de Bures (d. 1331) at Acton (Suffolk) (plate 11), which rank as some of the finest memorials ever produced. Though once thought to have been engraved in the late thirteenth century, they have now been redated on stylistic grounds to the 1320s and 1330s. Secondly, there are some small effigies which are all that survive of what were once floriated cross compositions. In these the brass effigy was either set at the intersection of the arms or, if the commemorated was shown kneeling, very likely placed at the foot of the cross. The inspiration for these very beautiful memorials came not from tomb sculpture but from stained glass windows or illuminated manuscripts.

English brasses in the middle ages remained very different from those manufactured in the Low Countries. The English engravers much preferred the 'separate inlay' technique to the Flemish rectangular plate. Only in the sixteenth century did they begin to use rectangular plates, and then only much smaller ones than the Flemish workshops had produced in their heyday. By and large the English shared the preference of the French and Polish engravers for sinking the component parts of the brass into separate matrices in the slab (plates 14, 16).

The majority of surviving medieval brasses came from workshops in London. The products of these workshops can be identified by certain stylistic conventions they adopted. We have to remember that most medieval effigies, whether tombs, incised slabs or brasses, were not portraits; they were stylised representations of the deceased. A client could ask to be shown in an up-to-date suit of armour. He could even request that his tomb be modelled on another that he had seen. But he did not expect his brass to be a physical resemblance. For this reason each workshop could develop its own standard designs which the master would pass on to the apprentices he trained, and even when these designs had to be up-dated to accommodate changes in fashion, stylistic continuity survived in the way that small details were portrayed. It is these details, or trade marks as it were, which enable us to identify the main schools of engraving in London over the two centuries up to the Reformation. Following the conventional classification, these are:

Style A (c. 1360–1410): their early knights are often rather clumsy; noses are engraved as if viewed from the side.

Style B (c. 1360–c. 1470): a prolific workshop in the first half of the fifteenth century, producing graceful though rather monotonous brasses identifiable by such motifs as a rose with four petals and four spines (e.g. in a canopy) and the criss-cross pattern for depicting grass below the feet (plates 12, 13a and b, 16).

Style D (C. 1410–c. 1485): this workshop may have taken over the business run by 'A'. They produced brasses more elaborate than those of 'B', and identifiable by the use of rose windows in canopies and flowery bases at the feet of figures (plates 14, 15).

Style F (c. 1475 onwards): perhaps the successor to 'B', their brasses can be identified by the bubbly, stalkless plants on the base and by the downward sloping horizontal bars of the capital H on inscriptions.

These were only the main work-

shops. We must not forget series 'C' and 'E', which were smaller businesses operating for a decade or so and then fading out. More importantly, there were also provincial workshops producing highly distinctive brasses at Norwich and York. What emerges, therefore, from a classification of surviving brasses along stylistic lines is something of the organisation of the engravers' trade. Even so, we have only distinguished the workshops, and not the men who worked in them. Can we discover any more about the engravers of English brasses than we could about their Flemish counterparts?

The men who made brasses were known as 'marblers'. The fact that they derived their name from work in stone suggests that brass engraving was carried on in workshops devoted principally to the production of tombs and tomb effigies. By a fortunate chance we still have the brass of one such 'marbler'. At Sudborough (Northants) is the brass of William West, his wife and their eleven children, one of whom, another William, is described as a 'marbler'. Now William West is known to have been a marbler in London in the 1430s, about the time that this brass, a standard product of series 'B', was engraved. If as seems likely, West was responsible for placing this brass in memory of his parents, in their local church, he would surely have ordered it from his own workshop. Perhaps, then, William West is the man behind series 'B'. We don't know for how long he remained in charge, but there is evidence that by 1454 the workshop was under new management. In that year John Essex, marbler, William Austen, founder and Thomas Stevyns, coppersmith, contracted to make an inscription for the tomb of Richard Beauchamp, earl of Warwick, at St Mary's, Warwick. Now the lettering of this inscription is of the style we find on series 'B' brasses. In other words, we surely have in Essex and Stevyns the men who took over the workshop after the retirement of West.

Having looked at the organization of the marbling trade, let us see briefly how brasses were made. What we call 'brass' was in fact an alloy of copper (75%-80% in the early fourteenth century), zinc (15%-20%), lead and tin, known by the term 'latten', and imported into England from the Continent. This was cut into plates up to 3' in length, which at some stage would be butted together and joined by a rectangular backing plate to make up a life-size brass like that of Sir John d'Abernon. Next, the design was sketched lightly on the surface, and the lines engraved to the required pattern using chasing tools and a burin. Cross-hatching was employed to show areas of shade. Like most medieval monuments, brasses were originally coloured. The lines were filled with black mastic, and the surface enamelled or gilded. When the brass was ready, it was fixed into the slab. The big, early brasses were heavy enough to be held down on a bed of pitch in the indent simply by the force of their own weight. Smaller brasses, however, needed to be secured by rivets driven into lead-filled sockets in the slab. The finished monument, slab and all, was then ready to be taken to its destination, along water routes wherever possible for reasons of both economy and convenience. Not surprisingly when we remember how bulky the finished product was likely to be, the expense of carriage added considerably to its final cost. A really lavish commission, like that ordered by Sir John de St Quintin in 1397, cost as much as 20 marks (£13.6.8). He wanted a marble stone and life-size brasses of himself and his two wives, to be laid at Brandsburton (Yorks). This brass still remains, and it is clearly the product of a workshop at York: Sir John saved on transport by ordering locally. Even so he (or his executors) did not get value for money. Only one wife was depicted, not two! Such evidence as survives suggests in fact that brasses could be ordered to suit every pocket. In 1471 the brass of Sir John Curson and his wife at Bylaugh (Norfolk), which is only half the size of Brandsburton, cost 8 marks (£5.6.8). Later still, in 1523, a 27in. figure of a priest, with shields and inscription, at St Alphege, Canterbury, cost only £4.10.0.

Because brasses were within the reach of the humblest trader or parish priest, they enjoyed a wide market from the fifteenth century onwards. Some 7,500 survive in England, more than in any other country in Europe. Many are superb works of craftsmanship, and all are valuable for the light they shed on changing fashions in armour (q.v.) and costume. Until recently they have attracted far more attention than stone or alabaster tombs simply because they are flat and can therefore be rubbed. This is unfortunate. Brass rubbings are certainly attractive to look at. But they are not essential to the study of brasses. Monumental sculpture was a thriving business in the middle ages, and, as we have seen, it is quite possible that tomb effigies, incised slabs and brasses could all have been manufactured in the same workshop. If we look more carefully at the other medieval monuments which fill our churches, we may end up by learning still more about brasses.

J. Page-Phillips, *Macklin's Monumental Brasses*, Allen & Unwin, 1969; M. Norris, *Monumental Brasses, the Craft*, Faber & Faber, 1978.

BRETIGNY, TREATY OF See, HUNDRED YEARS WAR.

BRISTOL Bristol was one of the two or three leading cities of medieval England and the most important centre of population in the west country. Our earliest evidence of the city's economic life is afforded by the chance survival of a couple of early eleventh century silver pennies, which indicate that it had a mint of its own by Ethelred the Unready's reign. From Domesday Book (q.v.) seventy or eighty years later we can sense that it had become a place of some importance, although, alas, the information provided by the survey is too incomplete to give any idea of the size of the local population or the trades they engaged in.

The town of Bristol itself was located in one corner of the royal manor of Barton Regis, near the junction of the Avon and Frome rivers. Across the Avon, on the Somerset side, lay the suburb of Redcliffe which was held by the Berkeley family of Berkeley Castle. Redcliffe enjoyed certain geographical advantages over Bristol itself, which enabled it in the thirteenth century to prosper at the expense of the older port. Needless to say, the burgesses of Bristol resented this competition, and the rivalry between the two communities culminated in attempts made by each to build harbour facilities to attract trade from the other. But it was not only with the port of Bristol that the men of Redcliffe found themselves at odds. Like burgesses elsewhere who chafed under what they regarded as the yoke of private lordship, they objected to having to hand over their profits to the manorial lord, and in 1305 their anger boiled over into attacks on Sir Maurice de Berkeley's property. The continued desire, whether successful or not we do not know, of the Berkeleys to tap the urban wealth of Redcliffe is hardly surprising in view of the trading wealth brought to Bristol and its suburbs in the late middle ages. The merchants throve on the long-established English tie with Gascony (q.v.). Further afield, they went to Spain, Portugal, and even to Madeira (Fig. 8).

Like their contemporaries elsewhere, the burgesses of Bristol invested some of their wealth in rebuilding or enlarging the local churches. The town had no cathedral of its own until 1542, when St Augustine's Abbey became the centre of a new diocese carved out of that of Worcester. But across the Avon at Redcliffe, it had in St Mary's a church of such magnificence that it was to be described by Queen Elizabeth as 'the fairest, goodliest and most famous parish Church in England'. Scale of architectural achievement is not always a reliable guide to urban prosperity in the middle ages, but in view of the trading links Bristol enjoyed, it seems likely that it escaped the worst of the economic decline that beset so many other towns at the end of the medieval period. All the same, we can agree that when John Cabot sailed from Bristol to America on 2 May 1497 he was opening a new era in the town's history.

B. Little, *The City and County of Bristol* (2nd ed., 1967).

BUILDING The size and magnificence of the cathedrals, abbeys and castles put up in the middle ages prompts us to ask how such enormous and complex structures could ever have been built. Let us not suppose that it is only by sheer luck that they have not fallen down. Certainly, the medieval builders had their disasters from time to time. But they knew more about mathematics and geometry than we sometimes give them credit for. We can say this because a good many sources about design and construction have come down to us, and from these we can piece together an account of how a great church or castle would have been built.

For sake of illustration let us visualize operations at their grandest by taking the example of a major church. The motives that led a bishop or a cathedral chapter to embark on a lengthy programme of reconstruction were various. At Canterbury it was a disastrous fire that caused the choir to be rebuilt after 1174. At Ely it was the collapse of the central tower. On other occasions it was the desire to create larger and more dignified surroundings for a saint's shrine.

Once the decision had been taken, money had to be raised. For this purpose a fabric fund would be opened. Churches like Canterbury fortunate enough to possess the relics of a popular saint were assured of a regular income from the offerings of pilgrims. Others had to supplement their ordinary revenues, just as we do today, by launching an appeal. Bishops organized preaching tours to create an enthusiasm for the project, and local landowners were persuaded to dig into their pockets.

As soon as the money started flowing in, the clergy were free to think about possible designs. So often in guide books we read statements attributing rebuilding operations to this or that bishop that we gain the impression that the clergy themselves were responsible for the execution of all the plans. Almost certainly this view is mistaken. Just occasionally the evidence points to the guiding hand of a clerk or monastic official, like Alan of Walsingham, the sacrist at Ely, who is usually credited with conceiving the Octagon; but more often the responsibility for architectural planning rested with the master mason. Here we must notice an important difference between medieval and modern building organization. Today it is the professional architect who draws the plans and the builder who supervises construction. In the middle ages, however, this distinction did not exist, and the master mason who had overall direction of the works and responsibility for the design would have begun his career years before as a trainee in the stonemason's yard.

Although responsibility for conceiving a design would be his, the master mason would need to take into account the wishes of those who were paying him. On the Continent the mason was often asked to construct a model to enable his clients to see what the completed building would look like. In England this does not seem to have been done, although we can hardly suppose that a cathedral chapter would authorize an ambitious scheme without first inspecting the plans. Whatever happened, we can assume that drawings would have been made at some stage, whether in a sketch book, like the one kept by an early thirteenth century Frenchman, Villard de Honnecourt, or on a plaster tracing floor, like the ones that have survived in upstairs chambers at York Minster and Wells Cathedral.

As soon as the designs had been agreed, work could begin on laying the foundations. Sometimes, as at Westminster Abbey in 1245, the old walls had to be demolished before erection of the new could begin. Elsewhere, particularly if it was an eastwards extension that was contemplated, the new foundations could be laid out around and

47

beyond the old work. Orientation was at first rather rough and ready, but the rediscovery of geometry in the twelfth century enabled builders to be more precise in working out the lines and angles, and accumulated experience no doubt counted for still more. Trenches were then dug — to a depth of as much as 31 feet for the tower of St Stephen's, Bristol — and filled with rubble as a footing for the walls. If the ground was marshy, it would be necessary first to reinforce the base by ramming in timber piles; the dangers that arose if this precaution were not taken appeared in 985 at Ramsey Abbey, where a newly-built tower gave way and had to be dismantled.

By the time the foundations were being set, arrangements would have been made for stone to be quarried. A few important churches enjoyed rights over a particular quarry, but others less favoured had to hire a quarry as needed, or simply buy stone on the open market. The celebrated quarry at Caen in Normandy was even used as a source by English builders after the Conquest. For churches like Canterbury it was probably cheaper to buy stone in France and ship it across the Channel than to cart it over-land from some English quarry. The most celebrated English quarries used in the middle ages were those at Barnack, which supplied stone for Norwich, Ely and Cambridge, Doulting, which supplied Wells, Chilmark, which supplied Salisbury, and Reigate, which supplied London.

When the stone had arrived, work could start on erecting the walls. The manner of construction varied according to time and place. Some walls would be composed of rubble, roughly hewn blocks of stone cemented by mortar, others, at least in part, of 'ashlar', regularly shaped pieces of stone so placed as to give a smooth surface. In Norman times the surfaces would usually be rough, and then plastered to receive frescoes, but later, as tools became more sophisticated, it became common, even if most of the wall was rubble, to give it a smooth ashlar finish. Once the walls started rising, scaffolding would be needed. There are plenty of illustrations in contemporary manuscripts showing the various forms of scaffold known to medieval man. One of the most ingenious was spiral scaffolding, probably devised to facilitate the construction of the circular towers which are a feature of military architecture in the thirteenth and fourteenth centuries. On most sites, however, the scaffolding would probably have looked little different from that in use today, except that it was constructed of wood instead of steel; and instead of planks, the walkways were made of wattled hurdles. When the walls had reached their full height, a wooden roof would be built, so that the job of erecting the stone vault could be carried out underneath in the dry.

One of the most difficult and dangerous operations must have been raising the stone up to the dizzy heights attained by some medieval towers. Large blocks like roof bosses, which had to be placed at the intersection of vaulting ribs, were fashioned either at the quarry or on the site, using a hammer and chisel. They would then have to be hoisted up by some sort of device, of which the simplest and earliest was a great hempen cable passed over a pivot. In the thirteenth century the treadwheel came into use, and the one that survives today in the tower of Salisbury Cathedral was very likely used in its construction in the fourteenth century. By the end of the middle ages another advance was made when cranes, for long in use on the quayside, were adopted for building purposes, and erected on roof-lines to hoist up stones and roof timbers.

How quickly was a building finished in the middle ages? There are no end of examples to show that construction of a cathedral nave could take the best part of half-a-century. By the 1180s, when the nave at Peterborough was completed, the Romanesque style in which it had been started was looking decidedly outmoded. On the other hand, work proceeded quite quickly at Salisbury, where the present cathedral (except the spire) was finished in 38 years (q.v. ARCHITECTURE, ECCLESIASTICAL). Certainly as far as ecclesiastical buildings were concerned what slowed down the pace of building was the irregular supply of funds: at St Alban's shortage of money brought work on the west front to a halt in the early thirteenth century, and the hard-pressed abbot had to organize preaching-tours to raise cash. In some of the greater churches as soon as construction finished at one end of the building, it was time to start again at the other. At York, for example, the commencement of work on a new nave in 1290 inaugurated a long and intermittent era of building that was not to end until the central tower was completed in 1472.

By looking at the cathedrals, the grandest creations of the middle ages, we can easily come away with the impression that most medieval building was done in stone. Nothing could be further from the truth. For most domestic, and even some ecclesiastical, architecture timber-frame construction was the rule. Wood was more widely available than stone, and in those parts of England where quarries were few, there was bound to be a forest that could provide supplies of oak. Carpenters never had to seek far for their raw material. But once they had obtained it, they rarely allowed it time to season. The result inevitably was that it warped, producing the rakish lines that today characterize so many timber-framed houses constructed in this period.

While the carpenters were cutting the timber to size, preparation of the foundations could go ahead. If the timber-frame were to be rested directly on the ground, the soil would be levelled and rammed down firm. But it made better sense, for avoiding rot, to erect the frame on a low stone wall to the height of about 3 feet or 4 feet. On the more substantial properties, this precaution would almost certainly be taken. When the groundwalks were ready, the end-frames would be erected. Sometimes these frames were assembled on the site, and sometimes at a distant yard, whence they were dragged to their destination and lifted into position. It was possible to use this prefabricated technique because of the construction method, based on the mortice and tenon, which enabled one timber to be locked into another. Once all the framing was in position, work could begin on filling the spaces between the timbers. This was usually done by the well-known method of 'wattle and daub', by which interwoven reeds or twigs were covered with plaster. The inside walls, as in a church, would very probably have been whitewashed and painted. As for roofing, thatch would probably have been employed most often in the earlier part of our period, and tiles or lead later on, by those who could afford it.

L. F. Salzman, *Building in England down to 1540*, Oxford, 2nd ed., 1967.

C

CADE'S REBELLION The man who gave his name to the rebellion against Henry VI's government in 1450 was a Kentishman called Jack Cade. His parentage and background remain obscure, indeed, infuriatingly so, because he could hardly have drawn the support he did from gentry as well as commons had he been an upstart peasant. The course of the rebellion recalls the Peasants Revolt (q.v.) of 1381. Towards the end of May the rebels gathered in Kent, and took over the capital. There they behaved so badly that the citizens, aided by the garrison of the Tower fought to regain control of London Bridge. A few days later a free pardon was offered and the rebels withdrew. But Cade's rebellion, far more than the Peasants Revolt, was a product of largely political grievances arising from corruption at home and defeat abroad. The dominance at Henry VI's court in the 1440s of the duke of Suffolk and his clique had given rise to wide-spread resentment which boiled over after the duke's murder on 3 May 1450. All the predictable complaints found expression in Cade's manifesto, a document embodying familiar ideas that had been the stock-in-trade of reform movements for the previous two hundred years. It blamed the evils of the realm on the 'false counsel' that the king had received from Suffolk and his progeny who, it said, should be dismissed and replaced by lords of the blood royal like the duke of York. Though the manifesto had been considered by the council at the end of May, it passed into oblivion once the rebels had been dispersed and Cade himself rounded up and killed. But, if it achieved nothing else, the rebellion did have the important consequence of encouraging York to hurry back from Ireland to claim the position in national politics sought for him by the commons of Kent.

CALAIS The town of Calais was England's bridgehead to the Continent in the late middle ages. In proportion to its size it was the most costly to win of Edward III's prizes in the Hundred Years War (q.v.), but also, as it turned out, the most important and the most long-lasting. Edward had defeated the French at Crecy (q.v.) on 26 August 1346. Overwhelming though his victory was, he wanted something more tangible to show for his efforts. So on 4 September he surrounded Calais, and began a siege that was to last for no less than eleven months. English losses were heavy, and when the town eventually surrendered on 4 August 1347 he was in no mood to be merciful to the burghers, whose lives, according to the famous story, he spared only after the pleading of his queen. And that was as far as his generosity went. He expelled them from the town, and repopulated it with English settlers. Calais became a part of metropolitan England in all but name.

The strategic advantages the English gained from the possession of Calais go without saying. They won control of both sides of the Channel; and they obtained a continental foothold from which to undertake future campaigns against France. The town was defended by a permanent garrison, which in the fifteenth century became a force to reckon with in the turbulent domestic politics of the time. Whoever won the captaincy of Calais had under his command a private army that he could use in the struggle for power in England. Warwick (q.v.) got the post in 1455, when the Yorkists temporarily had the upper hand, and it was from Calais five years later that he launched the invasion which culminated in his victory at Northampton on 10 July 1460 (q.v., WARS OF THE ROSES).

We can imagine that the Calais garrison would have followed their distinguished commander anywhere he wanted them to go so long as he was on the winning side. When his luck ran out in 1470 and he had to flee from Edward IV's England, he found the gates of Calais closed against him. The troops wanted not a refugee but a captain well placed at court who could make sure they were paid regularly. Access to the Exchequer mattered a lot to soldiers whose wages were usually months if not years in arrears. The problem was that Calais was dependent on Exchequer subsidies to the tune of some £1,500 *per annum* in peacetime and £3–£4,000 in wartime. How was this money to be found? The solution eventually reached was made possible by the establishment in 1363 at Calais of the 'staple' through which nearly all of England's wool exports to the Continent would pass. The setting-up of the Calais staple brought to an end the long and often bitter argument over the exporting of wool and the taxes to be paid on it. On the one hand, the king wanted to restrict the right of exporting to a group of merchants assured of making sufficient profit to enable them to lend to the Crown on the security of the customs and subsidy levied on wool. On the other hand, the growers favoured a larger consortium of merchants with whom they would be free to bargain for the best price they could get. In 1363 a compromise was reached. Edward III established at Calais a 'staple' or mart run by a broadly based company of some 200 merchants whose monopoly position would enable them to make loans, repayable later from the customs revenue. The Exchequer still retained responsibility for paying the garrison; but they could anticipate income by contracting loans with the Staplers. It was to be another century before they finally conceived what we would regard as the obvious and logical solution. This was the Act of Retainer, 1466, by which the Company of the Staple itself assumed responsibility for collecting the customs and subsidy on wool, out of the proceeds of which they would meet the cost of the Calais garrison.

The arms of the Company can be seen on brasses to Staplers at Thame (Oxon) and Northleach (Gloucs). These brasses (q.v.) constitute some of the few visible survivals of the English occupation of Calais. There is little to see at the town itself.

CAMBRIDGE Long before the scholars arrived, there had been a settlement at Cambridge. Here a number of roads converged at what was the most northerly point for effecting a passage from East Anglia to the Midlands before the Fens made communications impossible. The Romans had built an enclosure north of the river in the present-day Chesterton Lane area, but by the twelfth century the centre of life in Cambridge, as indicated by church building, had shifted southward to where the town centre is today. The first hard evidence for the existence of a community of scholars in Cambridge comes in 1209 when one of those periodic fights between clerks and townfolk in Oxford (q.v.) led to the migration eastwards of a group of the masters. Why they chose Cambridge we do not know. Was it because it was near to the rich and populous East Anglian counties?

In its organization and constitutional development Cambridge closely followed Oxford. The Chancellor of the University is first mentioned in 1230 within a year or two of the appearance of the same official in Oxford. In both universities the undergraduates lived in houses around the town rented by Principals which in Oxford were known as halls and in Cambridge as hostels. The colleges which characterize the two cities today were called into being to cater for the needs of graduates undertaking the long courses of study that would take them by their early thirties to a doctorate. The first Cambridge college was Peterhouse, founded in 1280 by Hugh de Balsham, bishop of Ely, for 'studious scholars living according to the rule of the scholars of Oxford called of Merton.' In the first half of the fourteenth century there followed King's Hall (before 1316), Michaelhouse (1324), University or Clare Hall (1326), Pembroke (1347), Gonville (1348), Trinity Hall (1350) and Corpus Christi (1352). Of these the most remarkable were King's Hall, originating as its name suggests in an endowment from the king, and Corpus, the only college in either university to be founded by the town guilds. For the next century there were no more colleges until the foundation of Godshouse in 1439 and King's by Henry VI (q.v.) in 1441. The early history of King's was chequered, for the collapse of the Lancastrian monarchy in 1461 brought work on its great chapel to a halt for

sixteen years until it was resumed by Edward IV in 1477 and then carried to completion by Henry VIII in 1515 (plate 6). Ninety-four feet high and nearly 300 feet in length this chapel of cathedralesque proportions must have towered even more than it does today over the country town which sheltered at its feet. Let us not forget as well that for the first century-and-a-half of its existence Cambridge was a smaller university than Oxford, probably less than half its size in terms of total numbers. Only in the fifteenth century did it start to catch up.

See also, UNIVERSITIES.

T. H. Aston, G. D. Duncan, T. A. R. Evans, 'The Medieval Alumni of the University of Cambridge', *Past & Present*, 86 (1980); N. Pevsner, *Cambridgeshire*, Harmondsworth, 2nd ed., 1970.

CANTERBURY The ancient cathedral city to which Chaucer's (q.v.) band of pilgrims made their way began its history as a Roman settlement called *Durovernum Cantiacorum*. In Saxon times it was the seat of the Jutish kings who ruled Kent. When Augustine and his fellow missionaries landed at Ebbsfleet in 597, they were assured of a sympathetic reception at the court because Bertha, Ethelbert's queen, was a Christian from the royal house of France. Bede tells us that she used a church on the eastern side of the city dedicated to St Martin of Tours which had been built by the Christians in Roman times. It is still standing today, and claims with some justice to be the oldest church in England. A couple of hundred yards to its west Augustine established the abbey of St Peter and St Paul, later known as St Augustine's because it received his body when he died in 605. Bede tells us that Augustine took over the site of another former Romano-British place of worship for the church, dedicated to Christ, which was destined to become Canterbury Cathedral. Later in the middle ages its archbishop, by virtue of his lineal descent from Augustine, claimed the title of 'Primate of All England'. Constitutionally Canterbury was a cathedral monastery. In other words, its services were sung by a community of Benedictine monks. The monastic precincts, rightly described as one of the best architectural mazes in England, survive on the northern side of the present cathedral, partly hidden under the later buildings of King's School.

The story of the present fabric begins with Lanfranc (q.v.), the first Norman archbishop, who rebuilt the church after his appointment in 1070. Only a generation later, however, the eastern half was rebuilt again, the crypt in the time of Prior Ernulf, the choir in the time of Prior Conrad. The former is the largest Norman crypt in England. Conrad's choir was destroyed by fire in 1174. Its place was taken by the choir and Trinity Chapel we see today, an early Gothic design with an affinity to Sens Cathedral in France easily explicable by the fact that one William of Sens was the architect (plate 2). The cathedral was completed in the fourteenth and fifteenth centuries, when the present nave, transepts and towers were built. Visually, Canterbury offers one of the most remarkable interiors in England. The view eastwards along the nave ends abruptly at the crossing. The strainer arches under the tower and the big flight of steps up the screen block any view further east into the choir. But why all the steps? The answer is that the crypt was hardly a crypt at all in the strict sense of the word, but rather an undercroft built at ground level. Consequently the choir had to be raised above it. The Canterbury crypt was large, larger than any other in England, because it housed so many saints' relics. Of these the most important were of course the bones of 'the holy, blissful, martyr', Becket (q.v.). Murdered in his own cathedral in December 1170, he was canonized four years later, and his cult soon made Canterbury the one pilgrimage centre in England of European importance. In 1220 the bones were translated to a new shrine in the Trinity Chapel behind the high altar where they were to remain until their destruction at the Reformation. They attracted countless pilgrims (q.v. PILGRIMAGES). Then as now Canterbury prospered on the tourist trade.

CARTHUSIANS In 1084 Bruno, a canon of Rheims, abandoned a brilliant career as a teacher to found a religious community at La Chartreuse near Grenoble. He was one of those men not uncommon in the eleventh century who chose to reject the vanities of the world in favour of the austerities of a life of contemplation. But rather than opt for the conventional life of the monk, he preferred to go back to an older tradition and re-create the eremetical life of the early desert fathers. He and his brethren did not eat and sleep in common; they lived in separate cells around the cloister. They followed St Benedict in dividing the day between work, reading and prayer; but they assembled in the church for only a few of the services, the rest being recited in private in the cell. What Bruno did on that rocky mountainside near Grenoble was to graft the ancient tradition of the hermits onto the communal tradition of orthodox Benedictine monasticism. Yet his achievement might have died with him, had not Guigo, the fifth prior, put his usage into writing, and encouraged the foundation of more Charterhouses in France.

The first English Charterhouse was established in 1178 at Witham (Somerset) as one of the monasteries founded by Henry II in atonement for the murder of Becket (q.v.). But it was only much later still, in the fourteenth and fifteenth centuries that the Carthusian ideal, as pure and as austere as in its earliest days, began to exercise a strong appeal over potential founders. Seven of their nine houses in England were founded between 1370 and 1420. Rather remarkably, the men responsible for this late flowering of the Order were members of the military aristocracy, like Sir Walter Mauny, who founded the London Charterhouse, Thomas Mowbray, earl of Nottingham, who founded Epworth, Thomas Holland, duke of Surrey, who founded Mount Grace, and King Henry V (q.v.) himself, who endowed Sheen in 1415. The Carthusians were among the beneficiaries of that growth of lay piety which characterized the late middle ages. What appealed to their high-born patrons was their preservation of a life of poverty and solitude to a degree remarkable among the Religious Orders. This they were able to do by remaining a small and select band and by adopting the Cistercian practice of annual chapters or meetings to legislate for the Order.

The manner in which the distinctive quality of Carthusian life influenced the lay-out of their priories can best be seen by looking at the ruins of Mount Grace in Yorkshire. Around the main cloister were ranged the church and the cells of the monks, fifteen in number and each with its own garden. To the south another and smaller cloister was built early in the fifteenth century to provide accommodation for six more monks. It says much for the popularity of the Carthusians that Mount Grace should have had to cater for rising numbers at a time when most houses did well to prevent them from falling.

See also, MONASTICISM.

CASTLES The history of castle-building in Britain begins with the Norman Conquest in 1066. It is not often in medieval history that we can be so definite about anything, but all the available evidence points to the introduction of private fortresses by the Normans. The Anglo-Saxons were well familiar with *communal* fortifications – burhs – which defended the entire population of a town, but the idea of a lord building his own private, heavily fortified residence (i.e., a castle) was foreign to their experience. The one or two castles known to have existed in England before 1066, Hereford and Clavering for example, are the exceptions that prove the rule, for they were built by Norman favourites of King Edward the Confessor who came and settled here. What necessitated a great wave of castle building all across England was the arrival in 1066 of a small band of invaders, numbering no more than a few thousand, who needed to make themselves secure in a newly-won country where they were surrounded by a hostile subject population. The castle was the perfect answer to the problems posed by occupying a conquered land.

The earliest Norman castles, whether built by the king or his barons, were simple affairs, laid out on the motte-and-bailey plan. The motte was a large mound of earth, crowned by a wooden palisade, at the foot of which lay an enclosure known as the bailey (Fig. 2a). The entire fortification would be surrounded by a ditch, and in most cases the bailey would itself be separated by another ditch from the motte, which was regarded as a strongpoint of last resort, capable of holding out long after the rest of the castle had fallen. These simple fortifications could be erected both cheaply and quickly because earth and timber were the only raw materials required. The Bayeux Tapestry (q.v.) shows the Normans heaping up a motte at Hastings before they went out to meet Harold in battle. According to the chronicler Orderic Vitalis, in 1068 William the Conqueror (q.v.) had castles built at Warwick, Nottingham, York, Lincoln, Huntingdon and Cambridge, all in the course of a campaign lasting only a few months. No doubt he

made use of conscript labour. Very few of these earliest castles, possibly only the great keeps of Colchester and the Tower of London, were built of stone right from the start. Most would have been built of timber, and then rebuilt in stone as soon as time allowed – or not rebuilt at all.

If any feature of military architecture is identified in popular imagination with the Normans, it is surely the keep. Yet the great stone keeps that often pass in the guide books as 'Norman' are more than likely to be twelfth century, not eleventh, and the creation of the Angevin kings, not their predecessors. As we have seen, Colchester and the Tower of London are probably the only stone keeps to date from the reign of the Conqueror himself. It was the long era of internal peace a generation later in the reign of Henry I (q.v.) that gave both king and barons an opportunity to

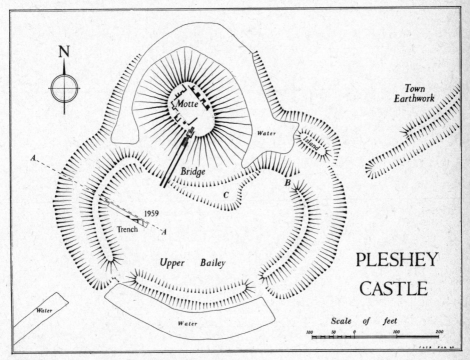

Figure 2a   A typical motte-and-bailey castle.

modernize and strengthen the old motte-and-bailey fortifications. By resorting to every device he could to wring money from his subjects, Henry I could dispose of resources that enabled him to raise up the splendid keeps we see at Norwich and Rochester. And, as always in medieval architectural history, if the king set a fashion, the nobility were quick to follow. The great keeps of William d'Albini at Castle Rising, Aubrey de Vere at Hedingham and Geoffrey de Clinton at Kenilworth could match in size and magnificence any of those the king built. The keep was designed principally to serve the military purpose for which the castle had been called into being, but it also contained the domestic quarters – the hall, solar, garrison rooms, cellars and so on. Hence the sheer size of the keep,

which was sometimes so large that the old motte had to be flattened to make way for it. As often as not, however, the wooden palisade crowning the motte would be replaced not by a square keep but by the circular structure we know as the shell keep. In this design the domestic apartments were ranged against the inside wall of the 'shell' (Fig. 2b).

How successfully did these twelfth-century castles stand up to the assaults of the enemy? Well enough, certainly, to cause the military engineers to devote all their energy and ingenuity to developing the science of siege warfare. For the castle's purpose was to afford a strong defensive point which had to be taken by the opposing force if it was to be free from attack in the rear. It is for that reason that sieges figure so pro-

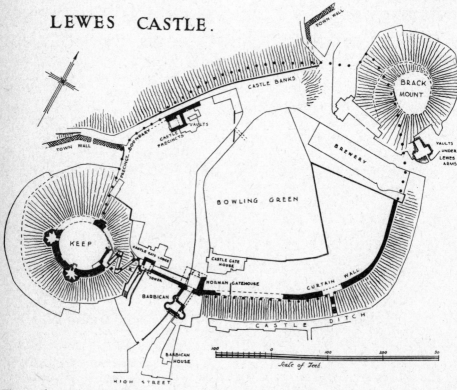

Figure 2b Unusual combination of two mottes and one bailey.

minently in twelfth-century history; it is for that reason that the civil war of Stephen's (q.v.) reign (1135–54) turned not on battles in the field but on sieges of castles like that at Faringdon, the fall of which, according to Henry of Huntingdon, decided the outcome of the war in Stephen's favour. The weapons at the disposal of besiegers were stone-throwing machines, like mangonels, and battering rams that could be used to breach a hole in the wall. If all else failed, the garrison could be starved into submission.

The value of the Norman castle, then, was its defensive strength. But by the end of the twelfth century military architects were thinking of ways that the besieged could turn the attack back onto the besiegers. This they did in two ways. First, they erected projecting battlements, or machicolations, on top of the walls so that the defenders could fire down with impunity on the men attacking them below. (And it was not just arrows and bolts that came down on the attackers. Boiling water and anything else to hand was used as well.) Secondly, they placed towers at intervals along the walls. Since the keep was already quite strong enough, these were usually placed along the much weaker perimeter of the bailey. An enemy attacking any part of the wall would then be exposed to fire from a flanking tower on each side of him. Mural towers of this kind first made their appearance at Dover (c. 1179–91), and were then taken up at Framlingham (c. 1200), where their implications for the future were apparent: for the keep was dispensed with altogether, leaving only the bailey. The castle had become a simple walled enclosure defended by the flanking towers. The old dichotomy of motte and bailey was abandoned in favour of an integrated fortification in which the defence was no longer concentrated on a single strongpoint but disposed equally around the walls.

This concept of military architecture found fullest expression in the castles which Edward I (q.v.) built in north Wales (q.v.) to encircle Snowdonia (Fig. 3). Conway (1283–87), for example, is planned as a rectangle, irregularly-shaped so as to exploit the contours of the rocky prominence on which it was built, and fortified by massive drum towers which punctuate the circuit of the walls. More sophisticated still, and the logical culmination of this line of architectural development, was the concentric castle. The principles upon which it was founded can easily be seen by looking at the plan of Beaumaris Castle in Anglesey (Fig. 4). One ring of fortifications encloses another, and the approaches to north and south were commanded by matching gatehouses. Where did the idea of the concentric castle come from? Very likely from the Middle East, where we find the majestic Crusader castles constructed on this principle. The earliest concentric works in England to which a definite date can be assigned are those at the Tower of London undertaken by Edward after he had returned from Palestine, filled with new ideas, in 1274. No sooner had Edward set his masons to work than one of his greatest subjects, Gilbert de Clare, earl of Gloucester, began building a completely new castle at Caerphilly (Glamorgan), which by the time of its completion was to become the purest concentric fortress of its day, and very likely a model for Beaumaris. Though the likes of Edward I and Gilbert de Clare commissioned these great castles, they did not of course design them. Can we therefore identify any master mason, or architect as we would call him now, to whom Edward's programme in north Wales can be attributed? The genius in question was almost certainly James of St George, a Savoyard who settled in England and developed the science of military archi-

tecture to a level of sophistication never to be surpassed in the middle ages.

For the truth of the matter is that Master James represented a climax, not a new beginning. Castles on the scale of

Figure 3 Recruitment of labour for Edward I's Welsh castles.

Conway, Caernarvon and Beaumaris were never to be built again. They were not needed. Indeed, the ring of fortresses encircling Snowdonia made Edward's Welsh conquests so secure that the two largest ones – Caernarvon and Beaumaris – were left unfinished. A few castles were still built from scratch in the late middle ages, notably Queenborough and Bodiam in southern England to meet the threat to the Channel coast from French marauders; but piecemeal improvement in the cause of greater comfort was more common. That commodious apartments could be accommodated within walls all too familiar with the sight of war is demonstrated by the remarkable tower-house which Henry Percy, earl of Northumberland built in the 1380s at Warkworth in the Scottish borderland. It was a sophisticated variation on an old

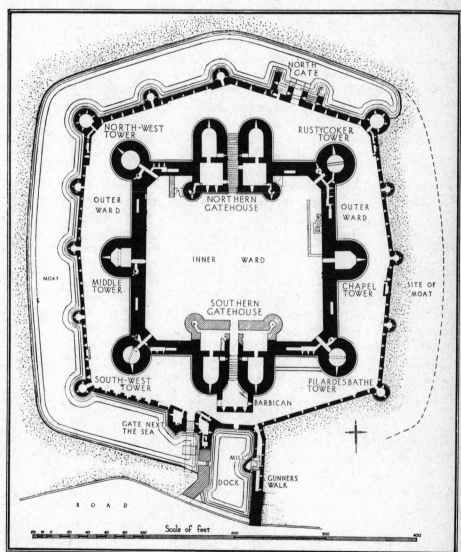

Figure 4 Beaumaris Castle, Anglesey, 1295-*c.* 1330.

theme – the keep perched on top of a motte. Yet it was not unique. In the late middle ages the idea of the keep or great tower enjoyed a remarkable revival, as we can see at Caister, Kirby Muxloe and most dramatically of all at Tattershall. Was this pure antiquarianism? Or a response to the collapse in public order of the Wars of the Roses (q.v.) of the mid-fifteenth century? More likely the latter. But in the last resort we must not underestimate the element of show-manship in it all. Tattershall was even built of brick, not stone!

Despite the emphasis on magnificence in fifteenth-century military architecture, internal peace in England was not so firmly established as to make the construction of serious fortifications a total waste of time. The Wars of the Roses did after all last on and off for the best part of 30 years. But whereas, say, the civil war of Stephen's reign was decided by one siege after another, the civil war of York v. Lancaster was decided by battles fought in the field. It is this transformation in military tactics which is wrapped up in the phrase 'the decline of the castle'. The point is surely that castles were rendered obsolete by their own strength. The more invincible the castle became, the longer and more expensive a successful siege would have to be. This is why the age of castle warfare in English history hardly saw out the thirteenth century. Once the king had come to dispose of such wealth that he could support large armies in the field for months at a time, it made better sense to adopt offensive tactics and decide the issue quickly in the field. Redundant as a fortress, the castle could now complete the transition to becoming a country house.

R. A. Brown, *English Castles*, Batsford, revised ed., 1962.

CAXTON, WILLIAM   Right at the end of the middle ages William Caxton brought the new-fangled art of printing to England. He was uniquely qualified to do so. He had spent 30 years of his life as a merchant in the Low Countries, where he had probably worked for a time in a printing-house. To a knowledge of how the processes actually worked Caxton was able to bring a keen interest in literature. He had translated the 'Recuyell of the Historyes of Troye', a work which he and a partner later printed at Bruges in the 1470s, When he returned to England, he established a printing-press in the precincts of Westminster Abbey, and in 1477 the first book was printed there. What sort of works did Caxton print for the English market? Perhaps the most famous was Malory's (q.v.) *Morte Darthur*, published in 1485, the year of Bosworth. But nearly half of the volumes that appeared before Caxton's death in 1491 were manuals of piety and devotion, like Jacob of Voragine's *Golden Legend*. We need not be surprised by this. It was merely a reflection of the tastes of the day. And what did the introduction of printing mean for the development of the language? It contributed to the evolution of an accepted written standard. At the risk of exaggeration, it did for written English in the late fifteenth century what the BBC is supposed to do for spoken English today.

CHAMBER   See, GOVERNMENT

CHANCERY See,   GOVERN-MENT

CHANTRIES   Elaborate   chantry chapels form so prominent a feature of the interior of our major churches that we are apt to get a misleading impression of what was involved in the foundation of a chantry in the middle ages. The provision of a chantry need not entail the erection of a chapel to go with it. A chantry pure and simple was no more than a private mass celebrated regularly at a side altar for the repose of the souls of the founder and any others named by him. What encouraged testators to set aside money in their wills for the celebration of such *post obitum* masses was a belief that a regular offering of the eucharist was the most effective way of 'drawing down the mercy of God'. The great surge in the popularity of chantries in the late middle ages was probably a response, therefore, to the increasing importance of the mass in the Catholic liturgy (q.v.), as evidenced by the pronouncement of the doctrine of transubstantiation in 1215 and the institution of the feast of Corpus Christi in 1264. Consequently, the money that had been invested in the foundation of monasteries in the eleventh and twelfth centuries was invested in chantries in the fourteenth and fifteenth.

If a founder were to endow a chantry in his life-time, he would usually require the mass-priest to celebrate masses for his current well-being and for the safe repose of his soul after death. More often, however, a testator made provision for the celebration of these soul-masses in his will. Wealthy prelates and politicians, weighed down by guilty consciences, ordered as many masses as they could afford. Ralph, Lord Cromwell (d. 1455) provided for 3,000, and the mighty Cardinal Beaufort (q.v.) for as many as 10,000. These were the kind of men who erected the lovely chantry chapels that line the aisles of churches like Tewkesbury Abbey and Win-

chester Cathedral. But it is important to remember that these only represent the foundations of the very rich. What led to the enormous proliferation of chantry masses in the late middle ages was the fact that they were cheap to endow, and well within the means of the middle and indeed some of the humbler classes. Robert Whittington of Pauntley, for example, provided in his will for a priest to celebrate masses in Pauntley church (Gloucs) for one year after his death for the repose of his soul, those of his parents, of John Brouning and Sibyl Staunton and of all the faithful departed. Provision for the celebration of masses for a limited period of time was quite a common arrangement. Robert Whittington said one year. Humbler testators could probably only afford a few weeks, or one every year for a year or two.

By the end of the middle ages, then, literally thousands of masses had been endowed. So many, in fact, that a whole class of humble chantry priests was called into being. William Langland (q.v.), the author of *Piers the Plowman*, was one. Many of these men served chantries whose revenues were so diminished in value with the passage of time that they could hardly support the priest. At St Paul's the position had become so acute by 1391 that Bishop Braybrooke carried out a reorganization of the chantries in the cathedral so as to reduce the number of chaplains from 57 to 31. A couple of decades later Bishop Repingdon performed a similar reorganization in his cathedral of Lincoln, cutting the number from 41 to 19.

Chantries came to an end in the sixteenth century, when the monasteries too were swept away. In 1547 an Act was passed dissolving all chantry foundations and transferring their property to the Crown for the relief of the poor, the endowment of grammar schools and the 'relief of the King's charges.'

G. H. Cook, *Medieval Chantries & Chantry Chapels*, John Baker, 1968.

CHAUCER, GEOFFREY In the fourteenth century England produced its two greatest poets of the middle ages, William Langland (q.v.) and Geoffrey Chaucer. They were living and working at about the same, within a few hundred yards of each other in London; yet for all they had in common, they might have lived worlds apart. With Langland, a humble chantry priest, we enter into the sufferings and grievances of the labouring classes; with Chaucer, an esquire of the king's household, we move in the polite society of the 'courtly makers'.

Chaucer was in fact born not into the gentry but into the mercantile elite of London, probably in about 1342. It was quite easy, however, for a young man of his birth to obtain a minor position at court or in a noble household, and between 1356 and 1359 he started off as a page in the service of Elizabeth, Countess of Ulster. In 1359–60 he joined Edward III's campaign in France, but had the misfortune to be captured. The king paid £16 for his ransom. What he did after his return to England we cannot be sure. Though Chaucer's life is copiously documented compared with Langland's, there are periods when he just disappears from view. Perhaps he travelled abroad. We know that after 1367, when he became a king's esquire, he made at least two visits to Italy on official business, one in 1372–3 to Genoa, the other in 1378 to Milan. These journeys were of great

importance for Chaucer's development as a poet because they brought him into direct contact with the work of Dante and Boccaccio. The latter's *Il Filostrato*, for example, forms the basis of Chaucer's *Troilus and Criseyde*, and *Teseide* the basis of *The Knight's Tale*. We can't be sure about the dating of all of Chaucer's works, but other poems likely to have been written in the early or middle years of his life were the *Boke of the Duchesse* (c. 1368–69), the *Hous of Fame* (c. 1380) and the *Parlement of Foules* (c. 1382). By the time that he embarked on *The Canterbury Tales* in about 1387, Chaucer was both more independent in his approach to poetry and also more mature in his outlook on life. For some years now he had been employed on royal service, and his importance at court made him a suitable person to hold local office in the county where he now resided, namely Kent: when not in Westminster, or at his house in Aldgate in the City, he lived at Greenwich with his wife Philippa. In October 1385 he was appointed a J.P. in Kent, and twelve months later served in parliament as an M.P. for the same county. By the 1390s, however, he was beginning to lay aside these public offices. In 1391, for example, he was replaced as clerk of the king's works, and compensated with the office, largely a sinecure one suspects, of sub-forester of North Petherton (Somerset).

One reason for his withdrawal from the public eye may well have been a desire to press forward with the great work for which he is chiefly remembered, *The Canterbury Tales*. On the suggestion of the Host, Harry Bailly, the pilgrims assembling at the Tabard Inn at Southwark agree to tell a couple of tales each on the outward journey to Canterbury and a couple on the return. This scheme, as it turned out, was far too ambitious. At any rate, Chaucer never produced that number of tales, and there are other signs in the work that the project was left uncompleted. But it remains an undoubted masterpiece. The prologue with which it opens is the most memorable portrait gallery in English literature. When we pass onto the Tales, we find Chaucer at his most versatile, equally skilful whether handling the story of Palamon and Arcite, as in the Knight's Tale, adapting a Breton lay, as in the Franklin's Tale, or just telling a good dirty yarn, as in the Miller's Tale. Chaucer was a born story teller. Does that imply that he was superficial? Certainly not. He was a man of the world, acute and perceptive in his observations. Though close to the court, he always steered clear of direct involvement in politics, preferring instead to stand on the side-lines watching how others acted in the drama of human experience. Unlike his great contemporary, Langland, however, Chaucer does not seem to have been a deeply religious man. In fact he is the first great English poet whose work is not religious in purpose or content. He is the first 'courtly maker', father of a long line of poets stretching down to Wyatt and Surrey in the sixteenth century.

He died on 25 October 1400, and was buried in the south transept of Westminster Abbey, the part later to become famous as Poets' Corner. His genius was recognized in his own lifetime, and lesser poets who followed, like Hoccleve and Lydgate, acknowledged him as their master. Chaucer's record of service to the Crown was matched, indeed exceeded, by that of his son, Thomas, who made himself an indispensable counsellor of the Lancastrian kings. A good marriage brought Thomas extensive lands in Oxfordshire and the south Midlands, and his only daughter and heiress, Alice (d. 1475), rose still higher, taking as her second husband William de la Pole, duke of Suffolk.

D. S. Brewer, *Chaucer*, Longman, 3rd ed., 1973; Chaucer, *The Canterbury Tales*, ed. N. Coghill, Penguin Classics, 1951.

CHICHELE, HENRY Unlike Archbishops William Courtenay and Thomas Arundel, his two immediate predecessors at Canterbury, Henry Chichele (born *c.* 1362) was not a scion of a noble family but the son of a merchant of Higham Ferrers (Northants). Perhaps through the good offices of John of Gaunt (q.v.), who was lord of the manor, he received an education at Winchester and New College, Oxford. This gave him a grounding in canon law he was to put to good use in the service of Richard Medford, bishop of Salisbury, from about 1396 to 1406. Chichele's obvious ability and his connections with the house of Lancaster were also bringing him employment at a more exalted level, first on an embassy to France and then a few years later in conciliar diplomacy. And when it was decided in 1409 to hold a Council at Pisa in an attempt to heal the Schism in the Church, he was one of the two principal English delegates.

Meanwhile at home the political stability of Henry IV's (q.v.) later years was threatened by a rift between the king and the Prince of Wales culminating in 1410 in the appointment of a Council under the latter, to which Chichele, by now bishop of St David's, was shortly to be admitted as a member. When we remember this past association with the man who was to be crowned Henry V (q.v.) in 1413, it is hardly surprising to find Chichele translated to Canterbury on Arundel's death in 1414. His primacy saw the English Church pass through some difficult times. The Schism was ended in 1417 with the election of Martin V, whose policy was to recover for the papacy the power that it had lost to the secular monarchies over the previous 40 years. The unfortunate Chichele therefore found himself under instructions to secure the repeal of the objectionable Statutes of Provisors and Praemunire, to which he knew there was no chance of the English parliament ever agreeing. In the world of ecclesiastical politics at home he once again had to tread carefully, most of all after Henry V's death in 1422, when the affairs of state passed into the hands of a child. He had to guard against the machinations of an ambitious rival, Bishop Beaufort (q.v.) who in 1426 finally procured the cardinal's hat which had been denied him in the previous reign. Moreover, he had to steer a middle path in the king's council between the rivalries of Beaufort and Humphrey, duke of Gloucester (q.v.)

Today, though, it is as a patron of learning that Chichele is best remembered. At Oxford he founded two colleges, St Bernard's (1438) for the Cistercians (q.v.) and All Souls (1438) for graduates in the arts and law. The former was later dissolved and incorporated in what is now St John's, but the latter lives on to perpetuate its founder's memory. Chichele died at Lambeth on 12 April 1443 and is buried in Canterbury Cathedral.

E. F. Jacob, *Henry Chichele*, Nelson, 1967.

CHRONICLES In the middle ages events were recorded and commented on by writers whom we call chroniclers. The chronicler was a kind of historian, but his outlook and approach were sufficiently different to merit a word of explanation.

Chronicles were really annals, a year by year record of events that were noteworthy enough to be written down. They seem to have been a by-product of the Easter tables that were compiled in the Dark Ages. Easter being a moveable festival, it was useful to have a table or calendar that would give its date for years ahead. Before long this purely liturgical data was accompanied by short notices of events, whether of national or local importance, that occurred in the outside world. In due course these annals acquired an existence, almost a momentum, of their own, but as late as the eleventh and twelfth centuries the nature of their origins can be detected in the kind of material that was included. For example, the Worcester chronicle commissioned by Bishop Wulfstan (1062–95) opens with an account of the early history of the diocese, and then gives the familiar Easter tables and lists of consuls, kings and bishops before launching into a universal history that interpreted English preoccupations in the light of God's general scheme for mankind.

This question of approach brings us onto the theological framework within which historical events were interpreted. Medieval chroniclers believed in the theory of the Seven Ages of the World. As set out in St Augustine's *City of God*, these were:

1. From the Creation to the Flood
2. From the Flood to Abraham
3. From Abraham to David
4. From David to the Babylonian Captivity

5. From the Captivity to the birth of Christ

6. From the birth of Christ till the Second Coming

7. The Eternal Sabbath.

Medievalists, writing as they saw it in the Sixth Age, would begin their histories with the birth of Christ or, if they were ambitious, with the Creation, drawing on the works of their predecessors for the early part of the story. For example, Bartholomew Cotton, the early fourteenth century chronicler at Norwich, used an earlier Norwich chronicle for the period from the Creation to 1290, when he drew on his own experience to bring the story down to his own day. It should be obvious by now that medieval explanations were therefore not so much historical as theological. History studied the gradual unfolding of the divine scheme for the world. If men were faithful, God would reward them; if they were sinful, he would chastize them. Inexplicable phenomena, natural disasters and the like could thus be seen as the expressions of God's anger, and the reigns of bad kings as a punishment for an errant people.

Artless and disjointed though it may appear, medieval chronicle writing was at least inspired by a way of looking at the past. It sought to reconcile the evident chaos of temporal affairs with the presumed coherence of the divinely created order. The chronicler could allow his story simply to unfold. He himself need do no more than commend the good and condemn the evil for the guidance of those readers who sought to lead a better life. Most writers, therefore, were content to hide behind the anonymity of their work. Only a few emerge as men of some ability and insight, deserving we might say of the title

of historian. In the Dark Ages, of course, there was Bede (672–735), whose *Ecclesiastical History* was to be a source of inspiration for the rest of the middle ages. In the twelfth century there was William of Malmesbury, like Bede a polymath, and one who could turn his hand equally to biography, hagiography, topography and history. And in the thirteenth century there was Matthew Paris (q.v.), the fiercely patriotic chronicler of St Alban's from 1236 to 1259.

William of Malmesbury is worthy of a little further attention at this stage because he was the most distinguished product of the revival of historical studies that followed the Norman Conquest. Intelligent observers could see that Hastings (q.v.) had effected a clean break with the past, and that things were never going to be the same again. The coming of the Normans bred a nostalgic renewal of interest in the Old English past; but it also stimulated solid research. Churches had to protect their lands from the encroachments of predatory Norman landowners and the reputations of their saints from the contempt of sceptical Norman clerics. Writers therefore had to start digging into the past to look after their ancient inheritance. Thus William of Malmesbury wrote the *De Antiquitate Glastoniensis Ecclesiae* to provide a cloak of historical justification for the mythical origins of Glastonbury Abbey, and the *Gesta Pontificum* to recall the memories of those Saxon bishops whose saintliness was being challenged. William travelled, looked at buildings and transcribed documents. In other words, he engaged in research. But he was not alone in so doing. Writers at Canterbury, Worcester, Evesham and Durham were also busy compiling cartularies (collections of charters) and writing chronicles and biographies in the cause of propaganda and self-justification.

The twelfth century saw medieval historical writing in England at its best. For the reign of Henry II (q.v.) we have some excellent writers like Robert of Torigni, William of Newburgh and Ralph of Diceto, not to mention all the biographers who recorded Becket's every word and deed. Most of these men were monks, but a few like Ralph of Diceto, who was dean of St Paul's, were secular clergy. By the thirteenth century we get the impression that every monastery of any consequence was keeping its own chronicle. The most voluminous compilation was that of St Alban's, started by Roger Wendover or an anonymous predecessor in the reign of King John (q.v.), and kept up by Matthew Paris and a succession of writers until as late as 1440. By the later middle ages, however, the position of the monks was being challenged not only by secular clerks like Diceto but by friars and members of the laity. Not all of this work can match the best twelfth century writing in terms of quality, but for modern historians the value of such a wide range of sources is beyond question. In the fourteenth century we can point to the *Scalacronica*, written by Sir Thomas Grey, a Northumberland knight, and the *Life of the Black Prince*, by the herald of one of the Prince's companions, Sir John Chandos. Many of these chronicles are, however, for reasons we have already mentioned, of anonymous authorship. The *Gesta Henrici Quinti* (*Deeds of Henry V*) was obviously written by a chaplain who was with the English army at Agincourt in 1415, but alas we do not know his name. Finally, we ought to mention the various town chronicles compiled in the late middle ages, of which the most important are the succession of London chronicles that give us such a valuable insight into the capital's often turbulent political struggles.

D. Hay, *Annalists and Historians*, Methuen, 1977.

CISTERCIANS   In those remarkable decades around 1100, when the renewed spirituality of western society led more men than ever before to become monks, a new diversity of approach crept into the once settled world of European monasticism. A feeling that laxity was gaining the upper hand in monastic life spurred groups of reformers to seek to recapture the original purity of St Benedict's Rule. One such critic was Robert, a monk of Molesme, who in 1098, led a small group of fellow brethren to seek a stricter life over in the Burgundian forests at Citeaux. From this modest beginning grew one of the great Orders of medieval Europe. By 1115 Citeaux had four daughter houses, including Clairvaux, of which the celebrated propagandist St Bernard became abbot; in 1153, by the time of Bernard's death, Cistercian houses numbered over 300.

Why were the Cistercians so popular? Perhaps simply because they met the vigorous spirituality of the twelfth century head-on by challenging not merely existing Benedictine monasticism but also the whole basis of feudal society. Unlike the Benedictines (q.v.), whose abbeys lay in the towns, the Cistercians chose rural sites. Unlike the Benedictines, whose estates were integrated within the manorial system, the Cistercians rejected feudal sources of income in favour of tilling land reclaimed from the wild. Unlike the Cluniacs (q.v.), who elaborated the liturgy (q.v.), the

Cistercians opted for a simple form of worship. In the time which had thus been made available the monks were to engage in manual work, reading and private prayer. Manual work did not rule out tilling the soil, but the monks could hardly provide all the labour they needed with their own hands. Cultivation of the lands that lay furthest away therefore fell to the lay brothers, who manned the granges on which the Cistercian economy relied. It was in the Cistercian houses that the lay brothers made their first appearance, but they were later to be employed by the Gilbertines (q.v.) and the Carthusians (q.v.) too. Bound to a life of almost total silence, they were men whose expectations in life could not have been high, and whose only reward lay in contributing to the needs of a pioneering religious community.

Just as radical as the alterations they made to the horarium (i.e., daily life) and the internal economy of the monastery were the measures the Cistercians took to secure the continued observance of their interpretation of the Rule. Unless uniformity was maintained by all the houses which claimed to be Cistercian, laxity, they feared, would soon set in. Their constitution broke new ground, therefore, in requiring the abbots to meet yearly at Cîteaux to legislate for the Order and in providing for an annual visitation of each abbey by the abbot of the house from which it had sprung. Never before, not even for the priories dependent on Cluny (q.v.), had such machinery been established to unite the houses of an international Order.

The first Cistercian house established in England was Waverley (Surrey), founded in 1138. But it was in the north that the Order was to make its greatest impact, and characteristically in a manner that makes a good story. The first Cistercian abbey in the north was that of Rievaulx (Yorks), founded in 1132 by Walter Espec, lord of Helmsley. Among its earliest monks were some of the Yorkshiremen who had been with Bernard at Clairvaux, and as they proceeded north they passed through York (q.v.), unconsciously provoking a crisis in the Benedictine abbey of St Mary, which lay just outside the city walls. The example of the Cistercians from Clairvaux encouraged a group of dissident monks, led by Prior Richard, to protest to the abbot that laxity was setting in. After initial hesitation the abbot resisted the demands of the prior and his supporters, and they turned for help to Archbishop Thurstan, who decided to visit the abbey on 17 October 1133. The prospect of a visitation was not well received by the abbot and his friends, and when the archbishop arrived he encountered such opposition that he was forced to flee, accompanied by the 13 dissidents. To provide them with shelter he gave them a site near Ripon, later to be distinguished by the name of Fountains.

The early Cistercians attracted men of distinction, and set for themselves rigorous standards of discipline. But for how long did they succeed in living up to them? In the first century of the Order's existence Cistercian abbeys would certainly have struck the visitor as different from those of the Benedictines. Their churches would have seemed bare, devoid of ornamentation, and colourless. The lay-out of the buildings would have been different because of the need to accommodate the lay brothers in quarters of their own on the western side of the cloister. By the fourteenth century, however, these differences would have seemed less pronounced. The prohibition on learning was soon relaxed, if we are to judge by the literary career of Ailred, abbot of Rievaulx (q.v.), one of the greatest writers of his day in England, and in the thirteenth century the Cistercians even followed the other Orders in founding a house for their monks in the University of Oxford (q.v.). The beautiful choir of Rievaulx Abbey, rebuilt in the thirteenth century, suggests that they were also succumbing to the temptation to replace their earlier buildings with grander structures characteristic of the Gothic age. At the same time the Cistercians had little option but to adjust their methods of economic organization. Faced as they were by the increasing reluctance of any but a few to contemplate a life so arduous, they had to abandon the use of lay brothers. Instead they took on hired labour. The change did little to affect the prosperity of the Cistercians, however, because they relied far less for their income on arable farming, which was labour intensive, than on sheep breeding, which was not. The sheep runs brought to the Cistercian abbeys of the Yorkshire dales those trappings of worldly wealth from which the founding fathers of the Order had done their best to escape.

D. Knowles, *The Monastic Order in England*, 2nd ed., Cambridge, 1966.

CLOSE ROLLS See, GOVERNMENT.

CLUNIACS The Cluniac family were far more important in the history of European monasticism (q.v.) than their modest numbers in medieval England might suggest. They took their name from the Burgundian abbey of Cluny, founded in 910. Under the rule of two able and long-lived abbots, Odilo (994–1049) and Hugh (1049–

1109) Cluny achieved a position of such eminence that in the age of monastic reform in the tenth and eleventh centuries she became a source not just of inspiration but also of active assistance in the revival of many religious houses. In the tenth century the working of Cluny's influence had been through informal ties between the great abbey and those who went from its walls to reform a house that had appealed for help. But how was Cluny to guarantee the permanence of the reforming spirit once the initial enthusiasm had passed? In the eleventh century abbot Odilo groped towards a solution to this problem by insisting that monasteries that adopted the customs of Cluny should enter into a relationship of dependence on the abbey. Thus the Cluniacs were not so much an Order in their own right as a family owing allegiance to a mother house. In this way they reconciled the desire of each Cluniac community to be self-governing with the need for supervision by the abbot of Cluny himself.

The chief characteristic of the Cluniac way of life was its elaborate liturgy (q.v.). The simple horarium of St Benedict, which had struck a balance between the demands of public worship, private study and manual labour, gave way at Cluny to an unceasing round of services in the church. This luxuriant ritual had its admirers; but it also produced a reaction in favour of simplicity from which the Cistercians were shortly to profit.

In their heyday the Cluniacs were remarkable for the number of friends they enjoyed in high places. In England they had the support of William the Conqueror himself and members of the aristocracy. The first Cluniac house in England, St Pancras', Lewes, was founded in 1077 by one of the Conqueror's principal lieutenants, William de Warenne, and his wife. From it sprang a family of daughter houses, including Castle Acre and Thetford in Norfolk. Even in the twelfth century, when their way of life was coming under fire, the Cluniacs still enjoyed the support of rulers like Henry I (q.v.), who founded Reading, and Stephen (q.v.), who founded Faversham, both staffed by Cluniac monks. Indeed, the success of the Order in England lay not so much in the size or number of its houses, in each case small, as in the prominence attained by some of its monks. Two of the most distinguished bishops in the twelfth century had been monks at Cluny itself – Henry of Blois, bishop of Winchester, King Stephen's brother, and Gilbert Foliot (q.v.), bishop of London, the long-standing opponent of Becket (q.v.). And the roll-call can be extended further if we include men like Robert, bishop of Bath and Wells, who were monks of Cluniac priories before being elevated to bishoprics. The prominence they attained in the corridors of power led the Cluniacs to develop distinctive ideas of their own about Church/State relations. They believed that the Church was less likely to be liberated from unwelcome secular interference by the more aggressive tactics of the Gregorian reformers than by opening the lines of communications, as Bishop Henry hoped to do with his brother, King Stephen. Few Cluniac houses in England have left extensive remains. The ruins of Lewes Priory suffered badly when the railway was driven across them in the nineteenth century. In Norfolk, however, there are extensive ruins at Castle Acre and at Thetford, where the complete ground plan of the buildings can be traced.

H. E. J. Cowdrey, *The Cluniacs and the Gregorian Reform*, Oxford, 1970.

COINAGE One of the most remarkable achievements of the Saxon kings was the creation of a sound and stable system of coinage based on a metallic standard. As trade recovered in the seventh and eighth centuries, so the need was felt for an acceptable medium of exchange, satisfied in the case of England by minting both gold and silver coins. After the last quarter of the seventh century, however, no more gold coins were struck in this country until the thirteenth century, and for the intervening 600 years the only denomination of the coinage was the silver penny. So far as numismatists are concerned, then, the Norman Conquest brought little change, except to the extent that the coins of the early Norman kings were slightly heavier than those of their immediate predecessors.

How did the English coinage come to have such an enviable reputation for stability in eleventh century Europe? The answer lies in the strong measure of central control that the king was able to exercise over the supply of coin. In William the Conqueror's reign, as in Edward the Confessor's, coins were struck at some 60 or 70 mints, most of them in central and southern England; but the tendency towards anarchy inherent in such decentralization was eliminated by insisting that the dies from which the coins were struck could be issued from only a limited number of die-cutting workshops. The king's monopoly over the supply of dies enabled him to reconcile easy availability of coinage with overall direction of the currency. Royal authority is demonstrated even more dramatically by the regularity with which these dies were changed. The purpose of these transactions seems to have been one of profit, because each time a change was effected the moneyers had to pay the king before receiving the new dies to take back to their mint. Methods of production changed little in the course of the middle ages. The coins were cut by hand from a pound weight of silver, and flattened and moulded to shape by the use of a hammer and anvil. Although they were supposed to be as nearly as possible of equal weight and size, no standard weight was set for individual coins until the reign of James I, and so long as the correct number was cut from a pound of metal small variations in weight from one coin to another were disregarded.

From the reigns of the first two Norman kings we have 13 types of coin, all of them inscribed 'WILLEM' without indicating either father or son, leaving us to guess on a roughly proportionate basis that, say, the first eight belong to the Conqueror and the remaining five to Rufus (plate 17a). The gradual deterioration in the quality of the coinage in the course of Rufus' reign goes some way in preparing us for the episode that took place in 1125 under Henry I (q.v.), when Bishop Roger, the justiciar, summoned all the moneyers to Winchester and sentenced them to mutilation for flooding the land with false money. After the accession of Henry II (q.v.) the regular changing of dies that we noticed earlier was abandoned, and the first type, introduced in 1158, lasted until the reform of 1180, which inaugurated the so-called 'short-cross' issue. The remarkable thing about the coins of this type is that, although they were in circulation under Richard I, John and the early years of Henry III they all bear the name HENRICUS. By 1247, however, clipping had become such a problem that a new coinage was issued, known this time as the 'long-cross' issue from the cross on the reverse which continued

right to the edge of the coin. Any pennies on which the four ends of the cross were not visible would not be considered legal tender.

As we have already seen, the only coin in circulation since the reign of the Saxon king Edgar had been the silver penny. Pounds, shillings and marks existed only as units of account. It was therefore a new departure when in 1279 Edward I (q.v.) introduced further denominations in the form of the groat (4d) and the farthing. At the same time the weight of the penny was reduced from 22½ to 22¼ grains. In appearance it differed little from Henry III's issue. On the obverse side is the crowned head of the king and on the reverse a long cross with three round pellets in each of the angles (plate 17b). Allowing for various permutations, this remained the standard design for silver pennies for the rest of the middle ages.

The striking of new denominations suggests that the mints were meeting a demand for a more flexible system of currency in the thirteenth century. If small change had been wanted in the past, it had been obtained by cutting a penny into halves or quarters. In the countryside petty transactions had very likely been settled by resort to barter – a coin worth a penny was not to be sneezed at when we remember that in the thirteenth century a labourer's daily wage was unlikely to be much more than that amount. On the other hand, as the pace of trade quickened, a coin of higher value was needed for use in international transactions. In Italy the great city of Florence responded in 1252 by minting a golden florin, the first golden coin to make its appearance in western Europe since the Dark Ages. English merchants, of course, did not want to be dependent in their trading on these foreign coins, so in 1257 Henry III (q.v.) put an English gold currency into circulation, in the form of a penny which would exchange for 20 silver pence. The gold coin met with a bad reception, very likely because it was undervalued. This is surely the implication of the decision later the same year to re-value it at 24 pence, but even so continuing lack of confidence led to its withdrawal by about 1270.

A second and more successful attempt to introduce what we know as the bi-metallic standard was made in 1344 in the reign of Edward III (q.v.), for reasons that continue to arouse debate among historians. In the 1330s we hear complaints in parliament about the shortage of good coin. These carry a ring of truth. The economic difficulties that had been building up were aggravated after 1337 by the financial demands Edward III was making in what were to be the opening stages of the Hundred Years War (q.v.). Massive expenditure undertaken abroad, whether to subsidize English allies in the Low Countries or to pay soldiers' wages, had the effect of reducing the amount of coin in circulation from about £1,000,000 in the 1290s to half that amount in the 1340s. Gold, on the other hand, was commanding a high price. This encouraged people to import it, so making the production of a domestic gold currency almost inevitable.

The initial issue of January 1344 consisted of three coins – a florin worth 6s, which would be used for international transactions, and a half and a quarter, known from the designs on their reverse sides as the 'leopard' and the 'helm' respectively. Unfortunately for Edward III, however, the florin met with a reception no more sympathetic than its predecessor had in Henry III's reign. This time it seems that the gold was too highly valued in relation to silver. Eight months afterwards, in August, the florin and its smaller denominations were withdrawn and replaced with the 'noble', worth 6s 8d, and its half and quarter. Without doubt these early gold coins of Edward III rank as some of the most beautiful ever minted in England. The obverse of the florin showed the king seated in majesty; on the noble this was replaced by the king standing in a ship, holding his shield and sword, perhaps an allusion to the naval victory of Sluys (1340) a few years before (plate 17c). The reverse of the florin, as of its successor, the noble, had a floriated cross as its main feature with a scriptural motto round the border.

The reign of Edward III also saw in 1351 the introduction of a multiple of the silver penny, known as the groat and worth 4d and supplemented by a half-groat worth 2d. After that few changes of any importance were made to the coinage until the reign of Edward IV, when two new gold coins were issued in 1465, one known from the design on its reverse as the 'rose noble or ryal', worth 10s, and the other, known from the design on its obverse as the 'angel', worth 6s 8d and replacing the noble. One more denomination was added to the list in the reign of Henry VII, to complete the picture. This was the famous gold 'sovereign', a large coin worth 20s featuring on the obverse the king in majesty and on the reverse a shield set against a luxuriant rose (plate 17d).

If the English coinage had one besetting problem in the middle ages, it was paradoxically that it was too good. Consequently we hear in the fourteenth century of poor quality coins, known at various times as lusshebournes and as crockards and pollards, coming in from abroad and, on the operation of what was later to become famous as Gresham's Law, driving out of circulation the better-quality English coins. The French kings debased their country's coinage. The English kings by and large did not before the age of the Tudors. Consequently their problem was how to ensure an adequate supply of high-value coins.

G. C. Brooke, *English Coins*, London, 2nd ed., 1950.

CORONER After the sheriff (q.v.), the coroner is the oldest of the local officials we have inherited from the middle ages. The office was established in September 1194 when the eyre justices were told to have three knights and a clerk elected in each county 'to keep the pleas of the Crown'. Coroners were authorized in the boroughs for the first time a few years later in 1200. It was the coroner's duty to hear appeals (q.v.), hold inquests on dead bodies, receive confessions from felons in sanctuary, who wanted to leave the realm, and record outlawries that were pronounced at sessions of the county court. Unlike his colleague the sheriff, who was appointed by the Exchequer and held office for a year at a time, the coroner was elected and held office for life. According to the order of 1194, coroners were to be drawn from the ranks of the knightly class, but before too long much humbler people were accepted. Like all local officials coroners were unpaid, but they had ample chance to profit from bribery and corruption.

R. F. Hunnisett, *The Medieval Coroner*, Cambridge, 1961.

CORRODY A corrody (Latin, *corredium*, provision for maintenance) was a form of pension or annuity given by monasteries. It might entitle the corrodian either to residence with the monks or to a ration distributed each day at the abbey gates. Corrodies were awarded not so much as an act of charity as on a strict calculation of financial gain. They could be given, for example, to the vicar of an impropriated (i.e., acquired) church instead of a money salary. Or they could be awarded to layfolk in exchange for property. In 1392, for instance, Robert Aleyn and Matilda, his wife, received from the monks of Westminster a corrody of 14 loaves and 14 gallons of ale per week and £6.13.4 per annum in return for granting to the abbey their mill at Stratford, Essex. On other occasions the sale of a corrody, very likely to someone wanting to provide for his old age, was a straight means of raising cash. The price would be pitched according to the means of the corrodian and perhaps, too, according to his life expectancy. Failure in these circumstances to make sound actuarial calculations could land a house with unwelcome financial burdens, as Merton Priory, Surrey, found when it sold a corrody to a man for the modest sum of 20s, hardly expecting him to survive, as it turned out, for another 29 years.

CRECY Like the equally famous engagements at Poitiers (q.v.) in 1356 and Agincourt (q.v.) in 1415, Crecy was one of those battles in which a small English army took on and defeated a much larger French one. Such a remarkable triumph was the outcome of a change of strategy on Edward III's (q.v.) part. Instead of pinning his hopes on a grand alliance between England and the princes of the Low Countries, as he had to little effect between 1337 and 1340, he sent one army down to south-west France and himself landed with another in Normandy on 12 July 1346. His intention was to march eastwards towards Flanders, creating as much havoc as possible, but near the village of Crecy in Ponthieu on 26 August he found his passage blocked by the presence of a large French army under King Philip VI. The enthusiasm of the French overcame their tactical sense, and they launched an attack on the English position that afternoon when their vision was blinded by the setting sun. The French knights charged across the field, only to be mown down by a storm of arrows from the English longbowmen. Among the casualties on the French side were the count of Flanders and the blind king of Bohemia. The English owed their success to the tactic they had developed over the previous half-century in the Scottish wars of combining archers with dismounted men-at-arms – a ploy which was to bring them victory again at Poitiers in 1356. The sequel to the battle of Crecy was rather more dispiriting from the English point of view. On 4 September they began to besiege Calais (q.v.). But it was to take eleven months to reduce the town to submission, and by then an outbreak of dysentery had badly thinned the ranks of the army.

CRUSADES On 27 November 1095 Pope Urban II preached the First Crusade at Clermont in central France. It was a memorable occasion by any standard. Accounts of what Urban said differ, but what is beyond doubt is the spontaneous enthusiasm he evoked, right from the moment when Adhemar, bishop of Le Puy, stepped forward after the pope's sermon to become the first man to take the cross. Adhemar was to be the pope's own representative in the army which set out to the East in the following year. Among its leading commanders under Adhemar's nominal direction were Raymond, count of Toulouse, Godfrey of Bouillon, duke of Lower Lorraine, and his brother Baldwin, Bohemund, son of Robert Guiscard, the Norman count of Sicily and his nephew, Tancred, and Robert, duke of Normandy, son of William the Conqueror. William Rufus (q.v.), King of England, was the most notable absentee. But if Rufus was an unusually secular-minded man for his day, most of his contemporaries had no hesitation in springing to the defence of Christ's heritage in the East. Their love of God, love of their fellow-suffering Christians, was the force that drove them on through thick and thin, until they had conquered the Holy City of Jerusalem. Crusading fervour, the reform movement in the Church and the monastic revival were all in their different ways expressions of the resurgent spirituality of twelfth-century Europe. It was to that spirituality that the popes naturally enough appealed in their crusading propaganda. As Cardinal Odo of Chateauroux said in 1245, when preaching a new crusade from France:

It is a clear sign that a man burns with love of God and zeal for God when he leaves country, possessions, house, children and wife, going overseas in the service of Jesus Christ . . . Whoever wishes to take and have Christ ought to follow him; to follow him to death.[*]

Love of God aroused the feelings of twelfth-century men. It probably counted for more in drawing men to the East than did economic motives like the quest for booty that were once used to

[*] Quoted by J. Riley-Smith, 'Crusading as an Act of Love', *History*, 65 (1980), p. 180.

explain the Crusades. But such idealism had to be presented in terms comprehensible to a feudal society. So love of God was presented as family love. Christ had been robbed of his hereditary patrimony by the infidel. It was a responsibility incumbent on all of his children to recover it for him. This, indeed, was what the Crusades were all about. They were not wars of conversion. They were Holy Wars authorized by the pope for the recovery of Christian lands from the infidel. But equally they could be and were directed against heretics and schismatics like the Albigensians in southern France, who constituted just as much a threat to the unity of Christendom as the Moslems did.

If we can understand how Pope Urban's appeal was so enthusiastically received in 1095, we still need to explain why he had to make it in the first place. Jerusalem had after all fallen to the Moslems as far back as 638. The problem was that the Eastern Empire was again under attack, this time from the Seljuk Turks who had defeated the Byzantine army at Manzikert in 1071. The Emperor Alexius Comnenus called on the pope for assistance. He must have been surprised, perhaps even alarmed, at the size of the armies that made their way towards Constantinople in response to his appeal. And little could he have envisaged the measure of success they were to enjoy. On 15 July 1099, three years after setting out, they captured Jerusalem, put its inhabitants to the sword, and set up a feudal state on western lines.

A crusade was in a sense a pilgrimage. Its participants took vows, and enjoyed the privileges of protection at home and Indulgence for the remission of sins. It followed, therefore, that when their vows had been fulfilled by the recon-quest of Jerusalem, they could return home. They left garrisons to defend the Kingdom, and built the splendid castles we can see in Israel and Syria today. But was that enough to guarantee the permanence of their achievement? It seemed not, when in 1144 the important city of Edessa fell to the Moslems. Fresh help had to be obtained in the West, and a Second Crusade was preached. But it ended in failure. And no sooner had the unsuccessful crusaders returned to Europe than Nur-ad-Din, the Turkish leader, extended his power into Egypt and completely surrounded the Latin state. In July 1187 his successor, the famous Saladin, defeated the crusaders at the battle of Hattin, and in October entered Jerusalem. In response the Third Crusade was preached. Armies set out from Germany under Frederick Barbarossa, who died on the way, from France under King Philip, and from England and the Angevin lands under King Richard (q.v.). They took Acre and Jaffa in 1191, and came within sight of Jerusalem, but that was all. Philip and Richard could agree on nothing, and the Crusade collapsed in the face of internal dissent. Philip returned home in October 1191, and Richard in the following year. It is a telling postscript that on the way he should have been imprisoned by Leopold, duke of Austria, for insulting his banners at the siege of Acre. Innocent III immediately preached a fresh crusade. It set sail in 1202, but never reached the Holy Land. The prospect of Constantinople proved too alluring. In 1204 the crusaders reached the city, deposed the emperor, and put Baldwin of Flanders in his place. The Byzantines did not recover possession until 1261.

In the meantime the western crusaders had adopted a new strategy for recovering Jerusalem. Instead of launching a direct attack on Palestine, they chose to invade Egypt, which was the power base of Saladin's empire. A Fifth Crusade set off in 1218 and captured Damietta on the Nile delta. The strategy very nearly succeeded. The sultan offered Jerusalem in return for Damietta, but the crusaders unwisely rejected his terms. They held out for too much, and in the end got nothing. St Louis, however, adopted the same strategy when he set sail for the East in 1249. He recaptured Damietta, and marched up the Nile. But at Mansurah the army was surrounded, and in the ensuing retreat the king was captured. After his release, Louis sailed for Acre (May, 1250) and spent the next four years in Palestine.

It was Acre that was the Lord Edward's destination when he led an English force to the East in August, 1270. This was an expedition composed largely of royalists who used the pretext of the crusade to obtain the Church's protection for the lands they had grabbed from their opponents in the baronial wars of the 1260s. There was little they could do when they reached their destination. The states of Tyre and Acre were at loggerheads. Edward patched up their disagreements as best he could, made a truce with the sultan and then set sail for home in 1272. Some 19 years later, on 18 May 1291, Acre fell, and what was left of the Latin Kingdom of Jerusalem ceased to exist. Crusading fervour, however, lived on, and late medieval popes lost nothing to their predecessors in the enthusiasm they brought to reuniting Christendom in an effort to win back Christ's patrimony from the infidel. But they could not confront external foes until internal ones had been eliminated. The suppression of internal dissent was seen as a prerequisite for the departure of another expedition to the East. In other words, crusades had first to be preached against heretics and schismatics. These may strike us, as they struck some contemporaries, as a monstrous perversion of the ideal; but strictly defined, they count as crusades all the same.

J. Riley-Smith, *What were the Crusades?*, Macmillan, 1977; S. Runciman, *A History of the Crusades*, Cambridge, 3 vols., 1951–4.

'DECORATED' See, ARCHITECTURE, ECCLESIASTICAL.

DEMESNE When a text says that X held his lands in demesne (Latin, *in dominico*), it means that he held them himself, and not from anyone else. Thus the royal demesne consisted of those manors held directly by the king, the revenues from which went to support the estate and dignity of the Crown. Similarly, the demesne manors of a great estate or feudal honor were those which the lord had not subinfeudated to any of his vassals.

If we turn now to the internal organization of the manor, the land which the lord himself cultivated was known as the demesne, to distinguish it from the land held and cultivated by the tenants. The demesne in this sense was a home farm, worked either by the *famuli* (or paid estate labourers) or by the labour services owed by the unfree tenants, the villeins. By the early fifteenth century, when high costs and low prices caused most landlords to abandon large-scale cultivation, manorial demesnes were usually put out to lease.

DIET   There are a number of ways we can find out what people would have eaten in the middle ages. Cookery books tells us what they were recommended to serve to their guests; archaeological finds tell us what actually was served or, to be more precise, what was thrown away afterwards. Cookery books pandered for the most part to the taste of those rich enough to be interested in laying on special dishes. Archaeological evidence, on the other hand, illuminates the dietary habits of rich and poor alike.

The nobility, as is known only too well, believed in entertaining on a lavish scale. The quantities they ordered for a good feast would seem shocking now to a weight-conscious public; but conspicuous consumption was what was expected of them, and conspicuous consumption was what was offered. Take, for example, the feast that was prepared to celebrate the enthronement of George Neville as archbishop of York in 1465. The larders were stocked up with 300 quarters of wheat, 300 tuns of ale, 100 tuns of wine, 6 bulls, 1,000 sheep, 304 calves, 400 swans, 2,000 geese, 2,000 pigs, 13,500 birds, 1,500 hot pasties of venison, not to mention the countless spices, custards and jellies. However large their appetites, the 6,000 or so guests could hardly have made any more than limited inroads into that mountain of food; but provided they went away singing the praises of the house of Neville, their host would no doubt have counted himself more than satisfied. If it is argued, with some justice, that this was hardly a typical banquet, we can cite instead the less pretentious but still very lavish standards set at the table of Chaucer's Franklin:

His bread, his ale were finest of the fine
And no one had a better stock of wine.
His house was never short of bake-meat pies,
Of fish and flesh, and these in such supplies
It positively snowed with meat and drink
And all the dainties that a man could think.*

To judge from the dishes with which contemporaries chose to indulge themselves at dinner, the medieval palate must have been very different in its tastes from the modern. To some extent the limited range of eating utensils known in medieval England imposed restrictions on the kind of food that could be served. Forks were unknown here before the seventeenth century. For that reason meats had to be chopped up beforehand into small, easily digestible portions that could be lifted to the mouth by hand, and grain and other foods pounded into a soft mess that could be sipped from a spoon. In the middle ages, when so much of the diet, particularly for the lower classes, was grain-based, eating could have been painful had not the roughness been moderated.

Yet these considerations, however important, hardly prepare us for the

* Chaucer, *The Canterbury Tales*, ed. N. Coghill, Penguin, 1951, p. 28.

extraordinary combinations of food that we find recommended in the recipe books. These days we aim to bring sympathetic and complementary tastes together on a dish; in the middle ages they mixed together ingredients without any consideration for possible incongruity. These days we try to cook our food in such a way as to preserve its taste; in the middle ages they seem to have prepared it in such a way as to destroy whatever taste it may once have had. The following recipe, given in a fifteenth-century cookery book, can stand for other concoctions that would seem revolting to modern taste:

Take some apples, stew them, let them cool, pass them through a hair sieve. Put them in a pot, and on a flesh day add good fat beef broth, white grease, sugar and saffron. Boil it, mess it out, sprinkle on good spices and serve.

Or alternatively we might contemplate the 'sop-in-wine', so 'well-loved' by Chaucer's Franklin. This was made by cutting up pieces of bread or cake, and pouring over them a sauce of wine, almond milk, saffron, ginger, sugar, cinnamon and cloves.

In the middle ages, as in the present day, it was the French who set the standards of cuisine which were followed by everyone else. When indulging their taste for the exotic, therefore, the English aristocracy were merely following the example set by their peers across the Channel. This liking for strange combinations of food stacked up in huge quantities seems to have lasted at least until the sixteenth century, when we hear that in the time of Francis I of France many families still ate from platters piled high with veal, beef, mutton and pork and vegetables. In the sixteenth century, as in the fourteenth, the principal meals of the day were still two in number, dinner taken

at 10 or 11 in the morning and supper taken at about 4 in the afternoon.

If we turn next from the plenty of the few to the poverty of the many, we shall not be surprised to find very different dietary standards. The quantity and variety of the food consumed by the peasants depended of course on the level of income they enjoyed, and also perhaps on where they lived. One dish that was popular in peasant households was pease pottage, which curiously enough has survived as the name of a Sussex village. It consisted of old pea soup left to solidify. Or, if that didn't sound too appetizing, there was pease pudding, which was made of soaked dried peas cooked together in a cloth with salted pork. By and large the bulk of the rural peasantry, certainly in the thirteenth century, must have lived on a diet which was weighted heavily towards carbohydrates. Of the cereals that they grew, wheat would have been sold to raise cash, and barley and oats kept for making into bread. According to Sir William Ashley in his study, *Bread of our Forefathers*, it was not until the eighteenth century that the rural population was regularly eating a wheaten loaf. In earlier times they would have been driven to reliance on grains like barley, rye or even oats for making flour. It is worth a mention, in passing, that on the tables of the polite, bread was served without its crust, for reasons about which we can only speculate. Was the crust too hard to eat? Or were the kitchens so unhygienic that it was thought too filthy?

If the prospect of bread and pottage became too dreary to contemplate, the peasants could turn to fish and meat for a change. Game would be a real delicacy, as likely as not to be won by poaching in some nearby park or in the royal forest. Sheep and cattle, however, would be kept in varying proportions in every medieval village. The sheep were slaughtered for their mutton when they were too old to be worth keeping for their wool. Bone deposits unearthed at Wharram Percy (Yorks.), a village deserted in the late middle ages, suggest that its inhabitants had enjoyed a meat diet that was 60% mutton, 30% beef and 8% pork. Their heavy consumption of mutton is hardly surprising in view of the predominantly pastoral economy of east Yorkshire.

How did people wash down the often strange combinations of food that they ate? Water was out of the question because it was undrinkable. For the rich there were many varieties of wine to choose from, imported mostly from Gascony (q.v.), France and the Rhine. For the great mass of the population, however, ale would have been the standard beverage, brewed after a fashion from barley or oat malt. The normal reckoning, in upper class households at least, was that 60 gallons of ale could be made from a quarter of malt. In the fourteenth century brewing was a sideline undertaken by many tenants in the village, quite a proportion of them women, but in the fifteenth growing specialization encouraged the emergence of professional brewers who ran their own ale-houses – or pubs, as we would call them today. Beer was unknown in England before the sixteenth century, when hops were introduced from the Netherlands 'to the detryment of many Englysshe men', as Andrew Boorde put it in 1542 in his *Dyetary of Helth*. It was presumably the more bitter taste of the new beverage that incurred his disapproval.

C. Platt, *Medieval England: a Social History and Archaeology*, Routledge & Kegan Paul, 1978; R. H. Hilton, *A Medieval Society: the West Midlands at the end of the Thirteenth Century*, Weidenfeld & Nicolson, 1966.

DISTRAINT Medieval England, of course, had no police force, no band of officers in the pay of the government whose duty it was to enforce the law. So if an indicted malefactor proved reluctant to turn up in court when summoned, some other means had to be found of compelling him. The common law did this by the process of distraint, or seizure of his lands and chattels. If an accused failed to attend a hearing, the sheriff would order the hundred (q.v.) bailiff to take possession of his lands and goods until such time as his attendance had been secured. Distraint was, and of course still is, used to effect the collection of debts. The term was also employed in a more specialized sense to describe the policy of compulsory knighthood which was practised from the thirteenth century onwards. Writs of distraint were sent to the sheriffs asking them to return the names of those eligible for knighthood who had not yet taken it up. By the early fourteenth century the qualification had become more or less fixed at an annual income of £40. Since these writs were commonly issued when the king was planning a military expedition, it seems likely that their purpose was to swell the number of knights in the English army. From those who persisted in declining to take up the honour of knighthood the king was still able to reap some financial advantage by imposing fines for exemption.

DOMESDAY BOOK This is the name given to the great survey of England undertaken in the last years of

William the Conqueror's (q.v.) reign. It became such an indispensable reference book that by the 1170s it had acquired the nickname 'Domesday', because like the Day of Judgement (doom = judgement), its sentence could not be quashed or set aside. Domesday Book survives in two volumes, now preserved in the Public Record Office, which are the oldest of our public records.

Just why this massive enquiry was undertaken remains one of the mysteries of Anglo-Norman history. Two historians, Richardson and Sayles, have even gone so far as to condemn it as a vast administrative mistake. If Domesday Book still remains something of an enigma, it is however equally hard to believe that so intelligent a ruler as William I could be responsible for wasting everyone's time. He set the wheels in motion at the Christmas court of 1085, when he ordered a survey of the whole of England, detailing the lands and possessions of all the barons, how much they were worth, and what services and payments were due from their tenants. Very likely this was not the first enquiry that William had ordered. It seems possible that it was intended to supplement earlier and more limited investigations. When these had turned out to be unsatisfactory, William ordered a more searching enquiry, which found expression in the work we know as Domesday Book.

The manner in which the information was collected carries a surprisingly modern ring. England was divided into seven circuits, each covering about five counties. To each of these circuits a group of commissioners was assigned. They went from county to county, collecting the information they wanted from juries that came before them in a session of the county court. These enquiries provided the commissioners with a vast amount of information, but if the resulting survey was not to be unwieldy, it had then to be reduced to a manageable size. Moreover, it had to be decided whether the information was to be assembled on a geographical basis, county by county, village by village, or on a feudal basis, landowner by landowner. In the event an uneasy compromise was reached. The arrangement was by counties, but within each county it was by landowner. In other words, the survey was converted from a gazetteer into a directory of feudal tenants. The returns for most of England were condensed in this manner to produce the main volume of Domesday Book, which may well have been complete by the time of the Conqueror's death in 1087, but those for the eastern circuit (Norfolk, Suffolk, Essex) remained separate and unabbreviated in volume two.

Once the evidence was written down in the form we have it today, it did not lie idle. It was kept in the treasury at Winchester, where it may well have been used to increase the yield from taxation, for a contemporary tells us that at that time 'the land was vexed with many calamities arising from the collection of the royal money.' But Domesday Book was not merely an elaborate eleventh-century tax return. The arrangement of the material within counties on a feudal basis suggests that it may also have been William's intention to take stock of the territorial revolution which had been a major effect of the Conquest. In any dispute about the ownership of land this great survey could be cited as a source of unimpeachable authority, not lightly to be set aside.

What can be learned from Domesday Book about William the Conqueror's England? As Professor Loyn has rightly written, 'it tells much, but it does not always tell what is wanted'. Thanks to the oddities of its internal arrangement we may well have to search around for the details concerning a single village. If, say, we want the description of the village of Harpswell (Lincs), which was divided into three manors, we need to look for the appropriate entry under each of its three lords – the king, the archbishop of York and Jocelyn Fitz-Lambert. Once these practical difficulties are mastered, Domesday Book becomes an invaluable guide to the social and economic history of eleventh century England. For example, the commissioners in most cases attempted to trace changes in the value of manors by recording their worth in 1066, at the end of Edward the Confessor's reign, and in 1086. From these figures we can see how the new Norman lords increased the value of their landed estates by exploiting them more intensively, and also how the taxable capacity of Yorkshire declined in this interval as a result of William's harrying of the north in 1069–70. But Domesday Book tells us more than anything else about the nature of the government that created it. It has no parallel in eleventh-century Europe; it is a tribute to the ability and ambitions of the new Norman kings and to the efficiency of the administrative machine which they had at their disposal.

V. H. Galbraith, *The Making of Domesday Book*, Oxford, 1961.

DOMINICANS Although the two Orders of friars, the Dominicans and the Franciscans (q.v.), came into existence simultaneously in the early thirteenth century, the ideas and aspirations of their respective founders were very different. Francis of Assisi was a man of the deepest spiritual insight who believed in teaching by example rather than by argument. In his view simplicity of life would be more effective than intellectual artifice. Dominic, on the other hand, believed that the time had come for an international Order of trained theologians to be sent out across Europe to combat the growth of heresy. Despite the different ends the two men had in mind, the very fact that their respective Orders took shape at the same time meant that in the early years of their existence each was bound to influence the other.

This point can be illustrated in a number of ways. First, we can take an example of the influence exerted by the Franciscans on the Dominicans. Following the ban on the creation of new Orders imposed by the Fourth Lateran Council in 1216, Dominic chose to base the institutions of his Order on those of the Augustinian Canons (q.v.). In 1220, however, reputedly after a meeting with Francis, he dropped the idea in favour of adopting the strict corporate poverty of the Franciscans. His followers, like those of Francis, were to become mendicants (i.e., beggars), dependent on the charity of others. For constitutional organization, on the other hand, it was the Dominican example which was followed by the Franciscans. The arrangements which Dominic conceived for the government of his Order were complex, but at the same time effective. He divided Europe into provinces, each headed by a prior. Once every year, the provincial chapter, composed of representatives from all of the constituent houses, would meet to elect a *diffinitor*, or representative, for the general chapter and four *diffinitores* to whom the business of the chapter would be delegated. The general chapter, which likewise met annually, ran in cycles of three years, for two of which it was composed of the *diffinitores* and for the third, of the provincial priors. At the summit of this organization was the master-general, who served for life and was elected by an *ad hoc* general chapter. The Franciscan constitution was much slower to evolve than its counterpart, but when it did, in the 1240s, it owed much to the Dominican model.

As we have seen, what had moved St Dominic to establish his Order was the necessity of combatting heresy. This the brothers were to do by force of argument, in other words by preaching: hence the name 'Friars Preachers'. But what was their impact in England? Numerically it was considerable. Within half a century of their arrival in 1221 they had established some 46 houses in this country, and their final tally of 53

was only five short of that of the Franciscans. But in terms of influence and distinction the Dominicans lost out to the Franciscans. The sheer popularity of the latter inspired so many of the most brilliant men of the day to don their grey habit that in the process the Order was transformed from one of simple apostles into one of scholars and intellectuals. In other words, the Franciscans took over the field marked out by the Dominicans for themselves. All the same, the Dominicans managed to attract large congregations for their sermons, as we can tell from the lengthy naves they built for their churches. The one still remaining at Norwich (St Andrew's Hall) is a good example. Extensive remains of other Dominican friaries, particularly of their domestic buildings, can be seen at Bristol and Gloucester.

R. B. Brooke, *The Coming of the Friars*, Allen & Unwin, 1975.

'EARLY ENGLISH' See, ARCHITECTURE, ECCLESIASTICAL.

EDMUND OF ABINGDON Many of the materials for the life of Edmund of Abingdon arise from the proceedings for canonization instituted after he died in 1240. For that reason they verge on the hagiographical. Our task today is to sort fact from fiction. Edmund was the son of an Abingdon burgess, Reginald, known as the Rich, and his wife Mabel.

He and his brother were sent to the schools at Paris to read the Arts, and after he had incepted as a Master, he returned to spend another six years studying the Arts at Oxford (q.v.). He then transferred, as was the custom, from the Arts to the higher faculty of Theology. He spent another four years at Paris, and came back to join the Oxford Theology faculty, on the most reliable estimates in or around 1214. It is a pity that we do not know more about his Oxford years, not just because he was an influential teacher at a crucial period in the early history of the University but also because of the association of his name with the site in the parish of St Peter-in-the-East later occupied by St Edmund Hall.

In 1222 he became treasurer of Salisbury Cathedral, and in September 1233 was elected archbishop of Canterbury. Even before he was consecrated in April the following year he found himself drawn into the maelstrom of national politics. Angered by the prominence of Poitevin-born favourites in the royal household, Richard the Earl Marshal had led an uprising against Henry III's (q.v.) government. Edmund used all his considerable powers of conciliation to bring king and rebels together again, a task admittedly facilitated by the news of Richard's death in Ireland in February 1234. In the years that lay ahead Edmund's relations with the king were in fact to be far from harmonious. And it was to be much the same with the monastic chapter at Canterbury Cathedral. The main bone of contention was Edmund's revival of an old plan to found a college at Maidstone to provide for the numerous secular clerks in his service. This the monks saw as a threat to their rights as the archiepiscopal electoral body. Neither side seemed ready to give way.

As for what happened next, we can choose between two possible interpretations. According to the accounts submitted for the canonization proceedings, Edmund withdrew into voluntary exile at Pontigny, already famous as the refuge of his great predecessors, Becket (q.v.) and Langton (q.v.). Allegedly to escape from the heat, he moved to Soisy, where he died on 16 November 1240. The reliability of this traditional hagiographical account has been called into question by Edmund's latest biographer, who points out that no contemporary sources mention that the archbishop chose to go into exile. On the contrary, one of the chronicles says that his purpose in leaving was to visit Rome. He had been summoned to a general council due to begin at Easter, 1241, and he was setting out early to enlist papal support in his dispute with the chapter at Canterbury. On the way he fell ill and died. Though depriving Edmund of his claim to a martyr's crown, this explanation does carry a ring of plausibility. The archbishop was an attractive man whose reputation for fairness and purity of life enabled him to set an example to contemporaries; but his years as archbishop were marred by a succession of disputes, not always of his own making, which meant that the expectations aroused by his appointment were never fulfilled.

C. H. Lawrence, *St Edmund of Abingdon*, Oxford, 1960.

EDWARD I The reign of Edward I was one of the most important in medieval history. The king raised the English monarchy to new heights of prestige, but in the end over-reached himself by attempting to conquer Scotland (q.v.).

He was born on 17 June 1239, the eldest son of Henry III and his wife Eleanor of Provence. In 1254, at the age of 15, he was married to Eleanor, half-sister of Alfonso X, king of Castile. Like all marriages arranged at this level of society in the middle ages, it was a diplomatic alliance, intended in this case to secure the southern frontier of Gascony. But Edward and Eleanor do seem to have developed great affection for each other, and after she died in

1290, he erected in her memory a series of crosses – the famous Eleanor Crosses – marking the places where her body rested on its final journey from Lincoln, where she died, to Westminster, where she was interred. Edward remained nine years a widower until in 1299 he took Margaret, sister of King Philip IV of France, as his second wife. The chroniclers say that he had long fancied a French princess, but as they were probably referring to Margaret's sister, it seems that diplomatic considerations once again lay behind the match.

Edward succeeded to the throne in 1272. His youth had offered little promise for the future. He had shown himself to be a rather shifty individual. In 1258 the attraction of Simon de Montfort's (q.v.) powerful personality seems to have drawn him to the baronial reform movement, but he repented of his early enthusiasms and by 1264 was fully committed to restoring his father's authority. In the civil war that followed he was captured at Lewes, but escaped and led the royalists to victory at Evesham in 1265.

When news reached him in December 1272 of his father's death, he was on his way back from a crusade (q.v.) to the Holy Land. By the time he finally returned in 1274, he had been away for four years, and furious allegations awaited him that local officials, both royal and baronial, had taken advantage of his absence to misbehave, line their pockets and usurp royal lands. Edward reacted by launching a thorough investigation into local government, the records of which are known as the Hundred Rolls (q.v.). It was largely in response to the evidence uncovered in these enquiries that he published the first Statute of Westminster, 1275, remedying many long-standing abuses, and the Statute of Gloucester, 1278,

initiating the 'quo warranto' proceedings which questioned the warrant whereby baronial franchise holders exercised their rights. These were but two of the many important statutes issued in the 1270s and 1280s. Edward was seeking both to assert his authority and to remove the grievances which had fuelled the baronial reform movement in the reign of his father.

These same decades also saw Edward complete the conquest of Wales (q.v.). Two short wars, in 1277 and 1282, were enough to win Snowdonia – all that was left of independent Wales – for the English. No doubt encouraged by this easy triumph, Edward thought he could do the same in Scotland when a disputed succession provided an excuse for intervention after 1290. But he was badly mistaken. He had started a war that he could not win. Rather his involvement had the effect of unleashing a nationalist movement that made Scottish resistance all the fiercer, and in Robert Bruce the Scots found a leader of genius who gave them the sense of purpose they needed. The long wars with Scotland, which dragged on into the reign of Edward's grandson, formed the backcloth to English politics for the next couple of generations. The problems of heavy taxation and military service to which they gave rise contributed to a serious political crisis in 1297, when dissident barons led by the earls of Hereford and Norfolk found themselves in alliance with Robert Winchelsey, archbishop of Canterbury, in resisting Edward's demands. Edward was embarking on yet another campaign in the north when he died at Burgh-on-the-Sands on 7 July 1307.

He was a forceful man, and his reign illustrates English medieval monarchy at its most dynamic. For all the opposition he aroused in his later years, it is significant that his opponents never succeeded in shackling him with a constitution as humiliating for the monarchy as the one that had been imposed on his father in 1258 in the Provisions of Oxford (q.v.).

M. Prestwich, *War, Politics and Finance under Edward I*, Faber, 1972.

EDWARD II In January 1327 Edward II became the first English king since the Conquest to be removed from the throne. He had reigned for 20 years. Arguably, it is less remarkable that he should have been deposed than that he should have lasted for as long as he did.

He was born on 25 April 1284 at Caernarvon, the eldest surviving son of Edward I (q.v.) and Eleanor of Castile. In 1301 he was created the first Prince of Wales. His early years revealed little in his character to inspire confidence, and already he was infatuated by a young Gascon knight, Piers Gaveston, whom his father was obliged to send into exile in February 1307. When the younger Edward succeeded to the throne later that year, Gaveston was immediately recalled and created earl of Cornwall. The first signs of trouble came at Boulogne in January 1308, when a group of barons swore to redress 'the oppressions which have been done and are still being done' against the people. This oath foreshadowed the additional clause inserted into the coronation oath in February 1308 requiring Edward to keep the laws and customs 'which the community of your realm' shall have chosen. This clause was almost certainly inserted to prevent Edward from going back on any future agreement with the barons in the way that his father had. Indeed it was invoked only two months later to secure the exile of Gaveston.

Exile him they might, but they could not indefinitely prevent his return, and by 1309 he was back at the king's side. Dissatisfaction with Edward and his friends continued to mount until in March 1310 the committee of Ordainers was appointed in parliament to reform the state of the realm (q.v., ORDINANCES). Their programme included the removal of Gaveston and the other favourites whose greed had impoverished the crown, and the return (or 'resumption') of royal lands they had been granted. Once again, however, Gaveston slipped back, this time to be captured at Scarborough, and executed by the earl of Lancaster a month later (19 June 1312).

The presence of unpopular favourites injected a note of exceptional bitterness into the politics of Edward II's reign, but as in the closing years of his father's life it was the Scottish war that continued to overshadow English affairs. Edward would neither give up the war nor pursue it with enough vigour to achieve any success. When he did finally lead a large force northwards, it suffered at Bannockburn (q.v.) one of the worst defeats ever to befall English arms in the middle ages (24 June 1314). Humiliation abroad, as so often in history, led to reform at home, and Edward had no alternative now to conceding Lancaster's demand for the enforcement of the Ordinances. Unfortunately for Lancaster, however, his efforts were thwarted by the terrible famines that followed the destruction by heavy rain of the harvests for 1315 and 1316. And by 1317 his position at court was being undermined by the rise of two new favourites, the Despensers, father and son. He withdrew from court, and did his best to frustrate the policies of Edward and the courtiers from the relative isolation of his estates in the north. A party of bishops strove tirelessly to reconcile the earl to the king, but with only partial success. The Treaty of Leake (August 1318), which was the outcome of their efforts, met Lancaster's demand for the establishment of a standing council, but with the earl himself bribed into dropping his claim to membership, the influence it exerted over the king amounted to precious little.

Although the bishop of Worcester noticed an improvement in the king's conduct in 1320 – he was getting up earlier in the morning – such optimism proved in the event to be unjustified. Edward fell increasingly under the influence of the two Despensers, the younger of whom took advantage of his position to extend the lands he held in Glamorgan into a territorial lordship embracing most of South Wales. His aggressive behaviour provoked almost the entire baronage into resistance, and Edward was forced to send him and his father into exile in July 1321. But like Gaveston before him, the younger Hugh was soon back. Edward now acted quickly. He had the decision against his favourites reversed, and set about crushing his opponents. They appealed to Lancaster for help. Characteristically he was too busy pursuing a vendetta of his own to come to their assistance. Edward scattered the opposition in the Welsh Marches, and then marched north against Lancaster himself, who was defeated at Boroughbridge on 17 March 1322, and then executed.

For the next four years Edward and the Despensers ruled without challenge, until a small party of rebels, led by Queen Isabella and Roger Mortimer, landed at Orwell (Suffolk) on 24 September 1326. With them they had the king's young son, Edward. Edward

II's government just collapsed, and the king himself was captured in November, according to some at Llantrisant, according to others at Neath. In January 1327 Isabella hastily summoned a parliament, and a delegation was sent to Edward to induce him to abdicate in favour of his son. He bowed to the inevitable, and was led away to confinement first at Kenilworth, then at Berkeley. According to the traditional accounts, he was murdered at Berkeley on Mortimer's orders on 21 September 1327. However, in recent years some credence has been lent to a document known as the 'confession' of Edward II. This purports to be a narrative dictated to Manuel Fieschi, a clerk of Pope John XXII, in which the deposed king tells how he escaped from Berkeley and travelled through France and Germany to his eventual abode in an Italian hermitage. It is difficult to know what to make of this document, and no adequate explanation of it has yet been offered. For the moment it is probably safer to accept that Edward did after all meet his end in Berkeley Castle in September 1327

M. Prestwich, *The Three Edwards*, Weidenfeld & Nicolson, 1980; N. M. Fryde, *The Tyranny & Fall of Edward II, 1321–1326*, Cambridge, 1979.

EDWARD III The bronze effigy of King Edward III on his tomb in Westminster Abbey shows an old man with a long silky beard. It is how he might have looked in his dotage; but in his prime he had been one of the most vigorous and successful rulers of his day.

Edward was born in November 1312, when his father Edward II was at loggerheads with the barons. After the defeat of the earl of Lancaster's rebellion in 1322, the king was totally dominated by the two Despensers, and his wife Queen Isabella used the excuse of negotiating a settlement of the Gascon war to withdraw to France and plot with her lover, Roger Mortimer of Wigmore. Once her son had joined them, they moved on to the Low Countries, where the count of Hainault lent them his support in return for the marriage of the young Edward to his daughter Philippa. Then in September 1326 they invaded England, removed Edward II and placed the prince on the throne (25 January 1327). Edward put up with their tutelage for three years, until he felt ready to take an initiative himself. In October 1330, when he was 18, he had the two of them arrested at Nottingham Castle. Mortimer was executed, and Isabella packed off to comfortable retirement at Castle Rising.

The middle years of the reign were of course to see the great English victories in France, but Edward had served his military apprenticeship in Scotland (q.v.). In 1328 Isabella and Mortimer had signed the Treaty of Northampton acknowledging Scottish independence. It was a humiliating surrender. But when Robert Bruce died in the following year, and his five year old son David became king, there was a chance of re-opening the war. In 1332 Bruce's rival, Edward Balliol, and a group of fellow exiles invaded Scotland. They scored an early success at Dupplin Moor on 11 August, but were driven out again the following year. Edward then moved in directly, and after a sweeping victory at Halidon Hill near Berwick (19 July 1333) placed Balliol on the Scottish throne. The tactic Edward employed in that battle of combining archers with dismounted men-at-arms was one he was to use again to great effect in France. After the onset of continental warfare in 1338, Scotland claimed less of his attention, but all the same it was on that front that one of the most remarkable victories of his reign was to be won – at Neville's Cross in 1346, when David Bruce was taken prisoner.

Edward III's interests had turned across the Channel in the later 1330s because King Philip VI had confiscated the duchy of Gascony (q.v.). Arguments about the status of Gascony had given rise to wars often enough before, but this time Edward chose to by-pass all those tricky questions about the terms on which the duchy was held by staking his own claim to the crown of France. He argued that as the son of their sister Isabella he was a nearer relation in blood to the last three Capetian kings than was Philip VI, who was only their cousin. He planned to attack France in the same way that his predecessors had by purchasing the support of allies in Germany and the Low Countries. This proved to be an expensive and ultimately ineffectual strategy, however, and apart from a naval victory at Sluys he had little to show by the time he returned home on 30 November 1340. But he learned from his mistakes. Thenceforth he abandoned the idea of building grand, but shaky continental alliances in favour of launching surprise attacks on France from bases around the periphery, like Brittany and Gascony. Acting on this strategy, and using the tactics worked out in the Scottish wars of the 1330s, he achieved a striking victory at Crecy (q.v.) in 1346, and his son Edward, the Black Prince (q.v.), a still more striking one at Poitiers (q.v.) in 1356, when King John 'the Good' was captured. With the king of France a prisoner in England, Edward's prospects were transformed. The French crown, his claim to which had been no more than a forlorn hope, now lay within his grasp. One more campaign and it would be his. But the expedition of 1359–60, intended to deliver the final blow, failed to live up to expectations, and when negotiations were brought to a conclusion at Calais in October, he had to abandon his regal pretensions in return for getting an enlarged Gascony in full sovereignty.

With the advantage of hindsight we know that the war was to be reopened to England's disadvantage in the last years of Edward's life. But in fairness to the king, he had good reason to reflect with satisfaction on his achievements over the 30 years up to 1360. The bitter struggles of Edward II's reign had given way to a long period of internal stability based on a community of interest between king and nobility. He had succeeded in raising the English monarchy from the depths to which it had sunk during the reign of his father; and his court was famed throughout Europe for its ethos of romance and chivalry. This cult Edward fostered to enhance his own political standing. In 1348 he founded the Order of the Garter, an exclusive brotherhood of 26 knights, each of whom had a stall in the royal chapel of St George in Windsor Castle (q.v.). Membership was an honour sought by many and gained by few. Likewise it was partly prestige, but partly also self-indulgence that led him to embark in the 1360s on the programme of rebuilding and modernization at Windsor Castle, which was to make it perhaps the grandest royal residence of its day.

But it was Edward's misfortune to live for too long. In the 1370s the erosion of England's possessions in France was accompanied by a failure of leadership at home. The crown was subjected to severe criticism in the 'Good Parliament' of 1376, when several of the king's ministers were tried by the new process of impeachment (q.v.). The most notorious courtier of all, though, was not a minister, but Edward's mistress Alice Perrers, whose property, seized after the king's death on 21 June 1377, was valued at no less than £2,626. The final doom-laden years of Edward's life made a sad ending to a reign that in its heyday had epitomized medieval kingship at its most successful. All the same, we may question whether Edward had purchased internal stability at too high a price. It can be argued that he allowed the nobility to win too great a share of influence, most of all in the shires, where the abuse of magnate power evoked strong criticism from the Commons in parliament. If that were so, we can understand why his grandson and successor, Richard II (q.v.), should have attempted, at the cost of his throne as it turned out, to shift the balance of power in favour of the crown.

M. Prestwich, *The Three Edwards*, Weidenfeld & Nicolson, 1980.

EDWARD IV The first and longest lived of the three Yorkist kings, Edward IV enjoyed a reign of some 22 years from 1461 to 1483, interrupted briefly by Henry VI's so-called 'readeption' in 1470–1. His principal achievement was to bring a period of stability to an England torn by the struggle for Henry VI's throne; yet the very policies he pursued contributed to the breakdown of that stability after his death.

Edward was born on 28 April 1442, the eldest son of Richard, duke of York, and his wife, Cecily Neville. His father's opposition to the policies of Henry VI (q.v.) and his ministers led at the end of the 1450s to the outbreak of the period of civil strife known as the Wars of the Roses (q.v.). In 1459 he and his son had to flee the country for fear of being seized and executed as traitors. The following year the tables were turned. They returned to crush their opponents at the battle of Northampton on 10 July 1460, and the duke of York was recalled and made heir to the throne. Yet only five months later, on 30 December he was defeated and killed at Wakefield. The mantel of leadership now passed to his eldest son. Paradoxically it was another defeat that was soon to make him king of England. In February 1461 Queen Margaret defeated the Yorkists at the second battle of St Alban's, and freed her husband, who had been little more than a prisoner for the previous six months. Having lost control of their puppet, the Yorkists could only cling onto power by creating a king of their own. So they put the new duke of York on the throne as Edward IV.

It was a shaky start, but on Palm Sunday, 29 April 1461, he made such an effective job of disposing of Queen Margaret's army at the battle of Towton that the Lancastrian threat to his newly-won throne was as good as over. In southern England the Yorkists had long enjoyed the advantage in popular favour, thanks to their skilful use of propaganda. It was only in the far north that they had to stamp out the dying embers of resistance, and that they did at the battle of Hedgeley Moor in 1464. The main threat to stability in England in the 1460s came less from the remaining Lancastrian partisans than from divisions within the Yorkist camp itself fostered by the king's own political mistakes. Prime among them was the Woodville marriage. In October 1464 he made known that a few months earlier he had secretly married Elizabeth Woodville, widow of Sir John Grey. The consequences would not have been so far-reaching had not Elizabeth brought with her to court a large coterie of ambitious relatives, including no less than half-a-dozen sisters who all had to be found suitable marriages. Few were more upset than Edward's most powerful supporter, Richard Neville, earl of Warwick (q.v.), who found it harder now to find appropriate husbands for his own two daughters. It must have become apparent to him as the years went by that Edward IV was not to be the pliable instrument in his hands for which he had hoped. In July 1469, therefore, he risked an armed throw. With the support of the king's untrustworthy brother, Clarence, he invaded England from Calais (q.v.), captured Edward and executed cronies of his like Richard Woodville, Earl Rivers, and William Herbert, earl of Pembroke. But it was one thing to capture the king, and quite another to try ruling the country in his name. Edward soon escaped, and Warwick fled to France, where he defected to Queen Margaret and the Lancastrians. On 13 September 1470 Warwick returned, and put Henry VI back on the throne. For the moment Edward had to take to his heels, but time was on his side. The mere sight of poor Henry VI again was enough to convince most people that the 'readeption' would never last. From his refuge in the Low Countries, therefore, Edward planned the invasion which led in the following year to Warwick's death at Barnet (14 April 1471) and Queen Margaret's defeat at Tewkesbury three weeks later (4 May 1471).

Edward IV, like Charles II, was determined never to go on his travels again. To that extent, after 1471 he avoided the kind of mistakes that had cost him the loyalty of his subjects in the first reign. But the success he enjoyed in restoring peace and prosperity did not extend to reconciling to each other the opposing factions at court. The most serious problem facing Edward in the 1470s was the quarrel between his own two brothers, George of Clarence and Richard of Gloucester, the future Richard III (q.v.), over the disposal of the earl of Warwick's inheritance, to equal shares of which they laid claim by virtue of their respective marriages to Warwick's two daughters. The dispute over this vast inheritance was, however, merely the ground on which Clarence chose to pick his fight between 1471 and 1475. He had been a constant source of trouble in the past, and he was jealous of the lands and offices which had been granted to his younger brother in the north. In 1477 charges of treason were brought against some of Clarence's servants, and Edward took the opportunity to encompass the downfall of the duke himself, who was executed – whether in a butt of Malmsey wine or not – in February 1478. 'False, fleeting, perjur'd Clarence' is surely an unworthy recipient of our sympathy, but what Edward IV did was, in the words of his latest biographer, 'judicial fratricide', and a sad exception to a record of generosity and magnanimity towards fallen opponents without parallel in fifteenth century England. Over and over again Edward had pardoned enemies like Henry Beaufort, duke of Somerset, who showed their gratitude by rebelling again as soon as they had the opportunity. His readiness, albeit sometimes misplaced, to forgive and forget was matched too by his generosity towards those who had assisted him in his time of need. These pleasant characteristics he enjoyed along with a taste for high living and for female company that once again remind us of Charles II. Perhaps it was this high living that hastened him to a premature death on 9 April 1483. Still, a peaceful end on a death-bed was not so very common for an English king in the fifteenth century.

So where did Edward IV go wrong? He was successful enough in his own lifetime, and in the present day he has won praise from many historians for restoring order to the crown's finances after a long period of insolvency. But he was unable to ensure the peaceful succession of his 13 year old son, Edward V (q.v.). Why? The answer is that he had failed to resolve the long-standing antagonisms between his wife's Woodville relatives and their enemies in the Yorkist affinity. The confusion that surrounded even his testamentary wishes was an open invitation to renewed blood-letting. Although he had apparently named Richard of Gloucester as Protector in codicils added to his will, he left his elder son firmly under the control of the Woodvilles at Ludlow Castle. In view of the distrust with which the Woodvilles regarded Richard (and vice versa) it is hardly surprising that a struggle for power should have followed. Richard felt he had to grab the throne simply to survive. The Lancastrian family usually managed to stick together; the Yorkists had a habit of tearing themselves apart.

C. D. Ross, *Edward IV*, Eyre Methuen, 1974.

EDWARD V The elder of the two sons of Edward IV (q.v.) was born in November 1470. When his father died on 9 April 1483, he was in the care of Anthony Woodville, Earl Rivers, at Ludlow. On the way to be crowned in

London, he was taken by his uncle, Richard, duke of Gloucester, and transferred to the Tower, where his younger brother, Richard, duke of York, was soon to join him as a fellow captive. Edward's coronation, planned for 22 June 1483 never took place, and he and his brother disappeared from view even before Richard III assumed the crown on 6 July. What sort of king the boy would have made we have few means of telling, but Dominic Mancini, an Italian visitor to London, commended his scholarly attainments and knowledge of literature.

The Usurpation of Richard III, ed. C. A. J. Armstrong, Oxford, 2nd edn., 1969.

EDWARD, THE BLACK PRINCE Though the soubriquet, 'the Black Prince', was not earned until the sixteenth century, Edward of Woodstock was famed in his own day as 'the perfect root of all honour and nobleness, of wisdom, valour and largesse', to use the words of his biographer, the Chandos Herald.

The eldest son of Edward III (q.v.) and Philippa of Hainault, he was born on 16 June 1330 at Woodstock (Oxon). He owed his exalted reputation in the eyes of contemporaries to the qualities of courage and generalship which he was to show in the struggle between England and France known as the Hundred Years War (q.v.). His first experience of active service came at the battle of Crecy (q.v.) on 26 August 1346, when he commanded the right wing of the successful English army. Crecy was a triumph in which father and son could share the honours between them. The next time the French were defeated, it was the Prince alone who reaped the glory. That was at Poitiers (q.v.) in 1356. It seems to have been Edward's plan in the mid-1350s to field two armies in France simultaneously. In 1355 he sent the Black Prince to Aquitaine, and in the next year Henry, duke of Lancaster, to Normandy, in the expectation that they would join each other somewhere in the Loire valley. But the demolition by the French of the bridges across the river prevented any such link-up, and instead the two commanders were forced to retreat in the face of an offensive led by King John VI. The French caught up with the Prince near Poitiers, and confident as they were in their massive numerical superiority forced him to give battle. In the clash that followed the Prince won the greatest victory of his career. King John himself was taken prisoner. When the long negotiations over the terms for his release finally proved abortive, Edward III and the Prince led a new expedition in 1359 to deliver what was intended to be the knock-out blow. Though it was not as successful as had been hoped, an agreement was reached at Bretigny conceding to the English one of their long-standing demands – Aquitaine held in full sovereignty.

Now that peace had come, the king had to find some useful employment for his eldest son. This he did in 1362 by creating him prince of Aquitaine with full responsibility for administering and defending the province. Aquitaine's security demanded that her two neighbours, France to the east and Castile to the south, be kept apart. So it was important to prevent Castile from drifting into the French orbit. In 1366 just that eventuality seemed likely to occur when King Pedro was overthrown by his half-brother, Henry of Trastamara, leading an army of French mercenaries.

In the interests of restoring stability on his southern frontier, the Prince therefore led an Anglo-Gascon force into Castile, defeated Trastamara at Najera on 3 April 1367, and reinstated Pedro on the throne. It was to be the last victory of his active career. During his stay in Spain he contracted a painful and debilitating disease, probably dysentery, which was to prevent him from taking the saddle again. In 1371 he returned to England, and in the next year surrendered Aquitaine to his father. He died on 8 June 1376, and was buried in Canterbury Cathedral. Arguably, the Black Prince acquired the enviable reputation he did because his powers of statesmanship were never put to the test. He never became king of England. And he did not rule Aquitaine long enough for the flaws in his character to reap their inevitable harvest in disillusionment. For flaws there were. We can detect a note of harshness, for example, in his dealings with his tenants in Wales and the earldom of Chester. In 1353 – to note but one instance of sharp practice – the county community of Cheshire bought off a threatened eyre visitation by paying him 5,000 marks, only to find themselves instead subjected to a trailbaston (q.v.) enquiry, which was the same thing under another name. In Aquitaine he ruled with an arrogance and haughtiness that bred resentment among the independent-minded nobility of the province. More recently he has been accused of cruelty for ordering the inhabitants of Limoges to be put to the sword when he took the city in 1370. Yet his conduct, merciless though it may seem to us, was entirely consistent with the laws of war, because the place had just defected to the French with the connivance of its bishop, an erstwhile ally of the English. The Black Prince was probably neither more nor less humane than most soldiers of his generation. In conclusion, we should mention his marriage to Joan of Kent, which seems to have been one of the few genuine love matches in an age of arranged matrimony. They had one surviving son, the future Richard II (q.v.).

J. Harvey, *The Black Prince and his Age*, Batsford, 1976.

ELEANOR OF AQUITAINE The turbulent 'black-eyed beauty' who achieved fame as the wife of Henry II (q.v.) was the daughter and heiress of William X, count of Aquitaine. Her first marriage, to Louis VII, king of France, ended in divorce in 1152. Louis has been criticised for his compliance in this separation, seeing that it meant the loss of Aquitaine; but since he could handle neither the duchy nor its duchess – both she and it were ungovernable – he was probably wise to recognize reality. The year that she was divorced Eleanor found a new husband in Henry of Anjou, the future Henry II of England. It was to be one of the most famous matches in history. Henry and Eleanor were both strong and independent personalities and quarrelled incessantly. And as if the quarrels between husband and wife were not enough, there were also the quarrels between father and sons, in which the parents naturally took opposite sides – Henry favouring John (q.v.), and Eleanor her eldest son, Richard (q.v.). Henry died in 1189. But Eleanor, like so many other domineering medieval women, survived long into widowhood. She finally died on 1 April 1204, in the reign of her youngest son John, and was buried in Fontevrault Abbey.

ESCHEATOR An escheat was a feudal tenement which lapsed in default of heirs or during the minority of an heir to the lord or descendant of the lord from whom it was held. To the greatest feudal lord of all – the king – escheated lands were a source of revenue of such importance that in 1232 responsibility for their collection was transferred from the sheriffs to newly-established officers called escheators, two of whom (later reduced to one) were appointed in each county. When a tenant died, it would be the escheator's duty to take his lands into royal custody until it was ascertained by a local jury who was the next heir and whether the king should exercise the right of wardship should that heir be under age. Unlike the coroner and other local officials who have survived to the present day, the escheator disappeared in 1660 when the feudal revenues he collected were abolished by parliament.

EXCHEQUER See, GOVERN-MENT.

EYRE The eyre was the most powerful instrument of centralized government ever fashioned by the English crown in the middle ages. For over a century-and-a-half, from the reign of Henry II to that of Edward II, the justices in eyre (*in itinere*) were sent on visitations of the shires to hear all manner of civil and criminal pleas. To be sure, Henry II was not the first king to think of sending out his justices in this way. We know that Henry I was despatching justices to hear pleas in the counties because the fines they collected are recorded in the Exchequer pipe roll of 1130. But after the long civil war between Stephen and Matilda, Henry II had to construct the system all over again, and this he seems to have done by 1166 when the first full eyre of the reign was undertaken.

There is no doubt that an eyre was an elaborate business. Indeed, that was to be one of its disadvantages. So how did it work? When the king announced a nation-wide eyre, he divided the country into circuits, each to be worked by a group of justices moving from one county to the next until they had completed their business. The justices held their sessions in a full meeting of the county court, and so long as they were there all subordinate courts suspended their hearings and handed over to them the indictments which had not yet been determined. When the juries from each hundred had assembled, the justices presented them with a series of questions known as 'the articles of the eyre', asking what crimes had been committed and what statutes contravened. The articles of 1194 served as the point of departure for all later sets of instructions to the justices. As the thirteenth century wore on, so many new articles were added, taking in business of an administrative rather than a judicial nature, that the eyre became bogged down in the sheer weight of its own bureaucracy. It became less an instrument for enforcing the law in distant parts of the country than a means of keeping a check on local officials like the sheriff, and of raising money through the imposition of heavy fines. The oppressiveness of the eyre soon caused county communities to dread the coming of the justices. Sometimes they were prepared to pay a fine to the king in order *not* to receive a visitation. By the reign of Henry III, therefore, it became the unwritten rule that no county was to have an eyre more than once every seven years.

In the reign of Edward II the crown

finally abandoned eyre visitations altogether. The reasons seem to have been largely financial. For a century or more the main value of the eyre to the king had been the money it raised in fines. By the 1290s, however, Edward I (q.v.) was turning regularly to parliament (q.v.) for grants of national taxation (q.v.). The counties would never have stood for eyre visitations and taxation at the same time, so it was the eyre which had to go. There were just two eyres in Edward II's reign, in Kent in 1313 and London in 1321, and one right at the start of Edward III's reign in the East Midlands in 1329–30. After that the eyre to all intents and purposes was dead.

A. Harding, *The Law Courts of Medieval England*, Allen & Unwin, 1973

F

FASTOLF, SIR JOHN A veteran of the Hundred Years War (q.v.), known to us from his correspondence in the Paston Letters (q.v.) and from the recollections of his secretary, William Worcester (q.v.), Fastolf in real life was very different from the drunken debauchee to whom Shakespeare gave a corrupted form of his name. He was a successful knight and a shrewd businessman.

Born in about 1380, the scion of an ancient though modest Norfolk family, he saw early service in the household of Henry IV's second son, Thomas of Clarence, but still ranked no higher than an esquire when he joined the Harfleur-Agincourt expedition in 1415. By 1416 he had finally been knighted, hardly a premature honour for a man entering his later 30s. His achievements in fact were to come late in life, in the reign of Henry VI (q.v.) rather than that of his father. At the battle of Verneuil (17 August 1424) we are told by Worcester that 'he won by the fortune of war about 20,000 marks' – presumably meaning that he took prisoners whose ransoms came to that amount. Already we can sense that he was careful with money. The most distinguished prisoner he took at Verneuil, and the one likely to yield the largest ransom, was the duke of Alencon; but after he was released a few years later, Fastolf complained that he had been deprived of his full share of the money. By 1426 Fastolf's reputation as a captain stood high enough to earn him election to the garter. But only three years later that very reputation was called into question when he found himself strongly criticized for his conduct at the battle of Patay (18 June 1429). He had beat a hasty retreat from the field, so it was alleged, leaving the lords Talbot and Hungerford to be taken prisoner by the French. Talbot was certainly angry. Yet accusations of cowardice, such as those made by the chronicler Monstrelet, are hardly borne out by the ample evidence of continued confidence shown in Fastolf by the duke of Bedford, the English commander in France. He continued to be a member of Henry VI's French council until 1439, the year before he returned to England to invest and enjoy the profits he had made in France. That he returned a rich man there can be no doubt. In 1445 his lands in England were worth £1,061 *per annum*, and to that total we then have to add the income he derived from the estates he held in France until the English collapse. What did he do with his money? Like most men of his standing in the middle ages, he invested it in lands and in buildings. He spent no less than £13,855 on adding to his estates. In about 1430 he started to rebuild his fortified manor house at Caister, though how much money that absorbed in the 30 years we are told the masons were at work we can only guess. By his early 70s Fastolf had become, in K. B. McFarlane's brilliant characterization, 'a close-fisted, litigious and irascible old man', reduced to 'a state of querulous and unmanageable senility.' His final months were divided between worrying about the £11,000 the government still owed him and making last minute amendments to his will. Since he was childless, Fastolf proposed to use his money to endow a college of priests at Caister. But in November 1459, two days before he died, he revised his earlier plan so as to assign full responsibility for the foundation to his friend John Paston, who in return for 4,000 marks was to have in fee simple all the lands of which he was trustee. The validity of the second will was of course called into question, and for years ahead the Pastons (q.v.) were to be plagued by incessant litigation, documented in their family correspondence.

Long after the dust had settled on Fastolf's deeds of conveyance, his fame was converted into notoriety by William Shakespeare. In the original draft of *Henry IV* Hal's drinking companion in the London ale-houses was called Sir John Oldcastle, but the name was changed to Falstaff when complaints about character assassination were made by Oldcastle's descendant, Lord Cobham. There is some evidence for the youthful notoriety of young Prince Henry, but none at all to associate him with Sir John Fastolf, who was less than ten years his senior.

K. B. McFarlane, 'The Investment of Sir John Fastolf's Profits of War', *Trans. Roy. Hist. Soc.*, 5th series, vii (1957).

FEUDALISM As it emerged in the tenth and eleventh centuries from the confusion of the Dark Ages, early medieval Europe assumed the form which we recognize as a feudal society. Though dangerously prone to jargon-ridden discussion, feudalism is a system quite easy to understand once we consider how and why it originated on the Continent in the age of the Emperor Charlemagne and his predecessors.

In the lands of the Frankish monarchy, particularly west of the Rhine, central authority was ceasing to be effective by the eighth century. The kings of the Merovingian dynasty were too weak either to repel external aggression or to enforce internal peace. Men therefore began to seek personal security by commending themselves to someone powerful enough to offer protection. In this process of commendation we can trace the origins of the feudal act of homage, whereby one free man became the 'vassal' of another, performing some agreed service, usually military, in return for the benefits of security and protection. To help his vassal to provide such military duties as might be demanded of him, the lord

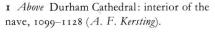

1 *Above* Durham Cathedral: interior of the nave, 1099–1128 (*A. F. Kersting*).

2 *Above right* Canterbury Cathedral: interior of the choir, 1175–84, designed by William of Sens and completed by William the Englishman.

3 *Right* Wells Cathedral: south transept looking into the nave, *c.* 1175–80. Note the carvings of the man with toothache and the man removing a thorn from his foot among the foliage capitals at the top of the right-hand pillar.

4 *Above left* Westminster Abbey: the choir, 1245–60. Gothic of the Ile-de-France style interpreted by Henry III's masons in an English idiom (*A. F. Kersting*).

5 *Above* Gloucester Cathedral: the choir, *c.* 1337–67. The earliest surviving large-scale work in Perpendicular (*Edwin Smith Collection*).

6 *Left* King's College Chapel, Cambridge: begun in 1443 and not completed until the following century (*A. F. Kersting*).

7a) *Above left* Stewkley, Bucks: a vaulted Norman chancel

b) *Above* Dinton, Bucks: Early English lancets.

c) *Left* Elsing, Norfolk: Reticulated tracery, *c.* 1340.

8a) *Above left* Cruck cottage at Didbrook, Gloucs. **b)** *Right* Interior of the Guildhall, Leicester, *c.* 1347. The trusses are of cruck construction (*Dixon Scott Collection, Public Record Office*).

9 Manor-house of 'upper-hall' design at Bosham, Sussex, as depicted on the Bayeux Tapestry. Harold and his retinue are having dinner before setting out on the journey that was to take them to William's court in Normandy (*Mansell Collection*).

10a) *Above* Stokesay Castle, Salop: the hall range, began *c.* 1285. **b)** *Below* Little Wenham, Suffolk: built *c.* 1270–80. On the left is the hall, on the right the chapel with solar above (*A. F. Kersting*).

11 *Left* Brass of Sir Robert de Bures, engraved *c.* 1320, Acton, Suffolk

12 *Above* Brasses of Sir Reginald de Malyns and his two wives, 1385, Chinnor, Oxon: London style 'B' (*British Museum*).

3a) *Left* Brasses of Sir Hugh Halsham and his wife, 1441, West Grinstead, Sussex: London
[sty]le 'B'.

) *Right* Brasses of Sir William Etchingham and his wife and son, 1444, Etchingham, Sussex:
[L]ondon style 'B'. Note how similar these two brasses are (*Victoria and Albert Museum*).

14 *Above* Brass of Sir Thomas
Brounflete, 1430, Wymington,
Bedfordshire: London style 'D'

15 *Right* Brasses of Robert Ingleton
and his three wives, 1472, Thornton,
Bucks: one of the most lavish products
of London style 'D'.

16 *Left* Brasses of William and Marion Grevel, 1401, Chipping Campden, Gloucs: London style 'B' (*The National Monuments Record*).

17a) *Below* Silver penny of William the Conqueror, 1066–87 (*British Museum*).

b) Silver penny of Edward I, 1272–1307: 'long-cross' issue (*British Museum*).

c) Gold noble of Edward III, 1344 (*British Museum*).

d) Gold sovereign of Henry VII, 1485–1509 (*British Museum*).

18 *Above left* Foundation charter of New Minster, Winchester, showing King Edgar, 959–75, offering the charter to Our Lord (*British Library,* MS Vespasian A.VIII).

19 *Above* Initial 'B' from the Psalms in the Winchester Bible, *c.* 1160–70, showing Christ driving out the evil spirits (above) and rescuing souls from Hell (below) (*The Dean and Chapter of Winchester*).

20 *Left* Scenes from the Book of Genesis, from a Bible picture leaf by W. de Brailes, *c.* 1230–50 (*Reproduced by permission of The Syndics of the Fitzwilliam Museum, Cambridge*).

21 *Opposite* St Omer Psalter, the Beatus page, executed *c.* 1325 for members of the St Omer family of Mulbarton, Norfolk, whose portraits appear in the row of medallions at the foot (*British Library* Add. MS 39810).

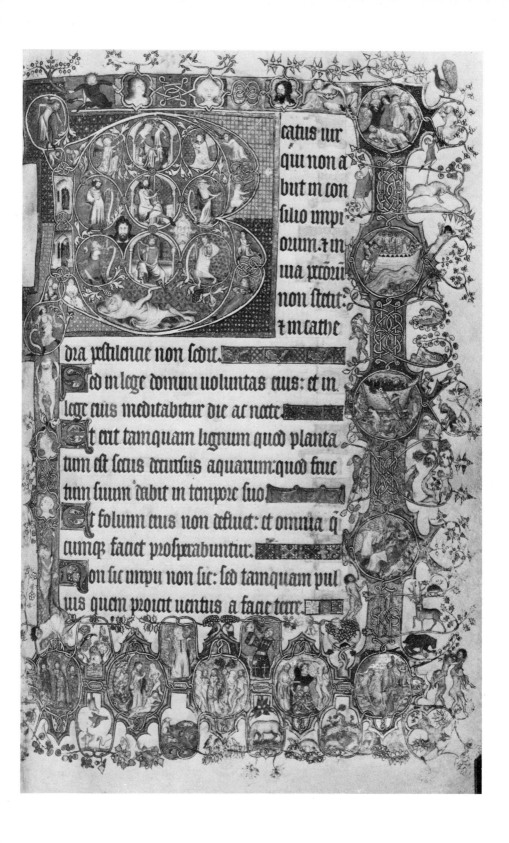

eatus uir
qui non a
but in con
silio impi
orum. ⁊ in
uia pctoui
non stetit:
⁊ in cathe

dra pestulencie non sedit.
ed in lege domini uoluntas eius: et in
lege eius meditabitur die ac nocte.
t erit tamquam lignum quod planta
tum est secus decursus aquarum:quod fru
ctum suum dabit in tempore suo
t folium eius non defluet: et omnia q'
cumqz facet prosperabuntur.
on sic impii non sic: sed tamquam pul
uis quem proicit uentus a facie terre.

22 *Above* The Luttrell Psalter, *c.* 1340: Sir Geoffrey Luttrell of Irnham, Lincs., being armed by his wife and daughter (*British Library* Add. MS 45130).

23 *Opposite* The Wilton Diptych, *c.* 1380–90 (*Reproduced by courtesy of the Trustees, The National Gallery, London*).

24 *Above* Sherborne Abbey Missal, *c.* 1400: detail from the border (*collection of the duke of Northumberland*). *Photo: George Skipper*.

25 *Above right* The Lovel Lectionary, *c.* 1400: the artist, John Sifrewast, presenting his book to John, Lord Lovel (*British Library,* Harley MS 7026).

26 *Right* Tinted drawing of John Lydgate presenting his poem *The Pilgrim* to Thomas Montacute, earl of Salisbury (*British Library,* Harley MS 4826).

Left and above

27a) The south door of Kilpeck Church, Heref., c. 1140–5.

b) Details from the arch of the south door at Kilpeck.

28 The font at Castle Frome, Heref., c. 1170. On the left is the Baptism of Christ. Then come a pair of doves. On the right is the Bull of St Luke, the first of a series of the signs of the Four Evangelists which fills up the remaining space.

29 *Left* The Bellfounders Window, York Minster, *c.* 1320–30, given by Richard Tunnoc, who is shown in the lower central panel kneeling before St William of York. The scene on his right shows bell-casting, and on his left probably tuning (*The National Monuments Record*).

30 *Above* St Peter Mancroft, Norwich, *c.* 1430–55, the chancel and east window (*A. F. Kersting*).

31 Lady Howard, *c.* 1485, one of a row of benefactors in the windows of the north aisle of Long Melford Church, Suffolk.

32 The Shambles at York, a view taken early this century.

sometimes bestowed a benefice, or fief (*feudum* in Latin) as it later came to be known. Not least among such lords were the Merovingian kings themselves, who assembled an army by seizing the lands of the Church and granting them to vassals for the promise of military service. In the eighth century these estates were used to endow well-armed soldiers, or knights as they were to become known, but later the kings also used them to provide maintenance for great officers at court. Vassals were granted fiefs, therefore, not just for the performance of military duties, but for other specified forms of service too. Later on such non-military forms of feudal tenure were known as sergeanties.

This deliberate policy pursued by the Frankish kings contributed to the spread of vassalage in the ninth century. Not only were the kings creating more vassals on royal and ecclesiastical estates but those to whom they granted benefices or fiefs then created vassals on their own lands. All that was needed to seal this process was a formal union between vassalage and the fief. This seems to have come by the early ninth century, when it was accepted that a vassal became liable for the performance of an agreed service once he had been granted a fief. In other words, feudalism was based on a contractual relationship between lord and vassal. This was created by the formal act of homage, when the vassal knelt down and placed his hands between those of his lord who received him as his man. After performing the act of homage, the vassal swore an oath of fealty, declaring that he would always be faithful to his lord.

Feudalism was therefore a product of Frankish society in the eighth and ninth centuries, nurtured by the weakness of central authority, and fostered by

monarchs who granted fiefs in return for the performance of future military service. If they thought that by so doing they would buttress the authority of the crown, they were to be sadly mistaken. In law the vassal held only a life tenancy, and on his death the fief reverted to the grantor who was free either to retain it or bestow it again, as he saw fit. In practice, however, the simple fact of possession came to favour the vassal, who could frequently regard the fief as his own and as his son's after him. The vassal's position was strengthened at the expense of his overlord's, even if that overlord was the king.

The structure of feudal relationships we have been examining developed in the lands of the Frankish monarchy, but not in Anglo-Saxon England. Certainly, many hundreds of free men were commending themselves to the protection of powerful lords in England in the tenth century, but the notion of dependent land tenure in return for the performance of a stated personal service never developed here, because the preconditions for its growth did not exist. Feudalism was introduced by the Normans after 1066. William began imposing the essential features of a feudal society on England quite soon after the battle of Hastings, and simply because he came as a conqueror to an occupied land he was able to impose feudal principles in a manner more thoroughgoing than had been customary in Normandy where they had been the outcome of a process of natural growth. Thus when he rewarded his followers for their success at Hastings William insisted that they should hold their newly-won lands in return for the performance of future military service, usually knight service or castle guard. The lords, whether secular or ecclesiastical, who held their lands in this way directly from the king were known as tenants-in-chief. They numbered about 150 in all. Each was made responsible for the provision of a certain quota of knights in the feudal host which, if all had assembled, would have totalled about 5,000. To perform this obligation, the tenants-in-chief could either keep the knights resident in their households or, more commonly as time went on, grant them fiefs from their own estates. By this process, known as sub-infeudation, the feudal chain linking lord and vassal extended further and further down the hierarchy.

One of the most remarkable features of the Norman settlement of England is the speed with which we find tenants-in-chief granting out large tracts of their estates to dependent knights. This is of course quite understandable in the case of those monasteries on whom William had inflicted knight service. We know only too well from the history of one distinguished house that the existence of a large body of knights domiciled within the precincts could ruin monastic life. At Glastonbury the remarkably ham-fisted Abbot Thurstan once called in his knights to intimidate the monks, and open fighting broke out in the church, where a number of them were gravely wounded. It is not surprising to find, therefore, that abbeys like Westminster and Bury St Edmund's which were assigned responsibility for a quota of knights started to solve the problem by granting them landed fiefs within 20 years of the Conquest.

However, it is less easy to understand why a powerful baron, proud of his position in society, should wish to divest himself of a fair part of his estates merely in order to provide his knights with land of their own. Yet this is just what happened in the years after William's death. To understand the reasoning behind 'subinfeudation', as it is known, we need to remember that when a lord granted a fief to a vassal he was not only providing for future military service but also creating a source of future income. How could a lord succeed in creating an income for himself at the same time as reducing his own landed resources?

The sources of income which we know as the 'incidents of feudalism' derived from the rights of ownership which a lord retained over a fief he had granted to a vassal. They were based on the belief, increasingly a fiction by the twelfth century, that the vassal was a life tenant, on whose death the fief would revert to the lord who had bestowed it. Theoretically, the lord was free to grant it out to whomsoever he chose, but it was the normal practice to allow the eldest son to succeed once he had paid an entry fine known as a 'relief'. Should the tenant die leaving a son under age, the lord was entitled to take the fief into 'wardship'. This afforded him the chance to exploit the estate for all it was worth until the son was old enough to succeed. If, on the other hand, the tenant died leaving only a daughter or daughters, their marriages were highly marketable commodities that could be used to make money. Faced in an emergency with a sudden need for cash, a lord was entitled also to take what was known as an 'aid' from his vassals. By the thirteenth century such occasions had come to be defined as the ransoming of the lord's person, the knighting of his eldest son and the marriage of his eldest daughter. These rules applied to the king in his dealings with his tenants-in-chief no less than to the latter in their own dealings with sub-vassals.

Seen from this point of view, therefore, feudalism was a nexus of financial privileges. It can be regarded not only as the means by which William I provided for his future military needs but also as a system of taxation. And it was in this direction that the future of feudalism was to lie. As early as 1100 we know that the payment of scutage (literally 'shield money') was allowing the king's tenants to escape the performance of their obligations in the feudal host. Instead of serving in person they sent money which was used to hire mercenaries. The feudal host of 5,000 knights is therefore a product of the historical imagination rather than a reality rooted in eleventh century military experience. It was as a source of revenue that feudalism was to be of more lasting importance to the king, indeed to any overlord in a position to profit from reliefs, wardships and other 'incidents of feudalism'.

The dependence of the crown on its income from feudalism helps to explain why such perquisites as reliefs and wardships figured prominently in disputes between king and baronage in the twelfth and thirteenth centuries. It was in the king's interest to mulct those who held from him – his tenants-in-chief – as intensively as he could. Indeed, he was limited only by the tenant's capacity to pay. For that reason it was laid down in 1100 that the king should charge only 'reasonable' reliefs. But since it was the king who decided what was 'reasonable', the barons were no better protected than they were before. So they decided in Magna Carta (q.v.) in 1215 to lay down for the first time just what constituted a 'reasonable' relief, and they named 100s for a knight's fee and £100 for a barony.

It was the financial worth of feudalism that ensured its survival in skeleton form long after it had ceased to serve as the flesh and blood of medieval society. The main turning point in the history of feudalism seems to have come in the reign of Henry II (q.v.). For a hundred years after the Conquest feudal society had centred on the honor, or barony – in other words, the assemblage of fiefs held from each tenant-in-chief of the crown. All the tenants of the honor were obliged to attend the meetings of the honorial court where matters of common interest were discussed and settled. Of the composition of the court and its procedure we know little, but what we can sense from the surviving evidence is its importance in giving a corporate expression to the ties forged between a lord and his vassals. After the reign of Henry II, however, the honorial court, and with it the honor, clearly dwindled in importance thanks largely to the king's legal reforms which lured business from the feudal to the royal courts. Matters which were once settled by custom in the honorial courts were now being settled by means of the writs which Henry made available to initiate actions in the hearing of his own justices (q.v., Justice). As a result of this process of judicial centralization, which strengthened the relationship between king and subject at the expense of that between lord and vassal, feudalism was dealt a lasting blow.

Surprisingly, feudalism was not formally abolished in England till 1660. Until then it had continued to form the basis of English land law, and as such it was valued by feudal lords for the lucrative rights which it gave them over their tenants. So far from dying, it actually enjoyed a revival in the age of the Tudors. In the reign of Henry VIII the two courts of Wards and Surveyors were set up to enable the crown to maximize the income it derived from feudal rights. In the reign of Elizabeth the queen's devoted minister, Lord Burghley, was Master of Wards, a position which gave him control over the upbringing of such young noblemen as the dissolute earl of Oxford and the earl of Southampton, Shakespeare's future patron.

The posthumous history of feudalism is even more curious than its resuscitation by the Tudors. The word 'feudal' did not exist in the English language until Sir John Spelman invented it in 1639. The 'feudal system', if the New English Dictionary is to be believed, had to wait till 1776 for its first appearance in the writings of Adam Smith, and 'feudalism' itself did not appear until 1839. 'Feudal' is of course derived from the Latin, *feudum*, a fief. It is this word which has had the misfortune to be picked up and used in a derogatory sense to describe a supposedly backward society which found its most appropriate expression in the anarchy of Stephen's (q.v.) reign. Far better it is to accept that the broader the sense in which the term is used, the less value it retains. If we were to tear away the inessentials, we would find that it was the contractual relationship between lord and vassal which lay at the heart of medieval feudalism.

F. L. Ganshof, *Feudalism*, London, 1952.

FINE We sometimes find that in the middle ages a word conveyed a different meaning from the one it has today. A good example is the word 'fine'. The medieval equivalent of the modern term would have been 'amercement' (q.v.), that is to say, a payment imposed by a court on someone found guilty of a trespass. A fine (<*finis*) in its medieval sense was an agreement reached in the king's court at the end of a fictitious suit. The practice of using the royal courts in this way to register agreements

over the tenure of land began in the reign of Henry II (1154–89), when the regular visitations of the justices in eyre (q.v.) encouraged litigants to seek licence to have their suit terminated and registered before a session of the court. At first the agreement was written down only in duplicate, one copy going to each of the litigants, but in 1195, probably at the initiative of the justiciar (q.v.), Hubert Walter, it was decided to make a third copy, known as the 'foot of the fine', which was filed in the treasury for easy reference in case of future disputes (see below). By the thirteenth

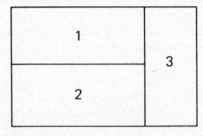

century most of the innumerable disputes which were terminated by fines were quite fictitious, undertaken solely for the convenience of having the conveyance registered in court. The feet of fines that survive in their thousands in the Public Record Office today are a valuable source for the study of family pedigrees and manorial histories.

FORESTS Despite centuries of internal colonization, vast tracts of forest land still stretched across England on the eve of the Conquest. Here the king and his thegns were able to indulge their taste for hunting. It was a sport which William I (q.v.) was to enjoy just as much if not more than his Saxon predecessors. As we know, he cleared south-west Hampshire to create what was called the 'New Forest'. But an enlargement of the area reserved for the chase was not the only consequence of the Norman Conquest. For the first time the forest was given legal definition: it embraced those parts of the country subject to the forest law. As Richard FitzNigel was to put it a century later in his *Dialogue of the Exchequer,*

The whole organization of the forests . . . is outside the jurisdiction of the other courts and solely dependent on the decision of the king . . . The forest has its own laws, based it is said, not on the common law of the realm, but on the legislation of the king.

In other words, the forest law was a matter for the king alone, and nothing to do with the custom of the realm. Its purpose was the preservation of the vert and venison – that is, the natural habitat of the forest and the game which it sheltered – and to that end forest offenders were punished with a severity hardly known under the common law.

In the course of the next century-and-a-half, however, the Norman and Angevin kings came to realize that the forest law could be put to other and more practical uses than simply the punishment of those who had dared to infringe it. It could be made to pay. It could be used to finance the needs of government. Henry I and his successors chose to enforce the forest laws not so much by death or mutilation as by inflicting heavy fines. In 1130 one of the king's justices handed over no less than 500 marks to the Exchequer in respect of the pleas of the forest he had heard.

The more the forest law weighed down on its hapless victims, high and low alike, the more it became an object of dislike. But it was not only the stringency of the law that attracted criticism; it was also the limits within which it applied. Let us not delude ourselves by thinking that a medieval forest was confined only to sylvan woodlands. Under William I, Henry I and particularly Henry II larger and larger areas were brought under the jurisdiction of the forest law, so that by the end of the twelfth century, when it reached its maximum extent, it applied to between a quarter and a third of England. To the far-reaching legal consequences for the inhabitants that we have already noted was added the administrative dislocation caused to private landowners who now found themselves hemmed in by restrictions on the exploitation of their own lands. It is thus hardly surprising to find that among the leading opponents of King John were lords from northern England who had suffered badly from the enlargement of the forests north of the Trent. Nor is it surprising to find that abuses arising from the forest administration were corrected in Magna Carta (q.v.). As it happened, John escaped lightly. Cl. 47 required him to disafforest all that he had afforested. But as it was not he but his father who had added most to the forest, that did not amount to much. He and his brother Richard (q.v.) had actually resorted to selling licences for *dis*afforestation as a desperate means of raising money quickly. All the same, in the century that followed the bounds of the forest and the law that applied within them remained as hotly contested as ever. Indeed, the subject was deemed to be of such importance that the clauses relating to it in Magna Carta were taken out in 1217 and enshrined in a separate document known as the Charter of the Forest.

It was not until the reign of Edward III (q.v.) that the forest ceased to be a major political issue. The reason was quite simple. It was no longer so important as a source of revenue. The rise of parliamentary taxation (q.v.) in the later thirteenth century assured the king of a regular supply of money, and freed him from dependence on the exactions of the forest justices. After the 1330s we hear little more of the bitter complaints that had been raised so vehemently in the past.

If we concentrate unduly on the political wrangles, we can easily come away with the impression that in the twelfth and thirteenth centuries forest dwellers lived in unrelieved hardship. No doubt they did suffer from the harshness of the law, otherwise they would not have complained. But the forest could also offer a life of freedom. It could give shelter to fugitives from justice. Sherwood Forest put Robin Hood (q.v.) and his men beyond the reach of the sheriff of Nottingham. And to Robin as to many ordinary folk on the verge of the woodlands poaching could provide a variety of diet (q.v.) denied to most peasants in medieval England. Provided of course you did not get caught.

C. R. Young, *The Royal Forests of Medieval England*, Leicester, 1979.

FORESTALLING AND REGRATING

One of the duties of a municipal corporation in the middle ages was to ensure an adequate supply of food for its citizens. The interests of the consumers had to be protected against those of the merchant victuallers who could have taken advantage of their position as suppliers to force up the price. For that reason in codes like the Coventry Leet Book we often find that steps were taken to stamp out the twin abuses known as 'forestalling' and 'regrating'. Forestallers were those who bought up supplies before they reached the market place. Regraters were those who held back goods so as to sell them later at a higher price. How effective these measures were we have no means of telling; but we should not pitch our expectations too high.

FORTESCUE, SIR JOHN

Among political thinkers of the middle ages Fortescue is hardly one of the most original; but not surprisingly for a man who was deeply involved in the political struggles of his day, he is one of the most practical-minded. Born in Devon in the 1390s, he joined Lincoln's Inn, and became a sergeant-at-law in about 1429. This legal training he pursued simultaneously with a political career which brought him to parliament as M.P. for a succession of West Country boroughs in the 1420s and '30s. Promotion in his chosen profession, when it came, was rapid. In 1441 he was appointed a king's sergeant, and in the following year, without any intermediate step, Chief Justice of King's Bench. By now, of course, Suffolk and the party dominant at Henry VI's (q.v.) court were coming under strong criticism for their alleged corruption and incompetence. But Fortescue was no trimmer. He was nothing if not a thorough-going Lancastrian. He was present at the Lancastrian debacle at Towton on 29 March 1461, and fled northwards to Scotland with the deposed Henry VI and his wife.

It may have been while on the run in the borderlands, or more plausibly while in exile in France after 1465, that he wrote the four tracts upholding the Lancastrian succession and the treatise *De Natura Legis Naturae*, in which he made his famous distinctions between 'Dominium Regale', or absolute monarchy, 'Dominium Politicum', or republican government, and 'Dominium Politicum et Regale', or constitutional monarchy. These ideas were taken further in the most popular of his works, *De Laudibus Legum Anglie*. He attributes the origins of absolute monarchy to military conquest, and of limited monarchy to the decision of a community of people to form themselves into a state. France he considered to be an absolute monarchy, England and Scotland (q.v.) constitutional monarchies. Fortescue came back with the temporarily ascendant Lancastrians in 1470–1, only to find himself on the losing side once again, this time at Tewkesbury on 4 May 1471. Edward IV (q.v.) now compelled him to make suitable amends for his past miscalculations. To recover his estates Fortescue had to refute his earlier writings and justify Edward's own title to the throne.

In the years that were left to him, in retirement at Ebrington (he died *c*. 1476), Fortescue wrote his last work, *The Governance of England*. Many of the suggestions he makes in this treatise had already been voiced many times over in parliament and elsewhere: that the king should live of his own, that former royal lands should be resumed and made inalienable, that the power of the great magnates should be curbed. But more original was his proposal that the Council should be transformed into a body of professional men, 12 secular and 12 clerical. Did he realize how far these measures to strengthen the crown would render more absolute the constitutional monarchy of which he had written so approvingly in his earlier works?

Sir J. Fortescue, *De laudibus legum Anglie*, ed. S. B. Chrimes (1942).

FRANCHISE A grant of franchise gave a lord the right to exercise within his lordship those functions of justice or administration which would elsewhere be exercised by the king's ministers. Among the most important liberties or franchises in medieval England were the earldom of Chester, the palatinate of Durham and the Isle of Ely. If any reason can be offered to explain the creation of these privileged enclaves, it must be that they enabled the responsibility for administration in some of the more distant parts of the country to be delegated to a local magnate better placed than the king to exercise effective authority. This is not to say that a franchise holder could act as a free agent in his liberty. Far from it. By launching the so-called 'quo warranto' proceedings (i.e., 'by what warrant') Henry III (q.v.) and Edward I (q.v.) sought to establish the principle that however they might have originated, franchises could only be justified in future so long as they served the public good. The result was that by the late middle ages a franchise was just another piece in the vast mosaic of local administration in England.

H. M. Cam, *Law Finders & Law Makers*, Merlin, 1962.

FRANCISCANS The Franciscans, or 'Grey Friars' as they were known from the colour of their habit, were the most successful of the orders of friars (q.v.) that settled in England. St Francis himself was not so much their founder as the source of their inspiration. Indeed, he can hardly be described as a reformer in the conventional sense of that term, still less as an organizer. What he believed in was teaching by example.

In David Knowles's words, he had a purely spiritual conception of his friars as 'followers of Christ in perfect poverty and simplicity, a new leaven to the world'. He therefore forbade them to own any property. He wanted them to gain their living by work or failing that by begging. Difficulties were bound to arise from the practical operation of this doctrine, but they were overcome by the legal fiction of vesting ownership of all the property needed by the friars in the pope.

If the simple evangelical ideal could sometimes be modified like this to accord with reality, it was still revolutionary enough to provoke controversy. Even before the death of St Francis in 1226 differences had arisen between those who wished to fulfil the founder's precepts to the letter and those who wished to relax them a little – differences which erupted into a bitter and protracted dispute that was only resolved a century later by Pope John XXII's bulls *Ad Conditorem Canonum* (1322), restoring to the friars full ownership of their property, and *Cum Inter Nonnullos* (1323) condemning the doctrine that Christ and the apostles had owned no possessions.

The English Franciscans were lucky enough to escape the worst excesses that the debate on poverty aroused on the Continent. That is not to suggest that they did not care about the issues involved. Indeed, right from the start they had attracted to their ranks some of the most brilliant men of their day, such as Adam Marsh, an Oxford graduate, and Haymo of Faversham, who became sixth Minister General of the Order in 1240. They wanted to attract talent, and they had no trouble in doing so because they were strong in the universities. When they first arrived in England, in 1224, they made for Oxford. And

thanks to the patronage of the learned Robert Grosseteste (q.v.), later bishop of Lincoln, the house they established there became a noted centre of learning. Among its most famous alumni could be numbered Roger Bacon (q.v.) and John Pecham, the first Franciscan archbishop of Canterbury.

For all the advantages it brought, this close association with the universities would probably have met with the disapproval of St Francis himself. It had the effect, as many historians have pointed out, of converting an Order of simple evangelists into an Order of intellectuals. St Francis wanted his followers to go from place to place inspiring devotion to the Christian faith by the very simplicity of their lives. We can recall the story told by the Lanercost chronicler of how an unfriendly knight was moved by the sight of two brothers walking barefoot near Oxford one winter, leaving bloodstains in the snow because their feet had been cut by the ice. But the more the Franciscans recruited from the universities, the more they risked forsaking apostolic simplicity for intellectual argument. What the Franciscans in fact were doing was usurping the very role intended by St Dominic for his own Order of friars.

Because the two mendicant Orders chose to base themselves in the towns rather that in the countryside, few of their buildings have survived the passage of time. So far as the Franciscans are concerned, the loveliest thing to see is the choir of their church at Chichester, now marooned in a public park. It is to excavations, such as those that have taken place at Oxford, that we must look for any additions to our knowledge of the surroundings in which the Franciscans lived. By all accounts it was during the years between 1270 and 1320 that they undertook their biggest building programme. They had decided by then to settle down, rather than wander from place to place, and they wanted houses in which to live and work. One or two of their churches were quite large – say, a couple of hundred feet in length – but even so were modest compared with the cathedrals, and hardly deserving of the strictures that came from the friars' opponents.

J. R. H. Moorman, *A History of the Franciscan Order*, Oxford, 1968.

FRIARS One of the most remarkable achievements of the medieval Church was its ability to create the kind of institutional framework that could harness the successive waves of religious revivalism that swept Europe between the tenth century and the fifteenth. In the twelfth century it was the monastic calling which summonded men to the service of God. In the thirteenth it was the ideals and teaching of St Francis of Assisi.

That St Francis was one of the greatest figures in the religious history of the middle ages we can accept without hesitation. But we should not allow the power of his name to blind us to the role of his contemporary, St Dominic, in founding the second new Order that took shape at that time. Dominic was a Spaniard by birth whose aim was to assemble a well-trained band of preachers capable by the force of their arguments of halting the spread of heresy in southern France. He had taken the Rule of St Augustine as his model, but after a meeting he is said to have had with Francis opted instead for the principal characteristics of the

Franciscan ideal. That was in 1220. In the following year Francis finally gave way to pressures to institutionalize his own fast-growing band of followers by submitting the so-called 'First Rule', which was abbreviated and formalized in 1223 in the 'Regula Bullata'.

Such in brief were the origins of the two main Orders of friars, the Franciscans (q.v.) and the Dominicans (q.v.), or the Minors and the Preachers as they were often called. What distinguished them from the Order of monks? First, they were an international brotherhood of individuals, not a community of houses. In other words, unlike the monastic Orders, in which each monk was a member of a house, the friars might go wherever they were needed. Secondly, St Francis, believing in the absolute poverty of Christ, forbade his followers to own any property; and his example was followed by St Dominic with respect to his own Order in 1220. The buildings that the friars needed for their headquarters were held to their use by the pope or some other patron. Thirdly, and following from this rejection of property, the friars fed themselves by manual labour or by begging. Hence they are often known as the 'mendicant' Orders (Latin, *mendicare*, to beg).

Favoured by rich and poor alike, the friars enjoyed a rapid success. The Dominicans were the first to arrive in England. They landed at Dover in 1221, and went via Canterbury and London to Oxford, where they were attracted by the University. The Franciscans, who followed three years later, preferred to disperse as widely as possible and within six years of arriving had founded communities in towns as far apart as Norwich and Hereford, Bristol and King's Lynn. By 1255 there were 49 Franciscan houses in England, and by about 1260 some three dozen Dominican houses. Why did the friars strike such a receptive chord in thirteenth-century society? Partly because they went out into the world instead of withdrawing from it. Partly too of course because their poverty contrasted with the growing wealth of the monks. And still more, perhaps, because they concentrated their pastoral work in the towns and cities, where large congregations of burgesses and artisans hungered after their preaching of the Word.

At first, the friars were welcomed by the monks and secular clergy, or at least they were shown no open hostility. But as the years went by, their popularity bred resentment and jealousy. The arguments crystallized over three main issues. First, the parish clergy were beginning to find themselves confronted with half-empty naves because their congregations preferred to go and hear the sermons (q.v.) of the mendicant preachers. Secondly, the friars showed themselves to be more competent than the parish clergy in hearing confessions. The Fourth Lateran Council of 1215 had enjoined all the faithful to confess to their parish priest at least once a year. If they were to confess their sins at all – and we can hardly suppose that everyone did – the faithful, it seems, preferred to confide in the friars rather than in the often ill-trained parochial clergy. Last but not least there were arguments over burial rights. As wills testify, people opted in increasing numbers for burial in the friars' churches, thus robbing the seculars' of the burial fees to which they had grown accustomed.

Unseemly disputes of this kind did nothing to lessen the growing criticism of the friars that we hear in the late middle ages. We are all familiar with Chaucer's Friar,

a very festive fellow.
In all Four Orders there was none so mellow,
So glib with gallant phrase and well-turned speech,*

but Langland (q.v.) too turned his pen to devastating effect against the mendicants. He complained that they used all sorts of dubious devices to extract money from patrons which they then lavished on building magnificent churches. In the universities Wycliffe (q.v.) was their foremost critic, accusing them of browbeating young people into joining their ranks.

No doubt a certain number of case-histories could be cited in support of these often vague assertions. But equally we cannot ignore the evidence which points in the other direction. Unpopular though they might have been with writers like Chaucer (q.v.) and Langland, the friars were still strongly favoured by fourteenth and fifteenth century testators. In 1459 John Langley of Siddington (Gloucs) left 2s 6d each to the Dominicans at Gloucester and Warwick, to the Franciscans at Coventry and Bristol and to the Carmelites at Gloucester. In 1490 his grandson Edmund left 6s 8d each to the Franciscans, Dominicans and Carmelites in Gloucester. In the decades leading up to the Reformation, therefore, we find little sign that the flow of benefactions was drying up. The zeal and freshness that had once commended the friars may have waned; but their admirers may still have outnumbered their critics.

D. Knowles, *The Religious Orders in England*, i, Cambridge, 1948.

---

* G. Chaucer, *The Canterbury Tales*, ed. N. Coghill, Penguin, 1951, p. 25.

G

GASCONY In 1152 Eleanor (q.v.), heiress of Aquitaine, married the future Henry II (q.v.) of England and Normandy. This eventful match created a union no less eventful, but a good deal more amicable, between their two countries that was to last for almost exactly three hundred years.

Eleanor was the ex-wife of Louis VII, king of France. Louis may have been content to let the duchy slip through his fingers, but his successors wanted to make up for what they saw as his neglect. They nibbled away at the frontiers of Gascony, and undermined the position of the king-duke by exploiting the rights of feudal overlordship. These rights were so ill-defined that they afforded ample opportunity for argument. But neither side wanted open war. So in 1259 in the Treaty of Paris they agreed on a compromise. Louis IX of France recognized Henry III (q.v.) as his vassal in Gascony on condition that the latter performed liege homage when requested. In other words, a straightforward feudal relationship was created. So far from easing matters, however, this agreement only made them worse. The French king's exercise of his sovereign rights, in particular his reception of appeals from the seneschal of Gascony's court at Bordeaux, exposed the duchy to the centralizing activities of the French royal officers. This caused more trouble than in the other great fiefs that lay on the borders of France because there were so few clear-cut boundaries. The potential for conflict was bigger, and the willingness to compromise was less. By the fourteenth century it had become apparent to the English that the only answer was to hold Gascony in full sovereignty, an idea that the French could never accept. It was this conflict over the status of Gascony that contributed more than anything else to the outbreak of the Hundred Years War (q.v.) in 1337. It was to be resolved only with the final expulsion of the English in 1453.

So long as it lasted, however, the link between England and Gascony profited both partners. Bordeaux, the capital, was a large town of some 30,000 people which flourished by exporting wine to London, and handling the cloth, leather, tin and fish which the ships brought back on the return journey. Bayonne, the next largest town, specialized in building and fitting out the ships that made the passage between Bordeaux and London (Fig. 8, P. 260). In a word, what the often turbulent Gascons valued most of all in the link with the English crown was the independence it gave them. Better a master 500 miles away in London than one half that distance away in Paris.

GAUNT, JOHN OF, Duke of Lancaster The third surviving son of Edward III (q.v.), John was born at Ghent in March 1340 while his father was based there in the early stages of the Hundred Years War (q.v.). A couple of centuries later, by the time that Shakespeare was writing, the city of his birth had become corrupted on the tongues of the English to 'Gaunt', and it is by that name that he is generally known today.

He acquired the title, duke of Lancaster, in 1362 by virtue of his marriage three years earlier to Blanche, daughter and eventual heiress of Henry of Grosmont, the first duke. The vast estates he inherited, spread across midland and northern England, brought him an annual income in the order of £12,000, considerably in excess of anything enjoyed by his peers in the nobility.

He rose to political prominence in the 1370s, when the king was in his dotage and his eldest son Edward, the Black Prince (q.v.) stricken with dysentery. It was a difficult time for the English, who were struggling against all odds to cling onto their conquests in France. In 1371 dissatisfaction with the handling of the war led to the replacement of Bishop Wykeham (q.v.), the Chancellor, and Bishop Brantingham, the Treasurer, by a government of secular ministers who looked to Gaunt for leadership. But the new men fared no better than their predecessors. Discontent boiled over in the 'Good Parliament' of 1376, and it fell to Gaunt to defend the court from the popular onslaught. Biding his time, he decided to make concessions while parliament was sitting and then to revoke them as soon as it had dispersed. That way he could cope with the M.P.s. But the man with whom he really wanted to settle scores was his old enemy, Bishop Wykeham, whom he suspected of being behind all the agitation. So he adopted an avowedly anti-clerical, anti-papal line, and to this end employed John Wycliffe (q.v.) to whip up public opinion. Wycliffe was a highly accomplished pamphleteer, but once the heretical nature of his ideas became clear, the embarrassment he caused to the duke outweighed his usefulness. He had to be dropped, but right to the end he was shielded by his former patron from prosecution by the Church.

On the death of Edward III in 1377 his ten year old grandson, Richard II (q.v.) became king. During the next ten years Gaunt's interests drifted abroad, towards Spain. After the death of his first wife Blanche in 1368, he had married Constance, daughter of Pedro the Cruel, king of Castile. When King Pedro was driven from the throne by his half-brother, Henry of Trastamara, Gaunt claimed to be the legitimate heir, and assumed the title and arms of king of Castile and Leon. In 1386, taking advantage of a Portuguese victory over the Castilians at Aljubarrota, he judged the time to be right to invade Spain in pursuit of his claim to the throne. Although his forces soon fell victim to disease, he remained sufficient of a nuisance to cause John I, Henry's successor, to pay him a substantial sum to depart.

In 1389 he headed back to an England which had been riven by civil war in his absence. Richard II's opponents had resorted to force to remove his unpopular favourites, Robert de Vere and Michael de la Pole. Gaunt's return, however, restored a moderating influence to English politics, and for the next eight years the tensions abated sufficiently to allow king and councillors to think of negotiating an accord with the French. The progress of these talks interested Gaunt deeply because in 1390 Richard had granted him the Duchy of Gascony (q.v.) *for life*. As a way of solving the long-standing Anglo-French dispute over the Duchy's status it was now proposed to settle it on Gaunt and his heirs *in perpetuity*. An ingenious suggestion certainly, but one that found little favour with the Gascons, who refused to accept any initiative tending to weaken the link with England and to draw them further into the orbit of France. The proposal was quietly dropped. Gaunt spent 15 months at Bordeaux pacifying the Duchy (1394–5), and on his return formalized his relationship with Katherine Swynford, his mistress of a quarter of a century's standing, whom he now took as his third wife. He died on 2 February 1399, a few months after his son and heir, Henry Bolingbroke, had been sent into exile. Richard decided to take the inheritance into his own hands, thus setting in motion the events that were to end in his own deposition before the year was out.

For all his fame and eminence Gaunt remains a rather enigmatic figure. We have no contemporary portrait, and the effigies of him and his first wife on their tomb in St Paul's Cathedral perished in the Great Fire. What emerges most strongly from the chronicle accounts is Gaunt's unpopularity. To some extent this was not his fault. He was the unlucky person who had to shoulder the blame for corruption at home and defeat abroad. On the other hand, it is hard to deny that he could sometimes be arrogant, overbearing and insensitive, as on the occasion in 1376 when he suggested replacing the Lord Mayor of London by a royal commissioner. The Londoners responded to this attack on their liberties by marching in such force to Gaunt's palace of the Savoy that he had to abandon his dinner and flee by the back door. He was no more popular with the peasants in 1381: they actually burned the Savoy to the ground. The most praiseworthy quality we may note in Gaunt, and in his brothers, is their consistent loyalty to the crown during the difficult years of Edward's decline and Richard's minority, when temptation might have led them to dissipate their energies in struggles of the kind that were to tear England apart 80 years later

in the reign of Henry VI (q.v.).

S. Armitage-Smith, *John of Gaunt*, London, 1904.

GEOFFREY OF MONMOUTH

Geoffrey of Monmouth's *History of the Kings of Britain*, completed in c. 1138, was a medieval best-seller; but it is not quite what we would expect a 'history' to be. It has little in common, for example, with the *Historia Novella* of Geoffrey's more sober-minded contemporary, William of Malmesbury. Geoffrey's book is more romance than fact, more literature than history. Indeed, as William of Newburgh, one of its few critics noted, it was a 'figment of the imagination'. In that case, why was it so popular? Because Geoffrey wrote a highly readable account of a period of British history so ill-documented that he was able to use his author's licence to elaborate it and embroider it as he saw fit. He begins by explaining that the name 'Britain' is derived from Brutus, a descendant of Aeneas who settled here after the fall of Troy. He moves on through the story of King Lear to the Roman settlement and then the Saxon invasions in the time of King Vortigern. At this point he introduces his hero, King Arthur, son of Uther Pendragon. Arthur halts the Saxon onslaught and carries the war into Gaul, but at the battle of Camblam he is mortally wounded, and is carried away under mysterious circumstances to the Isle of Avalon. Here, then, we find the Arthurian legend (q.v.) developed for the first time in full. Was it pure invention, or did Geoffrey have a source? He tells us in his preface that Walter, archdeacon of Oxford, had presented him with an ancient book written in the British language which set out the deeds of all the kings from Brutus to Cadwallader. Whether this book ever existed or not is hard to say. Knowing as we do that Geoffrey could hardly distinguish fact from fiction, there is reason to agree with those critics who denounce the preface as a tissue of lies. On the other hand, the fact that no such book has come to light is not in itself conclusive. We still have some early Welsh chronicles containing material that Geoffrey might have used. Who is to say that there was not another manuscript which has not survived the passage of time? Moreover, Walter the Archdeacon is known to have existed, and Geoffrey is unlikely to have invoked his name unless they were both conspirators in an elaborate literary hoax. Occasionally the two men appear as co-signatories to charters. Geoffrey evidently spent much of his life in Oxford, even if his name suggests Welsh extraction. Like most clerics of his day, he eagerly sought the favour of patrons who could bring him a benefice or two; doubtless that is why most surviving copies of his *History* open with a dedication to Robert, earl of Gloucester, the bastard son of Henry I (q.v.). Eventually he obtained the bishopric of St Asaph, but the wars then being fought on the Welsh border probably prevented him from even visiting the see, let alone collecting its revenues, before his death in 1155.

Geoffrey of Monmouth, *The History of the Kings of Britain*, ed. L. Thorpe, Harmondsworth, 1966.

GILBERTINES The one religious Order of English provenance, the Gilbertines took their name from St Gilbert of Sempringham (Lincs.), who in the 1130s founded some houses for the benefit of nuns and lay sisters. Gilbert wanted to create an opening for the many women for whom few opportunities existed in the male-dominated world of twelfth-century monasticism. The response was greater than he had expected, and before long he found himself at the head of a growing family of houses. Feeling himself ill-qualified to provide the leadership now expected of him, he asked the General Chapter of the Cistercians in 1147 if they would agree to take over his community. They declined on the grounds they could not admit women. It was almost by default, therefore, that Gilbert found that he would have to legislate for an Order of his own.

In so doing he faced certain problems. The women of course could neither celebrate Mass nor till the soil unaided. So he arranged for canons to minister to their liturgical needs, and followed the example of the Cistercians in introducing lay brothers to cultivate the land. In effect, he had revived the 'double' monastery, which had been a feature of seventh century monasticism. At the time of his death in 1189, according to the chronicler William of Newburgh, Gilbert had founded more than a dozen monasteries, of which ten were 'double'. It is said that they catered for as many as 1,500 sisters, but this figure, like most medieval statistics, may well be an exaggeration.

At the time of the Dissolution in the 1530s there were 26 Gilbertine houses in England. They were probably quite simple in construction and decoration, knowing as we do of Gilbert's respect for the Cistercian ideal of austerity. At Sempringham itself the church was 250ft long, and divided along its length by a solid wall broken only in the chancel by the saint's shrine. On the south side lay the nuns' church, and on the north that of the canons.

R. Graham, *St Gilbert of Sempringham and the Gilbertines*, London, 1901.

GLENDOWER, OWEN Among the writers of Tudor England Shakespeare was decidedly out of step in choosing to magnify the personality of Glendower. At that time he was normally regarded by polite writers in Wales, if not by the Welsh people themselves, as a failed rebel who had brought ruin and destruction on his native land. Only in the late eighteenth century did his posthumous reputation recover. Only then did he take his permanent place in the pantheon of Welsh heroes.

The date of Glendower's birth is not known for certain, but it is usually assigned to c. 1359. He inherited estates in North Wales worth £300 or more, making him a well-to-do landowner by the modest standards of the Principality. What led him to sacrifice the comfortable life of a country gentleman was a dispute with a neighbour of his, Reginald Grey, lord of Ruthin, whom he accused of seizing some of his lands. In 1400 Glendower and his men laid waste to Grey's estates, and Henry IV (q.v.), returning from Scotland, was obliged to go westwards to pacify the area. Little good did it do him, because the Welsh resorted to the time-honoured practice of retreating far into the mountains. Before long it was apparent that Wales was in the grips of a full national uprising, and it became a matter of urgency for the king to decide on a response. But his counsellors were divided. The Percys, notably Henry Percy (Hotspur), the Justice of N. Wales, seem to have had some sympathy for Glendower, particularly since their own support for Henry IV was beginning to wear thin. Reginald Grey himself, on the other hand, favoured a hard line. How poetic then that it should have been he who fell into the hands of the rebels in April 1402. Two months later he was joined by Sir Edmund Mortimer, Hotspur's brother-in-law. At this time Glendower was at the height of his power. Most of the Welsh castles had fallen to him, and although the defeat of his friends, the Percys, at the battle of Shrewsbury in 1403 weakened his control of South Wales, he was still powerful enough to establish in the Principality a shadow government of his own. By 1406, however, he was on the retreat. The king's son, Prince Henry, the future Henry V (q.v.), led a series of campaigns which in the next few years succeeded in re-imposing English rule. The fall of Aberystwyth in November 1407 and Harlech in the following year marked the final collapse of a rebellion that had dogged Henry IV for the best part of his ill-fated reign.

But Glendower himself, like the old soldier, didn't die; he only faded away. When Henry V came to the throne, he was still at large. The new king offered to receive him back into his favour before setting out for France in 1415, but he heard nothing. Rumour had it that he died at the home of one of his daughters, the wife of a Herefordshire squire, at Monnington in the Golden Valley. He is said to be buried in the churchyard there. The aura of mystery, so reminiscent of the conclusion of Arthur's reputed career, could hardly be more appropriate for one who was seen by his fellow countrymen as a national saviour in the tradition of the ancient British king.

J. E. Lloyd, *Owen Glendower*, Oxford, 1931.

GOVERNMENT In the middle ages the king was the source of all decision-making, and the branches of his household were the first government ministries. This was why medieval government acquired a domestic and informal quality which it retained right down to the sixteenth century. Ramshackle and ill-coordinated it may have been, but the dependence of all its parts on the king's will gave it some consistency of purpose and prevented it from sliding into chaos.

If we want to trace the origins of the medieval system of government, we must go back to the later Saxon period. By the tenth century the growing use of charters to guarantee title to land led to the organization of a royal writing office, and the levying of taxes to some sort of treasury. The early history of these two institutions is obscure to say the least. But that very obscurity suggests an important conclusion: bureaucratization could not have gone very far, otherwise more written evidence would have survived.

After the Norman Conquest the mists begin to clear. Let us begin by looking in a little detail at the writing office, or Chancery as it later came to be known. This was staffed by the clerks of the royal chapel, and headed by an official known as the Chancellor. Though an important man in the administration, the Chancellor was not yet the great officer of state he was to become later on. He was usually one of the king's chaplains, and would be rewarded in due course with elevation to a bishopric. Herfast, for example, the first Chancellor known to us by name, was appointed to the East Anglian diocese of North Elmham in 1070. The writing office which William the Conqueror took over in 1066 was the most advanced of its day in northern Europe because it had solved the problem of how to communicate the king's wishes to his people. This it did by means of the writ – a formalized written notification usually addressed to the officers and suitors of the county court. It then went on to solve the problem of authentication by attaching a splendid two-faced pendant seal to the bottom of every writ that issued forth in the king's name. Custody of this seal was the most important of the Chancellor's duties.

As the scope and activity of royal government increased under the Norman and Angevin kings, so too did the number of writs produced every day by the clerks in Chancery. If government were not to sink into chaos, it would be necessary to keep copies of letters and to file them according to their subject-matter. So in 1199, the year of John's (q.v.) accession, the Charter Roll was started for copies of charters, in 1201 the Patent Roll for copies of letters issued 'patent', i.e. open, and finally in 1204 the Close Rolls for letters issued 'close', i.e. sealed. Curious though it may seem, these copies were not kept in registers, but were transcribed onto long parchment membranes which were then stitched head-to-tail to form continuous rolls, one for each year.

For the first two centuries or so of its existence the Chancery itinerated with the rest of the king's household, but as its records grew ever more bulky, so it became necessary for it to have a permanent home. By the fourteenth century we know that the Chancellor himself did business in Westminster Hall, and it was there that some at least of the documents would have been sealed. As for the enrolments, they found a resting place in the 1370s in the House of the Jewish Converts in what is now Chancery Lane. This is the building better known today as the Public Record Office.

The secretariat of the late-Saxon monarchy seems to have been much more sophisticated than the parallel financial organization. We know that Ethelred II and his successors levied a complex land tax known as the geld (q.v., TAXATION). We know also that they kept their money in a treasury at Winchester. This was no more than a storehouse kept under lock and key by some local worthy dignified by the title of 'treasurer'. What measure of control was exercised over income and expenditure by the Norman kings we cannot be sure, but evidently very little, otherwise in the early twelfth century King Henry I (q.v.) and his minister Bishop Roger would not have needed to introduce regular audits at a new office called the 'Exchequer'. The name first appears in about 1110, and it is a milestone in English administrative history. It gave the king what he had hitherto lacked – a means of preventing corruption on the part of his local officials and of ensuring that they paid over every penny that they owed him. By the time that the Exchequer machinery had been perfected, it was cumbersome, but it was also thorough. How did it work?

Sessions of the Exchequer were held twice yearly. At the Easter session, known as the 'view of account', the sheriff paid in the first instalment of his 'farm' or income due from his shire. When he returned in Michaelmas, he paid over the final instalment, at the Lower Exchequer, where the sums were notched up on wooden tallies. He then went to the Upper Exchequer for his accounts to be audited. This was an occasion he dreaded. He sat before a table covered by a chequered cloth (hence 'Exchequer'), the vertical columns of which stood for units, tens, hundreds and so on. Since it was impossible to do complicated sums in Roman numerals, adding up and subtraction were done by placing or taking away as many counters in each column as were required. On one side of the table sat the sheriff. On the other sat the Treasurer and Barons of the Exchequer, that is, the lawyers who dealt with any litigation that arose. When the accounts had been audited to the Treasurer's satisfaction, they were transcribed onto long membranes of parchment secured at their heads with cords, and known from their appearance when rolled up as 'pipe rolls'.

The strength of the Exchequer was its ability to maximize the yield from existing sources of revenue. Its weakness was the time it took to collect it. Like the Chancery it had 'gone out of court', and settled down at Westminster. Again like the Chancery, its machinery had become cumbersome and inflexible – much too inflexible. A smaller and less rigid financial office was needed for providing the king and his household with money as they travelled around the country. At the beginning of the thirteenth century King John made use of the Chamber. However, under his successor, Henry III (q.v.) the Chamber was pushed into the background by the Wardrobe – for reasons that are not entirely clear. Perhaps it was because the Wardrobe enjoyed a closer relationship with the Exchequer: it was after all from the Exchequer that it received most of its money. Important as the Wardrobe had become under Henry III, it rose to still greater heights under Edward I (q.v.). During the 35 years of his reign bigger burdens were imposed on English government than ever before by the demands of war finance. Edward realized that the Exchequer could no longer cope, and therefore expanded the Wardrobe into a War Treasury in all but name. Theoretically subordinate though they were to the Exchequer, the Keeper of the Wardrobe and his staff acted in practice as free agents, organizing the collection of taxes and customs revenues and paying the wages of Edward's troops. This was all very well so long as income was sufficient to meet expenditure. But by the last years of Edward I's reign it was not, and the Wardrobe had to borrow heavily. For that reason, under Edward II (q.v.) there was a reaction in favour of Exchequer supremacy, and the Wardrobe's brief heyday as a War Ministry was over.

If a king like John or Edward I were to make use of a more informal office than the Exchequer for disbursing sums of money, he would also need some way of passing on his instructions more quickly. He could no longer turn directly to the Chancery: that, as we have seen, 'had gone out of court'. So he introduced a new seal, the 'privy seal', to authenticate letters he dictated personally. John is the first king we know for certain to have had a privy seal, because he used it to give warrants for the issue of letters under the Great Seal of Chancery. For the best part of the thirteenth century the privy seal was kept wherever the king happened to be, at first in the Chamber (see below) and later in the Wardrobe. But by the reign of Edward II the baronial Ordainers (q.v., ORDINANCES) decided to transfer its custody to a specially appointed official called the Keeper of the Privy Seal. The privy seal, like the great seal, had become institutionalized. It had 'gone out of court'.

What happened next was that the familiar process of evolution began all over again. Deprived of the privy seal as an instrument for his personal use, the king had a new seal made, known as the 'secret seal'. The first signs of its use

appear in 1313, two years after the Ordinances. It was kept in the most private place the king could think of – the Chamber, hitherto a private treasury from which he met such expenses as presents for his wife and children. Edward III (q.v.), however, had grander plans for an expansion in its activity, and the secret seal was associated with them. He wanted to make the Chamber the lynchpin of his system for mobilizing England's resources for the Hundred Years War (q.v.). He assigned lands for the support of the Chamber, and told the Chancery and Exchequer to recognize the secret seal, or 'griffin' as it was now called, as the official warrant for its business. The Exchequer put up with this for as long as it had to, but finally in 1356 reasserted its supremacy. The Chamber's existence as an estate office came to an end, and with it the use of the griffin seal.

When the secret seal reappeared in the 1380s, it was under a different name and in a new guise. Richard II (q.v.) called it the signet, and entrusted it to the custody of an official known as the 'secretary'. The use to which the young king put this seal was not to everyone's liking, because he made it the instrument of his own autocratic will both to give direct orders to local officials and to 'move' the great and privy seals. So when his opponents came to power in 1386, Archbishop Arundel, their nominee as Chancellor, refused to accept the signet as a warrant for the issue of letters under the great seal. After this setback both signet and secretary receded into the background, and it was not until the reign of Henry VI (q.v.) that they experienced a revival. Thomas Beckington, who was appointed secretary in 1437, made himself a great man of affairs. But his successors were figures of less importance, and it was not yet clear whether the man made the office, or the office the man. Certainly, the successive bouts of insanity which afflicted Henry VI in the 1450s diminished the standing of the secretary as the official closest to the king.

Wielded by an able and vigorous king, however, the signet could be made to get the administrative machine moving again. And when Edward IV (q.v.) recovered his throne in 1471 he used this seal to initiate more and more business. If anything, it came to overshadow the privy seal. Certainly its keeper, the secretary, was set on the way to becoming a great officer of state, and in the holders of the office at the end of the fifteenth century we can see the forebears of Thomas Cromwell and William Cecil in the sixteenth. Important as it was, however, the signet was only an instrument, a means to an end. It was the policies it initiated that mattered. And here we must point to the importance of the Chamber in boosting the landed revenues of the Yorkist and early Tudor kings. Realizing as some of their predecessors had that the Exchequer was utterly inadequate to the task of increasing the income of the crown, Edward IV and Henry VII turned once again to the household agencies to bring about a recovery. Lands were transferred from the control of the Exchequer and entrusted to the management of specially appointed keepers who were accountable to the Chamber for the rents they collected. This very personalized approach to government reached its culmination in the age of Thomas Cromwell. The final reassertion of Exchequer control that occurred in 1554 in the reign of Mary takes us out of the middle ages and into a period which had distinctive problems of its own to cope with.

S. B. Chrimes, *An Introduction to the Administrative History of Medieval England*, Blackwell, 1952.

GRANGE The economic organization of the estates of the Cistercian (q.v.) monasteries centred on the unit known as the grange. What distinguished the Cistercians from the Benedictines (q.v.) was the fact that they chose to establish their houses outside the reach of feudal society, in an uncultivated district which could then be organized as a single estate. Dependent though such an estate would be directly on the monastery, if it was of some size its more distant parts would need to be administered from a farm – in other words, a grange. Its buildings would have comprised store-rooms, an oratory and sleeping accommodation for the lay-brothers on whom the Cistercians relied for the manual labour involved in clearing and cultivating the land. So well suited was the grange to the administration of a large estate that it was soon adopted on the estates of other Orders, and one of the best examples to survive to this day is the grange of the Benedictine nuns of Shaftsbury at Tisbury (Wilts).

GROSSETESTE, ROBERT Contrary to the impression given by his unfortunate name (literally 'Fathead'), Robert Grosseteste was without doubt the most distinguished intellectual to grace the bench of bishops in thirteenth century England.

He was born at Stradbrook (Suffolk) in *c.* 1168 of humble parentage. Of his earlier years we have but the barest outline and hardly that. In 1193 he was a clerk in the household of the bishop of Hereford. During the years of the Great

Interdict, provoked by Innocent III's quarrel with King John (q.v.), he probably studied in Paris, acquiring experience he was to put to good use when he returned to Oxford, in about 1214. It is an indication of his renown as a scholar that in 1221 he became Chancellor of the University, and is reckoned the first of the long line of holders of that office. Early in the 1230s he held a lectureship with the Oxford Franciscans (q.v.), encouraging and assisting them in their studies. By this time he had begun what was to be a lifetime's work bringing hitherto unfamiliar Greek and Hebrew texts to the attention of a Latin audience. It was Grosseteste, for example, who gave Europe its first complete translation of Aristotle's *Ethics*.

He continued these studies even after his elevation to the see of Lincoln in 1235, when he was well past the age of 60. As Sir Maurice Powicke has observed, it is hard to believe that the busiest and most active bishop of his time did his hardest work when he was between 65 and 83 years of age. That he was a conscientious diocesan we know only too well from his enthusiasm for reforming the morals of both clergy and laity and from his inflexible insistence in 1239 on making a visitation not just of the diocese but also of the cathedral of Lincoln in the teeth of fierce opposition from the dean and chapter. The principle which constantly guided him in the exercise of his pastoral duties was 'the supreme importance of the cure of souls'. It was this belief which enabled him to combine devotion to the idea of papal supremacy with ringing denunciation of the pope when the latter's 'provision' (q.v.), or appointment, of an unworthy candidate to a benefice placed the cure of souls in danger. As the sun gives light to the moon and stars, he once wrote, so the pope imparts power to his bishops, and they to their subordinates. Grosseteste was no constitutionalist. It is doubtful, for example, if he would have spared much time for those in the next century who argued that the Church was a corporation in which 'head and members' jointly exercised the plenitude of power. As a papalist of unflinching conviction, Grosseteste's solution to these problems was a personal one. He would appeal to the pope directly, as he did in 1250 against the visitation procedures of the archbishop of Canterbury. More dramatic still was his refusal in 1253 to accept the provision to a prebend at Lincoln of the pope's nephew. 'I do not obey, I reject, I rebel against the contents of this letter', he wrote to the papal notary. Later that same year, on 9 October, he died, and was buried at Lincoln Cathedral. Grosseteste was a man who set the highest standards of personal rectitude; to those who fell short of them we may suspect that he would have extended little sympathy.

Robert Grosseteste: Scholar and Bishop, ed. D. A. Callus, Oxford, 1955.

GUILDS Of all the institutions of medieval society the guilds are surely the best known and at the same time the least understood. Quite simply the word describes a form of association or friendly society found in the towns (q.v.). But familiar as we are with the protean nature of so many medieval institutions, it comes as no surprise to learn either that the guilds changed greatly in nature and purpose during the middle ages or, to confuse matters further, that they could pass under a number of other names, such as 'misteries' or 'crafts'. It is important to bear these points in mind before we go any further.

The guilds made their first appearance in Anglo-Saxon England as societies of a social or religious nature whose activities sometimes stretched to the defence of their members' trading interests. To that extent they anticipated the 'guilds merchant' which emerged in most large towns after the Conquest. Composed of most if not all of the burgesses of the town, the 'guild merchant' was often concerned not only to defend the trading privileges of its members but also to become the spokesman for the town as a community. Consequently, it was sometimes through the guild merchant that a town obtained its charter of incorporation. In which case it was more than likely that the same men would hold office in both the guild merchant and the borough.

If this dominance of both the guild merchant and the borough council by the same group of men was a source of strength, it could also be a source of weakness. These men were usually rich merchants. So it is hardly surprising that some of the lesser crafts felt themselves left out, and took steps to improve their position. For example, in the great cloth towns, which were dominated by the merchants who made their money in the finishing trades, the weavers and fullers retaliated by forming guilds of their own (q.v., INDUSTRY). These were what we know as 'craft guilds'. They sought to secure for their members the monopoly of engaging in that particular trade within the town.

Not all of these early guilds lasted for very long, and even the guild merchant itself faded into the background once the boroughs had won the right to run their own affairs and to elect their own rulers. But in the late middle ages new life was breathed into the old idea of craft associations. As peoples' devotional habits came increasingly to be focussed on the parish churches, so fraternities and brotherhoods were formed for the simple purpose of maintaining a chaplain or paying for a candle to burn on a side-altar in the local church. Such fraternities need not necessarily have been craft-organized, but many of them were. For that reason they recommended themselves to the hard-pressed urban authorities when they were seeking agencies onto whom to devolve the ever-increasing burden of control and regulation. The guilds, in other words, fitted conveniently into a pattern of urban life akin to what we would now call a corporate society. The main object of economic policy in the towns was to concentrate local trade in the hands of the burgesses, ensuring at the same time by means of an elaborate code of regulations that the consumer did not suffer as a result.

What better way of achieving this than through the guilds? They laid down rules of admission to the craft, imposed a long period of apprenticeship, normally seven years, and ensured that products were up to standard. The sheer extent to which the economic life of the towns was regulated from above through such agencies as the guilds may be somewhat uncongenial to a society like ours disillusioned with the fruits of economic planning, but it fully accorded with the precepts of a mercantilist age.

Aside from their economic functions, the guilds also provided social and charitable services for their members. For such purposes they built halls and chambers, where feasts could be celebrated, for example on the anniversary of the patron saint of the fraternity. The guildhalls at York and Leicester are good examples (plate 8b). Once they became property owners, of course, the guilds needed protection at law. Like the borough communities of which they were part, they achieved this by seeking incorporation by royal licence. In 1453, for instance, the king granted permission to 15 tailors of York to found a guild of a master and four wardens 'of the said Mistery and other persons, brethren and sisters, in honour of St John the Baptist in York'. Of the social activities of the guilds the most well-known are the drama productions known as the 'mistery plays' (q.v.). The religious side of their work was curtailed at the Reformation when the chantries (q.v.) were dissolved and all property held by the guilds for devotional purposes confiscated. In London and other cities, however, they have survived to the present day in the respectable guise of the livery companies.

HASTINGS The engagement fought on 14 October 1066, though known by the name of Hastings, took place about six miles to the north where the town of Battle now stands. On Edward the Confessor's death on 5 January 1066 Harold, earl of Wessex, had become king, but before long his title was challenged by two claimants, Harold Hardrada, king of Norway, and William, duke of Normandy (q.v.). The Norwegian invasion came to a bloody end at the battle of Stamford Bridge near York on 25 September, when Hardrada himself was killed and his army shattered. No sooner had Harold recovered from this challenge, however, than news reached him of William's landing on the Sussex coast at Pevensey on 28 September. Immediately he began the long march southwards, reaching London on or about 6 October, and setting out for the Sussex Weald a day or two later, no doubt with a view to taking his enemy by surprise. In the event the tables were turned. It was the English who were caught unawares. They awoke on the morning of 14 October to find the Normans facing them across the valley: alerted in the night to Harold's approach, William had led his men some six miles out of Hastings to a position at the foot of a low Wealden ridge. At daybreak the English formed their ranks along the top of this ridge, to the distance of about 300–400 yards on each side of Harold's standard. It was a solid defensive position for an army composed entirely of foot soldiers. Duke William's one advantage was that against them he could deploy cavalry as well as infantry.

When hostilities began, at 9 a.m. we are told, Duke William launched first his infantry and then his knights against the English, but to little avail. At one point in fact, the Norman left flank actually began to give way, and some of Harold's men came pouring down the hill-side in hot pursuit. It is said to have been this episode which gave William the idea, once order had been restored, of luring his enemy from the ridge by the ruse of a feigned retreat. Though some of Harold's men were rash enough to abandon their hill-top security only to be cut down by the Normans, the majority stood firm. William therefore rallied his cavalry, and sent them once more against the English. At the same time he ordered his archers to fire their arrows high into the air so that they rained down on Harold and his men. It was presumably at this stage that Harold himself was killed. The English position finally broke, and by nightfall William was in command of the field.

Estimating the size of medieval armies is always hazardous, but according to the most reliable guesses Harold may have marshalled about 7,000 men, William rather fewer. The Conqueror commemorated his victory by founding the monastery known as Battle Abbey, the high altar of which was reputedly reared on the place where Harold met his death.

See also, BAYEUX TAPESTRY.

R. A. Brown, *The Normans and the Norman Conquest*, Constable, 1969.

HENRY I Few English monarchs of comparable importance have left so faint an impression on the pages of history, we are told, as Henry I.* He is a king who leaves nagging doubts in our minds. Was his rule perhaps viewed less sympathetically by those who lived under it than by those writing later, in the civil war of Stephen's (q.v.) reign, who looked back nostalgically on what they saw as a lost golden age?

Henry was the youngest of the three sons of William the Conqueror (q.v.), and if the tradition is true that he was

* R. W. Southern, in *Medieval Humanism*, Blackwell, 1970, p. 206.

born at Selby in 1068, the only one of the Norman kings to have been born in England. He was therefore probably bilingual, though the later legend that he was a considerable scholar, which by the fourteenth century had earned him the surname 'Beauclerk', rests on no firmer foundation than that he could read Latin.

When the Conqueror died in 1087, his dominions were divided between the two elder sons. Henry got nothing but a legacy of £5,000 in silver. However, he invested it wisely, and by 1088 had set himself up in the Cotentin peninsula in Normandy, which he had purchased from Duke Robert. He happened to be with the hunting party in the New Forest when Rufus was killed there on 2 August 1100, and whether or not he was an accomplice to any assassination plot, the speed with which he slipped off to secure the crown certainly shows how determined he was to be the next king. He needed to act quickly because his elder brother Robert had just returned from the East, and his friends in the nobility were urging him to make a bid for the English throne. Henry therefore decided to win allies by offering a number of political concessions. He published a coronation charter. He welcomed back Archbishop Anselm (q.v.), who had gone into exile rather than endure any longer William Rufus's attacks on the Church. And he imprisoned Ranulph Flambard, Rufus's unpopular minister. When Robert did finally mount an invasion of England in 1101, he could still count on a few fifth columnists to support him, notably the powerful Robert, earl of Shrewsbury, but rather than risk a pitched battle, he decided to compromise. He signed away his claim to the crown in return for an annuity of 3,000 marks. So the final resolution of the contest for power between the two brothers was post-poned until 1106, when Henry invaded Normandy, and defeated Robert at Ticherbrai. The duke was captured and imprisoned in Cardiff Castle, where he languished till his death at the age of 80 in 1134.

Now that England and Normandy were again under a single ruler – and were to remain so for the next 30 years – methods of government had to be adjusted accordingly. How, for example, was England to be run while the king was in Normandy? To supervise the government of England while he was himself abroad, Henry turned to Roger, bishop of Salisbury, a remarkable administrator who is considered to be the first of our Justiciars (q.v.). He was the man on whom Henry relied not only to run the judicial machine but also to raise money: for he may have disposed of his brother, but his problems had not disappeared. He still had to defend his territories against a formidable coalition of enemies led by Louis VI, king of France. He therefore needed money, and lots of it. It was these financial demands that led to an increasing formalization of financial procedures in England in this period. Onto the Treasury at Winchester, which received the king's revenues, was grafted the Exchequer, where the accounting was done (q.v., GOVERNMENT). Henry wanted to make sure that no money slipped through his fingers. However, he needed not only institutions but men – reliable men, like Bishop Roger. Here the rebellions at the start of his reign provided him with the chance he needed. He took the lands of those who had been disloyal, and regranted them to supporters of his, 'men raised up from the dust' in the words of one chronicler, **who owed everything** they had to Henry I. Thus he never again had to face a rebellion in England.

Successful though Henry I might be in his conduct of government, the permanence of his achievement was called into question by one of those accidents which sometimes change the course of history. On 25 November 1120 the White Ship ran aground off the Norman coast with the loss of almost everyone on board. Among the many distinguished casualties was the king's only legitimate son, William. In the following year Henry remarried, but there were no more children. He therefore brought back from Germany his daughter Matilda, widow of the Emperor, and made the barons swear that they would uphold her succession to the throne. To neutralize the threat from Anjou, Normandy's traditional enemy on the southern frontier, he married her to Geoffrey, the son of the count of Anjou. So far as the barons were concerned, the arrangements that Henry had made were not only offensive, but positively dangerous, carrying as they did the prospect of an Angevin succession. Small wonder, then, that after Henry died on 1 December 1135, they forgot their oaths to Matilda and welcomed Stephen as king instead.

For Henry the tragedy was that, though he had fathered more bastards than any other English king – 19 in all – he had only two legitimate children, William, drowned in 1120, and Matilda. Both were by his first wife Edith, a descendant of the Saxon royal house, who assumed the name Matilda on her marriage. His second wife was Adeliza, daughter of Godfrey, duke of Louvain. With Henry the Norman house came to an end in the male line. He was the most competent of the Conqueror's sons, an able ruler, yet in the end unsuccessful – and not simply because of the absence of a male heir. His administration was too harsh, and his financial demands too burdensome, to ensure the peaceful obedience of the baronage after his death. They wanted to recover the power and privileges they had lost to Henry's 'new men'; so there would very likely have been a reaction even if a disputed succession had not followed Henry's death in 1135.

R. W. Southern, 'The Place of Henry I in English History', reprinted in his *Medieval Humanism and Other Studies*, Blackwell, 1970.

HENRY II One of the most able and energetic men ever to govern England, Henry II was a monarch whose rule extended over so many territories and whose career embraced so many fields of activity that it is hardly possible to form an overall view of his reign. The quarrel with Becket (q.v.) is therefore best dealt with separately.

Henry was born on 4 March 1133 at Le Mans, the eldest son of Geoffrey of Anjou and his wife Matilda, Henry I's daughter and designated successor. His earliest involvement in English politics came during the civil war occasioned by his mother's bid to wrest the crown from the usurper Stephen (q.v.). In 1147, shortly before Matilda abandoned the struggle, he crossed to England with a small force, but in view of his weakness thought it wise to accept Stephen's offer of a sum of money to go home. He made another visit in 1149, and again in force in 1152. By then it was Henry, not his mother, who led the opposition, and even those barons who had been prepared to accept Stephen as king for his own lifetime were coming round to the view that Henry of Anjou should succeed him. In July 1153 Henry's army came face to face with Stephen's across

the Thames at Wallingford, and the reluctance of either army to fight to the finish enabled negotiations to begin. As it was finalized at Westminster, the treaty that ended the long civil war provided for Stephen to remain king for his lifetime, and then to be succeeded by Henry.

Stephen died less than a year later, on 25 October 1154, and Henry found himself the ruler of dominions stretching from the Cheviots to the Pyrenees. From his father he had inherited Anjou and Maine, from his mother England and Normandy, and from his wife Eleanor (q.v.), whom he had married in 1152, the vast duchy of Aquitaine down in the south-west.

So far as England was concerned, Henry's first task was to restore order after the preceding 15 years of civil war. He needed to tread carefully because when they had accepted him as their next king, the English barons were bargaining from a position of strength not weakness. In making his first appointments, therefore, Henry made sure that each of the main interest groups was represented – the baronage by Robert, earl of Leicester, the knights by Richard de Luci, co-justiciar with Leicester, and the Church by Thomas Becket, his Chancellor. Although the new king drew his advisers from all ranks, and from those who had fought against as well as for him, he soon showed that he intended to be master in his own house. In 1155 he expelled the Flemish mercenaries whom Stephen had employed, and set a time limit for the demolition of all unlicensed castles that had been erected during the Anarchy.

Still more important was the need to sort out the conflicting claims to land that had contributed so much to the feuding in Stephen's reign. Disputes over the descent of land were heard in the court of the feudal superior from whom the fief was held, whether the king's court in the case of tenants-in-chief or the honorial court in the case of sub-tenants (q.v., FEUDALISM). But what recourse was open to a plaintiff who was dissatisfied with the verdict that had been given in a feudal court? The very fact that there was none led Henry II to introduce the writ 'of right' which ordered the lord to do right to a plaintiff, if the sheriff were not to take up the case himself. Though intended only to remedy defects of justice, the writ of right eventually undermined the feudal courts by destroying their finality: it was now open to any aggrieved plaintiff to transfer an action to the royal courts.

In the 1160s Henry II succeeded in making royal justice more attractive still by offering a quick remedy to those who had been ejected from (or 'disseised of') their lands. The Assize of Novel Disseisin instructed a jury to enquire before the king's justices if the plaintiff had been unjustly disseised. Other 'assizes', as they were known, followed in the 1170s, the most important being Mort d'Ancestor, which enabled a deprived heir to recover his inheritance. These actions all involved the use of a jury, empanelled by the sheriff, to decide a simple question of fact. If, however, a more complex case made its way into the courts, the old practice would have been for it to be decided by ordeal or by battle. With judicial procedures becoming as sophisticated as they were, this method was soon condemned as obsolete, and in 1179 Henry II offered trial by jury as an alternative. This was known as the 'grand assize'.

Henry II's reforms laid the foundations of the English common law. The assorted body of Old English, Danish and Norman customs gave way to a unified code of law regulated by the writs that activated the king's new assizes. The king's courts, however, were only open to those of free birth. So the legal reforms also had the effect of emphasizing the difference between the freeborn and the villeins. The increasing popularity of royal justice was not without its implications for the barons either, for in the long run it was to spell the demise of their own feudal courts. And as the royal courts became busier, so the king became more powerful. The lives of more and more people were affected by the judgements he made (q.v., JUSTICE).

The developments did not pass unnoticed. The steady drift of power from the barons to the king, which took place in the first 20 years of the reign, helps to explain why so many lords were prepared to support the rebellion, or 'great war' as it was known, against the king in 1173–4. Although it was in origin only a family quarrel, it developed into a major rebellion which convulsed all the Angevin lands, and exposed them to attack from the king of France. Once Henry had overcome the rebels, he made sure that they would never again be able to mount such a powerful campaign against royal authority. He received former opponents with favour, but he disarmed them by taking and demolishing the castles which had made their resistance possible.

The last years of the reign were marred by bitter family quarrels between husband and wife, father and sons. After he had married Eleanor of Aquitaine (q.v.), Henry must have come to realize why her former husband, Louis VII of France, had decided to divorce her. By the early 1170s the two were living apart, Henry with his mistress, Rosamund Clifford, Eleanor in confinement in Winchester to prevent her from inciting her sons to rebellion against their father. In fact, they needed little inciting, because in their eyes the old man was too keen to cling onto the reins of power. After the death of Henry, the young king, in 1183, Richard (q.v.), the second-born, became heir to the Angevin lands. But by 1189 he had gone over to Philip Augustus, king of France, and the two were marching into Anjou when Henry died on 6 July 1189.

Henry II, Eleanor and Richard are all buried at Fontevrault Abbey in France. Henry was a mighty king, yet curiously unkingly in manner. He was unkempt in appearance and indifferent to what people thought about him. Pomp and display were qualities that in the 1150s he had left to his Chancellor, Becket.

W. L. Warren, *Henry II*, Eyre Methuen, 1973.

HENRY III The thirteenth and fourteenth centuries are each dominated by a single long reign. In the fourteenth century it is Edward III's (q.v.); in the thirteenth, Henry III's.

Henry was born at Winchester on 1 October 1207, the son of King John (q.v.) and his second wife, Isabella of Angouleme. His accession to the throne in 1216 on the death of his father inaugurated the first royal minority in English history since the Conquest. For its duration the country was governed by a regency council under William Marshal, earl of Pembroke (d. 1219), whose task it was to negotiate a settlement of the civil war that had broken out between King John and the barons. The council brought the minority to an end in two stages, the first in 1223, the second in 1227 when the king declared himself of full age.

The years of his personal rule from then until 1258 were marked by periodic clashes with the baronage into which the king was drawn by a child-like innocence in matters political and from the consequences of which he had often to be rescued by the better judgement of his brother Richard, earl of Cornwall. After the death of William Marshal, Henry relied heavily for advice on Hubert de Burgh, until a coalition of his enemies brought about his replacement in 1232 by two Poitevins, Peter des Roches, bishop of Winchester, and Peter des Rivaux. A rebellion led by Richard Marshal resulted in their downfall as well two years later in 1234. The reason was quite simply that they were foreigners. Anti-alien sentiment forms a powerful undercurrent in Henry III's reign, and being something new in the thirteenth century merits a few words of explanation. The loss of Normandy in 1204 had left England an island state once again, free to develop its own national identity. The identity found expression in the concept of the 'community of the realm', which we hear so much about in this period; and the stronger this sense of community became, the less popular foreigners were going to be in England, particularly at court or in the Church. We might also mention that as the nobility became more detached from events on the continent, so they became less and less interested in supporting the attempts Henry made to recover the lost Angevin possessions in France.

Unsuccessful though these attempts turned out to be, they were hardly as misguided as the king's decision to accept the Sicilian crown on behalf of his second son, Edmund. Till Henry said yes, Pope Alexander must have been losing hope that anyone would take up this dubious offer. The catch was that

Sicily, though in the pope's gift, was not in his possession. It was occupied by his enemies, the Hohenstaufens, and whoever accepted the crown would have to conquer the country, and moreover pay for the privilege of so doing himself.

By 1258, even before he had set out, Henry had accumulated debts of 135,000 marks. He could only hope to escape from his commitments by turning to the barons for assistance, and their condition was that he should accept the constitution known as the Provisions of Oxford (q.v.). The revolutionary nature of this document can hardly be exaggerated. It took the government of the country out of the king's hands and vested it in a council of 15, so that, in the words of one historian, 'the king reigned, but the council ruled'. Henry endured this thraldom for a couple of years, but in 1261 the pope released him from his oath and he resumed power. Deadlock was reached, and in 1263 both sides, king and barons, agreed to submit their differences to St Louis, the French king. His arbitration, given in January the following year, gave Henry everything he asked for, and the barons, led by Simon de Montfort (q.v.) realized that they had no alternative but to fight. At Lewes (14 May 1264) the baronial army gained a decisive victory over the royalists, and both the king and his son Edward (q.v.) were taken prisoner. After his escape, however, Edward rallied the royalists, and led them to victory at Evesham on 4 August 1265. During the closing years of his father's reign, which ended in 1272, it was Edward who exercised the decisive influence over policy.

Henry III derived his political ideas both from home and abroad. His devotion to the cult of the Saxon king, Edward the Confessor, suggests a desire to identify with English traditions which found expression in the choice of name for his eldest son and in the rebuilding of Westminster Abbey, where the Confessor was buried. But at the same time he sought inspiration in the court of Louis IX of France, St Louis. This explains why he and his masons chose a French model – Rheims Cathedral – for the abbey which was the coronation church of the English kings. Henry, incidentally, was the first of our post-Conquest kings to be buried in the abbey. His widow, Eleanor of Provence, died some years later in 1291, and was buried at the nunnery of Amesbury, in which she had spent her retirement.

F. M. Powicke, *King Henry III & the Lord Edward*, Oxford 1947.

HENRY IV The coup that gave Henry of Bolingbroke the throne in 1399 was not the first successful deposition of an English monarch – Edward II (q.v.) had been removed in favour of his son in 1327 – but it did establish an unfortunate precedent in setting aside the normal rules of descent to allow the succession of a challenger whose strongest claim was force.

Born in about 1366, Henry was the only legitimate son of John of Gaunt, duke of Lancaster (q.v.). His relations with his cousin, Richard II (q.v.), do not always seem to have been easy, and in the crisis of 1387–88 he ranged himself alongside the king's opponents. Twelve months later Richard recovered the initiative, and with political harmony apparently restored, Henry was able to think of going on crusade to Prussia. He led two expeditions, the second of which, in 1392, developed into an extended pilgrimage to the Holy Land taking in a fair number of

Europe's courts on the way. By 1397, however, life in England was becoming more dangerous for those who had rebelled against the king ten years before. In July three of them were arrested. Bolingbroke and Mowbray remained free, though both had reason to feel they could no longer trust the king. Very likely moved by such fears, Mowbray is said to have warned Bolingbroke that Richard might still punish them for their rebellion a decade before. Reports of this conversation reached the king, who cut through the problem of choosing between Bolingbroke's word and Mowbray's denial by ordering the two men to fight a tournament. At the last moment, as we know from Shakespeare's play, Richard cancelled the duel, and both men were sent into exile.

To Richard's misfortune, the question of Bolingbroke's future was reopened a few months later when John of Gaunt died (3 February 1399). Was Henry to be allowed to return to inherit his father's lands? Richard decided not, and thus sealed his own fate. By confiscating the family patrimony he offended against the deepest susceptibilities of the age and aroused the distrust of the propertied classes. When the king sailed for Ireland on 29 May, Henry seized the chance to return to England to regain his birthright. He obtained crucial support from the Percy family, and confronted Richard at Conway. For some inexplicable reason the latter surrendered himself to Henry, who packed him off to the Tower. If he had ever seriously considered limiting his ambitions to the recovery of the inheritance, he soon stepped up his demands when he observed the swift collapse of Richard's government. He claimed the throne, partly by birth, partly by conquest; and once Richard's

abdication had been procured, he was crowned King Henry IV.

It turned out to be a troubled reign. High expectations had been placed on this popular and chivalrous aristocrat, and however hard he tried he could hardly have hoped to fulfil them. He had no difficulty in disposing of a plot hatched by some of Richard's friends in 1400. But a rebellion led by his former allies the Percies in 1403 was a more serious matter. It culminated in the battle of Shrewsbury, where they were defeated (21 July 1403). Young Hotspur was killed; but his father, the earl of Northumberland, who was not present on the field, escaped punishment and remained at large to continue stirring up trouble. In 1405 he conspired with Richard Scrope, archbishop of York, to lead yet another uprising. Henry nipped it in the bud, and promptly had the archbishop executed. Northumberland himself was rounded up and killed at Bramham Moor three years later.

Internal peace-keeping on this scale cost money, and the repeated demands for taxation which Henry was forced to make led to a worsening of relations with parliament. In addition, he had to finance commitments in Scotland and, more ominously, in Wales (q.v.), where Owen Glendower (q.v.) held the English at bay for eight years. How successful was Henry in coping with all these problems? There is no doubt that he had the misfortune to rule at a difficult time, and in addition to political disaffection he had to face family problems too. His eldest son, the future Henry V – Shakespeare's Prince Hal – is a figure around whom many legends have grown up, but what we can say for certain is that by 1410 he was politically at odds with his father. However, the differences were never so serious as those which had divided Henry II (q.v.)

from his sons, and before too long harmony seems to have been restored. Reflecting on these 13 years then, we can sympathize with those contemporaries who felt that Henry IV had not matched up to their expectations. But he had weathered the storm, and passed on a secure throne to his son and successor, Henry V. He died on 20 March 1413, and was buried in Canterbury Cathedral.

K. B. McFarlane, *Lancastrian Kings and Lollard Knights*, Oxford, 1972.

HENRY V Few English kings have accomplished so much in so short a time; and few have had so many legends gather around them. The familiar picture is the one fostered by Shakespeare of the dissolute youth who reforms himself to become a great war leader. But how near does it come to the truth?

Henry was born at Monmouth on 16 September 1387, the son of Henry of Bolingbroke and his first wife, Mary Bohun. It was after his father became king in 1399, and his eldest son heir to the throne, that we begin to hear stories about the riotous behaviour of Prince Hal. There is certainly strong evidence that he was responsible for robbing his own receivers and that he went around in low company. Perhaps, like other heirs apparent, he had too little to do, though on the face of it this seems unlikely. From 1400 to 1408 he was leading the effort to crush Glendower's rebellion in Wales, and in the later years of the reign muddied his feet in the waters of English domestic politics. Relations between father and son reached crisis point in 1410–11; but whatever the differences that might have separated them, they were not serious enough to prevent a reconciliation before Henry IV died on 20 March 1413.

All the chroniclers confirm that on succeeding to the throne Henry became a new man. He directed his energies towards the affairs of state, foremost among them renewing the claim to the crown of France which had lain in abeyance for a couple of generations. Before looking across the Channel, though, he had to deal with two minor rebellions at home – Oldcastle's Lollard (q.v.) uprising in 1414 and the curious conspiracy led by the earl of Cambridge detected on the eve of Henry's departure for France. Once these people were out of the way, Henry V never again had to face internal dissent.

Henry's first expedition to France set sail on 11 August 1415, and landed in Normandy to embark on the siege of Harfleur. This turned out to be a more lengthy operation than expected, and by the time the town fell (22 September), the English army was riddled with dysentery. Despite his losses Henry was rash enough to march across northern France to Calais, trailed by a large French army, which finally caught up with his at Agincourt (q.v.). The result was the most celebrated English victory of the middle ages (25 October 1415), and it ensured that the king would be hailed as a national hero when he returned home.

So far as furthering Henry's ambition of winning the French crown was concerned, however, the Agincourt campaign counted for little. A more thorough-going policy of conquest was needed, and it is just that which Henry undertook when he invaded Normandy in 1417. It was the Norman conquest of England in reverse. By 1420 the whole of the duchy was occupied, and the estates of its lords shared out among the English conquerors. How had Henry V been able to achieve such astonishing success? The truth is that a bitter civil war between the two factions competing for power under Charles VI left France incapable of resisting the enemy. On 10 September 1419 matters were made still worse when the Dauphin and his men murdered John, duke of Burgundy, at a meeting on the river bridge at Montereau. To gain revenge for this atrocity, Philip, the new duke, turned to Henry, and it was this Anglo-Burgundian alliance that brought about the peace settlement agreed at Troyes on 21 May 1420. King Charles VI disinherited his son, the Dauphin, and recognized Henry of England as his heir and successor. Only Henry's premature death at Vincennes on 31 August 1422 robbed him of the chance of uniting England and France under his rule.

In less than nine years Henry V had succeeded where Edward III had failed. He had won the French crown. We know that in the end it all came to nothing because he left a one-year old child to succeed him. But could the settlement have been made to stick had he lived? The whole of southern France after all lay in Dauphinist hands. Piecemeal conquest could hardly have given reality to Henry's title, but in the long run patient diplomacy might have done. Henry was a determined and purposeful man, there can be no doubt about that. All the same, we may well feel misgivings that someone so gifted should have devoted his energies to a seemingly sterile campaign of foreign conquest. The way that Henry saw it was that by creating the dual monarchy he was advancing the cause of the unity of Christendom. But the tragedy was that he was attemping to do so at a time when the English and French nations were drawing further apart.

K. B. McFarlane, *Lancastrian Kings and Lollard Knights*, Oxford, 1972.

HENRY VI 'Woe to thee, O land, when thy king is a child', said Thomas Kerver of Reading in 1444. By that time Henry VI had all but lost the crown of France. Fifteen years later he had lost the crown of England as well.

Born on 6 December 1421, the only son of Henry V (q.v.) and his French bride, Catherine of Valois, Henry had the misfortune to become king when he was only nine months old. He was heir to the dual Anglo-French monarchy founded by his father. For the 15 years of his minority the administration in France was led by his elder uncle, John, duke of Bedford, and in England by his other uncle, Humphrey, duke of Gloucester (q.v.). Inevitably, the governing councils were divided by rivalries between the great lords, notably between Duke Humphrey and the crown's biggest creditor, Cardinal Beaufort (q.v.), but considering the difficulties they faced, they coped adequately enough. In France Bedford proved an effective regent. Try as he might, however, he could only delay and not prevent the slow erosion of Henry V's conquests. At the Congress of Arras in 1435 the Burgundians, who had sided with Henry V in 1420, decided to switch allegiance to Charles VII of France, the king they had once helped to disinherit. And in April the following year the French re-entered Paris.

Matters were not helped, and perhaps were hindered, when Henry VI came of age in 1437. It is not always possible to tell whether he or his councillors initiated policy, but whoever made the decisions they were rarely such as to inspire confidence. All would have agreed that it was necessary to provide some diplomatic fig-leaf to cover England's retreat from France, and this was provided at Tours in May 1444, when a two year truce was negotiated, and a marriage alliance arranged between Henry VI and Margaret of Anjou. But in 1445 Henry went much further, apparently on his own initiative, by offering to surrender Maine to the French in return for a full settlement. The man entrusted with carrying out the negotiations was William de la Pole, duke of Suffolk, an able man, but so tainted by suspicion of corruption that he had to face impeachment in 1450.

The eventual collapse of English rule in France did a lot of damage to Henry VI's reputation. The shortcomings of his government at home did still more. Patronage was monopolized by a circle of courtiers centred on the Queen and the Beauforts, from whom the duke of York, heir presumptive to the throne since 1447, was conspicuously excluded. When Jack Cade (q.v.) and the Commons of Kent rose in rebellion in 1450, York's return was at the top of their list of demands. Popular support, however, counted for little in the face of Queen Margaret's hostility. It was only the onset of King Henry's insanity that rescued York from oblivion. In March 1454 he was named Protector of the realm, a title he held for the next nine months. But as soon as Henry recovered his senses, he was out in the cold again. A council was summoned to meet at Leicester in May 1455, and he and his men feared they would be arrested, so they planned to intercept the king at St Alban's. The battle that followed in the narrow streets of the town (22 May) is considered to be the first engagement in the long struggle we know as the Wars of the Roses (q.v.). In fact it was not immediately followed by further hostilities. Four years of uneasy peace followed, until a further attempt by Queen Margaret to marshal her supporters, at Coventry in November

1459, convinced the Yorkist leaders that they would have to take to their heels. They returned in the following year, and at the battle of Northampton (10 July 1460) had the good fortune to capture King Henry. Paradoxically, it was a Lancastrian success that brought his unhappy reign to an end. At Wakefield on the last day of 1460 York was killed, and two months later Henry was retaken by his wife. Without an anointed king to legitimize their actions, the Yorkists had to make one of their own. On 4 March 1461, therefore, York's son was crowned king as Edward IV (q.v.).

For Henry his deposition marked the beginning of ten years' exile, spent mainly in Scotland. Whatever the state of his own mind, his wife Margaret was quite sure of hers – she wanted to regain power. The chance came in 1470, when Richard Neville, earl of Warwick (q.v.) – the Kingmaker – overthrew Edward IV, whom he had helped to put on the throne less than ten years before, and reinstated Henry. The 'readeption', as it was known, stood little chance of lasting. In April the following year Warwick fell at the battle of Barnet, and Edward re-entered London on 21 May. That really did spell the end for Henry VI who was executed shortly afterwards. His remains were interred in Chertsey Abbey, and later transferred to St George's Chapel, Windsor.

It is possible that Henry VI's bouts of insanity were inherited from his maternal grandfather, Charles VI of France, but contemporary descriptions suggest that his ailment was a different one. What Henry suffered from in 1453-4, and seems never fully to have recovered from, was sheer mental collapse. He was, we are told by Dr Griffiths, totally unresponsive. The problem for the historian is then to decide whether in his saner moments he was downright malevolent or just a helpless simpleton. He was, we know, intensely devout. His concern for good works was reflected in his twin foundations of Eton and King's College, Cambridge. But he was also prurient and responsible for allowing a gross misdirection of patronage. The Yorkist claim to the throne would surely never have been heard of had it not been for the appalling kingship of Henry VI.

B. P. Wolffe, *Henry VI*, Eyre Methuen, 1981; R. A. Griffiths, *The Reign of King Henry VI*, Ernest Benn, 1981.

HERALDRY According to the most satisfactory working definition so far offered, heraldry is 'a system of identifying individuals by means of hereditary devices placed upon a shield'.*

The fact that heraldic charges are displayed on a shield is a significant pointer to the military origins of the science. When knights rode into battle covered from head to toe in mail suits, and their faces concealed beneath closed helms, identification became quite impossible. To overcome this difficulty they adopted the simple expedient of showing a pictorial device which everyone would recognize. This would be displayed on the shield and on the linen surcoat worn over the armour to protect it from the elements – hence the familiar terms 'coat armour' and 'coat-of-arms'.

In an illiterate society armorial bearings provided the means by which a knight could not only identify himself in the field but also authenticate charters and other important documents. It is because charters were preserved as

deeds of title that the personal seals attached to them by witnesses provide our earliest surviving insight into the use of heraldry. In England the first armorial device we have comes from Stephen's (q.v.) reign, just before the outbreak of the civil war, when Waleran, count of Meulan and earl of Worcester, made a seal (*c.* 1136-8) showing him on horseback, holding in one hand a shield and in the other a lance flag, on both of which can be discerned the checky coat used by his family. Across the Channel, too, we find in the first half of the twelfth century our earliest evidence of the adoption of hereditary armorial devices. At Le Mans we have the famous enamelled plate said to have covered the tomb of Geoffrey, count of Anjou (d. 1151) and now preserved in the local museum. The count is shown beneath a semi-circular arch holding a shield of golden lions on a blue field and wearing a cap also charged with a lion. This device, like the checky coat of Count Waleran, can be accepted as truly heraldic because it was transmitted from one generation to the next: on the Great Seal of King Richard I (q.v.), Count Geoffrey's grandson, we find the arms *three lions passant guardant* – destined to become famous as the lions of England.

By the thirteenth century we can tell that heraldry had become an established science because it was acquiring a technical vocabulary of its own. We obtain our first taste of this corrupted French jargon in the Rolls of Arms drawn up by the heralds to record the arms of knights who were present at some special occasion like a tournament. Perhaps it is worthwhile pausing to run through some of the most common terms in an attempt to overcome the problems of comprehension that make heraldry so baffling to the uninitiated; for, despite

* C. Mackinnon, *Observer's Book of Heraldry*, London, 1966, p. 1.

the impression fostered by the luxuriant quarterings of a later, and more decadent, age, the basic rules of heraldic design are straightforward, and their terminology precise.

To start with, we must learn the names of the 'tinctures'. These embrace the two metals – gold (or) and silver (argent) – and the five colours – red (gules), black (sable), green (vert), blue (azure) and purple (purpure). To eliminate possible confusion in the identification of a shield, the convention arose that a colour must never be placed on a colour, nor a metal on a metal. Very few shields, however, have a plain field. If there was not to be a danger of overlapping, 'divisions' had to be introduced for sake of variety. These are eight in number, and are best represented diagrammatically (see below). From the divisions we next move on to the 'ordinaries', which are the oldest and most important of the charges on a shield. Once again, there is an exact

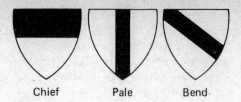

Chief   Pale   Bend

Fess   Chevron   Cross

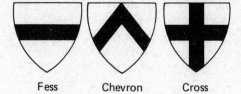

Pall   Saltire   Pile

terminology, similar in many instances to, and derived from, the descriptions of the principal divisions (see above). Simple forms like these, variously arranged, proved more than adequate to construct some of the earliest and most beautiful coats of arms. Practical necessity, however, led in the direction of greater complexity. How were the arms of a son, a brother or a nephew to be distinguished from those of the head of the family? Since the purpose of heraldry is to identify *individuals*, differences were introduced, known in the case of children as 'marks of cadency':

a. The eldest son, *a label*.
b. The second son, *a crescent*.
c. The third son, *a molet*.
d. The fourth son, *a martlet*.
e. The fifth son, *an annulet*.

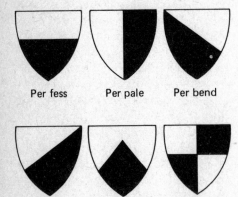

Per fess   Per pale   Per bend

Per bend sinister   Per chevron   Per cross, or quarterly

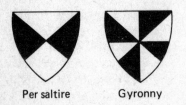

Per saltire   Gyronny

a   b   c   d   e

The evolution of this body of rules begs a lot of questions about the degree of control exercised over the adoption and use of arms in the middle ages. How was it, for example, that two knights did not by accident adopt the same device? Just occasionally they did, but the rarity of such occurrences seems odd. Part of the explanation may lie in the way that heraldic devices were adopted. Camden observed centuries ago in an oft-quoted passage how men began 'to bear arms by borrowing from their Lords Arms of whom they held in fee.' He was almost certainly right. In the fifteenth century, for example, the Talbots of Fincham (Norfolk) were using the device *six gauntlets, in the order, three, two, one,* which clearly followed the arms of the Wauncy family from whom they held their lands. Arms derived in this way from a common root would usually be differenced adequately enough to prevent overlapping. Then again there were 'canting' coats of-arms, those which involved a pun on the owner's name: the shells of Shelley and the trumpets of Trumpington are two of the best known examples.

When men assumed arms in these various ways, can we tell whether they did so with or without authorization? In other words, just who was entitled to use a coat-of-arms in the middle ages? This is perhaps the most difficult question of all, and one which left contemporaries rather perplexed. In the 1380s the French writer Honoré Bovet had to admit that it was treated satisfactorily in none of the earlier textbooks. One that he consulted must have been that of the celebrated jurist Bartolus of Sassoferrato who came to the conclusion in 1356 that any man could assume arms on his own initiative, but those granted by a prince were of higher authority than the others. On the other hand, only active knights who used arms for identification on the field would really need to have them; a knight who never saw military service would well understand the predicament of Otto de Maundell, who in 1393 had to obtain from Richard II a confirmation of arms granted to his father because the original letters patent had been lost. From what little evidence we have for England it seems that arms could be bestowed by the king (though royal grants are rare) or by earls and barons on their retainers, or could simply be assumed, as Bartolus said, without authority. The consequence, as Nicholas Upton complained in the 1440s, was that many humble men were taking up arms on their own initiative. What caused this freedom to be curtailed was the growing assumption in the fifteenth century that possession of a coat-of-arms implied the quality of noble birth. Some of the early writers had been conscious that there might be a connection between dignity of blood and a grant of arms by the king. This is certainly the assumption behind the letters patent that Richard II issued in 1389 in favour of John Kingston, saying he would receive him into the estate of gentleman and make him an esquire with the right to bear the arms *Argent, a chapeau azure with an ostrich feather gules.* The knights and esquires, born of noble and gentle blood, felt that their superiority over those of only free birth was marked by their armigerous status. If armorial bearings were to become a mark of privilege, then it followed that the right to assume them would have to be limited. In England this was done by delegating to the heralds sole responsibility for the granting of arms. The first moves in this direction came in the reign of Henry V (q.v.), when the responsibilities of the heralds were defined. In

1417 the king created the new office of Garter King of Arms, with jurisdiction over the other heralds; and a few months later the duke of Clarence published a set of ordinances defining the relations of Garter and the other Kings of Arms and enjoining them all to seek out the noble and gentle men living in their respective provinces, and especially those who ought to bear coats-of-arms in the service of the king. In this ordinance we can discern the origins of the later system of heralds' visitations.

How did the heralds come to be given these duties? Such evidence as we have, and it is mainly of a literary nature, suggests that their earliest duties were connected with the organization of tournaments (q.v.). They were sent far and wide to summon knights to take part, and when the day came they were expected to recognize the combatants and to exercise whatever control they could over the conduct of these often disorderly occasions. Once it was all over, their knowledge of armorial insignia made them the obvious people to ask to draw up a roll of arms celebrating the occasion. Somewhat later the heralds were entrusted with undertaking diplomatic errands, and finally in 1417 they were assigned responsibility for not only identifying but granting coats-of-arms.

At just this very time, as we have seen, the duke of Clarence was seeking to clarify the relative claims to precedence of the officers of arms. This he did by assigning a territorial jurisdiction to each of the senior heralds, known as kings, under the overall primacy of the newly-created Garter King of Arms. North of the Trent lay the province of Norroy, and south of it the province of Clarenceux King of Arms. The kings were the principal officers of what was later to become by incorporation in 1484 the College of Arms.

It is worth stressing in conclusion how unique the English system of heraldry is in European historical development. Only in England was the granting of arms delegated by the king to an institution like the College of Arms; and only in England were the claims of the armigerous investigated regularly by heralds' visitations of the shires.

Sir A. Wagner, *Heralds and Heraldry in the Middle Ages*, Oxford, 2nd ed., 1956.

HERIOT Heriot was a death duty paid by a tenant to his lord (Old English, *here*, army, and *geature*, military equipment). Thus a lord would be entitled to a suit of armour, for example, on the death of one of his military tenants. More usually, however, heriot described the payment due to a lord whenever a villein tenant died and on some estates, also, whenever villein land changed hands between tenants. The heir would be expected to hand over the best beast or chattel to the lord, and the second best beast to the parson as a mortuary payment. By the thirteenth century liability for such payments as heriot and merchet (q.v.) was one of the distinguishing marks of villein (i.e. unfree) status. After the Black Death (q.v.), when the position of the tenantry was much improved, villeins struggled to shake off these burdens, and heriot often gave way to an agreed money payment that soon became incorporated within rent.

HERLAND, HUGH Medieval England excelled above all in the art of carpentry. Some of the finest work was done by the three men who successively held the office of king's carpenter in the fourteenth century – William Hurley (d. 1345) and William and Hugh Herland. Hugh was probably born in about 1330. By 1366 he had evidently been in royal employment for some time because in that year he received a grant of 10 marks (£6.13.4) in recognition of his long service. In 1383 he retired on the grounds that he was getting old, but was back at his job again in the 1390s when Richard II (q.v.) commissioned him to design the roof for Westminster Hall. Herland, like most of the master craftsmen in the king's pay, also did part-time work for other clients, most notably in his case for William of Wykeham, bishop of Winchester (q.v.), with whom he dined several times in the 1390s. It may well have been his work on the chapel of the bishop's new college at Winchester which persuaded Richard to invite him to crown the newly-rebuilt Westminster Hall with a magnificent timber roof. This was to be his masterpiece. It was the earliest large-scale design of hammer-beam construction in England, and measures 240ft in length and 70ft across.

Herland died in 1405. He is very likely the 'carpentarius' whose kneeling figure appears in the east window of Winchester College chapel, alongside those of two men he must have known – William Wynford (q.v.), Wykeham's architect, and Simon Membury, his clerk of the works.

HUMPHREY, Duke of Gloucester

Soldier, political adventurer and patron of learning, Duke Humphrey was one of the most versatile figures of fifteenth century England.

The youngest son of the future Henry IV (q.v.), Humphrey was born in 1391. When his elder brother, Henry V (q.v.), died in 1422, leaving a nine-month old child as his heir, he claimed the office and title of protector of the realm, citing as his authority a codicil added to the late king's will. Such bold pretensions, however, were not well received by the lords of the council, who chose instead to divide the powers of government between Humphrey and his brother, John, duke of Bedford. Significantly enough, one of Humphrey's critics on this occasion was Bishop Beaufort (q.v.), the man destined to be his life-long rival and adversary. The differences between the two were both personal and political. Beaufort was judicious, Duke Humphrey impetuous. Beaufort believed in extricating England as honourably as possible from the war in France, Duke Humphrey in prosecuting it vigorously and in defending English maritime interests in the Channel. Humphrey could argue a good case, but confidence in his judgement was weakened by the failure of his expedition in 1424–5 to recover the inheritance of his wife Jacqueline of Hainault. Jacqueline had already been married to John of Brabant, but Humphrey claimed the contract to be invalid. He lost the argument, and afterwards married Eleanor Cobham, one of her ladies-in-waiting. For all his impulsiveness, however, Gloucester was a force to be reckoned with, because the support he enjoyed in the country balanced, if it did not outweigh, his unpopularity at court. Henry VI (q.v.) was clearly suspicious of him. In 1447 he summoned him to a parliament at Bury St Edmund's, and had him arrested. He died a few days later (23 February) under circumstances that suggested foul play.

Among the mourners must have been

the Chancellor and Scholars of the University of Oxford. Over the years they had benefited much from his generosity in gifts of books and manuscripts, and it was to house these that they built another storey over the Divinity School known to this day as 'Duke Humfrey's Library'. History, science and rhetoric were among the duke's special interests, but the books which he donated include works on theology and the classics too. He is supposed to have been no less devoted to pleasures of the flesh, but it is as a sponsor in England of the new learning of the Renaissance that he best deserves to be remembered. He was buried in St Alban's Abbey, where his chantry chapel can still be seen.

K. H. Vickers, *Humphrey, duke of Gloucester*, London, 1907.

HUNDRED It is in the tenth century that the hundred (or its alias in the Danelaw, the wapentake) first emerges as the next administrative unit below the shire. Its two principal officers were the bailiff, who served writs on behalf of the sheriff, and the constable, who was responsible for the hue and cry. According to ancient custom, the hundred court met every four weeks, when those who attended would transact a wide range of minor administrative and judicial business. By the late middle ages it met less often because by then its importance lay not so much in the business that was determined before it as in the drawing up of indictments which would be heard later before a session of the J.P.s or the king's justices. The empanelling of juries from the hundreds was in fact the standard way in which thirteenth and fourteenth century governments collected the information

they needed. Never was this appetite for information demonstrated more dramatically than in the enquiries launched by Edward I (q.v.) when he came back from crusade (q.v.) in 1274. Commissioners were appointed in each county to investigate allegations of corruption and malpractice, and this they did by putting a series of questions or 'articles' to the hundred juries who came before them. The replies, submitted in writing and known to us today as the Hundred Rolls, were lengthy and detailed enough to convince Edward that reforms were needed, and over the next ten years the Statutes of Westminster I (1275), Gloucester (1278), and Westminster II (1285) were published to rectify the encroachments and injustices uncovered.

H. Cam, *The Hundred and the Hundred Rolls*, London, reprinted 1963.

HUNDRED YEARS WAR As a historical concept, the 'Hundred Years War', like the 'Wars of the Roses', is of little antiquity. It was coined in the nineteenth century, and has since passed into general use to describe the period of Anglo-French hostilities that opened with Philip VI's confiscation of Gascony (q.v.) on 24 May 1337 and ended with the final expulsion of the English from the duchy in 1453. The inadequacies of the phrase are all too clear: it describes a period that was longer than a hundred years and a war that was broken by long periods of truce. But for all that, there is something to be said for the view that the Anglo-French hostilities of the late middle ages were different from, and perhaps more bitter than, those which had gone before.

By way of background we need to remember that even if the war ended as a struggle between two nation states, it began as one between two feudal confederations. William the Conqueror's victory at Hastings (q.v.) had created a cross-Channel dominion embracing England and Normandy (q.v.). Henry II's accession nearly a century later in 1154 merged this into a much larger 'empire' embracing Anjou, Poitou and Aquitaine as well. Even though Normandy was lost in 1204, and Anjou a decade or two later, the king of England still clung onto the duchy of Aquitaine, or Gascony as it was later known. The precise terms on which he held it were ill-defined. In 1259, therefore, in the Treaty of Paris, Louis IX and Henry III decided to sort things out. Henry was made a vassal of the king of France, from whom he was to hold Gascony as a fief in return for the performance of liege homage. Instead of resolving the conflict, however, the treaty managed to make it worse. The assumption behind any feudal relationship was that the interests of lord and vassal were identical. But those of the king of France and his vassal in Gascony were not. So the king engaged in undermining the authority of the English, and this he did by hearing appeals from aggrieved Gascons who wanted to overturn judgements given in the ducal court at Bordeaux. If goodwill had existed on both sides, the relationship created by the Treaty of Paris could have been made to work, but in the event it did not. In the peace negotiations of 1359–60, therefore, the English demanded that Gascony should be held in full sovereignty.

Had the status of Gascony been the only issue at stake, though, we would have been hard pushed to explain why the Hundred Years War lasted so long and became so difficult to resolve. The duchy had after all been confiscated twice before, in 1294 and 1324, without provoking anything more than a short war. What complicated matters in the 1330s was the determination of the French to link the Gascon problem with a settlement of the long-standing Anglo-Scottish dispute. Ever since Edward I had begun his attempt to subdue them in the 1290s, the Scots had turned to France for help, and the treaty of Corbeil (1327) committed them to intervening on the French side in the event of any future Anglo-French hostilities. In May 1334 David Bruce, driven from power in Scotland (q.v.) by Edward III, took refuge in France, where he was welcomed by Philip VI and allowed to set up court. Thereafter the French insisted that there could be no settlement in Gascony without a corresponding settlement in Scotland. And when in 1336 Philip moved what had been intended to be a crusading fleet from the Mediterranean to the Channel, Edward had good reason to fear that an invasion of England was imminent. His own invasion of the Low Countries in 1338 may well have been undertaken to prevent just that eventuality.

What Edward did after he landed in Flanders brings us to the third factor in the origins of the Hundred Years War. At a ceremony at Ghent on 26 January 1340 he assumed the arms and title of king of France. His claim to the throne, though late in coming, was well-founded. In 1328 Charles IV, the last surviving son of King Philip the Fair, had died childless. The nearest heir was his sister Isabella, widow of Edward II of England; if her own claim was inadmissable because she was a woman, it was the belief of her son Edward III that she could transmit it to her heir. Back in 1328 Edward's case had gone by default because he was still a minor, and the count of Valois had taken the throne as Philip VI. A decade later, as we have seen, Edward resurrected his claim. How serious was he? Did he think he had a realistic chance of winning the crown? Or was it just a bargaining counter to be discarded as need be in return for more tangible concessions, such as possession of Gascony in full sovereignty? We can hardly answer these questions to full satisfaction: Edward no doubt adjusted his claims according to the tide of fortune. Suffice it on this occasion to observe that the objective could not have been quite so unrealistic as we might suppose, or Henry V would never have been recognized as heir to the crown of France in 1420.

After a lengthy round of diplomatic preliminaries, hostilities got under way in 1338, when Edward transported himself and his army to Flanders. His strategy was the time-honoured one, practised long before by King John in 1214 and by Edward I in the 1290s, involving the mobilization against France of a grand coalition centred on England, Germany and the princes and urban patriciates of the Low Countries. It all turned out to be wildly over-ambitious. The princes took the pensions that Edward offered, but declined to move. All through the winter and spring of 1338–9 he was condemned to idleness. When in September he finally marched into the Cambresis, he was abandoned by the count of Hainault, and such hopes of success as he still entertained were dashed by the refusal of the French to meet him in open battle. The first, inconclusive phase of the war was terminated by the truce of Esplechin (25 September 1340) and Edward had little to show for his efforts apart from the naval victory off Sluys on Midsummer Day 1340.

Without more success than he had achieved so far, he would be unlikely to receive further grants of taxation from parliament. He therefore had to review his strategy. He abandoned the idea of a frontal attack from the north-east in favour of a simultaneous series of assaults launched from the peripheral provinces of France. Gascony itself, though much shrunken in size by the 1340s, provided one such foothold. Brittany provided another. A succession dispute in the duchy between Charles of Blois and John de Montfort, who held the English earldom of Richmond, provided Edward with the opportunity to intervene on the latter's behalf in return for recognition of his title as king of France. He was also able to make use of the assistance from time to time of French malcontents like the Norman lord, Godfrey d'Harcourt, and Charles the Bad, king of Navarre. In other words, the essence of his new strategy lay in exploiting the resentments felt by the feudal princes against the centralizing policies of the Valois monarchy. To that extent the Hundred Years War can be seen as a French civil war.

Normandy, Brittany and Gascony therefore provided Edward's commanders with three bases from which to operate. If English armies were to land in each of these theatres, Philip VI would hardly know whence to expect the next attack. He might march down to Gascony, only to find himself drawn north again by an English landing on the Cotentin. This is just what happened, for example, in 1346 when Edward relieved the pressure on Henry of Grosmont in the south by drawing the French northwards to fight at Crecy (q.v.) on 26 August – a decisive English victory as it turned out. Ten years later

Grosmont in Normandy and Edward, the Black Prince (q.v.), in Gascony adopted the tactic of simultaneous attacks once again. This time the laurels went to the prince, who captured King John of France at Poitiers (19 September 1356). If ever Edward III were to win the crown of France, this was surely his chance. In 1359 he set out at the head of an expedition that he thought would culminate in his coronation at Rheims Cathedral. Rheims, however, resisted all assaults, and he was obliged to come to terms the following spring at Bretigny. The agreement reached there, and ratified at Calais, granted Edward an enlarged Aquitaine in full sovereignty in return for surrendering his claim to the throne.

This settlement, though arguably giving Edward less than he had wanted, marked the end of the most successful period of warfare for the English in the fourteenth century. When hostilities were resumed in 1369 in the years of Edward's decline, the advantage of leadership had passed to the French. John of Gaunt led a march or *chevauchee* across France in 1373 which, profitable as it may have been in terms of booty, did nothing to reverse the steady attrition of the former English conquests. Under these circumstances it was in the English interest to renew negotiations. A peace treaty in the event was never reached because the two sides could not agree about Gascony; but in 1396 at Leulinghen they settled for the next best, an extended truce of 28 years sealed by a marriage alliance between Richard II and Isabella, the six-year old daughter of Charles VI of France.

Just as the collapse of effective authority in England in the later years of Edward III's reign had encouraged Charles V to reopen the war in 1369, so

a similar, but more disastrous, collapse of leadership in France in the early fifteenth century encouraged Henry V to renew hostilities in 1415. Charles VI (1380–1422) was afflicted by recurring bouts of madness. Into the power vacuum created by his inability to rule stepped the dukes of Burgundy and Orleans, respectively uncle and brother of the king, and men whose rivalries were to divide the nation into two warring camps. After the murder of Orleans in 1407, nothing could prevent open war between his partisans and those of John, duke of Burgundy. It was to this background that Henry V took the initiative once again, negotiating with both French parties simultaneously. When his demands, as he no doubt expected, were rejected, he landed at the mouth of the Seine, besieged Harfleur, and then began the arduous march to Calais (q.v.) that culminated in the victory of Agincourt (25 October 1415). One victory, however distinguished, was not of course the same as winning the war. In 1417, therefore, still exploiting the internal divisions that weakened France, he began the systematic conquest and settlement of Normandy. What finally enabled him to convert these military successes into a political triumph was the murder by the Dauphin Charles of Duke John of Burgundy at Montereau in 1419. The Burgundian party were driven into the arms of the English. The dauphin was disinherited, and Henry recognized as heir to the crown of France (Treaty of Troyes, 21 May 1420).

Unfortunately for the English, Henry was to be dead within two years. He passed away on 31 August 1422, leaving an infant son to inherit the crown of England and, two months later on the death of Charles VI, the crown of France as well. For the next 15 years, during the king's minority, conduct of affairs in France lay in the capable hands of John, duke of Bedford, who appreciated that continued success depended on the Anglo-Burgundian alliance. The English, as the prior of Dijon Charterhouse put it, had entered France through the duke of Burgundy's skull. So long as remembrance of the duke's murder kept the Burgundians at odds with the Dauphinists, the English were safe. But Philip, the new duke, could not ignore the revival in French fortunes after Joan's relief of Orleans, still less after the coronation of the Dauphin as Charles VII in 1429. If he wanted to retain any influence in French affairs, he would have to come to terms with Charles. That is just what he did at Arras in 1435. The loss of the Burgundian alliance and the collapse in morale under the incompetent Henry VI sealed the fate of the English in France. The surprising thing is not that the French recovered the conquered lands, but that they took so long to do it. Normandy fell at last in 1450 and

Gascony the next year. John Talbot, the famous war veteran, tried to stage a comeback in 1452 by leading an army to Gascony in support of a local uprising; but at Castillon on 17 July 1453 he was defeated and killed. That really did mark the end. Only Calais was left.

The French monarchy, whose abasement had allowed the English to register such sweeping conquests, recovered because it became symbolic of the national will to expel the invader. The war, whether the English liked it or not, was over. Charles VII was king once more in his own land, his hold over the French people immeasurably strengthened as a result of the sacrifices he had called on them to make. But no peace followed the conclusion of hostilities. The French did not need one; and the English could not face one. It was not until 1802 in the Treaty of Amiens that an English king in the person of George III finally surrendered his ancient title to the crown of France.

E. Perroy, *The Hundred Years War*, Eyre & Spottiswoode, 1965.

i

IMPEACHMENT The idea of a prosecution in parliament (q.v.) by the lower house before the upper emerged clearly for the first time in the 'Good Parliament' of 1376 when the Commons, led by Sir Peter de la Mare, their Speaker, were seeking the removal of a group of Edward III's ministers. The Commons decided to bring a list of charges against them, first and foremost

against the Chamberlain, Sir William Latimer. When Latimer asked who was accusing him, de la Mare, speaking on behalf of the Commons, said that they would maintain the charges together. This was the essence of impeachment: the Commons, acting in the king's name, would assume the role of a community of accusers. In proceeding in this way, Peter de la Mare and his friends had fashioned a useful parliamentary instrument for putting unpopular ministers on trial. They used it again to prosecute Michael de la Pole, the Chancellor, in 1386. However, its future value for this purpose was effectively undermined by the ruling of the judges in 1387, when questioned by Richard II (q.v.), that ministers and justices could not be put on trial by the Lords and Commons without the king's permission. After an unsuccessful revival in 1450 against the duke of Suffolk, impeachment lay dormant until the seventeenth century, when it was resurrected in James I's reign to bring Sir Giles Mompesson to trial.

INDUSTRY Although the majority of the population worked on the land, English medieval society was complex and sophisticated enough to stimulate the growth of a modest manufacturing sector.

The industry which had developed furthest along capitalistic lines based on the division of labour was clothmaking. In the thirteenth century this was centred chiefly in the old-established towns of eastern England – Beverley, York, Lincoln and Northampton, for example. One advantage it enjoyed right from the start was an ample supply of wool from the sheep flocks for which England was justly famous. Oddly enough, though, the cloth towns lay at some distance from the main wool-producing areas, which were over in Herefordshire, the Cotswolds and of course along the Pennines.

The first stage in the process of manufacture was sorting, because the mixture of different qualities of wool in a single cloth was forbidden. Next came carding or combing, the purpose of which was to make the wool ready for spinning into yarn. Spinning itself was traditionally done by women. The yarn was then ready to be woven into cloth. For this operation a horizontal, flat bed-loom was used, at one end of which was the warp beam and at the other a roller onto which each section of finished cloth was wound. The weaver operated his loom by using pedals to raise the lower alternate warp threads, at the same time as passing the shuttle with the weft threads across them from one side to the other. Next the raw cloth had to be fulled – in other words, thickened by being beaten in troughs flowing with water and fuller's earth. The latter was an absorbent form of earth found in deposits at Nutfield and Reigate in Surrey. The cloth would then be stretched back to its original shape and passed onto the finishers whose business it was to draw all the loose fibres by using teazles. By now it was ready for dyeing, a process which involved both colouring the raw material and fixing it. Madder was used for scarlet, vermilion for bright red, saffron for yellow and woad for blue. The woad plant, of course, had been grown in this country at least from Saxon times, but by the late middle ages the dyers were finding themselves ever more reliant for this, as for the other dyes, on imports from abroad. Whatever colour was chosen, it was fixed by a mordant, usually alum for scarlet and potash for other colours. All that remained, then, once the cloth had dried, was for it to be packed and sent off to market. The standard broadcloth woven in England by these methods was 24 yards long and 1½–2 yards wide.

The cloth trade was probably medieval England's biggest industrial employer. One estimate is that it gave jobs to some 15,000 people in 1400 – though we have to qualify that by saying that some of those would only have worked part-time. Cloth production was also a long and complex business. That very complexity soon encouraged the growth of specialization, to the extent that by the thirteenth century each stage of the process was performed by artisans skilled in their own craft. Of these the men who emerged as the most powerful were the dyers, because the necessity of importing dye materials from abroad gave them international trading links. Indeed, in thirteenth-century Leicester the dyers had emerged as a class of mercantile entrepreneurs controlling not only the local production of cloth but also the marketing of it. The weavers and fullers were prepared to put up with this only for so long. They responded by forming themselves into guilds (q.v.). But the very strengthening of their position encouraged the dyers to transfer their custom to textile workers in the countryside, who could be paid less. As imports from Flanders grew in volume in the thirteenth century, it became all the more important for them to cut their costs. The erection of fulling mills on country streams, which historians once considered so important, was therefore less a cause than a consequence of the general decline of urban textile making.

Despite these setbacks, the cloth industry lived to fight another day. But when it experienced a revival, as it did under the stimulus of providing cheap clothing for the armies of Edward I and Edward III, its geography looked very different from a century before. Some of the old-established manufacturing towns, like Salisbury, were still flourishing; but it was the newer centres that were meeting the mass demand for cheaper cloths. First and foremost there was the West Country – Stroud and Cirencester in Gloucestershire, Brad-

ford and Castle Combe in Wiltshire, and Frome in Somerset. And in East Anglia there were Sudbury, Lavenham, Worsted and other villages, whose late medieval prosperity is attested by the magnificence of their parish churches.

When we turn from cloth to the other trades, we find that the numbers employed were far fewer, and the methods involved usually less sophisticated. One exception was glazing. It did not employ great numbers; but it did require a measure of specialization. Glass *making* was carried on at Chiddingfold in Surrey. It involved taking sand, lime and potash and melting them in a clay pot in a furnace. Glass *painting*, on the other hand, was a quite separate process carried on in the workshop of a master glazier at somewhere like London, Norwich or York (q.v., STAINED GLASS). Although armorial windows became very popular in upper-class houses in the late middle ages, the main demand for painted glass came as it always had from the Church. Bell-founding was another industry that flourished under ecclesiastical patronage. Richard Tunnoc, goldsmith and bellfounder of York, was so proud of his trade that he donated the so-called 'bellfounder's Window', in the north aisle of the Minster (*c.* 1320). It depicts various stages in the craft of bell-making. In one panel we see the master and two assistants casting the bell, and in another Tunnoc and an assistant either polishing or tuning it (plate 29).

Mention of bells brings us onto metal-working in general. In the thirteenth and fourteenth centuries the iron and metal trades may actually have engaged more men in the great Midland city of Coventry than textiles did. The supply of iron came from the Forest of Dean which contained the most extensive mines in medieval England. By the fifteenth century, however, they were being matched by the Wealden workings in Kent and Sussex which supplied the London market. Tin, another component in bellfounding, came from Devon and Cornwall. Since 1198 the tin-miners of the locality had been organized under the aegis of the Stanneries Court, which guaranteed them immunity from villein (q.v.) dues and exemption from normal taxation. Instead, the Crown levied a due on all tin produced. And how much was produced in the middle ages? It is hard to get reliable figures for the level of activity in the extractive industries, but we know that in the early fourteenth century, a period of unusually high production, between 560,000 and 817,000 lbs of tin were being presented each year to be taxed.

For warmth in their homes people relied on charcoal and wood. In the north-east of England the coal mines that had lain idle since the departure of the Romans were brought back into use in the twelfth century, but mainly to supply the kilns that were used for lime-burning, brewing and baking. Coal was apparently not popular as a heating fuel, at least not with the Londoners who complained in 1307 that it was infecting and corrupting the air. There is no evidence that coal-mining in the middle ages was a highly capitalized activity, and it was presumably only the seams close to the surface that were exploited. All the same, enough was extracted to bring prosperity to late-medieval New-castle-on-Tyne, which was the centre of the coastal carrying trade.

Finally, we should note the salt trade. In the middle ages salt was the essential preservative. Along the east coast of England it was produced by the process of evaporation from sea water; inland it was extracted from the brine springs of Droitwich (Worcs.) and Nantwich (Cheshire). In the early middle ages England was probably self-sufficient in the commodity, indeed a net exporter, but by the fourteenth century was reliant on imports from the Bay of Bourgneuf area of western France,.

L. Salzman, *English Industries of the Middle Ages*, Oxford, 1923.

IRELAND Geography has been unkind to Ireland. Too far from Europe, too close to England, the country has found itself cut off from the mainstream of European development, and yet prevented from establishing its own political and cultural identity by a fatal combination of English influence and internal disunity. At the very time in the eleventh and twelfth centuries, when kings and princes elsewhere were fashioning strong, feudal monarchies, Ireland was condemned by the fact of its geographical isolation to remain politically immature. Local princelings competed with one another for the empty title of 'high king'.

Like the rest of Europe, Ireland had had to face the Viking onslaught in the ninth century; and before it had passed, colonies of Norsemen were established in towns like Dublin and Waterford along the east coast. The next wave of outside influence came with the Anglo-Normans in the 1170s. The events that led to the founding of their settlement are an apt commentary on Irish history in this period. In 1152 Dermot McMurrough, king of Leinster, had abducted Devorgilla, wife of Tiernan O'Rourke of Breifne in Meath. Although Devorgilla soon returned to her husband, Tiernan was determined to get revenge, and in 1166 allied with Rory O'Conor, the high king, to drive his rival out of Ireland. Dermot turned up at the court of Henry II (q.v.) seeking allies. The king was not yet prepared to intervene himself, but allowed the Irishman to enlist the support of members of his baronage. First to go, in 1169, were Robert FitzStephen and Maurice FitzGerald. However, the biggest contingent to answer Dermot's call was that led by Richard de Clare, earl of Pembroke, known to history as Strongbow. By the end of 1170 he had taken Dublin and Waterford. He married Dermot's daughter Eva, and on her father's death in 1171 succeeded to the kingdom of Leinster. All this was evidently too much for Henry II. Worried that these adventurers might become too powerful, he crossed to Ireland himself in 1171 to secure the submission of both the new settlers and the native princes. Strongbow had to surrender Dublin to the king; but he was re-enfeoffed with the rest of Leinster. So at the end of the day he could consider himself well satisfied.

Henry also established the rudiments of an administration in Dublin; but it is rather to King John (q.v.) that we must give the credit for putting the Anglo-Norman colony on a firmer basis. What provision did he and his father make for its government? The king himself was represented in Dublin by a justiciar – or lieutenant, as he was known by the fourteenth century. The rest of the Irish administration mirrored its counterpart in England (q.v., GOVERNMENT). There was a council which advised the justiciar, a chancery which wrote his letters, and an exchequer which collected the revenues. By the thirteenth century there was also a parliament, to which in due course (though later than in England) representatives of the Commons were summoned.

If the future of Anglo-Irish society looked promising when John returned to England from his visit in 1210, that appearance was deceptive. The 'conquest' of Ireland had nothing in common with the conquest of England in 1066. When Harold fell at Hastings, England fell with him. But Ireland had not one king but many, and they were all still in power. England in 1066 had a central government machine that could simply be taken over. Ireland did not. As we have seen, it had to be created. The Norman conquest of England was a state-directed enterprise. The Anglo-Norman settlement of Ireland was a private affair, and largely allowed to remain as such. And the momentum which had driven it forward in the later twelfth century began to falter by the mid-thirteenth. Ireland remained only half-conquered, half-feudalized. If one consequence of this state of confusion was that tribal dynasties still continued to skirmish with each other, another was that the process of racial assimilation went forward. So alarmed by this did the government become that at the Kilkenny parliament of 1366 the famous statutes were passed defining the areas of English influence in Irish society. The English colony was limited to the territory in the east known as the Pale – by implication any attempt to subdue the rest of Ireland was abandoned – and its population was prohibited from marrying into the native Irish or adopting their way of life. This was not so much an aggressive piece of legislation as a defensive reaction by a settler community afraid of losing its identity; and if it sounded draconian, its terms, like those of most medieval laws, could easily be circumvented by the purchase of a licence.

The Kilkenny statutes were published at a time when the English government was making a new and determined effort to halt the slow but steady erosion of the Pale. In 1361 Edward III (q.v.) sent his son, Lionel, duke of Clarence, over to Dublin as lieutenant. For all the advantages that Lionel was able to bring to the job – for example, he was married to the heiress of the earldom of Ulster – it is unlikely that he made much headway before returning to England in 1366. Nothing daunted, Edward III tried again three years later. In 1369 he appointed William of Windsor as lieutenant with £20,000 to spend on supporting the administration of Ireland. Handsome though this subsidy was, it was insufficient, and Windsor's high-handed efforts to raise still more money from the Irish aroused such opposition that he was recalled in 1371. By then the reopening of the Hundred Years War (q.v.) prevented the English government from undertaking any fresh initiatives, and the problems of Ireland were relegated to the background until the next reign. Richard II (q.v.) had made a long truce with the French, and the lull in hostilities allowed him to make the first personal intervention in Irish affairs since King John. He led two expeditions to Ireland, the first of which, in 1394, was very successful, and the second of which, in 1399, was cut short by news of Henry of Bolingbroke's landing in England. Ireland was left in a state of confusion; but that was hardly likely to worry the newly-crowned Henry IV (q.v.), who had problems enough of his own to worry about.

Of the lieutenants appointed in the fifteenth century few made any impact. In the struggles between York and Lancaster known to us as the Wars of the Roses (q.v.) Ireland lent its support to York, who held large estates there, inherited from his Mortimer ancestors. After the accession of Henry Tudor in 1485, Ireland became the home of lost causes. In 1487 Lambert Simnel made Ireland the base for his attempt on the throne. A few years later in 1491 Perkin Warbeck turned up in Cork claiming to be Richard, duke of York. It was the fear that the Irish parliament might lend its support to these pretenders that lay behind the passing in 1494 of a law which allowed the Dublin assembly only to pass such measures as had first been approved by the king and council in England. This famous law perpetuates the name of Sir Edward Poynings, who was deputy lieutenant at the time. It represents as good a point as any to terminate an account of Irish medieval history, because the subordination to the authority of Westminster which it created was to last for the next three centuries until 1783.

A. J. Otway-Ruthven, *A History of Medieval Ireland*, London, 1968; T. W. Moody & F. X. Martin, *The Course of Irish History*, New York, 1967.

J

JEWS In the middle ages, when usury was condemned by the Church, moneylending was conducted mainly by the Jews. That is not to say that there were no Christian moneylenders. On the contrary, Henry II (q.v.) borrowed heavily from William Cade of St Omer, a usurer who had agents in every part of western Europe. England had its Christian moneylenders too, but the Jewish community here was more prominent than it was, across the Channel say, in Normandy.

The Jews had been introduced into England after the Norman Conquest. Though free in law, they in fact belonged to the king, who commended them to the protection of the keepers of his castles. In the reign of Henry I (1100–35) they resided only in London, but the civil war of Stephen's reign seems to have had the effect of dispersing them. Early in Henry II's reign there were communities at Norwich, Lincoln, Cambridge, Thetford, Northampton, Oxford and in Gloucestershire, Wiltshire and Hampshire. In 1221 there were recognized communities in 17 of the larger towns – a recognized community being one which possessed an *archa*, or office for the registration of Jewish bonds.

Let it not be supposed that the Jews derived their entire livelihood from usury. If Aaron of Lincoln (d. 1186) and Jurnet of Norwich (d. *c.* 1197) had cash to lend, it was because they had already amassed a fortune from trade (though we know little of which trades they engaged in). But once they had acquired enough capital, they used it to earn more. In the thirteenth century their clients ranged from monasteries in need of money to improve their buildings to hard-up knights reduced to paying off one debt by contracting another. If a borrower entered into a bond for a capital sum, he could pledge either land or moveable property as security. Should he then default in payment, the Jewish creditor would simply sell the moveables or make arrangements for the disposal of the land. Being a town dweller, the Jew did not usually enter into possession himself. One consequence, therefore, of the failure of improvident borrowers to acquit themselves was the growth of an active market in encumbered estates, which enabled a skilful speculator like Walter de Merton in the 1260s to accumulate the properties that went to endow his college in Oxford.

Their trade as moneylenders did not necessarily make the Jews unpopular. A few of them were on close, through not perhaps on intimate, terms with the great. The reign of Henry II (q.v.) was their heyday. After his death and the accession of Richard the Lion Heart (q.v.) the rise of crusading fervour bred a wave of anti-semitic hysteria. In 1190 the Jewish community at York was massacred. Hostility towards the Jews gathered strength again in the baronial wars of the following century. In 1264 there were pogroms in London and other towns. In November 1278, after peace had returned, Jews all over England were arrested on suspicion of coin-clipping. The end finally came in 1290 when Edward I (q.v.) expelled them.

Why should the king turn against a community his ancestors had striven for so long to protect? Was he coming to the relief of hard-pressed landowners driven by necessity into dependence on the moneylenders? It seems unlikely, since he took over the bonds himself. The debtors simply exchanged one creditor for another. The expulsion was a straightforward act of plunder. By 1290 the Jewish community, which had once numbered 3,000 or so was reduced in both numbers and wealth. Edward had no need of their money-lending facilities. Italian bankers could provide him with extensive credit on the security of parliamentary taxation (q.v.). The Jews no longer played a significant role in the national economy. So he could take what was left of their wealth and expel them.

H. G. Richardson, *The English Jewry under the Angevin Kings*, London, 1960.

JOHN King John is one of the notoriously bad kings of English history, his name forever associated with the humiliation inflicted on him at Runnymede in June 1215. Yet there is a strong case for believing that he was not so much purposefully wicked as just unlucky.

Born in 1167, probably at Oxford, he was the youngest and favourite son of Henry II (q.v.). When his brothers had long been provided for, John was still lacking any estates of his own – hence the nickname John Lackland. In 1172, therefore, his father decided to give him the three castles of Chinon, Mirebeau and Loudon. At the best of times the members of the Angevin family found it hard enough to get on with each other, but on this occasion the territorial pro-

vision that Henry II intended to make for his youngest son provoked such a violent reaction from the eldest, who claimed the castles as his own, that civil war followed. A few years later Henry provided for John by giving him Ireland (q.v.), but he did little good there, and by the time of his father's death in 1189 had joined his elder brother Richard (q.v.) in rebellion. It was to be evident once again in Richard's own reign that loyalty was a word of which John hardly knew the meaning. He was too busy thinking ahead to the time of his own accession.

When news came of Richard's death in 1199, it was not completely clear who would follow him on the throne. Richard had designated John, but the other candidate with a claim was Arthur of Brittany, son of John's now deceased elder brother Geoffrey. John acted quickly, seizing the Angevin treasure at Chinon, and sailing for England where he was crowned in Westminster Abbey on 27 May. As for Arthur, he was rounded up in 1202, and died in captivity a year or two later. The quite justified suspicion that their ruler might have been murdered provoked the Bretons into rebellion. They enjoyed a powerful ally in Philip Augustus, king of France, who had long nursed the ambition of driving the Angevins from Normandy (q.v.) and now moved in for the kill. The Normans' will to resist seems to have crumbled, and by midsummer 1204 the duchy and its capital had fallen to the French.

There was something symbolic about the loss of Normandy. John still retained the more distant territories further south, like Poitou and Aquitaine, but the duchy, which had enjoyed the longest and closest links with England, was gone. Yet the loss of Normandy was of much more than symbolic significance, for John's attempts to re-conquer it form the central theme of the next ten years. The strategy which he employed was a good one, and was to be employed by other English kings like Edward I (q.v.) in the years to come. He intended to invade France from the south-west himself and to rely on allies in Germany and the Low Countries to do likewise from the north-east. This ambitious plan for a war on two fronts, with all that it entailed in raising money and mobilizing men, inevitably had repercussions at home, and to make matters worse John could hardly have made such demands at a more unfortunate time. Since the 1180s England had been afflicted by an acute inflation, the effect probably of an influx of bullion from abroad. Simply to keep pace with prices John needed to increase his income proportionately; but to undertake ambitious campaigns on the Continent as well, he had to push his demands still further.

On top of this he had the misfortune to become embroiled in a dispute with the Church at a time when it was led by Innocent III, perhaps the most powerful pope ever to preside over medieval Christendom. When Canterbury fell vacant in 1205, John was anxious to secure the election of his close adviser, John de Gray, bishop of Norwich, but the pope had other ideas. His nominee was Stephen Langton (q.v.), an Englishman influential in the papal curia. The monks of Canterbury, meanwhile, had elected a third candidate, Reginald, one of their own number. The pope quashed this election, and suggested that they elect Langton, which they obligingly did. But so vehement was John's opposition to the new archbishop that he denied him entry into the country, and in 1208 an Interdict was imposed. In other words, the churches were closed, and the clergy ordered to cease performing their duties. This order was followed by the excommunication of the king in 1209. Unpopular though the Interdict may have been, it paradoxically had the effect of easing the royal financial pressure on the taxpaying classes, because so long as it lasted John took the revenues of the Church.

How, then, did the reign reach its dramatic climax? John was prepared to put up with the Church dispute so long as it could be kept in isolation, but by 1213 Philip Augustus had forged an alliance with the pope on whose behalf he proposed to invade England. Operating on the time-honoured principle of 'divide and rule', John submitted to Pope Innocent, who now became his ally. Philip continued fitting out his invasion fleet all the same, and moved it to Damme in Flanders. There it had the misfortune to be discovered at anchor by John's fleet, and attacked with the loss of 100 ships and many more cut adrift (30 May 1215). Encouraged by this success, John decided in the following year to launch the invasion of France on which he had lavished so many years of careful preparation. It was all to no avail. When he got to Poitou, he was deserted by the local barons. And over in the Low Countries, his German allies were defeated so decisively at Bouvines (27 July 1214) that his own hopes were shattered into the bargain.

Even before news of Bouvines reached England, opposition to John was building up. It was led by the northern lords, who objected to serving abroad, but John's arbitrary rule and exorbitant financial demands, which fell heaviest of all on the baronial class, turned a movement led by a few extremists into a more general opposition front. By early 1215 full civil war had broken out, and after the fall of London in May John had to come to terms. At Runnymede in June he agreed to the famous charter of liberties we know as Magna Carta (q.v.). It ended one war and started another; it was too extreme to satisfy the king, too moderate to satisfy the extremists. In August John was released by the pope from his oath to uphold the charter, and he was still fighting his opponents when he died at Newark in October 1216.

What would have happened had he lived we can hardly tell. Now that he had the pope on his side, John doubtless expected the full armoury of papal diplomacy to be brought to bear on his opponents, and perhaps even a crusade to be preached against them. They in the meantime had deposed John, and awarded the English crown to Louis, son of the king of France. There were all the makings of a very bitter struggle indeed. For John, however, this like most of his earlier campaigns was dogged by moments of ill-luck: there was the occasion when he is supposed to have lost his baggage in the Wash. But his entire reign can be seen as an unequal struggle against the forces pitted against him. Administratively, he was far and away the most competent of the sons of Henry II. Yet his very efficiency in exploiting all available sources of revenue, particularly feudal (q.v.) perquisites, merely added to his unpopularity. Had he recovered Normandy, he might have purchased some tolerance, even acquiescence. But what he enjoyed in administrative skill, he conspicuously lacked in military prowess.

Even so, all this hardly explains why John was apparently so hated in his own day. The problem is that he received a bad write-up from the chroniclers, particularly from Roger Wendover at St Alban's Abbey. It is Wendover who tells us about wicked King John extracting teeth from the Jews, slitting the noses of papal servants and imprisoning Geoffrey of Norwich in a leaden cope, to mention but the most lurid of his anecdotes. Wendover's famous epitaph, 'Foul as it is, hell itself is defiled by the fouler presence of John', was repeated by nineteenth century historians as if it were the unbiased verdict of a reliable contemporary. Quite the contrary. Chroniclers writing in monasteries were hardly likely to be sympathetic to a king who had brought a papal Interdict down upon England. John was certainly no angel, but an indication that he was not without some conventional piety is given by his devotion to the cathedral at Worcester, where he chose to be buried between the shrines of St Oswald and St Wulfstan.

W. L. Warren, *King John*, London, 1961.

JOHN OF SALISBURY Perhaps the most learned man of his day, John of Salisbury was not only a scholar and writer but a man of affairs too. His modern reputation rests principally on two works, the *Polycraticus* and the *Metalogicon*, both completed in 1159 and dedicated to his friend and patron, Thomas Becket, at that time Henry II's Chancellor.

All that we know about his early years is told to us by John himself in an autobiographical chapter in the *Metalogicon*. He was born between 1115 and 1120 at Salisbury. In 1136 he went abroad to continue his studies, drawn to the Hill of St Genevieve in Paris, as so many of his contemporaries were, by the reputation of the great Abelard. When Abelard gave up teaching in the following year, he went to the school at Chartres, where the study of classical literature had been revived by such men as Bernard and William of Conches. His years at Chartres were important for his intellectual development, for it was very likely there that he acquired the un-affected Latin style, so unusual for a medieval scholastic, which distin-guishes his writing.

In 1140 or 1141 he returned to Paris. By the time that he left again in about 1148, he had spent some 12 years of his life in study. All this was a more than adequate preparation for the career that he chose to pursue in ecclesiastical administration. After going to the Council of Rheims in 1148, he spent the next four years at the papal curia, where his experiences were to inspire him later on to write the *Historia Pontificalis*. Then in 1153 he took advantage of letters of recommendation he had ac-quired from Bernard of Clairvaux to become the counsellor and secretary of Theobald, archbishop of Canterbury.

It was while he was at Canterbury that he wrote the two works for which he is remembered today. The *Poly-craticus* is a rather discursive treatise in nine books, the first five dealing mainly with the idle vanities that beguile the courtier and the last four with theories of the State. John takes an organic view of society. The commonwealth is likened to a human body in which the priesthood corresponds to the soul, the prince to the head, the judges to the eyes, the soldiers to the hands and the husbandmen to the feet. Written as it was more than half a century before Aristotle's *Politics* became available in the West, the *Polycraticus* is wholly medieval in outlook, and not in the least influenced by the revival of Classical ideas that began in the twelfth century. The *Metalogicon*, by contrast, equally medieval though it may be in its philo-sophical preoccupations, succeeded in breaking new ground. It was the first work to make use in their entirety of Aristotle's philosophical treatises known as the *Organon*.

John's political views determined his attitude to the great struggle between Becket (q.v.) and Henry II (q.v.) which he was privileged to observe at close quarters. He believed that human laws could only be derived from the Christian faith; in that case the Church was entitled to have a say in their for-mulation. Church and State, in other words, were both part of the same commonwealth. Whatever misgivings he may have felt about Becket's hand-ling of the dispute, John had no alter-native but to support the stand that he took and to share with him the hardship of years in exile. When in 1170 it seemed that a settlement had been reached and Becket returned, John almost certainly came back with him. He was only a few rooms away on that fatal day in 1170 when the archbishop met his death.

For the next few years John probably remained at Canterbury. But in 1176 he was elected bishop of Chartres, an office that he held until his death four years later on 25 October 1180. He was bur-ied at the monastery of Josaphat, just outside the city. Less original perhaps than the famous Abelard, John was nevertheless a learned and widely-read scholar, an accomplished letter-writer and a perceptive commentator on the world around him.

C. C. J. Webb, *John of Salisbury*, London, 1932.

JUSTICE As Maitland, the great legal historian, once wrote, hardly a rule remains unaltered, and yet the body of law that now lives among us is the same body that Blackstone described in the eighteenth century, Coke in the seventeenth, Bracton in the thirteenth and Glanvill in the twelfth. In few fields of English historical study is the feeling of continuity more pervasive than in legal history and in few fields of life has the legacy of the middle ages been more influential than in the formulation of the system of common law we still cherish today.

It is impossible to understand the system of justice that operated in medieval England without glancing first at its origins in the Old English period. The laws of the Anglo-Saxon kingdoms were the unwritten customs their peoples had always known and accepted, preserved in popular memory, and declared when need be in the folk moot. Law was there to be discovered, not made or created. With the arrival of the Christian missionaries in the seventh and eighth centuries, Mediterranean influences began to permeate Saxon society, and we find kings like Ethelbert of Kent and Ine of Wessex who followed the example of the Roman emperors in publishing written codes of law. The coming of Christianity also promoted the idea that new laws could be made, because the institution of Church property created the need for legislation that would have been inconceivable in pagan society. Another twist was given to the story in the ninth and tenth centuries as the tie of lordship gradually superseded the tie of kinship as the principal bond of society. People thought of the law, and the duty of preserving the peace, as belonging to someone, usually to the person in whose court infringements of that law were punished. Thus the king reserved to his own court cases which he considered to be breaches of his own peace, such as fighting at court, robbery on the highways and obstructing his officials. This category was to be the basis of the 'pleas of the crown' we meet later on – namely, those crimes serious enough to be heard by the king's professional justices in the court of King's Bench.

On the eve of the Conquest there was a hierarchy of courts in England, ranging from the king's court at the top, through the shire court, down to the hundred court and the private court of the manorial lord. William the Conqueror took over this judicial system as he found it, and made few alterations except to transfer the hearing of spiritual pleas from the shire court to the jurisdiction of the Church. In other words, we have in this move the origins of the separate Church courts of the later middle ages. If he tampered little with the existing public courts, William was nevertheless responsible for erecting alongside them a new system of feudal justice, based on the courts of the 'honors', to adjudicate pleas arising out of feudal tenure (q.v., FEUDAL-ISM). The settlement in these courts of matters of mutual interest to the tenant-in-chief and the honorial barons who held their lands from him was to form the essence of life in a feudal society for the next hundred years.

The next turning point in English legal history came with the reign of Henry II (q.v.), a period often said to have witnessed a 'great leap forward' in the development of royal justice. The civil war of Stephen's reign presented Henry on his accession with a legacy of violent crime and conflicting claims to land to which he responded by making changes in the law known as 'assizes'. Of the changes that concerned the handling of criminal business the most important was the Assize of Clarendon in 1166, which provided for juries from each of the hundreds (q.v.) to present the names of suspected wrongdoers to the sheriff. This assize, as recent research has emphasized, marks the beginning in England of the idea of the public prosecution of crime, conducted moreover in the peculiarly English form of the 'grand jury'. This still survives in the United States long after it has vanished in its country of origin. Juries were also used in the so-called 'possessory assizes' which rank as Henry II's greatest achievement in the area of civil (as opposed to criminal) jurisdiction. These were legal actions intended to resolve the conflicting claims to land which had built up during the civil war and before, and their novelty lay in the employment for the first time of the returnable writ and jury of recognition. If we take Novel Disseisin as an example, we can see how these assizes worked. A plaintiff recently disseised (i.e., dispossessed) of his land would purchase from the king a writ of Novel Disseisin instructing the sheriff to summon a jury to decide the simple question of whether he had been ejected unjustly and without the judgement of a court. If the answer was yes, the sheriff was obliged to reinstate him. One or two observations need to be made about this and the other possessory assizes, like Mort d'Ancestor. First, they asked the jury to decide not a question of right, only one of fact: had the plaintiff been disseised or not? That made for speedy settlement of the case. Secondly, these writs were obtainable from the king and could be heard only in his courts. The effect was to attract before the king's justices a vast and increasing volume of business which would once have been heard in the honorial courts. If Henry II did not set out intentionally to undermine feudal justice, he made the superiority of royal justice so apparent that the honorial courts of the tenants-

in-chief went into a slow but definite decline. Thirdly, the royal courts were only open to men of free birth. Those who were unfree, the villeins as they were known, were confined to litigating in the court of their lord, which usually meant the manorial court.

The enormous popularity of these new-fangled assizes gave Henry II the chance to carry out a policy of judicial centralization. This he did by reviving Henry I's policy of sending out the royal justices on periodic visitations, known from a corruption of the Latin word 'iter' as 'eyres' (q.v.). From 1166 until their cessation in the early fourteenth century the eyres were the most dramatic manifestation of the king's judicial omnipotence, welcomed at first for their success in deterring the violent criminals, but later resented for the element of fiscal extortion that entered into their work. By the later thirteenth century we find county communities paying the king in order *not* to be visited by the eyre justices.

The final breakdown of the eyre in the 1320s, though a setback, was not necessarily a blow to the judicial and administrative power of the Crown because other courts were ready to step into the breach. For a start there were the twin courts of Common Pleas and King's Bench into which the former 'curia regis' (king's court) had been divided in 1234. In the fourteenth century King's Bench, though normally based at Westminster, undertook periodic visitations of the shires in much the same way as the eyre justices once had. There were also the commissions of oyer and terminer which could empower one or two of the king's justices with a few laymen to hear and determine a specific case. And finally we have the rise of the keepers of the peace, or the justices of the peace as they became in

1361, when they acquired the power to pass judgement on, and not just to receive, the indictments brought before them. It was the bench of J.P.s which ended up succeeding to the position the shire court had once occupied as the centre of social, political and judicial life in the county. Its quarterly sessions became a major local event.

Having sketched in outline the historical evolution of the English legal system, let us now see how it would have worked in practice. What would have happened to a malefactor suspected, let us say, of larceny in the reign of Edward III (1327–77)? Had he been apprehended in the act, and the coroner (q.v.) called in, the case would have been straightforward. But let us suppose that he escaped in possession of stolen goods, and was pursued in vain by the local constable after the hue and cry had been raised. A number of courses then lay open. The plaintiff could, if he or she wished, proceed by way of appeal (q.v.), which entitled him formally to accuse the suspect in the county court according to certain precisely regulated rules and then offer to support the charge by combat. In fact very few appeals ended in a duel, for there were procedures which allowed the issue to be decided by an inquest jury or terminated by out-of-court settlement. Though appeals were still being heard at the end of the middle ages, it became more common to proceed by way of indictment. Our offender, suspected of the crime either because he had been witnessed in the act or because he was a notorious local malefactor, would have been named either by the hundred jury next time the sheriff made his tourn of the hundred courts or by the keepers of the peace. All medieval crimes fell into the two broad categories of felony and trespass,

and under which heading a case of larceny came depended very much on the preference of the jurors. If indicted of a plea of trespass, our malefactor would probably have been summoned to appear before the shire court at an appointed date. Had he been caught in the act, the sheriff could detain him in prison pending trial. But if he had been lucky enough to get away – and here was the main weakness in the system – there was no incentive for him to attend in court at all. Under normal circumstances a trial could not proceed in the absence of the accused. In that case the process of outlawry would be invoked, entailing the seizure of the accused's goods and chattels until such time as he did make an appearance in court.

If, on the other hand, it was felt that the case of larceny was serious enough to be considered a breach of the king's peace, then the indictment might well reach King's Bench for hearing before the justices in Westminster or in the shire concerned next time a visitation was undertaken. In the central courts, whether King's Bench or Common Pleas, the pleading would be undertaken by the sergeants-at-law. These were the men who would aspire in due course to become judges: the link between bench and bar which has endured to the present day was forged in the middle ages, probably before the mid-fourteenth century. The case was then put to the jury – the petty jury, to be precise, to distinguish it from the grand or indictment jury. This method of establishing the question of guilty or innocent gradually replaced the old-fashioned methods of trial by ordeal. But let us not suppose that medieval jurors were models of impartiality or that they were denied contact with the parties to the dispute as jurors are today. Quite the contrary. Both parties were expected to acquaint the jury with their version of events, to 'labour' them, in the language of the day – though not to offer them bribes.

When the jury returned to give their verdict, the accused could count himself distinctly unlucky if it was one of 'guilty'. So many notorious malefactors got away scot free that we are bound to ask why. One problem was that conviction for felony automatically carried the death penalty, and jurors would naturally be reluctant to condemn a man so long as even the slightest shadow of doubt remained. They had to feel sure that the evidence presented to them by the hundred jury was reliable. All too often it was not. As we know from complaints made in parliament, indictments were often brought maliciously, and jurors had to be on their guard against convicting innocent men. If the result was to allow guilty men to go free, then that was a price they were prepared to pay. Another problem was the ease with which those convicted could procure pardons from the king. Who would be willing to convict a notorious malefactor well placed at court, knowing full well that in a year or two he would be back, ready to wreak vengeance on those who had convicted him? By the fourteenth century there is an air of ineffectiveness surrounding the courts of common law. They were slow and cumbersome. Cases dragged on for so long that when they finally disappear from the records it is not because a verdict has been given but because the parties in desperation have opted to make an out-of-court settlement. The justices were known to be corrupt, even if they were not all of such ill-repute as Chief Justice Sir Richard Willoughby who was said to have sold the laws of England as if they were cows or oxen. What chance had a humble litigant of gaining impartial justice when the cards were so heavily stacked against him? Little enough to make him turn elsewhere for redress. In 1397, for example, Lewis and Alice Cardigan, who were claiming the manor of Ladbroke (Warks.), took their case before the King's Council on the grounds that they could not afford the cost of a long action and that to deny them justice because they were poor was against 'law and conscience'. An extension of the jurisdiction of the King's Council was one response to the inadequacy of the courts of common law in England in the late middle ages.

F. Pollock & F. W. Maitland, *The History of English Law*, Cambridge, 2nd ed., 2 vols., 1898; A. Harding, *The Law Courts of Medieval England*, Allen & Unwin, 1973.

JUSTICIAR For more than a century the justiciar was the highest officer in England under the Crown. The origins of the office are to be found in the early twelfth century when England and Normandy (q.v.), divided after 1087 between the sons of William the Conqueror (q.v.), were reunited by Henry I (q.v.). In the long period of internal peace that followed England had to accustom itself to the periodic absence of the king–duke in Normandy, and Normandy to his periodic absence in England. So how was government to be carried on if the king was away? In England Henry I solved the problem by delegating to someone who could act in his name. After about 1120 that person was Roger, bishop of Salisbury, who is generally reckoned as the first of our justiciars. It is not clear that a successor was appointed to Roger after his arrest by King Stephen (q.v.) in 1139, but when peace was restored by Henry II (q.v.) in the 1150s not one but two co-justiciars were appointed – Robert Beaumont, earl of Leicester, an erstwhile supporter of Stephen's, and Richard de Luci, a member of the knightly class. After Earl Robert's death in 1168, Richard served alone until his retirement ten years later. He was then succeeded by Ranulph Glanvill, the reputed author of the famous treatise on the laws of England.

So long as the king had to divide his time between his English and his continental dominions, a justiciar would continue to be needed. But when Normandy fell to the French in 1204, and the king was henceforth resident in England, the office became unnecessary. In 1234 it was allowed to lapse. After 1258 it experienced a brief revival, however, when Hugh Bigod was appointed by the baronial reformers to investigate the many complaints that were made against Henry III's government.

F. J. West, *The Justiciarship in England, 1066–1232*, Cambridge, 1966.

L

LANFRANC The partnership between William the Conqueror (q.v.) and Lanfranc was one of the most successful between any king and archbishop of Canterbury. Together they were responsible for making some important and long overdue reforms in the life of the English Church.

The first fairly definite date we have in Lanfranc's career is 1042, when he entered Bec as a mature scholar. That means he could have been born no later than the second decade of the century, say about 1010 at the earliest. His town of origin is known, even if his exact date of birth is not. He was the son of a 'lawman' of Pavia in northern Italy. How far the young Lanfranc followed in his father's footsteps professionally we cannot say, for in about 1030 he made a clean break with the past by crossing the Alps into France. He went from place to place until he reached Avranches in Normandy, where he settled down as a schoolmaster. Then in about 1042 he underwent a religious conversion, and joined Herluin and the band of monks who had recently founded the abbey of Bec. Three years later he became prior. Bec represented a new depature in the history of Norman monasticism. It had been founded by a retired knight who longed, like the Cistercians in a later generation, to return to the life of simplicity and seclusion from which he felt that the monks of his own day had strayed. But however strongly Lanfranc may have been attracted by the ascetic ideal, he also wanted to start teaching again, and he obtained Herluin's permission to open a school at the abbey. In the course of these years at Bec he acquired a formidable reputation as both a teacher and a scholar. In our eyes today he is overshadowed by the fame of his pupil

Anselm (q.v.). But we cannot ignore the word of those contemporaries to whom he was the brilliant star that God had given to lighten Europe's darkness.

It was in his closing years at Bec that Lanfranc became drawn into a celebrated dispute with his former master, Berengar of Tours, on the nature of Eucharist. Berengar had argued that the Bread and Wine were only symbols of Christ, and that they could not therefore be changed materially into the flesh and blood of His Body. Though the doctrine of transubstantiation had not yet been clearly formulated, Berengar's views and the force with which he propounded them caused sufficient alarm for him to be summoned to recant in 1059. He complied, but subsequently repudiated his oath, and went on debating the Eucharist. It was at this point that Lanfranc brought his powers to bear in the treatise, *The Body and Blood of the Lord*. The argument he put forward, that though their outward appearance remains the same, the Bread and Wine are converted in their being into the flesh and blood of Christ by ways beyond our comprehension, was to be regarded by his own and subsequent generations as the definitive, orthodox reply to Berengar.

By the time he had finished writing the book, in 1063, Lanfranc had been appointed first abbot of Duke William's new foundation of St Stephen's, Caen. There he spent the next seven years of his life, until summoned to England in 1070 to become archbishop of Canterbury. We are told that he only accepted with reluctance; be that as it may, he turned out to be one of the most outstanding holders of the chair of St Augustine. The key to his success lay in the harmonious relationship he enjoyed with his friend and patron, King William. As Professor Douglas has

written, their association was so close that it is always difficult to decide which of the two was actually initiating policy. This partnership flourished, we must remember, at just the very time when Pope Gregory VII (1073–85) was calling into question the very right of a lay ruler to intervene in the affairs of the Church. Lanfranc ignored some of the more radical demands of the pope, while showing in the reforms he made in the English Church that he was fully aware of the need to bring English usages into line with those in the rest of western Europe. He held three important synods, at Winchester in 1072 and 1076, and at London in 1075, at which measures were taken against such recurrent abuses as simony, clerical marriage and vagrant clerks and monks. As for the monasteries, Lanfranc was limited in his scope of action. The right of appointing bishops and senior abbots was one that the king chose to exercise himself, though no doubt only after consultation with his archbishop. Normans were of course appointed, among them Lanfranc's own nephew, Paul, to St Alban's. The archbishop's influence was felt most of all in two ways: in the letters he wrote to those who turned to him for advice, and in the Monastic Constitutions he composed for Canterbury Cathedral Priory, which were later adopted by at least nine other communities, including St Alban's, Durham and Westminster.

Lanfranc survived the Conqueror to die on 24 May 1089. For a man whose life, or later life at least, is so well known, Lanfranc still presents us with several problems of explanation. Why did he leave Pavia? Why did he then abandon his career as a teacher in favour of the monk's habit at Bec? How did he come to be such a close friend of Duke William? It is difficult to reconcile the young Lanfranc, the dialectician and wandering scholar, with the pragmatic statesman of later years. He remains a curiously elusive figure. The truth of the matter may be that, judging by his surviving work, he was never quite the profound scholar some of his pupils and contemporaries took him to be. His writings, though competent, are marked by a certain superficiality. And his policy as archbishop is characterized by an aloof detachment from the Gregorian reform movement that was to render his kind of personal solution to the problem of Church/State relations obsolete by the time of his death. Arguably his weaknesses as a scholar proved to be his strength as a politician.

M. Gibson, *Lanfranc of Bec*, Oxford, 1978.

LANGLAND, WILLIAM Virtually all that we know about this great fourteenth century poet is derived from the autobiographical passages in *Piers Plowman*, the poem that was his life's work. As a boy he was provided with some schooling in the Scriptures, at the expense, so he tells us, of his father and some friends. When these friends died, he was left without any patrons. He moved from the west Midlands to London, and there he sank into the clerical underworld, making such money as he could by singing Masses for the souls of the dead in St Paul's and other churches. He could hardly have risen above Minor Orders because on his own admission he kept a wife and daughter.

His experience in life no doubt led him to identify with the poor and downtrodden, whose sufferings he describes with such insight in *Piers Plowman*. The popularity which this poem enjoyed right down to the sixteenth century (by which time its dialect was found too difficult) is evidenced by the large number of manuscripts which have survived – no fewer than 51, in three different versions. The earliest, the so-called A-text, was composed in the 1360s. Langland was evidently dissatisfied with this because he rewrote it at greater length in the 1370s in the form we know as the B-text. He then subjected it to further revision, so as to achieve clarification of the main theme, in the C-text of *c.* 1387. The poetic form that Langland adopted was alliterative verse. Relying for its effect on the repetition of the initial letter or syllable of a number of words in the line, this was a favourite literary form of the Anglo-Saxons, kept alive in northern and western England in the years after the Conquest to blossom forth again in the fourteenth century (q.v., LANGUAGE). Though it would have been regarded as old-fashioned by a courtly poet like Chaucer (q.v.), alliteration provided a perfect vehicle of expression for Langland's great allegory.

Structurally the poem falls into two halves, 'The Vision of Piers the Ploughman', comprising the first seven books or 'passus' of the B-text, and 'The Vision of Do-Well, Do-Better and Do-Best', comprising the last thirteen. The allegory is described and interpreted by Langland's persona, who falls asleep one May morning on the Malvern Hills, and dreams of a plain thronged with people going about their worldly business. After the allegorical figure of Lady Mead has been introduced, to symbolize the corruption of society caused by love of money, Reason calls on the people to begin the quest for Truth. Piers speaks up, and offers to guide the people to the Mansion of Truth. As remission for his sins, he is given a pardon by Truth, but finds himself tricked by its promise of salvation only to those who do well. Piers now disappears from the poem, and the dreamer begins the long search for Do-Well. Two friars suggest that he should turn to Thought and Intelligence, but their answers proving unsatisfactory he consults instead the representatives of Learning, Study, Clergy and Scripture. The poem approaches its climax in the Founding of the Holy Church on earth, but the dreamer falls asleep in the middle of the Mass and sees the Holy Ghost equipping Piers to establish a Christian society. The conclusion finds Conscience still searching for Truth, personified by Piers the Plowman, just as humans are still searching for the religious meaning that lies behind their lives.

Piers Plowman does not make easy reading. It requires perseverance, but if we make the effort we are rewarded by a poem rich in satire, humour and imagery. For the historian it is valuable for the author's comments on contemporary grievances. Langland is critical equally of the papal taxers, the friars and the cardinals. Yet he does not descend into heresy. It is significant that he is as remote from the eucharistic beliefs of the Lollards (q.v.) as he is from the courtly circles of Geoffrey Chaucer.

W. Langland, *Piers the Ploughman*, ed. F. Goodridge, Penguin, 1959.

LANGTON, STEPHEN If he was chiefly known in the middle ages as a preacher and Biblical commentator, and to a lesser extent as a theologian, Langton is remembered today more for the part he played in the political struggles of John's reign.

Such knowledge as we have of his parentage and early years was put together half a century ago by his biographer, Sir Maurice Powicke. Stephen was in all probability the son of Henry Langton of Langton-by-Wragby (Lincs.). In that case he would have been born in about 1165. We hear nothing of him until his arrival at the schools in Paris. There he studied, and later lectured on Theology. His reputation was such that in 1206 Pope Innocent III summoned him to Rome to become a cardinal. He had hardly been at the Curia for more than a few months, when at the pope's initiative he was chosen by the monks of Canterbury to be their next archbishop. King John (q.v.), however, had other ideas. He wanted the see to go to his faithful adviser, John de Gray, bishop of Norwich. There was a straight conflict of interest here, and neither party was prepared to give way. When John refused to allow Langton into the country, Innocent retaliated by imposing an Interdict.

The new archbishop, like Becket before him, spent his years of exile at the abbey of Pontigny in France. John was quite content to hold out so long as the pope was acting in isolation. But in 1213 a papal sentence of deposition was passed against him, the execution of which was entrusted to King Philip of France. An alliance between France and the papacy was too dangerous to contemplate. So John, by one of the remarkable *volte-faces* of which he was capable, gave in and allowed Langton to enter England.

On his return in July 1213 Langton tried to heal the wounds that had been opened over the previous five years. But it was difficult. Quite apart from the problems raised by lifting the Interdict, the baronial movement against the king was gathering such strength that it was bringing the country to the brink of civil war. John was forced to come to terms – those terms being embodied in Magna Carta (q.v.). Langton now had to choose between his conscience and his duty of obedience to the papacy. In the eyes of Innocent III the barons were rebelling against a king who since his submission had become a vassal of the Church, and moreover a crusader. But Langton was on the spot. He could see what John was really like. By the autumn of 1215 he found himself at such variance with the declared policy of the pope that he was suspended from office. He went to plead his case in Rome, and in due course obtained the revocation of the sentence on condition of his staying away from England. He was not able to return to his see until the restoration of peace in 1218.

In the closing years of his life Langton immersed himself in the day-to-day affairs of the Church, to which through force of circumstances he had been able to devote little time in the past. In 1222 he called a Council of the English Church at Osney Abbey, Oxford, to discuss the application in this country of the important decrees passed at the Fourth Lateran Council, held at Rome seven years before in 1215. If historians today are inclined to question the effectiveness of the constitutions passed at this and later Councils, there is no need, however, to doubt the sincerity of Langton's personal commitment to the cause of reform. He died on 9 July 1228 at his manor of Slindon (Sussex), and was buried in Canterbury Cathedral.

F. M. Powicke, *Stephen Langton*, London, 1928, repr., 1965.

LANGUAGE AND LITERA-TURE Whether we are interested in the formation of the English language or in the literature of which it was the medium of expression, few periods have a stronger claim on our attention than the middle ages.

England has enjoyed a long tradition of writing in the vernacular. The earliest surviving fragment of poetry we have comes from as far back as the seventh century. It is the song of Caedmon of Whitby which Bede preserved in his *Ecclesiastical History*. The language in which it is written is a Northumbrian dialect of 'Old English' (O.E.). Not surprisingly, when we remember where the Anglo-Saxons came from, O.E. bore strong similarities to German. It was what we call an inflected language. In other words, it identified the relationship of one word to another not by its position in the sentence but by use of case-endings. Likewise it employed gender, and required each adjective to agree with the noun it qualified. In the tenth and early eleventh centuries the coming of the Vikings to eastern and northern England added a distinctly Scandinavian flavour to the vernacular spoken in those parts of the country. But as Alfred and the Wessex kings gradually extended their rule into Danish England, so they took with them their own dialect of the O.E. tongue. It is that dialect which became the language of government in the century or more before the Conquest.

Literature at the end of the O.E. period was either heroic or religious – concerned, that is, with celebrating noble feats of arms or with imparting Christian beliefs. For poetic effects the Anglo-Saxon writers, from Caedmon on, relied on alliteration, or the repetition of a letter or set of letters usually at the start of each word. The following lines, taken from the *Song of the Battle of Maldon*, written soon after the event in the 990s, illustrates the point well:

Thaer geflymed weard
Nordmanna brego, nede gebaeded
to lides stefne lytle weorode;
cread cnear on flot, cing ut gewet
on fealone flod, feorh generede
(There the leader of the Northmen was put
to flight, driven by necessity to the prow of
the boat with a small troop; the galley
hastened to sea, the king went out on the
dark sea, (and) saved his life.)

Each line was broken in the middle by a caesura, the two halves being held together by the use of alliteration. In other words, the effect was created not, as we would expect today, by rhyming sounds at the end of each line but by the repetition of stress within the line or group of lines. This absence of rhyme makes the distinction between prose and poetry much less clear in O.E. literature than in modern. Tenth and eleventh century writers like Aelfric and Wulfstan relied on alliteration so much in their sermons that it is difficult for modern editors to know whether to print their texts in verse or prose!

The Norman Conquest dealt a savage blow to O.E. The linguistic position in England after 1066 became more complex than in any other country in western Europe. The Norman invaders made their own tongue (a version of French developed on English soil) the language of polite society and Latin the language of government. The kings themselves spoke mainly French until the fourteenth century. O.E., once a medium for both business and literature, was condemned to a long period of cultural eclipse from which it was only to emerge about three centuries later in the form we know as Middle English (M.E.).

Within half a century of the Conquest alliterative poetry as it had been composed in the O.E. period was a dying art. But that is not to say that it had died out completely. We cannot explain the great alliterative revival of the fourteenth century without supposing that an informal tradition of such writing survived during the centuries after 1066. And survive it did, though in a form much modified by French and other influences. For example, there was Layamon's *Brut*, an isolated piece of historical writing in vernacular alliteration composed by a priest of Areley King's (Worcs.) in or around 1200. Telling the history of Britain from the time of the supposed landing here of Brutus (hence the title), a descendant of Aeneas, it was the only important vernacular chronicle written in the early M.E. period (c. 1100–c. 1300). And from the literary point of view it is important for marking a transition between old-fashioned alliteration and the new, rhymed verse which was coming in from France.

We depend, of course, for our knowledge of the vernacular literature of this period on the extant manuscripts, which in their uneven incidence of survival may give a sadly incomplete or distorted view of what people read. If we go solely by the number of surviving manuscripts we are left in no doubt that devotional literature commanded the largest audience. That may well be because it was mainly sermons and religious treatises that were written down. Short popular songs and poems which a baron heard in his great hall would be transmitted orally, thus reducing their chances of survival. So when we look at the literature which has come down to us from the early M.E. period, we must not be surprised to find how much of it is religious in content. Judging from the number of manuscripts which have survived, one of the most popular works was the *Ancren Riwle* (Anchoresses' Rule). Written originally in about 1200 by an unknown author for the guidance of three well-born young ladies who had become anchoresses, this attractive piece was revised between about 1215 and 1222 for the benefit of a wider community in the form known as the *Ancrene Wisse*. This is written in a West Midlands dialect, a point of some significance remembering that Layamon, author of the Brut, and William Langland (q.v.) came from that part of England too. Internal evidence suggests that it may have been composed by a canon of Wigmore Abbey for the benefit of one or other of the two groups of nuns who were living nearby and to whom he probably acted as confessor. As a devotional manual the *Ancrene Wisse* acquired a wide circulation, and was read well into the fifteenth century. It was matched in popularity in the fourteenth century by the works of the mystic writers, of whom the most important was Richard Rolle of Hampole (Yorks.), who died in 1349. He wrote several prose tracts in his native Yorkshire dialect, which for their quality and style have earned him a justified place in the history of English prose and religious thought.

Before looking at the revival of alliterative poetry in the fourteenth century, we must first of all go back and see how far the form and content of poetry had changed in the meantime. For changed it had. The romance had supplanted the epic. In that simple disarming sentence is comprehended the most profound shift in ideas to have occurred between the collapse of the Ancient World and the rise of the Romantic movement. Gone were the great epics, gone were the heroic sagas of the Germanic peoples; in their place came the rhymed lyrics celebrating courtesy and love. What lay behind this new way of

looking at the world is hard to say, but we are surely justified in associating it with that general cultural rebirth known to historians as the 'Twelfth Century Renaissance'. The first stirrings of the new mood can be heard in Provence and Aquitaine in the late eleventh century, when the troubadours began composing their love lyrics. They emphasized the gentler side of life. Their knights did not engage in blood feuds or slaying dragons; they performed valorous deeds for their ladies. The character and conventions of this poetry varied according to time and place, and from our point of view in tracing English literary history it is probably the longer romances inspired by the legend of King Arthur (q.v.) which matter most.

That Arthur should have occupied such a prominent position in English literature right down to the age of Tennyson was largely due to Geoffrey of Monmouth (q.v.), who first presented the legendary sixth century king to a medieval audience in the 1130s. In the course of time, as the legends became embroidered, the emphasis passed from the king himself to the knights – the Knights of the Round Table as they were later known – whose exploits were the subject of celebration in their own right. The greatest M.E. poem deriving from this tradition is *Sir Gawayne and the Green Knight*, written in c. 1370 in a north-west Midlands dialect. It tells of the arrival in King Arthur's hall of the Green Knight, clad in green armour, with green hair and astride a green horse. He challenges any of King Arthur's knights to attack him with his huge axe – a challenge accepted by Sir Gawayne who strikes off his head. Little good does it do him because the Green Knight picks up his head and rides off, challenging Gawayne to meet him in a year's time at the Green

Chapel. The rest of the poem describes Gawayne's journey, his encounter with the Green Knight and his failure in a chastity test. The poem has preserved the secret of its inner meaning as successfully as its author has preserved his anonymity. All that we can say about this undoubedly inspired man is that he also wrote *Pearl*, *Patience* and *Cleanness*, three poems so-called from their opening words which are found with *Sir Gawayne* in the same manuscript. Although these poems are inspired by the alliterative revival of the fourteenth century, they experiment in breaking the monotony of the long line by combining rhymed and alliterative verse: in the case of *Sir Gawayne*, for example, the long alliterative lines are followed by a sequence of five short ones, rhyming 'ababa'.

The most celebrated poem of this revival is of course Langland's *Piers Plowman*, a great allegory which stands comparison with *The Pilgrim's Progress*. Once again there is a connection with the west Midlands. The setting is the Malvern Hills, where the poet falls asleep and dreams of Piers's quest for truth. After the Arthurian romances, *Piers Plowman* brings us down to earth with a bump. No longer are we with the knights and damsels at court but with the common people. *Piers Plowman* is a work of social satire, but if it shows sympathy with the labouring folk it is devoid of sentimentality because Langland (q.v.) is prepared to criticize all ranks of society. *Piers Plowman* was one of the most popular of all medieval poems, not least with John Ball and the peasant rebels who quoted it in 1381.

The author of *Sir Gawayne and the Green Knight* is unknown, and William Langland remains a shadowy figure. It is a different matter, however, when we come to consider Geoffrey Chaucer (q.v.). He is often regarded as the first English poet. To say that, as we have seen, would be misleading. But with Chaucer we are clearly moving into a very different world, where the poet is writing not so much for a didactic purpose, but partly for pleasure and partly in response to the demands of his patron. If Chaucer is not the first English poet, he is at least the first 'courtly maker'. *The Canterbury Tales* is his most ambitious work, indeed too ambitious because it was left unfinished. However, it was preceded by a number of earlier poems of which *The Book of the Duchess*, *Troilus and Cressida* and *The House of Fame* are the most important.

What is the place of Chaucer in the history of English literature? In a sense it is a curiously isolated one. As several writers have commented, the two great poets of the age – Chaucer and Langland – contemporaries and both at some time residents of London, seem to have had no knowledge of each other's work. They inhabited different worlds not only socially but intellectually. Although a poet who was to enjoy a long popularity, Langland was himself old-fashioned to the extent that in England if not in Scotland he was among the last of the long line of alliterative poets. Chaucer, on the other hand, stands at the head of a line of versifiers stretching down to Wyatt and the earl of Surrey in Tudor England. All the same, he remains in a class by himself. John Gower (c. 1330–1408), a friend of his, was a competent enough though not brilliant poet who could write equally well in English, French or Latin – the last English author of any note to be able to do so – and he included some valuable political comment in his work. In the next generation or two the poets were of much lower calibre. There was Thomas

Hoccleve (*c.* 1368– *c.* 1450), a clerk in the Privy Seal Office who regarded himself as a disciple of Chaucer. His main work *The Regement of Princes*, was addressed to the future Henry V (q.v.), and written in an easy, rather slipshod style that is at least devoid of the scholarly pretence that besets John Lydgate (*c.* 1370–1452). A monk of Bury St Edmund's, Lydgate was a prolific poet whose popularity is attested by the patronage he received from noblemen like Humphrey, duke of Gloucester (q.v.) and even from Henry VI himself (q.v.). To the modern reader, however he seems terribly long-winded. It must have been after ploughing through his main work, *The Troy Book*, a history of the Trojan Wars in no fewer than 29,626 lines, that Joseph Ritson, a nineteenth century critic, spoke of 'this voluminous, prosaick and driveling monk'. The fifteenth century certainly produced no Brahms to follow Chaucer's Beethoven. But by way of compensation it did succeed in bringing the Arthurian legends to a fitting climax in Sir Thomas Malory's *Morte d'Arthur* (q.v. MALORY). A great work of prose, this is the fullest exposition of the Arthurian romances in the middle ages, and its appeal was recognized by Caxton (q.v.) who printed it in 1485.

Until the arrival of printing, which had the effect of introducing standardization, great variety was to be found in M.E. spelling and vocabulary. Certainly, Chaucer had succeeded in making M.E. a respectable language of literature once more, but that is not to say that he found it, as it were, ready for use, because the vocabulary was as yet incomplete. Every time M.E. could not supply him with the word he needed, he had to borrow one from French or Latin. It has been calculated that of the 4,000 words from Romance languages found in Chaucer, as many as a thousand had not appeared in any English text before. We have to bear in mind, of course, the possibility that a number of these words might have passed some time before into spoken use, or even into written use in texts that have not survived. But the most recent work that has been done in this field goes to confirm that French loan-words passed into the vernacular later rather than earlier in the M.E. period. French and English lived alongside each other for a long time, and the former only began to influence the latter in terms of vocabulary when its dominance was beginning to wane.

The process by which the upper classes began speaking English once again is one that by its very nature is ill-charted. What people read is attested by written evidence, what people said is not. If the records of the royal government are anything to go by, the change-over came quite late. Henry V (1413–22) was the first of our kings since the Conquest to use the vernacular as the everyday language of government. But an indication that English had come to prevail over French in polite speech a lot earlier is given by a famous passage which John Trevisa interpolated into his translation of Higden's *Polychronicon*:

For Johan Cornwal, a mayster of gramere, chayngede ye lore in gramerscole and construccion of Freynsch into Englysch; and Richard Pencrych lurnede that manere techyng of hym, and other men of Pencrych, so that now, the yer of oure Lord a thousand threehondred foure score and fyve (1385), of the secunde kyng Richard after the Conquest nyne, in al the gramerscoles of Engelond childern leveth Frensch, and construeth and lurneth an Englysch. . . .

In 1385, then, it was general for schoolchildren to translate from Latin into English, not French. It is interesting to find as well that a couple of decades earlier in 1362 a statute was passed permitting the use of English in courts of law; and from *c.* 1370 we have the first surviving monumental inscription in English, on a brass to John the Smith at Brightwell Baldwin (Oxon.) In the keeping of records, particularly those of the Crown, the struggle was not only between English and French, as it was in speech and informal writing, but also between English and Latin. The weight of bureaucratic inertia ensured of course that in this quarter change would come much later than elsewhere, but a turning point was reached in the reign of Henry VI (1422–61). The main government offices started using English in the 1420s, and in the next decade English petitions started creeping into the official roll of parliamentary proceedings.

The English language as it re-emerged in the later fourteenth century was very different from the form spoken by the Anglo-Saxons. Before the Conquest, as we have seen, it was the Wessex dialect which was winning general recognition. But when English became respectable again in the later fourteenth century, it was a Midland dialect which triumphed. We have to bear in mind that in the middle ages, as indeed in modern Chinese society, the written and spoken forms of the language did not necessarily coincide. So although modern English is based on a uniform written standard which emerged towards the end of the middle ages in London, the dialectal forms from which that standard evolved were transmitted by the spoken word. Until the mid-fourteenth century it was the East Anglian dialect which exerted greatest influence on English as spoken in the capital. After the mid-fourteenth century it was the dialect of the east Midland counties of

Northamptonshire, Huntingdonshire and Cambridgeshire. In the age of Chaucer, however, we still find wide variations in spelling, indicating that written uniformity had not yet been achieved. What completed the process was the adoption in the 1430s by the scribes in the king's Chancery of a form of the language, combining both London and east Midland forms, that was to become the basis of modern English. Immigration into the capital must have had something to do with this evolution.

Explaining how the Midland, as opposed to any other, dialect came to achieve this supremacy is one question. Explaining why French gave way to English in the first place is quite another. To answer that we need surely do no more than look to the upsurge of nationalism occasioned by the outbreak of the Hundred Years War (q.v.) with France in the 1330s and encouraged by such victories as Crecy (q.v.) and Poitiers (q.v.).

See also, MISTERY PLAYS.

W. P. Ker, *English Literature: Medieval*, Home University Library, London, 1932; *Fourteenth Century Verse & Prose*, ed. K. Sisam, Oxford, 1921, repr. 1970; M. L. Samuels, 'Some applications of M. E. Dialectology', *English Studies*, 44 (1963).

LITURGY By liturgy we mean the forms of worship used in the Church. In the pre-Reformation world these forms were common to all the countries of western Europe, comprising as they did a single Christian community dependent on the authority of the pope in Rome. Yet there was seemingly infinite scope for local variation. The rites practised in England differed from those in Norway and Spain, and within England the rites practised at, say, Salisbury differed from those at York or Hereford. Eventually it was the Salisbury arrangements – what we know as the Use of Sarum – that triumphed over all the others and came to be adopted in cathedrals and parish churches as far apart as Glasgow and St David's.

The liturgical programme used in the cathedrals and secular churches followed the routine mapped out many centuries before by the Benedictine monks (q.v., MONASTICISM). In other words, the clergy were committed each day to celebrating High Mass and to saying the seven canonical offices, or 'hours' as they were known – Matins, Lauds, Prime, Terce, Sext, Nones and Compline. At Lincoln in 1400 High Mass was celebrated at 10 a.m. and Evensong at 3 in the afternoon. In this daily ritual the Mass obviously occupied a position of especial importance. In fact it came to be viewed with ever greater respect by the faithful as the middle ages wore on, the more so after the pronouncement of the doctrine of transubstantiation at the Fourth Lateran Council in 1215 had lent weight to the sacredness and mystery of the service. The Mass, so men believed, was a re-enactment of Christ's supreme sacrifice for the purpose of obtaining forgiveness of sins. What better way could there be of attracting the mercy of the deity than by offering his Son 'for the well-being of the living and for the repose of the dead'? For that reason every testator in the fourteenth and fifteenth centuries who could afford it provided in his will for the celebration of soul-masses regularly on the anniversary of his death in the hope of curtailing the trials of Purgatory. Private masses of this sort would be sung by chantry (q.v.) priests at side altars in churches or in chapels built specially for the purpose like those we can see today in Winchester Cathedral. As belief in the potency of the Mass intensified, so it seems that churchgoers received the sacrament less often. This was because communion was administered only after the faithful had confessed their sins to the priest, an operation so thorough that it was normally undergone but once a year, before Easter. That in turn meant that most people communicated no more than once a year. It may also be the increasing reverence shown towards the Host that explains why the Church slowly abandoned administering the sacrament in both kinds. Until the twelfth century the congregation had been given both the Bread and the Wine. Thereafter it was normal to offer only the Bread, concealing beneath it the flesh of Christ.

High Mass on Sunday, then as now, would have been the best attended service of the week. The faithful were of course encouraged to attend the other services, particularly Matins, but such evidence as we have suggests that empty churches were not a uniquely mid-twentieth century phenomenon. In 1291, for example, Archbishop Pecham wrote to his Archdeacon at Canterbury complaining that Sunday was being poorly observed and urging him to persuade more people to go to Church. And that was Sunday! As for the daily offices, a priest would hardly expect anyone to turn up. He might say Prime and Terce alone before the congregation arrived for Mass, and then Nones and Sext after they had gone.

Nowadays we are used to having the liturgy conveniently available within the confines of a single volume like the Church of England's Book of Common Prayer. Thanks to the luxuriant growth over the years of the Roman liturgy, however, no such remarkable feat of compression was possible in the middle ages. There were just too many variations in the services, too many accretions and additions. The problem was solved in a common-sense fashion by providing not one but a number of books, one for each service or part of the service.

In due course a great cathedral would acquire in its library quite a collection of these service books, many of them masterpieces of the illuminator's art. A parish church, on the other hand, would make do with far fewer. Which were the most important of these books for the purposes of daily worship? Which were the ones that every church would need? To start with, there was the Missal, or Mass book. Setting out as it did all the variations of the service required for Sundays, festivals and saints' days this was likely to be a truly bulky volume, one to keep on the altar rather than to carry around. In the greater churches and cathedrals, where the ritual was at its most elaborate, the Missal would be supplemented by other books containing specialized parts of the rite. For example, the deacon would have a Gospel Book from which he would read a passage appropriate for the day of the year, the sub-deacon an Epistle Book, containing the New Testament epistles, and the choir the Grail or Gradual, setting out the music. Apart from the Mass, there were a number of other sacramental services. For these a quite separate book was provided, known as the Manual and containing the offices of baptism, marriage, visitation of the sick and burial of the dead. This had to be a volume small enough for the parson to carry around, because he would need to take it when, for example, going to a house to administer the last rites to a dying parishioner.

As the liturgy grew more complex, the advantages became clear of compiling an abbreviated edition of the daily hours (Matins, Lauds, Prime, Terce, Sext, None, Compline), the main prayers and collects. Though referred to as the Breviary, this book might well be far from brief. A blockbuster edition could extend to four volumes, one for each season of the year, and include such optional extras as the *placebo* and the *dirige*, respectively the evening and morning offices for the dead. We should note in passing as well that two of the service-books would be used not only by the clergy but by lay-folk too. These were the Psalter and the Book of Hours. The former brought together all the Old Testament psalms in a form convenient for private devotion. The latter was the most popular of all medieval devotional books, as evidenced by the large numbers that were written for private patrons. Its contents included the Hours of the Blessed Virgin, the seven Penitential Psalms, the fifteen Gradual Psalms, the Litany, the *placebo* and *dirige* and the commendations. The office in honour of the Blessed Virgin reflected the enormous popularity that her cult enjoyed in medieval England – a cult reflected as well in the building of Lady Chapels at the eastern end of churches and cathedrals.

The richness of the medieval liturgy can be sensed in some measure by looking at the beautiful service books that have come down to us – for example, the St Omer Psalter and the Winchester Bible (plates 19, 21). Not all of them, however, would have been so richly ornamented. A Breviary used in a rural parish church would have matched the humility of its surroundings. Indeed, we must remember that, if the liturgy meant something to the literate and the educated, it may have meant little or nothing to the bulk of the congregation. If they were lucky enough to be able to see what was happening in the chancel, they would have been luckier still actually to hear it, bearing in mind that so much of the service was whispered by the celebrant or spoken *sotto voce* – and in Latin, of course. The effect may well have been principally one of mystery and symbolism, reinforced by the visual message conveyed, at least to the more sensitive of the congregation, by sculpture (q.v.), painting (q.v.), music (q.v.) and stained glass (q.v.).

J. C. Dickinson, *An Ecclesiastical History of England: the Late Middle Ages*, London, 1979; C. Wordsworth & H. Littlehales, *The Old Service Books of the English Church*, London, 1904.

LOLLARDY The fourteenth Century Oxford theologian, John Wycliffe (q.v.), inspired a movement of disciples known as the Lollards. This nickname was probably derived from the Dutch 'lollaerd', meaning someone who mumbled his prayers; but it had the advantage too, from the point of view of their detractors, of sounding conveniently like the English 'loller', a loafer or idler.

The Lollards comprised three main groups of people, each of whom may have had little or no contact with any of the others. To begin with, there were Wycliffe's immediate followers at Oxford. Among them could be numbered men like Philip Repton, Nicholas Hereford and John Aston, all faithful to the master so long as he was in Oxford, but forced to reconsider their positions once he had left. The effect of Archbishop Courtenay's visitation of the University in 1382 was to produce submissions from Repton and Aston

that autumn, and from Hereford a few years later in 1391. Lollardy's link with the academic community at Oxford was largely broken.

The second group was never brought into the open by the Church. There were the handful of knights at the court of Richard II (q.v.) whom the chroniclers accused of harbouring Lollard sympathies. That such allegations were not the product of idle gossip is proved by evidence from other sources which testifies to their heretical beliefs. Three of the knights, for example, made wills which contain Lollard characteristics like the prohibition of funerary pomp and vehement contempt for bodily flesh. How long these well-placed knights were able to escape censure is hard to say, but there is nothing to suggest that their sympathies ever brought them into open collision with the Church.

The third group were not so fortunate. They were the humbler followers who Lollardy attracted and on whom the mantle of Wycliffe's faith descended, once his disciples in the university had been broken or dispersed. Among them were men like William Swinderby, nicknamed William the Hermit, an unbeneficed preacher from Leicester whose activities across central and western England continued to make him an embarrassment to the authorities until his final disappearance into Wales in 1392. It was people like Swinderby who seem to have been most attracted by the puritanical, evangelical streak in Lollardy. Nor were they always clerks. The passage of Lollard beliefs owed as much to the laymen, often literate laymen, who would meet in small groups or congregations to discuss the Bible, which had so recently been made available to them in its entirety in English. Ill-educated these sympathisers may have been, but they had that insatiable appetite for first-hand knowledge of the scriptures which was to be shared by the Puritans in the seventeenth century.

This characteristic of the Lollards introduces us to one of the central tenets of their philosophy. They respected the Bible as the sole authority for the Christian religion. It followed that the Vulgate should be made available to all in the vernacular. At first the Church was slow to react, because partial translations had been made before, at the initiative of princes and members of the nobility, without repercussion. The Lollards themselves had made two translations before the clampdown came in 1407. By then the implications for the Church of making the Bible available to all had become apparent. Once the Scriptures were respected as the sole source of authority, the mediatory role of the priest was bound to be called into question. The next demand would be to get rid of the clergy altogether and to redistribute their wealth among the people. But there was more to Lollardy than just old-fashioned anti-clericalism. It was anti-sacramental, and openly sceptical towards Catholic teaching on the doctrine of transubstantiation. And last but not least it drew on a strong fund of anti-papalism: in Lollard epistemology the Bishop of Rome was denounced as anti-Christ.

Unaccustomed to coping with heresies, the English Church was at first slow to react to this novel phenomenon. A vigorous example was set by Archbishop Courtenay in 1382 in reimposing orthodoxy at Wycliffe's own university of Oxford, but the other bishops were slower in stirring themselves into action. The earliest Lollards, like Hereford and Aston, were therefore permitted considerable freedom of action and expression before the long arm of the ecclesiastical law finally began to catch up with them in the later 1380s. The problem then that exercised the minds of the authorities was the absence of any penalty that would deter others from straying along the path to heresy. How could the Church's armoury be re-inforced? The remedy was provided in the reign of Henry IV (q.v.) in 1401 when burning was for the first time in England made the penalty for obdurate heretics.

In the event the fires were only kindled twice in the reign of Henry IV. Lollardy by then was a nuisance rather than a serious threat, not so much a nation-wide movement of dissent as a discredited rag-bag of doctrines shared by scattered communities of believers. Still, it retained sufficient strength to mount an organized rebellion against Henry V (q.v.) in 1414. The ringleader was Sir John Oldcastle, a Herefordshire knight who wanted to replace the house of Lancaster with a Lollard state. He planned to kidnap the king and his brothers and occupy London, but the government, evidently forewarned, experienced no trouble in rounding up the motley army of rebels that converged on St Giles's Fields on the night of 9–10 January 1414. That Oldcastle was able to assemble any rebel gathering at all nevertheless implies that local congregations were able to keep in touch with each other, perhaps through the network of Lollard preachers. He drew little support from his own county of Hereford, rather surprisingly in view of William Swinderby's missions there, but perhaps it was too far for sympathisers to make their way to London. Bristol, on the other hand, still a good way from the capital, provided the largest single contingent of all. In eastern England there were again marked local disparities, with Essex providing generous support and Norfolk and Suffolk very little. In the Midland counties Lollardy drew strongest support from the towns, Leicester and Coventry for example.

These were roughly the localities that were to afford continued evidence of Lollard attachment for the rest of the fifteenth century. But there were smaller, more localized pockets as well. Indeed, Lollardy was something of a hydra-headed monster. As soon as it was suppressed in one area, it sprang up in another. In the Thames valley, for example, the Buckinghamshire Chilterns sheltered a colony of Lollards until 1414, thanks to the patronage of the Cheyne family; but once the heretics there had been stamped out, a new colony popped up south of the river in Berkshire. That Lollardy did live on in the fifteenth century in such areas as these can hardly be doubted, because recent research has thrown up so much evidence of prosecutions for heresy. In that case how far did the lingering influence of the Lollards shape the early stages of the English Reformation? The very least that we can say is that some of the essential doctrines of Protestantism had been anticipated a century-and-a-half earlier in the writings of John Wycliffe, and that the survival of Lollardy helped to prepare the ground for the reception of Lutheranism. But this is not to say that the work of Wycliffe and his disciples helped to advance the Reformation. Quite the contrary. Lollardy failed because it became proletarian. The Reformation succeeded because it was promoted by the king.

K. B. McFarlane, *John Wycliffe and the Beginnings of English Nonconformity*, London, 1952; J. A. F. Thomson, *The Later Lollards*, Oxford, 1965.

LONDON So long as our kings spent their lives on horseback, travelling from place to place, they had little need of a capital city. But as soon as government became so bureaucratic that they could no longer carry their records and account rolls around with them – and that time had come by the early thirteenth century – they had to settle down more or less in one place. The place they chose was Westminster. It was a natural choice. Just up the road was London, England's greatest city, and the only one that could compare in size with the great cities of the Continent, like Paris, Ghent or Florence. Estimates of London's population vary, but a figure of close on 50,000 before the Black Death (q.v.) would not be too wide of the mark.

The Romans were the first to appreciate the blessings that geography had bestowed on London. The city was equally accessible to all the great ports and cities of north-west Europe; it was the first point at which the Thames could be bridged; and it would be made the focus of England's road (q.v.) system. To the Romans may be attributed the building of the first London bridge, which was probably a wooden structure on a site a little to the east of the present one. It lasted until the 1170s when, according to the Waverley Abbey chronicler, Peter, vicar of St Mary, Colechurch, began rebuilding it in stone. This was the bridge that was ultimately to spawn the crowded superstructure of buildings so familiar to us from Hollar's engraving of 1647. At its southern end lay Southwark, never formally a part of London in the middle ages, but all the same a busy community in its own right. It boasted the Tabard Inn, whence Chaucer's (q.v.) pilgrims set off for Canterbury (q.v.).

Northwards the bridge led directly into the city. Though a large place, as we have seen, London was unusual among medieval towns in never having to enlarge its walls to accommodate a rising population. The line of the Roman fortifications, some two miles in length, fixed the city bounds for as long as it was necessary to have walls at all. At the south-east corner of the perimeter lay the great fortress built by William the Conqueror (q.v.) known as the Tower of London. It figures prominently in contemporary views of the Thames-side scene. But what above all else dominated the sky-line of the medieval city was the great cathedral of St Paul's, at 644ft the longest ever built in this country. Thanks once again to Hollar's engravings we can obtain a good idea of the appearance of Old St Paul's before its destruction. Inside the west door the view extended eastwards along the Norman nave, past the choir and lady chapel, rebuilt in the Decorated style between 1251 and 1312, towards the lovely rose window at the far end. On the south side of the nave lay the chapter house and cloister, rebuilt in the 1330s and among the earliest essays in the Perpendicular style of architecture. All that has gone. But, despite the damage wrought by the Great Fire, a good deal of medieval work survives among the churches of London. St Olave's, Hart St, St Helen's, Bishopsgate, and the priory church of St Bartholomew's, Smithfield, are three that have survived more or less intact. It goes without saying that London, like most medieval English towns, enjoyed a super-abundance of parish churches: by the thirteenth century there were at least a hundred, or one for every 3½ acres.

Being so populous and so close to the seat of government, London in the middle ages exercised a weighty influence on the affairs of state. In 1135 the citizens helped to secure the throne for Stephen. In 1141 they expelled his rival Matilda when she was within an ace of being crowned. In 1215 they welcomed the barons who had taken up arms against King John. But if the Londoners were capable of speaking with one voice at a time of national crisis, particularly when their own liberties were at risk, on other occasions they were torn apart by internal feuds and rivalries. There were the familiar struggles of rich and poor, rulers and ruled. But in the fourteenth century it was the ruling class itself that was divided. In Richard II's reign the victualling guilds, led by Nicholas Brembre, a grocer, tried to get a monopoly of the import of foodstuffs into the city. They were challenged by the non-victualling guilds led by John of Northampton, a draper, who whipped up popular agitation against his rivals. Brembre being a protege of the king, Northampton turned for support to his opponents. Although Northampton's cause was eventually to fail, he had his moment of satisfaction in 1388 when the Appellant earls, temporarily in the ascendant, despatched Brembre and other friends of Richard II to the executioners's block.

These events prompt a consideration of how London was governed in the middle ages. In the Norman period the most important officials were the two sheriffs, who were responsible for collecting the farm, or sum of money, that the city owed the king. The first major concession the citizens wrung from a reluctant monarchy in the reign of Henry I was that of choosing their own sheriffs and raising the money themselves. By the end of the twelfth century, however, civic aspirations had advanced very much further. In 1191 while Richard I was in the East, the Londoners created their city a 'commune', in other words, a self-governing community under a mayor. The mayor eventually superseded the sheriff as the most important official in the city, and his installation each year on October 28 provided the occasion for a great display of pageantry that has lasted to this day. Once elected, the mayor found himself presiding over an intricate structure of courts and councils that had been grafted onto the city's government one by one whenever it was found necessary. The oldest was the folkmoot, where outlawries (q.v.) were promulgated. Very likely nearly as old was the court of husting, which assembled in the Guildhall to hear pleas relating to land. The affairs of these assemblies were guided, if not managed, by the aldermen who formed an inner council of 24, one from each of the city's wards. These were the men who counted in medieval London, the charmed circle from whom most of the mayors were chosen. It was to counter this strong tendency towards oligarchy, so common in all medieval urban administrations, that the 'common council' was formed in the fourteenth century. Like the court of aldermen its members were elected by the wards, apart from a period of eight years between 1376 and 1384 when they were chosen by the crafts.

For administrative purposes Westminster, down the road, was never a part of the City of London. On the other hand, it naturally developed close social and commercial links with its mighty neighbour. The king was dependent on the city merchants for loans; and they were dependent on him for business. For that reason if no other they must have been glad when king and government settled down for good at the ramshackle palace between the Abbey and the Thames.

C. N. L. Brooke & G. Keir, *London 800–1216, The Making of a City,* London, 1975.

M

MAGNA CARTA   The Great Charter of 1215 is the most famous constitutional document to have come down to us from the middle ages, and justly so. It was the first written programme of political reform ever imposed on an English king by his subjects.

What drove them to taking such desperate measures? Here it is hard to separate Magna Carta from the myths that have grown up around the name of the king who was obliged to set his seal to it in June 1215 – King John (q.v.). In many ways King John was merely an unlucky prince who had to pay the price for what his predecessors had been doing. Magna Carta was the outcome of a crisis attributable as much to long- as to short-term causes.

The long-term cause of the Magna Carta crisis was quite simply the arbitrary nature of the government of Henry II (q.v.) and his sons. Indeed, we can go back further still, to find some of the demands of Magna Carta foreshadowed in the concessions which Henry I (q.v.) chose to make in 1100 in his coronation charter. The problem which faced the Norman and Angevin kings was that they had to resort to irregular and highly unpopular financial exactions in order to finance their policies. What they had at their disposal has been described as 'less a system of taxation than a system of plunder'. And so it was. The one source of national taxation (q.v.) which the Normans had inherited from the Saxons – the geld – was allowed to fall into disuse from the 1160s because its yield was so low. Consequently, kings became ever more reliant on the profits of justice (q.v.) and the lucrative but irregular sources of revenue we know as the 'incidents of feudalism' (q.v.). These included relief (paid by a son who succeeded to his father's lands), wardship (custody of lands during a minority) and aids (emergency taxes). The main disadvantage of these feudal revenues was that they fell not on all the king's subjects, as do modern taxes but only on those who held their land on feudal terms from the king – in other words, the tenants-in-chief, a group pretty well synonymous with the barons.

By the reign of Henry II the barons were well aware that they were being squeezed to the limit by the king. The pressure became still worse under his son Richard I (q.v.), when money had to be found to pay for the king's ransom. By the time of John the financial position of the crown had become almost impossible, because strong inflationary pressures had set in. Between about 1180 and John's death in 1216 prices rose at least threefold. Simply in order to stand still, therefore, John had to increase his money income proportionately. In fact, however, he needed to increase it more than proportionately in order to pay for the defence, and after its loss to the French in 1204, the attempted recovery of Normandy (q.v.), which was the largest demand on his pocket. Normandy had been joined to England ever since the Conquest in 1066. It did lasting

damage to John's reputation, therefore, that he should have been the king to lose it a century-and-a-half later. He subordinated everything to trying to recover it, and made financial demands to that end which might have been excusable had he met with success. In fact, however, he did not. Defeat abroad was inevitably accompanied by demands for reform at home.

Magna Carta as it was presented to John in June 1215 was not suddenly produced out of nowhere. It was the product of many months work by the barons. The first draft, known as the Unknown Charter, was probably formulated in the early months of 1215. It consisted of Henry I's coronation charter supplemented by a dozen new clauses. By June, however, events had moved so fast that the Unknown Charter had become outmoded, and a new document, known as the Articles of the Barons, was drawn up. This contained most of the essential clauses that were to be in Magna Carta and a few more extreme ones that were not, indicating that in the course of the next few weeks initial demands were watered down in order to produce a document on which moderate barons could agree too. Thus Magna Carta as we have it today – though King John would hardly have believed it – was not a document created by a group of hardline militants but a charter of liberties secured by a broadly based opposition movement. John was forced to subscribe to it because he had a civil war on his hands. At Brackley in April the barons had met to renounce homage to him, and in the following month they took London (q.v.). That was a fatal blow for John. By June, therefore, when he was staying at Windsor, he was obliged to negotiate. At that time the barons were based at Staines, and they chose to meet the king on the banks of the

Thames at Runnymede, simply because it was half-way. It is difficult to reconstruct exactly what happened there, but it seems likely that there were several encounters between the two sides. At the first, on June 10, broad agreement was reached on the basis of the Articles of the Barons; at the second, on June 15, further discussion very likely produced the document we know as Magna Carta; and at the third, on June 19, a firm peace was made and homage renewed. Thus King John certainly never signed anything at Runnymede; and he may not have sealed anything either.

What were the terms agreed at Runnymede and embodied in Magna Carta? To a modern reader the Charter may well come as a disappointment. It can hardly be seen as a medieval equivalent of the American Declaration of Independence. There are no grand-sounding Jeffersonian declarations of liberty. It is not a charter of liberty; it is a charter of liberties. The prominent part that financial oppression played in provoking the crisis is recognized in the large number of clauses limiting the king's ability to exploit the 'incidents of feudalism'. For example, reliefs, which in the past had been regulated only by the convention that they should be 'reasonable' were now fixed at £100 for a barony and 100s for a knight's fee (cl. 2). The rights of minors were safe-guarded during a wardship (cls. 4 & 5), and the rights of widows were protected (cls. 7 & 8) so that they would not be sold against their will to the highest bidder as they had by Henry II and John. Such details, perhaps dry to us today, were the very spice of feudal society. Other clauses aimed to prevent King John's corruption of the workings of justice, which once again had been occasioned by his need for money. Thus in cl. 40 John agreed, 'to no one will we sell, delay or deny right

or justice'. Characteristically, John had simply been using all the tricks his father Henry II had been using – like accepting bribes – only on a bigger scale. It is when we look at these clauses about justice however that we can understand how Magna Carta acquired its lasting fame. In cl. 40, for example, we read that 'No free man shall be taken or imprisoned . . . except by the lawful judgement of his peers or by the law of the land.' The barons could not afford to allow Magna Carta to become a purely sectional document, securing only their own privileges, otherwise they would have lost support. The concessions they extracted from the king were therefore applicable to all free men. For the villeins, however, for those who were not free, the Charter offered nothing. But then, nor did any other like document in any country in the thirteenth century.

Granted that King John was only brought to terms under compulsion, how was Magna Carta to be enforced? What was to stop him going back on his word? The barons anticipated this in the so-called security clause (cl. 61). They set up a committee of 25 to whom breaches of the Charter were to be referred. If within 40 days John still failed to offer redress, the committee were empowered to move against him. This procedure was set out with a view to ensuring that John restored the castles which he had confiscated in the course of his reign (cl. 52). John naturally seized every chance to drag his feet, so that by August aggrieved barons like Nicholas de Stuteville were complaining that they had still not recovered their property. To force John to comply, the 25 began ravaging his lands. It was therefore the operation of cl. 61 that provided the legal cover for the renewal of hostilities that ended only after John's timely death in October 1216.

Magna Carta was born in a crisis, and so far from ending it, it merely provided additional material for argument. Nevertheless it survived to become one of the corner-stones of the constitution. If England can be said to have a written constitution at all, it consists of such documents as Magna Carta, 1215, and the Bill of Rights, 1689. But Magna Carta became permanent only insofar as it became less contentious. When it was reissued in 1216 and 1217, it was reissued by the king's friends. So the radical clauses restricting royal power were removed. The process was taken further still in 1225 when the slimmed-down Magna Carta was republished and its forest clauses hived off and supplemented in what became known as the Charter of the Forest. Thereafter, in any settlement of grievances between king and baronage, as in 1297 and 1311 for example, it was the custom to begin by confirming 'the Charters'. Magna Carta was launched on its career as a document of symbolic significance.

Magna Carta survives in four 'originals' – two preserved in the British Museum, one at Lincoln Cathedral and one at Salisbury Cathedral. Historians now doubt whether there was ever a master copy, which King John or one of his clerks would have been called on to seal at Runnymede on 15 or 19 June. Later in the month, however, copies of it were certainly being written out for distribution to the shires, and it is these which are the four surviving contemporary versions we have today.

J. C. Holt, *Magna Carta*, Cambridge, 1965.

MALORY, SIR THOMAS The association of Malory's name with *Le Morte d' Arthur* rests on a paragraph at the end of the edition Caxton (q.v.) printed in 1485, where the author reveals his identity, prays for deliverance from prison and says that he wrote the book in the ninth year of Edward IV's reign (1469). Malory is usually identified with the Warwickshire knight, Sir Thomas Malory of Newbold Revell, a lawless character whose criminal career affords little promise of the creative turn that his mind would take during confinement. He first appears as a young esquire in the service of Richard Beauchamp, earl of Warwick. In 1443 he succeeded to his family estates. Two years later he was returned to parliament as a knight of the shire for Warwickshire. So far so good. But in August 1451 an indictment was submitted at Nuneaton (Warks.), accusing him of a succession of violent crimes over the previous 18 months, culminating in two attacks on Coombe Abbey. Soon afterwards he was arrested, and he spent the next few years in and out of prison. After Edward IV came to the throne in 1461 he received a pardon, but there is no hard evidence that he was ever at large again. As we have seen, he had once enjoyed the favour of the Beauchamp earls of Warwick, but he seems to have been regarded as expendable by their Neville successors. He died in 1471, and was buried at Greyfriars, Newgate, which suggests that he must have spent his last day behind bars in the sheriff of London's prison at Newgate.

It was of course in these unlikely surroundings that the imprisoned knight whiled away the time writing the stories of King Arthur (q.v.). Malory's career must surely remind us that, however ruffianly these medieval gentlemen may appear, they were well acquainted with popular ballads and romances which someone with a gift for telling a tale could turn to good use. In the preface to his edition of *Le Morte d'Arthur* Caxton hints at the sources Malory had consulted. He says that the 'copye' he was publishing was one which Sir Thomas 'dyd take oute of certeyn bookes of Frensshe and reduced it into Englysshe'. These French books from which Malory derived his inspiration are not known to us today by name, but probably included the most popular French versions of the Arthurian romances, most of them quite easily obtainable in fifteenth century London. All the same they were not the only sources he used. *The Tale of King Arthur and the Emperor Lucius*, for example, was derived from a fourteenth century English poem, the alliterative *Morte Arthure*. Malory's achievement was to re-write these earlier chivalric romances in a form acceptable to a late fifteenth century audience. This involved rejecting the old-fashioned narrative technique of interweaving one story with another in favour of the 'modern' technique of progressive exposition. In other words, he started with Arthur and Lucius, moved onto the stories of Sir Lancelot and Sir Tristram, and ended up with Mordred's treachery and the deaths of Arthur and Guinevere.

But does this mean that he conceived of the stories as comprising a single book? Almost certainly not. The idea of editing the stories under the title of *Le Morte d'Arthur* was one that occurred to Caxton when he published the text in 1485. For the next four-and-a-half centuries this edition of Caxton was the nearest that editors could approach to the lost original manuscript – until in 1934 a hitherto unidentified manuscript came to light in the library of Winchester College. It was one of those rare discoveries that transform our knowledge in a particular field. Although it was not an autograph copy, it was obviously much closer to the author's original than Caxton's edition, which was now shown

to have taken considerable liberties with the text. The sequence of stories is the same in the Winchester MS as in Caxton. But internal evidence supplies valuable indications that he conceived of each of the tales as a book in its own right, and not as episodes in a continuous cycle. In fact Caxton's appropriation of the title *Le Morte d'Arthur* to identify the whole work is an absurdity because it refers only to the last book, in which Malory describes the downfall of Arthur's court. Though Malory can no longer be credited with welding all the Arthurian legends into a coherent whole, his achievement is real none the less. He was a skilful writer bringing to his art a fluent English prose style, the development of which can be appreciated in reading *Le Morte d'Arthur*.

See also, LANGUAGE AND LITERATURE

The Works of Sir Thomas Malory, ed. E. Vinaver, 3 vols. Oxford, 2nd ed., 1967; C. Carpenter, 'Sir Thomas Malory and 15th Century Local Politics', *Bull. Inst. Hist. Res.*, liii (1980).

MALTOLT The nickname the 'maltolt' ('bad tax') was quickly coined to describe the levy of 3 marks (40s) imposed by Edward I (q.v.) in 1294 on each sack of wool exported from the realm. He needed to raise substantial sums of money to pay for the war with France. This he had originally proposed to do by seizing all wool, selling it and taking the profit; but in the face of fierce opposition from the merchants he settled instead for heavy customs duties. Edward was forced to abolish the maltolt in 1297, but his grandson Edward III (q.v.) succeeded in bringing it back in the 1330s and eventually establishing it as a permanent element in the revenues of the English crown.

See also, TAXATION.

MANOR Although often used as if synonymous, the terms 'village' and 'manor' describe different, but related concepts. A village is a small rural community in which agrarian occupations predominate. A manor, on the other hand, is a unit of lordship which may or may not happen to coincide with the village. If manor and village do coincide, the chances are that the lord will derive his income from three sources: the sale of produce grown on the home farm or demesne (q.v.), rents from the dependent tenantry and the profits of jurisdiction exercised in the manorial court. These constituents would have varied in importance, of course, according to the relative proportions of demesne and tenant land in the manor. When we talk about the estates of a particular lord, we mean the collection of manors that he held.

MATILDA, 'The Empress' See, STEPHEN.

MERCHET This was a licence paid by a villein (i.e., unfree) tenant to his lord for permission to marry off a daughter. Like heriot (q.v.), it was a mark of unfree condition, and by the fifteenth century became incorporated with the money rent, or disappeared altogether. On the manor of Minchinhampton (Gloucs.) in the thirteenth century merchet payments varied from 1s 6d to 6s 8d.

MISERICORDS Some of the most delightful wood carvings to have come down to us from the middle ages are to be found on misericord seats. In a characteristically medieval way these liftable seats provided the carver with the chance to turn practical need to creative advantage. The monks or canons who had to spend many hours singing in the choir needed some way of easing the strain on their feet; and this was achieved by so constructing the seats that when tipped up they exposed on their underside a bracket against which the priest could lean during the long service (*misericordia* = act of pity).

The first mention of misericords occurs in the twelfth century in connection with the convent of Hirsaugh in Germany. In England the earliest to survive are the thirteenth century set in Exeter Cathedral (*c.* 1230–70). The shape of the seats usually provides a rough guide to their date. In the thirteenth century they were given a front edge of convex form; in the fifteenth they were more usually polygonal with a pointed projection in the centre. Throughout the middle ages, however, misericords followed a consistent pattern of design, involving a central feature flanked by supporters. The subject matter of the carvings was derived from the entire range of Christian imagery, secular literature and drama. One of the most popular sources of all was the Bestiary, a Christian text available in the vernacular which used animals to illustrate the perennial theme of good and evil. On the other hand, there can be no doubt that a goodly number of misericord subjects were carved for no better reason than that they appealed to the carver's fancy. What else are we to make of the one at Beverley Minster of a wife thrashing her husband? Or of the knight falling from his horse at Lincoln Cathedral?

Sets of misericord seats survive in many of our cathedrals and greater churches, notably at Exeter, which has 50, Beverley Minster and Winchester which have 68 each, and Lincoln Cathedral with no fewer than 108. Perhaps the best of all are those for which a talented school of carvers was responsible in northern England, at Ripon, Chester, Manchester and Carlisle. These four churches offer a dazzling display of the carpenter's art.

MISTERY PLAYS A rich corpus of religious drama has come down to us from the late middle ages in the form of the plays performed by the craft or 'mistery' guilds (mistery, *métier* = trade). Like so much of the medieval cultural heritage, the plays were devotional in inspiration and didactic in purpose – in other words, they set out to impart the Biblical message to an audience many of whom would have been illiterate.

It may strike us today as curious that companies of laymen should have assumed responsibility for performing what was essentially religious drama. A word or two of explanation is needed. The mistery plays of the late middle ages had grown out of the dramatic dialogues which had sometimes been interpolated into the liturgy (q.v.) for the purpose of making sacred events more real to lay congregations. The parts would have been taken by clerics speaking in Latin. This evolution, of course, explains at the same time too much and too little, because a sense of theatre permeated so much of the medieval Church that it is difficult to pinpoint a direct connection with the later vernacular plays performed by the guilds. We are offered a clue if we remember that many of our surviving cycles of mistery plays were known as Corpus Christi plays – so called from the festival when they were performed. First established in 1264 by Pope Urban IV, Corpus Christi became a regular date in the Church's calendar by the fourteenth century, and falling as it did on the Thursday after Trinity Sunday, so close to mid-summer, afforded an excellent opportunity for processions and outdoor pageants. From this ritual, centred on the completion of the sacrifice of Christ, developed, appropriately enough, the idea of presenting a dramatic cycle extending from the Creation through the life and death of Christ to the Last Judgement. It is this extended theme which provides the subject matter of most of the plays, and accounts for their sometimes enormous length.

The English Corpus Christi plays are always thought to have been acted as processional cycles. A cycle was composed of a series of plays, each one assigned to a guild or group of guilds (q.v.). They were then performed on horse-drawn wagons, or pageants, which were moved from station to station through the town, so that an audience at any one station would see the entire cycle acted out in full in front of them, play after play – provided they were prepared to wait long enough. Calculations that have been made suggest that if they wanted to see an entire cycle, the onlookers, whether standing or looking from upstairs windows, would have had to rise at daybreak for the first performance and wait till late into the night for the last. At Chester, in fact, the performance was spread over three days. These practical problems encountered in production have led to the suggestion that one of the longest cycles – that of the York guilds – must have been performed indoors, but in the absence of any conclusive evidence either way the question must remain open. Whatever the case at York, it seems that elsewhere the plays were generally enacted outdoors, in prominent positions around the town. When Margaret, Henry VI's queen, visited Coventry in 1457 to see the Corpus Christi cycle, she stayed at the house of Richard Woods, which overlooked the first of the stations or acting-places. She witnessed all the plays, we are told, except Doomsday, which could not be performed for shortage of daylight.

Official texts of the cycles, copied from manuscripts in the hands of the guilds themselves, were kept by the town authorities, and were added to and altered from time to time. It was these official registeres which were called in for inspection at the Reformation so that expressions of religious sentiment contrary to reformist ideas could be eliminated. Stripped of their 'popery', the plays lived on, and indeed experienced a revival early in Elizabeth's reign. After the 1580s, however, we hear of no more performances.

Bearing in mind their instructive purpose, the mistery plays come across, even today, as works of extraordinary force and power. It is a fair assumption that the plays were the works of clerics, and in view of the orthodox nature of their content, rather conservative ones at that. They relied for their success on powerful visual effects, achieved through the use of stage props, and on strong characterization, communicated not only by speech but by gesture and expression. Herod, for example, the first medieval villain, was depicted as a ranting tyrant. In the work of the Wakefield Master, perhaps the most remarkable playwright of the fifteenth century, he was transformed into an overbearing magnate. Not one to stand back from his work the Wakefield writer used his medium to complain about such contemporary grievances as unruly magnate

retainers and the corruptibility of ecclesiastical lawyers. Like all medieval artists he chose to present the past in terms of the present. The strength of these plays lay in their very directness. How much more dramatic still they must have been when performed with all the paraphernalia on which the guilds lavished so much of their money. As for how they managed the dividing of the Red Sea, we can only wonder.

E. K. Chambers, *The Medieval Stage*, Oxford, 1903; A. H. Nelson, *The Medieval English Stage*, Chicago & London, 1974; *English Mystery Plays*, ed. P. Happe, Penguin, 1975.

MONASTICISM Monasticism involved a communal life of prayer and devotion in accordance with the three vows of poverty, chastity and obedience. Its origins lie in the East in early Christian times, when strict ascetics like St Anthony began to adopt the life of hermits in the Egyptian desert in the belief that only by withdrawing from the temptations of the world could the Christian lead a pure life in contemplation of God. Though he sought a life of solitude, St Anthony set an example which was followed by others who retreated into the desert in protest against what they saw as the growing worldliness of the Church. Some lived singly, but others joined together to live as communities, or monasteries as we call them.

In the course of the late fourth and fifth centuries the contemplative life started by the desert fathers spread to Western Europe, where it was given the shape it was to have for the rest of the middle ages in the Rule of St Benedict of Nursia (c. 480–550). Though this was not a work of such originality as was once thought, it still remains of great importance for establishing a moderate, balanced set of rules which adapted the tradition of the desert hermits to the communal approach to life more favoured in the West. In Benedict's view a monastic community should be self-supporting, dependent only on home-grown produce, and self-contained, because it was not the task of monks to undertake social or pastoral work. He laid down guidelines for an horarium, or division of time within the day. Some four hours were to be spent in liturgical prayer in the church, four hours in reading and private prayer and the remaining six waking hours in manual labour. Almost certainly the labour intended by St Benedict was not heavy work in the fields but domestic or artistic work.

In early Anglo-Saxon England monasteries were founded in Kent by Augustine and his fellow missionaries soon after their arrival in 597, and in the north by Celtic missionaries who came from Iona. But these abbeys, right from Lindisfarne down to Ely, suffered badly in the period of the Viking invasions, and despite a revival in the tenth century it was left to the Normans after 1066 to infuse new life into English monasticism.

In 1066 about 48 monasteries remained in England, all of them situated south of a line drawn from the Humber to the Severn. After the Conquest the Normans soon began to make their mark in founding new monasteries and in reviving old ones. Battle, Shrewsbury, Chester, Colchester, St Mary's, York, and Tewkesbury were all new foundations of the late eleventh century: Whitby, Jarrow and Wearmouth were revivals of once famous northern communities that had lapsed during the Viking onslaught. Equally striking was the increase in the number of recruits to the cloister. Worcester rose from 12 to 50 under Bishop Wulfstan (1062–95), Rochester from 22 to over 60 under Bishop Gundulf (1077–1108) and Gloucester from 10 to a hundred under Abbot Serlo (1072–1104). What changes would these monks have noticed around them with the coming of the Normans? To us today the most obvious characteristic of the new Norman abbots is their enormous appetite for building, manifested for example in the abbey churches we can still see at Tewkesbury, Ely and Peterborough (the last two now cathedrals). But they also reformed the internal regime of the English monasteries by introducing the customs and observances of the Norman houses from which they came.

In the years immediately after the Conquest, then, the main source of inspiration for the reform of the abbeys lay in Normandy. But in the late eleventh and early twelfth centuries another strong influence from abroad was provided by the great Burgundian abbey of Cluny (q.v.), of which several dependent houses were founded in England, notably at Lewes (1077) and Reading (1121). More significant in the long run for the development of monasticism on this side of the Channel was the arrival, indeed almost the invasion, of the Cistercians (q.v.) in the reigns of Henry I and Stephen (q.v.). The puritanism of the Cistercians represented a challenge to the norms of Benedictine monasticism which evoked an enthusiastic response from twelfth-century Europe. Still more, they had in St Bernard of Clairvaux one of the greatest propagandists in the middle ages. By the time St Bernard died in 1153, there were 343 Cistercian abbeys in Europe, of which 36 were in England.

All these Orders of monks claimed to

be following the Rule of St Benedict. Those who felt that 'a spiritual malaise' had infected the older Benedictine abbeys would reinterpret the Rule with a new strictness, only to find themselves outflanked soon afterwards by a stricter interpretation still. It was however a challenge to the existing order in some respects more radical than that posed by the Cistercians when the Regular Canons appeared on the scene in the decades before 1100. A canon was a clerk in holy orders who lived according to a rule; a monk, on the other hand, was simply one who vowed to pursue a life of prayer apart from the world. There was always a tension in medieval monasticism between the active and the contemplative life, between the view so strongly advocated by St Bernard that monks should withdraw from the world, and the contrary view that they should undertake good works in the community. It was to this latter need that the Orders of canons especially ministered, because they were prepared to undertake responsibilities in the parishes. Accordingly many of their early houses were founded in the towns. The main Orders of canons were the Augustinians (q.v.) and the Premonstratensians (q.v.), both of whom made swift advances in England in the reign of Henry I (1100–35).

There were numerous smaller monastic Orders, and England even gave birth to one of its own, that of St Gilbert of Sempringham, which revived the old idea of the double monastery embracing both men and women. But the principal Orders represented in England by the end of the twelfth century were the Benedictines, Cistercians and Augustinian Canons. If the sheer number of new foundations is anything to go by, the twelfth century was pre-eminently the monastic century in England. In the late middle ages the only Order to make significant advances were the Carthusians (q.v.), perhaps because they preserved their original austerity for longer than the other monks. By the end of the twelfth century, too, the monopoly which the monasteries had enjoyed in the world of learning and teaching was coming to be challenged by the rise of the universities (q.v.). It is true that the monks themselves established houses in Oxford and Cambridge, to enable some of their number to study, but we find all the same that in the fourteenth century the most gifted thinkers were living and working no longer in the monasteries, as they had in the age of Lanfranc (q.v.) and Anselm (q.v.), but in the friaries and the universities. The monasteries had lost the intellectual primacy they had once enjoyed.

The two principal Orders of friars, the Dominicans (q.v.) and the Franciscans (q.v.), had made their appearance in England in the early thirteenth century. As they grew in popularity, so the monks tended to become jealous of them; but their way of life, which took them out into the world to preach, was not so much a challenge to the Regular Orders as a parallel development, a new departure in the search for the 'apostolic life'. The friars are sometimes known as the mendicants, since their renunciation of all property obliged them to rely on begging for subsistence (Latin, *mendicare*, to beg).

How did the monks pass their time? Their life was governed by the horarium or timetable that prescribed the offices which had to be celebrated in the church. These offices were composed of psalms, lessons and anthems (q.v., LITURGY). The horarium varied according to the season, but we can take as an example the winter arrangement. The day would begin at about 2 a.m., when the monks would sing Nocturns, or Matins as they would now be called. Lauds, the next office to be recited, came at dawn, followed by Prime at about 6 a.m. The monks would then read in the cloister until 8 a.m., when they would return to the dormitory to wash. Their next office in the church was Terce, following which they assembled in the chapter house for the daily meeting or 'chapter' of the community. Between chapter and Sext, at mid-day, the monks devoted themselves to pursuits like reading, writing or illumination of manuscripts. Sext was followed by sung High Mass and the recitation of Nones. Then at 2 p.m. (or mid-day in summer) the community would proceed to the refectory for dinner – not without haste, one imagines, for this was the first meal of the day. After dinner they devoted themselves to reading until about 5 p.m. Then came Vespers, and at 6.15, after some refreshment, Compline. The community retired to the dormitory at about 6.30 for their seven hours rest before the routine began again at 2 the next morning. The peculiarities of the horarium, and in particular the provision of a siesta after dinner in summer-time, are largely attributable to the origins of monasticism in the hot climates in the East, and the failure to modify it to the requirements of the cold North. To what extent flexibility was introduced into its observance is a question to which no certain answer can be given, but it seems likely that by the thirteenth century the rules on silence would have been eased. Discussion would need to take place not only about matters spiritual or scholastic but also, for example in a great Benedictine community, about the innumerable business transactions that were created by the day-to-day running of a large estate.

St Benedict provided simple but last-ing guidelines for administration as he did for every other aspect of monastic life. He envisaged that the monastic community would be ruled by an abbot, assisted by a prior and by no more than one or two officials such as the cellarer, who provided for the material needs of the monks. By the eleventh century the cellarer had been joined by two other officials of importance – the precentor, who supervized the liturgical and literary activities, and the sacrist, who took charge of the fabric and contents of the church. Of these the most important remained the cellarer, for it was he who controlled the purse-strings. By the twelfth century this centralized system of administration was beginning to break up, in the Benedictine houses at least. First of all, the lands of the monastery were divided between those of the abbot and those assigned for the support of the community. Secondly, the revenues assigned to the monastic portion no longer passed through the hands of the cellarer but were divided among separate departments headed by monk 'obedientiaries' who derived their income either in money or in kind from lands and manors allotted for their support. This could have been a convenient system, but its disadvantage was an absence of central direction. As a result we commonly observe a retreat back to something like the old centralized system of administration. At Canterbury Cathedral Priory, for example, the obedientiary system, which had been instituted by the 1130s, was amended sometime between 1163 and 1167 to allow the appointment of central (monastic) treasurers from whom the cellarer, chamberlain and sacrist each received their rents. The new arrangements, coupled with the elaborate audit each Michaelmas, prevented overspending by the subordinate obedientiaries.

As for the surroundings in which the monks lived and passed their lives, we can gain a clear idea from the churches and ruins which still survive. The visitor entering the precincts of an abbey by the kind of grand gateway that adorned a Benedictine foundation like Bury St Edmund's would first encounter the outbuildings – the stores, granary and guest house, for example. Ahead of him would be the main buildings, ranged around the cloister court. Unless, as at Malmesbury and Canterbury, local topography dictated otherwise, the cloister was usually situated to the south of the church. The purpose was to take advantage of the sun, but even so the cloister walks must have been cold and draughty in winter before it became common in the late middle ages to insert glass. In most abbeys the only rooms certain to be heated by fires during the winter were the calefactory (warming chamber) and the infirmary. On the north side of the cloister lay the church, where so much of the day was spent. Its interior would be broken up by screens and partitions to an extent which it is difficult for us today to visualize unless by visiting the former Benedictine abbey of St Alban's. Towards the far end of the nave lay the rood screen, so named from the rood or crucifix which towered above it. On its western side there was a nave altar, for use by the local people if the abbey doubled as a parish church or by the lay brothers if the abbey was Cistercian. Two doors flanking the nave altar gave access to the central space under the tower, which was separated by another screen, known as the pulpitum, from the monks' choir in the eastern half of the church. We have already seen that after singing the office known as Terce the monks proceeded from the church to the chapter house, which usually lay along the eastern walk of the cloister,

adjacent to the south transept. There the community would meet daily, and there too the early abbots would sometimes have been buried, as at Rievaulx (N. Yorks.). The rest of the east walk was usually taken up by the dormitory, and the south walk by the refectory. Along the west range the plan was subject to greater variation. In Benedictine or Augustinian foundations the abbot's quarters or the cellarium might be found. In Cistercian houses, however, the lay brothers' quarters were almost invariably placed along the west walk, and one of the most splendid surviving ranges of monastic buildings is the long cellar at Fountains (W. Yorks.) with the lay brothers' quarters on the first floor. The infirmary and calefactory would then be tucked away outside the cloister, often as at St Mary's Abbey, Sherborne and Fountains, behind the east range (Figs. 5 and 6).

The English monasteries were dissolved in the reign of Henry VIII – the lesser ones in 1536, the greater houses in 1538–40. Their buildings met with differing fates. Five abbey churches became cathedrals of newly created dioceses. A few more churches, situated in the towns, were taken over for use as parish churches, as for example at Selby and Tewkesbury. But all too often abbeys which did not have the good fortune to survive as either cathedrals or parish churches were pounced on as quarries by the local townsfolk. For this reason hardly a trace remains of the once great abbeys of Burton, Abingdon or Winchcombe. With the buildings of the Cistercians, situated as they were in the countryside, it was a different story. Some like Buckland (Devon) and Forde (Dorset) were converted by their new owners into country houses. Others survived roofless, but otherwise intact. In the eighteenth century they appealed

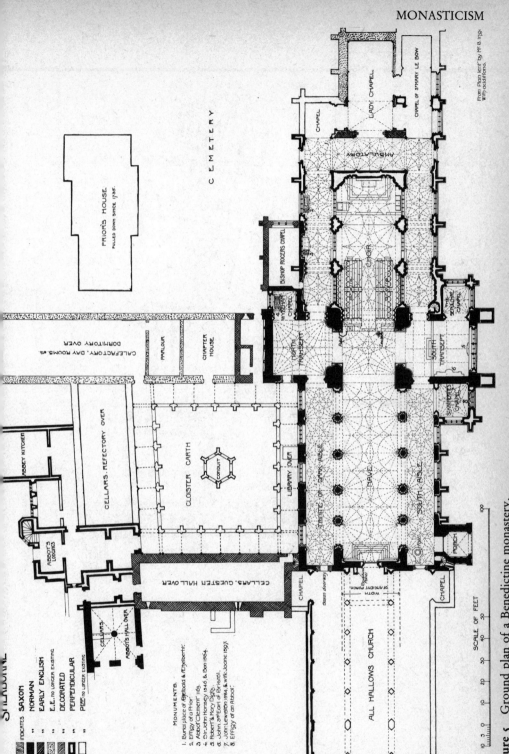

Figure 5 Ground plan of a Benedictine monastery.

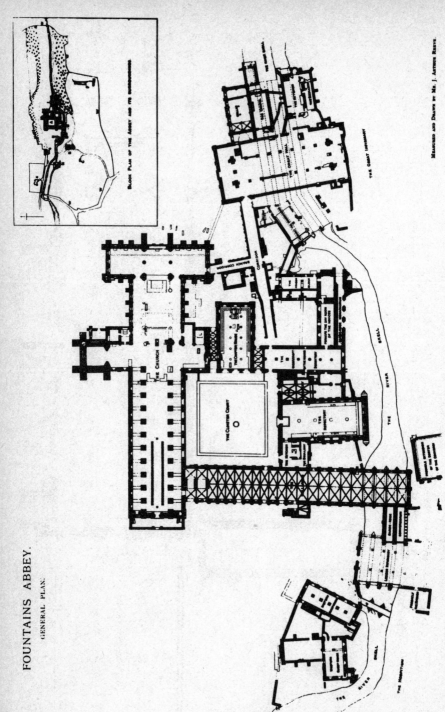

FOUNTAINS ABBEY.
GENERAL PLAN.

Figure 6   The Cistercian plan. The long range on the west side of the cloister contains the cellarium below and the lay brothers' dormitory above.

to that sense of the picturesque which inspired landowners to preserve gothic ruins in the parks which their landscape gardeners created. Thanks in large measure to the Aislabie family, who lived nearby, the untamed wilderness which the first monks found at Fountains in 1133 became the rural arcady we see today. And it was not only at Fountains that monastic ruins set against a sylvan landscape exercized a strong appeal over the Romantic imagination, if we remember that Wordsworth wrote some of his finest lines while overlooking the remains of Tintern Abbey on the river Wye.

D. Knowles, *The Monastic Order in England, 940–1216*, Cambridge, 2nd edn., 1963; *The Religious Orders in England*, Cambridge, 3 vols., 1948–59.

MONTFORT, SIMON DE

A Frenchman by birth, Simon became an Englishman by adoption. A royalist and an authoritarian by temperament, he became a rebel and a populist by necessity. These paradoxes lie at the heart of Earl Simon's career.

Born in c. 1208, he was a younger son of Simon IV de Montfort, who had led the crusade against the Albigensian heretics in southern France. Young Simon's claim to an interest in English affairs derived from the marriage of his grandfather, Simon III, to Amicia, daughter of Robert Beaumont, earl of Leicester. When the last Beaumont earl died childless in 1205, the inheritance should have been divided between his two sisters, but Amicia's portion was in fact taken first by the king and then by the earl of Chester. Young Simon therefore had to come to England in person to claim what he regarded as his rightful inheritance. In 1231 he was granted the

lands, and in 1239 the title, of the earl of Leicester.

For a man who had started off as a near-landless younger son, Earl Simon was doing remarkably well. In 1238, the year before his recognition as earl of Leicester, he had married Eleanor, sister of Henry III (q.v.). Although endorsed by the king, this marriage aroused the hostility of the baronage, who complained that they had not been consulted. At this stage of his career Simon was evidently regarded as a king's man, no different from all the rest of Henry's foreign-born favourites. So how did he come to change sides? It is easier to trace the long process of Simon's estrangement from the court than to account for it. For example, we can say with some certainty that the first big row between Henry III and Simon took place in 1239, the year after the earl's marriage. But we do not know what caused it. Good relations, so far as we can tell, were restored, but a decade later they were upset by a second and more serious rupture. In 1248 Simon was sent to reduce Gascony to some degree of governability. He set about the job with the same degree of ruthlessness and sense of purpose that had characterized his father's campaign against the Albigensians nearly half-a-century before. Inevitably, complaints and protests filtered back to England, and in 1252 Simon was recalled and made to answer them. He must have felt badly let down by his brother-in-law.

For Henry himself the reckoning came in 1258. His grandiose plans for installing his younger son Edmund on the throne of Sicily had landed him with enormous bills he had no hope of paying off without assistance from the barons and the community of the realm. They were only prepared to grant such assistance on condition that he accept the constitution known as the Provisions of Oxford (q.v.). Simon played little part in the political crisis that led up to the Provisions because he had gone to France to help negotiate a peace treaty between Henry III and Louis IX. Nevertheless, Henry's comment that much as he dreaded lightning, he feared Simon even more, suggests that he regarded the earl as a baronial partisan even at this stage. In the years that followed Simon certainly made a consistent stand in favour of the enforcement of the Provisions. But he was a difficult man to work with, and the disunity that soon began to weaken the baronial ranks enabled Henry to regain control in 1262. Simon took refuge in France. What brought him back six months later in April 1263 was the crisis unleashed by an uprising along the Welsh Marches. Edward, the future Edward I, tried to restore order, but his efforts were not merely fruitless but positively counter-productive because he offended the Marcher lords by bringing along a force of foreign mercenaries. The lords now chose to lend their backing to Earl Simon once more as the man most likely to reimpose law and order. On Simon's return the Provisions were of course enforced again, but only for as long as the barons were united in support of them, and that was unlikely to be for more than a few months. By the end of the year Simon was acquiescing reluctantly in the suggestion that the differences between himself and the king should be submitted to King Louis IX of France for arbitration. Confident though he always was of his own rectitude, he could surely have entertained little hope of convincing Louis that he was right. But all the same, in the absence of any better suggestions, the arbitration went ahead. When Louis' judgement came, in the Mise of Amiens, January 1264, it was a decisive statement in favour of Henry. Simon had little option but to fight. He marched south towards the Channel coast so as to prevent any French army from intervening on Henry's behalf. At the same time Prince Edward moved west from Winchelsea. The two armies met at Lewes on 14 May 1264. The battle was a great victory for Simon, and Henry III and Edward were taken prisoner. He used his moment of triumph to impose a new constitution known as the Mise of Lewes, which appointed a Council of Nine to govern in the king's name. But for how long could he continue to overawe the king in this fashion? And for how long could he continue to keep Edward, the heir to the throne, in confinement? As Sir Maurice Powicke has so aptly put it, Simon could neither legalize his authority nor surrender it. Supreme as he was for the moment, his position was soon undermined by the defection of those who had once been his supporters. Gilbert de Clare, the young earl of Gloucester, was warning the lords of the Welsh Marches that the arrogance and power as he saw it of the de Montfort family constituted a threat to the liberties of them all. By May 1265 the Marches were ablaze. Simon went to quell the disorder. But worse news awaited him. On 28 May Edward had escaped from custody, and made for the Mortimer stronghold of Wigmore (Heref.). To compensate for these defections Simon sought to appeal to a wider public by summoning representatives from the shires and the boroughs to a parliament (q.v.) in June. A bold propagandist move that may have been, but it was hardly enough to save him from the armed challenge of Edward and the Marcher barons. On 4 August 1265 the two sides met in battle at Evesham, and Simon was defeated and killed.

Before long the monks of Evesham,

who had taken in the body of the dead earl, found themselves growing rich from offerings made at his tomb. But was Simon a martyr, or simply a rebel and a traitor? Opinions have differed sharply, but of one thing we may be sure. He was no constitutionalist in the modern sense. If he was devoted to the kind of conciliar government envisaged in the Provisions, he was also authoritarian by instinct. He turned to the knights and burgesses not out of choice, but out of desperation. In so doing, however, he displayed a shrewd appreciation of where the mainsprings of his support were to be found. Simon voiced the grievances of the gentry – the knights and esquires in the counties. It was their demands for the elimination of corruption and for the appointment of local men to local offices which he took up and made his own.

F. M. Powicke, *King Henry III and the Lord Edward*, 2 vols., Oxford, 1947.

MORTMAIN Alienation into mortmain means the conveyance of land to the Church. It raised a number of problems in the middle ages. If an estate passed into the hands of the Church, it would be lost to the land market for ever; and if it was held in frankalmoign (free alms), as most Church land was, the Crown lost knight service. Moreover, since the Church was an undying corporation, the overlord lost the feudal incidents to which he would normally have been entitled. Not surprisingly, therefore, ecclesiastical tenure earned the nickname 'mortmain' – dead hand. It was very likely to meet the objections of landlords who had been deprived of feudal incidents as a result of such alienations made by their sub-tenants that Edward I enacted the Statute of Mortmain in 1279. Echoing similar legislation passed in other countries, this prohibited all acquisitions of land by the Church in future. Draconian though its terms may have sounded, it in fact did little more than introduce a licensing system. Before an alienation was made, an inquisition *ad quod dampnum* was held in the appropriate shire to determine what feudal incidents would be lost. The alienor would then be charged a fine roughly in proportion to the scale of financial loss involved. If it ever had the serious object of limiting the acquisition of land by the Church, the Statute came much too late in the day: by 1279 the Church had already acquired most of the land it was ever to acquire in the middle ages.

S. Raban, 'Mortmain in Medieval England', *Past & Present*, 62 (1974).

MUSIC What did most to shape the evolution of early medieval music was its association with the Church. The link between music and worship had been forged by the Jews, and it was to be reinforced by the Christians. Much of the music that has come down to us from the middle ages is therefore religious. Much, though by no means all. Medieval people liked to relax to the sound of light music as much as we do today. They gave us the love lyric. But what is common to practically all surviving medieval music, whether religious or secular, is that it is vocal.

The oldest form of Christian music is known as plainchant. In a large basilica the spoken voice would soon be lost in the aisles. So, to improve audibility and to lend an air of solemnity, it made good sense to intone the texts. In simple plainchant a melody of two phrases is sung without accompaniment, and repeated for each verse of the text, the two melodic phrases corresponding to the two halves of a verse. Plainchant, though associated with the name of Pope Gregory the Great (590–604), was in existence well before his time. As it spread throughout Europe, it became the standard chant for the divine offices sung in Church; and at the hands of the monks, whose principal employment was to sing it, it became a musical form of singular beauty.

The essence of the chant was its simplicity; but, human nature being what it is, before long men thought to improve on it. The liturgy (q.v.) was enriched by interpolations of melody or text, or both, which are known as 'tropes'. By the beginning of the twelfth century, when the fashion had run its course, every office had been troped, and even the tropes themselves were troped.

If we look at the earliest manuscripts of plainchant, one of the first things we notice is that rhythm is not indicated at all, and pitch not very exactly. This must mean that both pitch and rhythm were part of what is usually called 'performance practice' – that is, they were learned, understood and passed on orally, and did not need to be codified. What these early sources tell us is the shape of the melody and its construction, that is all. They were an adjunct to a tradition that was still basically oral. But once a composer, no longer satisfied with simply interpolating a trope, chose to superimpose one tune on another, written notation was bound to be necessary if singers were to keep in time with one another. So in the course of the next century western music acquired the written forms it still uses today. And once that was done, the way was open to polyphony. The two Winchester Tropers, dating from the late tenth and early eleventh centuries, contain a number of polyphonic settings which were used for the major festivals of the Church year. There are indications, however, that the Normans may not have viewed polyphony with such favour. And, besides, the Church did not allow every part of the liturgy to be elaborated without limit by the addition of more voice parts.

One of the happiest forms of medieval polyphony was the motet. This entailed a tenor chanting plainsong as a background to one or more upper voices, each with a different text. The potential for variation was almost limitless. The sacred tenor could find himself accompanied not by a devotional text but by a love poem, sung not in Latin but in the vernacular. This combination might be one which modern listeners would find at best bizarre, at worst in bad taste. We prefer harmony. The medieval audience, however had an ear for contrast. Most of the early vernacular motets we have are in French. Almost the only one in English is 'Worldes blisse, have good day' over the tenor 'Benedicamus Domino', which dates from the later thirteenth century. The secular motet apparently exercised less appeal in England than it did on the Continent. But another polyphonic form – the Round or Canon – took no time to establish itself in the English repertory. A round is a song in which the singers come in one after the other with exactly the same text. The most famous example is 'Sumer is icumen in', written at Reading Abbey in about 1240. It is unlikely that this attractive piece is the spontaneous work of a monk overjoyed one afternoon by the thought that summer was approaching. In the manuscript the English poem is written above a Latin text, 'perspice Christicola'. The evidence suggests that the Latin text is the earlier and that the composer then made a setting of the English poem as a 'contrafactum'. In that event we are dealing with a very skilled artist indeed.

This discussion of 'Sumer is icumen in' has taken us far from the field of secular polyphony. And it is time for us to pause and take stock of the changes that had taken place in the form and content of secular music. For changes there had been, and momentous ones too. Europe had awoken in the twelfth century to the sound of the courtly love lyric (q.v., LANGUAGE & LITERATURE). The troubadours of southern France had begun to sing of beauty and love. Their tender songs began to filter northwards after 1137, when Eleanor of Aquitaine (q.v.) married Louis VII, king of France. Bernard of Ventadorn, one of the greatest musicians of his day, came north with her. Later, of course, she was divorced by Louis, and married the Angevin Henry II (q.v.), who inherited the English crown in 1154, but the second marriage does not seem to have borne the fruitful musical consequences of the first. Even though French was, and was to remain for another century or more, the vernacular language of our nobility, the troubadour genre did not strike roots here. From the famous story of Richard I (q.v.) we know that Eleanor's favourite son inherited her musical interests. While a captive of Leopold, duke of Austria, Richard was discovered by his faithful minstrel Blondel, who went from castle to castle singing a song known to them both, until finally a refrain from a tower told him he had reached his master's prison. Some songs composed by Richard have in fact survived. Yet his tastes do not seem to have been shared to any great extent by the nobility. English composers could turn their hand to some delightful rounds like 'Sumer is icumen in'. But before the late fourteenth century there is an almost total absence of anything corresponding to French courtly polyphony. Is this just an optical illusion caused by the loss of the music? Or does it indicate that the English kings and nobility had different musical tastes from their peers in France? Had many more songs been written, they would surely have survived in even modestly greater numbers than they have. So the preponderance of Mass pieces and Latin motets may be a not unfaithful reflection of what was composed in the middle ages. Part of the problem may have lain in the Chapel Royal in the fourteenth century. None of the minstrels whose names are recorded in the account books of the king's household can be connected with any piece of written music that has come down to us. Nor for that matter can the name of any clerk be connected with any non-sacred composition. John Aleyn, a canon of Windsor (d. 1373) wrote a liturgical motet. But there the list ends. A gulf separates performance from composition. With the approach of the fifteenth century, however, it is a happier story. From the 1390s we have a collection of songs made by Thomas Turk, a Fellow of Winchester, to pass away the long evenings around Christmas and the New Year. And at court the king himself was a source of inspiration, to judge from the two compositions in the Old Hall manuscript ascribed to 'Roy Henry', probably Henry IV or V.

Shortly before 1400 the influence of 'Ars Nova' began to be felt in England. 'Ars Nova' was a new current of musical thought which took its name from a highly influential book written by the Frenchman Philippe de Vitry in about 1325. Philippe sought to distinguish the old method of notating motets in longs and breves from the new one in shorter values, of semi-breves and minims. The new rules he prescribed encouraged musicians to break free from the old rhythmic patterns and to employ all types of semi-breve and minim combination. The Old Hall manuscript which we mentioned earlier is the best collection of English music illustrating the new influences. It contains an important composition ('Veni creator spiritus/Veni sancte spiritus') by John Dunstable, the most distinguished English composer of the fifteenth century. But the bulk of Dunstable's work, amounting to some 60 compositions in all, is preserved in foreign manuscripts, an indication perhaps that his influence was felt more directly in France and Burgundy, where he spent the most active years of his life, than it was in England.

Seeing that we have concentrated in large measure on vocal forms, let us not lose sight of the developments in instrumental accompaniment in this period. By the ninth century we hear of organs being made in England. By the time of Bishop Athelwold (963–84) Winchester Cathedral had an organ so big that we are told 70 men stood perspiring as they worked its bellows.

The church organ had soon established itself as an indispensable accompaniment to sacred music. For the performance of secular music there was a dazzling array of instruments to choose from. String instruments included the rebec, held to the chin like a violin, and the viele, which was held upright on the lap. Both were played with a bow. The psaltery, which is known to have been played by St Dunstan, is an example of a string instrument that was plucked. The range of wind instruments included the flute and the recorder, and of percussion instruments, the triangle, cymbals and castanets. But in the middle ages instrumental sound served mainly as an accompaniment to voices, and not as a musical form in its own right. The move towards independence was to come later, during the Renaissance.

The Pelican History of Music: i, ed. A. Robertson & D. Stevens, Harmondsworth, 1960; *Medieval English Songs*, ed. E. J. Dobson & F. Ll. Harrison, London, 1979.

NEVILLE, RICHARD, Earl of Warwick 'Warwick the Kingmaker', as he is better known, is the most notorious over-mighty subject of the late middle ages, and significantly one of the few medieval noblemen of whom a full-scale biography has been written.

The Nevilles of Raby (Co. Durham) were a remarkable clan. They and their old rivals, the Percys, had long held sway in the north. But it was only with Ralph

Neville, earl of Westmorland (d. 1425) that the family rose from regional to national prominence. From Ralph's first marriage, to Margaret Stafford, descended the earls of Westmorland. From his second marriage, to Joan Beaufort, descended the line from which Warwick sprang. Richard, their eldest son, became earl of Salisbury, and his son and heir was our Richard. He inherited his father's earldom, and acquired that of

Warwick by his marriage to Anne, daughter and eventual heiress of Richard Beauchamp.

Warwick played a prominent part in the Wars of the Roses (q.v.). He shared in the triumph of the Yorkist lords when they invaded England from Calais (q.v.), and defeated the Lancastrians at Northampton on 10 July 1460. Early the following year, however, he was less successful. At the second battle of St Alban's (17 February) Queen Margaret's forces came out on top. Whatever opinion we may have of him as a field commander, and it may not be a good one, there can be no doubt that Warwick's support, political and military, was crucial in putting Edward IV (q.v.) on the throne in March 1461. It was his first exercise in king-making, and it was not to be his last. The problem was that Edward turned out to be no mere cipher. Warwick therefore formed an alliance with Clarence, Edward's feckless brother, with a view to their jointly reasserting control over the king. That was easier said than done. Warwick was driven into exile, and while staying in France transferred his support to Queen Margaret and the Lancastrians. It was an astonishing *volte face*, but justified in his eyes by a desire to regain the power he felt to be his. On 13 September 1470 he landed near Dartmouth, put Henry VI (q.v.) back on the throne, and compelled Edward IV to flee to the Low Countries. His second exercise in king-making proved to be short-lived, however. Equipped and supported by his Burgundian allies, just as Warwick before him had been by the French, Edward soon returned, and defeated and killed the Kingmaker at Barnet on 14 April 1471.

The outlines of Warwick's career can be sketched clearly enough, but it is more difficult to tell whether he was any more than just an over-mighty baron, born with a lust for power and determined not to be denied it. It has to be admitted right away that what we know of Warwick's character is rarely to his credit. His snobbish dislike of Edward's queen, Elizabeth Woodville, and her relatives, was admittedly shared by other well-born members of the nobility. But his merciless attitude towards fallen opponents contrasts sharply with Edward IV's generosity. After his triumph over Edward's army at Edgecote in 1469 he was responsible for the arrest and execution of Earl Rivers, the earl of Pembroke, the earl of Devon, Sir Thomas Herbert and Sir John Woodville. Those who crossed the Kingmaker's path were not given the chance to do so again. Though he gives the impression of being a crudely insensitive man, he certainly knew how to win support by open-handed generosity, in the City of London for example, and he was adept in the use of propaganda. Warwick knew all about the use and abuse of power. It was the appetite for wealth, the appetite for power, that motivated and eventually destroyed him.

P. M. Kendall, *Warwick the Kingmaker & the Wars of the Roses* (Sphere Books, 1972).

NORMANDY It is interesting to note that not once but twice in the eleventh century England lost its national independence. In 1017 Canute made the country part of his Baltic empire. Then in 1066 the country was conquered again, this time by William, duke of Normandy. The cross-Channel entity he created, so important for understanding contemporary events at home and abroad, lasted for a century-

and-a-half until the expulsion of King John (q.v.) from Normandy in 1204.

William (q.v.) himself ruled England and Normandy as a single entity. For the future, however, he proposed dividing the two dominions on the lines laid down by the customary Norman rules of inheritance. In other words, Normandy, the family patrimony, would pass to Robert, the eldest son, and England, acquired in the father's lifetime, to William, known as Rufus (q.v.), the second son. Henry (q.v.), the youngest, had to be content with a large sum of money. This arrangement lasted until 1096 when Robert, wishing to raise money for his expedition on the First Crusade, pawned the duchy to Rufus for 10,000 marks in silver. This brief period of renewed unity was abruptly terminated by Rufus's death in the New Forest in 1100. Robert returned from crusade (q.v.) just in time to recover Normandy, but not soon enough to prevent Henry from grabbing the throne of England. Robert longed to get England just as much as Henry did to get Normandy. It was clear that partition was not going to last for long, and in the end it was Henry who effected reunification by defeating and capturing his elder brother at Tinchebrai in 1106. Henry was the last of the Conqueror's sons, and after the loss of his own son and heir in the wreck of the White Ship in 1120, he sought to keep England and Normandy together by making the barons swear to uphold the succession of his daughter Matilda, wife of Geoffrey, count of Anjou. In the event, on his death in 1135 it was not Matilda but his nephew Stephen who won the throne. Stephen (q.v.), however, proved unable to secure a foothold on the other side of the Channel, and Geoffrey of Anjou, whose family had long coveted Normandy, began moving in from the south, conquering the whole

of the duchy by 1144. The two halves of the Anglo-Norman realm were severed once more, and were not to be reunited until Matilda's son Henry became king of England in 1154.

When they were brought together again that year, it was as part of a much larger and less tightly-knit confederation than before. Henry II (q.v.) was not only king of England and duke of Normandy, but also count of Anjou by descent from his father and duke of Aquitaine by courtesy of his marriage to Eleanor (q.v.). Between 1154 and 1204 the old Anglo-Norman connection was but one link in a long chain of territories. It finally broke in 1204, when Philip Augustus achieved his long-standing ambition of winning the duchy for the French crown. John (q.v.) spent the next ten years trying to get it back, but never succeeded.

If we try now to look in a little more detail at the ties linking England and Normandy in this period, we can see what it was that held the two dominions together for so long. When William conquered England in 1066, he confiscated the estates of the old English aristocracy, and gave them to his own followers. The great Norman baronial families, the Beaumonts, the Montgomeries and so on, henceforth held lands on both sides of the Channel. It was therefore in their interest to see the two countries ruled by the same man. For as soon as they were partitioned between two quarrelling sons, each wanting the half ruled by the other, then a conflict of loyalties was bound to arise. After 1100, for example, Robert, earl of Shrewsbury, was faced with losing his lands in Normandy if he was loyal to Henry I of England, or with losing his lands in England if he was loyal to Duke Robert. That was why the Anglo-Norman aristocracy had a vested interest in preserving the unity of England and Normandy, and that was why it was so disastrous for them when there was a prolonged separation like the one that occurred during Stephen's reign. To say that it suited the nobility to have England and Normandy under one ruler is not to imply that it ever occurred to that ruler to tie the two lands any closer together administratively. England had its own institutions of government, and so did Normandy. During the long period of internal peace under Henry I from 1106 to 1135 there may have been some movement towards assimilation, but if so it was halted by the break-up that occurred under Stephen, and there is no evidence that when Henry II succeeded as king-duke in 1154 he gave the lands under his rule any greater semblance of unity than that represented by a common allegiance to his own person. The Angevin 'empire' was less an empire than a kind of confederation. Simply by dint of their forced marriage a century earlier England and Normandy were linked more closely to each other than they were to the other lands Henry II ruled, but as the years went by the ties gradually became weaker. And all the time the Capetian kings of France were keeping up the pressure that was to culminate in their conquest of the duchy in 1204.

As we have seen, John spent the next ten years trying to get it back. In the event he was doomed to failure because the common interests that had once bound the cross-Channel dominion together were no longer there. Nevertheless, the recovery of Normandy remained an objective, however unrealistic, of Henry III's foreign policy until he was finally brought to surrender his claims in the Treaty of Paris in 1259.

And that seemed to be that. But in 1415 the Hundred Years War (q.v.) was reopened by Henry V (q.v.). He renewed the English claim to the crown of France and invaded Normandy. In 1417 he began the systematic conquest of the duchy, and by 1419 had all but completed the job: the Norman Conquest in reverse, it has been called. Just as Duke William had rewarded his commanders with estates in England, so King Henry rewarded his with estates in Normandy. Exeter got Harcourt, Clarence got Pontaudemer and so on. He expected the duchy to pay its way, but allowed it the maximum autonomy consistent with allegiance to the English crown. However, after the loss of the alliance with Burgundy in 1435, the position of the English in France became increasingly untenable. A big French offensive in 1441 was halted by the duke of York. But the final reckoning came at the end of the decade. In October 1449 Rouen fell, and in the following year Caen and Cherbourg. That was the end of the English in Normandy. When Gascony (q.v.) went three years later, Calais was the only foothold left on French soil.

J. Le Patourel, *The Norman Empire*, Oxford, 1876.

NORWICH   Norwich, the capital of East Anglia, first appears in the records in the early tenth century, which suggests that its origins lay in the period of Danish occupation of eastern England from *c.* 870 to 917. By 1086 it was the third or fourth largest town in England, a reflection of the importance it derived from being the economic and administrative centre of a large and prosperous hinterland. Although the Normans inherited a town already well established, they transformed it socially and topographically. By 1075 they had built a castle and founded a new borough alongside the old one; and 20 years later

Bishop Herbert de Losinga moved the seat of the E. Anglian diocese there from Thetford and began work on the present cathedral. The works undertaken in the first half of the twelfth century at both the cathedral and the castle added up to the biggest building programme Norwich was to see until the circuit of stone walls was erected between 1297 and 1344. These enclosed an area as big as the City of London, while containing only a quarter of its population. Medieval towns may have been squalid and unhygienic, but in Norwich at any rate overcrowding was not a problem except in the Market area.

In the later middle ages the production of worsted cloth was the main manufacturing trade carried on within the city.

Worsted exports fluctuated sharply. Whether the prosperity of the citizens fluctuated correspondingly we cannot be sure, but one thing is certain. If it did, it did not prevent them from plunging their money into the rebuilding of churches. Norwich has more medieval churches than any other city in England, and many of the 31 which survive today were rebuilt, often on a large scale, in the fifteenth century. At roughly the same time Elm Hill and Princes St were acquiring the frontages they still retain today. These two streets, popular with tourists and photographers alike, offer the best medieval ensembles remaining in the city.

J. Campbell, 'Norwich' in *The Atlas of Historic Towns*, Scolar Press, 1975.

OCKHAM, WILLIAM OF 'There seems no way round Ockham', Professor Jacob once wrote. 'Sooner or later he confronts every worker in later medieval history.' Ockham was undoubtedly one of the greatest English thinkers of the middle ages. As a logician he was without rival. As a destructive genius he has few equals in history.

The main facts of his life can be summarized quickly. Born in about 1288 at Ockham in Surrey, he became a Franciscan and was educated at Oxford. While studying for his Master's degree he began writing a book on theology, the allegedly heretical implications of which were drawn to the attention of the papal curia in 1324. He was summoned to

Avignon for examination. During the three years he had to wait there while the judges made up their minds, he met Michael of Cesena, the Franciscan minister-general who was struggling to uphold his Order's traditional ideal of absolute poverty against Pope John XXII, who was equally determined to revise it in the light of current conditions. Ockham shared Michael's doubts about the orthodoxy of the papal arguments. Fearing they might soon be arrested, they fled from Avignon in 1328 and found refuge at Pisa with Pope John's implacable enemy, the Emperor. Ockham spent most of the rest of his life at Lewis's court conducting pamphlet warfare with the papacy. He died in about 1349, probably a victim of the Black Death (q.v.).

The tracts that flowed from his pen over a period of more than 20 years were numerous and sometimes turgid. But the logic they employed was rigorous in the extreme – hence the term 'Ockham's razor'. What Ockham did was demolish the synthesis between faith and reason so carefully put together between 1266 and 1272 by Aquinas. The gradual reception over the century or so before 1250 of the large corpus of Aristotelian thought had posed a problem for thinkers steeped in the tradition of St Augustine. Augustine had taught that divine inspiration was the source of all knowledge. In the twelfth century Anselm (q.v.) had expressed a similar idea when he spoke of 'faith seeking to understand'. He believed that a deeply spiritual personality could with the powers of reason attain a knowledge of God. For him as for Augustine truth could only be revealed truth. The reception of Aristotelianism, however, changed all this. It dignified the human intellect by recognizing its autonomy; but at the same time it questioned the capacity of that intellect to comprehend divine truths of which it could have no direct experience. The task that faced thirteenth century writers, then, was that of reconciling intellect and faith, Aristotle and Augustine. Thomas Aquinas' solution to this problem can be summed up in his famous sentence, 'Grace does not destroy nature; it perfects her'. He worked from effect to cause in discussing how to approach God. The material world around us is an effect deriving from God as first cause. This world of matter is something unaided reason can understand; but the divine mysteries, incapable as they are of proof or comprehension, can only be approached through faith. In Thomism, therefore, reason and faith each found

their own sphere.

Ockham blew this synthesis sky high. He went to the very foundations of Thomism by attacking its metaphysic of being. Every finite being, Thomas had said, is made up of essence and existence. For example, we could conceive of the essence of a dinosaur, while acknowledging that dinosaurs are extinct and no longer exist. This is because, though existence is unstable, the essence of a thing is found in God. But all this, argued Ockham, is incapable of proof. The mind cannot abstract essence from the thing known because the mental process of abstraction cannot be shown to exist. 'Nothing', he wrote, 'can be known in itself naturally save by intuitional knowledge.' This 'Nominalist' epistemology denied to the thinker any right to knowledge of the extra-sensory universe save the intuitive knowledge of individual things, and in effect therefore denied that any metaphysical knowledge at all was possible. The existence of God was not demonstrable by the powers of reason. It could only be accepted as a matter of faith. Hence all the proofs for God's existence which had been worked out over the centuries, whether by Anselm, Aquinas or anyone else, were invalid.

Reason and faith, which Aquinas had laboured so hard to reconcile, were therefore driven as far apart as possible. As a result of confining the mind to the realm of human experience, Ockham awarded to God an absolute power, an absolute freedom to act as He would. Pursued to its logical conclusion, this doctrine carried devastating implications. It followed, for example, that God could, if He so wished, command a man to hate Him. He could dispense with charity and grace if He wanted. Grace as a quality of the soul was superfluous; it existed only as long as

God pleased. So the whole system of merit and reward fell to the ground.

A consequence of God's freedom of action was man's freedom of action too. And when dealing with men Ockham saw no distinction between the pope and any other mortal. The pope had no claim to infallibility, so it made better sense to vest supreme authority in the Church in a general council. At the same time Ockham and his fellow exile at Lewis IV's court, Marsilius of Padua, developed an autonomous secularist view of the state which, they said, should be free from any subjection to ecclesiastical sovereignty. One consequence of Ockhamist political thinking was to be seen in the early years of the fifteenth century, when the idea of a general council was revived as a means of healing the Great Schism in the Church. In the field of theology, however, the effects of 'Nominalism' were to be shattering. The Thomist synthesis, one of the most accomplished intellectual creations of the middle ages, was gone for ever. But the older tradition was not without its defenders, the most important of whom was Thomas Bradwardine (c. 1290–1349), an Oxford mathematician and Fellow of Merton. His answer to Ockham's emphasis on free-will was an assertion of divine determinism, which later in the century in the hands of John Wycliffe (q.v.) was to become what McFarlane called the 'grisly creed' of predestinarianism.

D. Knowles, *The Evolution of Medieval Thought*, London, 1962; G. Leff, *Medieval Thought: St Augustine to Ockham*, Harmondsworth, 1958.

ORDINANCES The Ordinances of 1311 represent the last major attempt at baronial 'constitution-making' in the middle ages. On 16 March 1310 the committee of Lords Ordainers was appointed by an unwilling Edward II (q.v.) to reform the state of the realm. They produced the first six Ordinances within three days of their appointment, and the remaining 35 eighteen months later.

What led to the appointment of the Ordainers was dissatisfaction with the government of Edward II. Unlike his father, Edward was not a commanding personality. He much preferred to be led, usually by low-born favourites, than to lead. Moreover, there was the terrible situation on the Scottish border, where Edward I had bequeathed a war which could never be won but which his son was reluctant to give up. Its financial consequence was to bankrupt the Crown.

The Ordainers, led by the earls of Lancaster and Warwick, therefore drew up a lengthy code of reforms to remedy the evils of the day. They aimed to improve the finances of the Crown by removing those who had been responsible for its impoverishment in the past. So the notorious Piers Gaveston and others like him were expelled from the kingdom (cls. 20–22); and the lands and gifts which the king had wasted on them since March 1310 were recovered, or 'resumed', so as to replenish the royal demesne (cl. 8). A financial purpose lay behind other clauses, but such reforms would have stood little chance of success had the Ordainers evaded the political problem that ultimately made them necessary. Some means of supervising the king's actions was needed. This they aimed to provide by holding regular sessions of parliament, to be called once or twice a year (cl. 29), by having the officers of state appointed in the presence of the baronage in parliament (cl. 14), and by appointing a committee of lords in each parliament to receive complaints against the king's ministers (cl. 40). By regular meetings of this nature, at which they themselves could meet and consult, the Ordainers expected to be able to enforce their programme of reforms.

Were their hopes fulfilled? Right from the start lack of co-operation from the king rendered much of their work nugatory. Moreover, Thomas of Lancaster was the only one of the earls prepared to make a stand on the enforcement of the Ordinances, and he alone could do little because of the distrust with which he was regarded by Edward. The real need was for some kind of conciliar supervision of the king along the lines of the Council of 15 set up under the Provisions of Oxford (q.v.) in 1258. Just such a council *was* set up in 1318, but it achieved little because Lancaster was not a member. Having therefore stood on the statute roll, largely unenforced and unenforceable for over ten years, the Ordinances were finally repealed after the suppression of Lancaster's rebellion in 1322. Unlike Magna Carta (q.v.) the Ordinances did not enter popular mythology, but the doctrines they embodied continued to be voiced by the Commons in parliament (q.v.) until the 1340s, and the idea of 'resumption' was revived in the fifteenth century.

English Historical Documents, iii, 1189–1327, ed. H. Rothwell, Eyre Methuen, 1975.

OUTLAWRY If an accused failed to turn up in the shire court to answer charges brought against him, sentence could not be pronounced in his absence; instead, the process of outlawry had to be invoked. A writ of *capias* was issued ordering the sheriff to attach him, and if on the third summons he still could not be found, then the exigent was issued. This was a formal demand that he be exacted, or compelled to attend. After the award of the first exigent, he forfeited his goods and chattels to the king, and after the fifth he was outlawed. Until such time as he answered for himself in the court to which he had been summoned, he was placed outside the protection of the law. The consequences of outlawry could be serious, and sometimes were when we remember that until 1329 a man outlawed for felony could be killed with impunity. But in practice its severity was tempered. Outlawry applied only to the county in which it had been pronounced. So all an outlaw needed to do was flee from his own county to the next. There is no doubt that the outlaws were quite a numerous band in medieval England, because in rough terms for every man convicted by the courts another ten were outlawed. As we know only too well from the Robin Hood (q.v.) ballads, they found ample cover in forests like Sherwood where they were able to defy authority for years on end. But why were these refugees from justice elevated to the status of heroes by the medieval ballad writers? Almost certainly because the king's courts and the lawyers who practised in them were so notoriously corrupt that those who succeeded in defying conventional 'justice' won the admiration of the downtrodden and oppressed.

OXFORD In the twelfth century Oxford had been but one of several English towns sheltering a congregation of masters and scholars. In common with these other towns it had a variety of advantages which made it an attractive venue for students. What is hard to explain is why Oxford flourished, and these other places – Northampton, for example – did not. Oxford was convenient geographically and well-served by communications. So too was Northampton. Yet Oxford grew into a university and Northampton did not. This is not to imply, however, that Oxford's progress to educational distinction was smooth and unchecked. Far from it. Feuds with the townspeople culminated in 1209 in the temporary dispersal of the University and the migration of some of the masters to Cambridge (q.v.). There they chose to stay, and England's second university was born. The stability, and indeed the very existence of the University, were threatened too by the rivalries between the Northern and Southern scholars which led to perpetual feuding and on one occasion, in 1334, to the temporary migration of the Northern masters to Stamford (Lincs.). It was to ease the tensions between the rival groups that two proctors were appointed annually, one to represent the Northern masters, and the other the Southern. We first hear of the proctors in 1248, and to this day of course they remain the principal disciplinary officers of the University.

Surprisingly few of the buildings which make a visit to Oxford one of the most memorable architectural experiences in England actually come from the middle ages. To start with, the Colleges began to appear on the scene no earlier than the late thirteenth century, and then only as communities of graduate scholars. The undergraduates lived in houses around the town known as halls. These were rented by Principals who provided lodging and instruction for their student tenants. Of these medieval halls only St Edmund Hall survives by name (its buildings are later),

though remains of others lie hidden behind later shop fronts along the High Street.

What inspired benefactors in the late middle ages to endow Colleges was a wish to provide for hard-up graduates wishing to pursue the long courses of study that led to the higher degrees. University (1249), Merton (1270, 1274), Balliol (1282), Exeter (1314), Oriel (1324) and Queen's (1341) were the earliest Colleges to be founded, but the Chapel, Hall and Mob Quad of Merton are the only buildings to come down to us from this period. Their irregular outline forms a striking contrast to the ordered symmetry of William of Wykeham's (q.v.) New College (1379), a foundation which marked as radical a departure in its arrangement of Hall and Chapel back-to-back along the northern side of the quadrangle as it did in its provision of tutorial teaching by the senior for the junior members of the foundation. If we seek the origins of the Oxford tutorial system, we will not go far wrong in looking to Wykeham's statutes of 1379. All Souls (1438) and Magdalen (1458), the two most important foundations of the fifteenth century, both owed much to the inspiration of New College, particularly in ground plan and architectural conception. As for University as opposed to College buildings, the most impressive survival is the Divinity School, with Duke Humfrey's Library above it, built in the fifteenth century when, paradoxically, theological studies in Oxford were at their lowest ebb for the middle ages.

See also, UNIVERSITIES.

F. Markham, *Oxford,* Oxford: Mowbray, 2nd edn., 1975.

P

PAINTING Medieval art demands from us an effort of imagination that the artistic masterpieces of the Renaissance and later do not. If we are to appreciate the pictorial heritage of the middle ages, as it has come down to us in frescoes, wall paintings and stained glass (q.v.), but principally in illustrated (or 'illuminated') manuscripts, we need to bear in mind the ideas and aspirations which called it into being. First of all, we have to remember that it is Christian art. It is the essentially religious content of medieval art which distinguishes it from that of later periods. The best artists of the day were engaged to decorate Bibles, psalters and towards the end of the middle ages Books of Hours (q.v. LITURGY). But even though they were working in a religious setting, the medieval painters seized every chance they could to introduce picturesque vernacular detail into their work. The second thing we need to remember is that medieval art was in a sense abstract. The artist did not portray nature as he saw it, but as he needed to represent it for his purpose. Here again it is the Renaissance which marks a turning point in Western history. Until then it was considered no part of the artist's job to portray man as man or, for that matter, a city as a city. Symbolism was what mattered. Thus anatomical modelling was ignored, and the rules of perspective undreamt of. For the Heavenly City we see merely a collection of roofs and towers crammed within a circular wall. When all that has been said, we are not entitled to decry the medieval artist. Naive his work might sometimes appear, but often it possessed a power, an emotional intensity, which has never been surpassed.

The earliest flowering of English medieval art came in seventh-century Northumbria, where Saxon, Celtic and Mediterranean influences came together to produce such well-known masterpieces as the Lindisfarne Gospels. The Northumbrian school was extinguished by the Viking onslaught of the ninth century, and when artistic excellence reappeared it found its centre in southern England at Winchester. In the reign of King Edgar (959–75) Dunstan, archbishop of Canterbury, and Athelwold, bishop of Winchester, led a revival in monastic life which stimulated the production of illuminated manuscripts. The artists responsible for this work evolved a style, known as the 'Winchester style', which prevailed in England until a generation after the Conquest. It marks a definite break with the Hiberno-Saxon art of Northumbria three hundred years before. The chief characteristics of the Winchester style can be seen in one of its finest manuscripts – the foundation charter of New Minster, Winchester (966). In the centre we have King Edgar presenting the charter to Our Lord who is enclosed within a mandorla supported by winged angels. The figures themselves are full of movement, easily recognizable for their swirling, fluttering drapery; and enclosing the scene is a rich border, loaded with heavy acanthus ornament (plate 18). The most enduring legacy of this school was its technique of outline-drawing, employed on the New Minster charter for the angels. Sketched in ink and only lightly coloured, these rely for their aesthetic effect solely on the use of line. The artists of Winchester and Canterbury probably derived the 'outline-drawing' style from Continental exemplars, but they invested it with such vigour that it became a characteristically English idiom.

So far as manuscript illumination is concerned, the Norman Conquest of England was a non-event. To adapt a well-worn epigram, the Normans had little to teach and much to learn from the Anglo-Saxon artists. A change did come, but it is to be associated less with the arrival of the Normans than with the wider cultural revival known as the Twelfth Century Renaissance. English art was subjected to a wave of Continental influence that was strongly Byzantine in inspiration – not surprisingly, when we remember that the Crusades were bringing Europe into closer contact with the Near East. As a result the informal sketchiness of the Winchester style became more severe, more monumental. This transformation first found expression in about 1120 in the Albani Psalter, a volume produced at St Alban's but now preserved at Hildesheim (Holland). In place of the gaiety which invigorated Saxon art, it is solemnity that pervades the work of the Albani artists. But perhaps for that very reason the Albani style represented too strong a reaction from the traditional tastes of the English artists, and in the later work of the twelfth century its rigidity gave way to a style more rhythmical while still monumental. This is what we see in the greatest Romanesque manuscript produced in England – the Winchester Bible (begun c. 1140–60), preserved in the library of the Cathedral there.

This, like many other medieval books, has been shown to be the work of not one but a number of artists, very likely drawn to Winchester by the patronage of Bishop Henry of Blois, King Stephen's brother. Of these men the most brilliant was the so-called Master of the Leaping Figures who began but did not finish the two capital 'B's at the head of the Psalms (plate 19). The name by which he is known to modern scholars sums up his style. His figures, though intended to be clothed in the characteristic twelfth-century 'damp-fold' drapery, have overcome the early stiffness, and instead leap and swirl in a highly emotional manner. The Continental influence of the twelfth century also took its toll of the heavy acanthus leaf borders of the Anglo-Saxon artists. Instead, miniatures are neatly surrounded by frames within which the familiar Hiberno-Saxon interlace pattern makes a reappearance. From what little wall-painting of this period that has survived in a satisfactory state of preservation it is clear that the monumental style of the twelfth century was not confined to manuscripts. In St Anselm's chapel, Canterbury Cathedral, we can see high on the wall the celebrated painting of St Paul shaking the viper into the fire. The convention in which the draperies are shown points to a hand closely associated with the Master of the Leaping Figures, a hand clearly capable of combining careful modelling with powerful and dramatic handling of design. It is these qualities which make the painting one of the masterpieces of later twelfth-century art.

At the beginning of the thirteenth century English art sustained another wave of influence from abroad. This time it was largely French-inspired, and associated with the evolution from Romanesque to Gothic. The movement that in architecture saw heavy Norman buildings give way to light, slender

Gothic structures also saw the profound, monumental style of the twelfth century in illumination give way to a smaller-scale, more human form in the thirteenth. The main features of the new mood are well illustrated in the Fall of Man from a Bible of *c.* 1230–50 in the Fitzwilliam Museum, Cambridge (plate 20). The grandiose proportions of the Winchester Bible (23ins.×15¾ins.) have given way to more modest dimensions (10ins.×7ins.). And this preference for a smaller format was accompanied by a change in the manner of illumination. Artists came to favour a narrative approach, enclosing each scene within a medallion – a technique often found in the stained glass of the period. In the Fitzwilliam Bible, for example, the six oval medallions down the centre of the page portray scenes from Genesis, and the roundels along the border tell the story of Adam and Eve. This manuscript also serves to demonstrate the main decorative change that becomes noticeable in the thirteenth century – the reappearance of the wide border that had distinguished the pre-Conquest 'Winchester style'. It was in the border that ever increasing decorative embellishment was to be concentrated as the century wore on. What this reflected was a release from the serious mood of the twelfth century, which allowed the artist to lavish as much if not more attention on the periphery as he did on the central subject of the page. He was able to indulge his taste for the irrelevant once more. He introduced rabbits, squirrels, monkeys, not to mention animal grotesques, all of them creeping in and out of the luxuriant foliage. For the moment, though, we must note in passing that it is in the thirteenth century that we can start identifying by name some of the artists who worked on these manuscripts. For example, the

Bible in the Fitzwilliam was signed by 'W de Brailes', perhaps William de Brailes the illuminator who is known to have worked in Oxford. Another artist who signed his work was Matthew Paris (q.v.), the chronicler, to whose scriptorium at St Alban's we are indebted for the revival in England of the technique of outline drawing.

These characteristics of thirteenth century art form the background to the evolution of the 'East Anglian style', so called from the number of works produced there, in which English medieval illumination found its most glorious expression. If we look at the capital letters or the magnificent borders which decorate their manuscripts, we will have no difficulty in understanding why the East Anglian artists were so highly regarded. By the early fourteenth century painters probably spent less time working on Bibles than on devotional books like Psalters and Books of Hours commissioned by private lay patrons. Of these perhaps the finest is the St Omer Psalter, begun in about 1330 for the family of that name resident at Mulbarton (Norfolk). All the elements of the East Anglian style are present on its 'Beatus' page – the Psalter's opening folio on which the illuminator lavished all his skills (plate 21). The 'B' encircles a Jesse tree in which the interlace technique puts in another appearance. Small and intricate as it is, the letter is matched by the exquisite medallions which adorn the border; and out of the interstices in between them grow a variety of foliage motifs in which a peacock, a snail, a stag, a monkey and even a unicorn can be identified. With the St Omer Psalter the East Anglian artists produced a masterpiece that was never to be surpassed. When we move onto the later manuscripts of the school, signs of incipient decadence unfortunately creep in. The Luttrell Psalter (c. 1340), though one of the most popular of all medieval manuscripts for its delightful scene of Sir Geoffrey being armed by his wife and daughter-in-law, is nevertheless the first major manuscript of the school to show unmistakable marks of this decline. Its margins are filled with grotesques like the famous monkey wagoner which are frankly more absurd than amusing (plate 22).

Just as the exuberance of Decorated architecture gave way to the rectilinear simplicity of Perpendicular, so the excesses of the later East Anglian school gave way mid-century to a simpler style in which these decorative borders received less emphasis. The 1350s in fact show little evidence of any artistic achievement, and it took a wave of French and Italian influence to breathe new life into English art in the later years of Edward III's reign. The principal characteristics of this 'International' style, as it is called, can be seen in the Bohun Psalter (c. 1370–80), the Italian inspiration of which is suggested by the beady black eyes and black hair of Christ and his apostles. But foreign inspiration did not last for long. And when English artists once again produced works of the highest excellence, it was purely domestic influences that were at work. Leadership by now had passed from the East Anglian artists to the Court school, which operated under the patronage of the young Richard II (q.v.). Although several of his Court artists are known to us by name, sadly we do not know which of them were responsible for the two most famous works of the reign, the Wilton Diptych (plate 23) in the National Gallery and the 'coronation' portrait of the king himself in Westminster Abbey. The latter has been so heavily restored that it would be unwise to come to any firm conclusion about its style or possible provenance. But the Wilton Diptych is another matter. It displays all the fondness for animals so characteristic of English art, and if we are right in dating it to about 1395 then either the king's painter Gilbert Prince or his successor Thomas Litlyngton could have been responsible. The delight in the portrayal of wild animals experienced by whoever painted the Diptych was shared by another artist whose work has come down to us. This was the Dominican, John Sifrewast, to whom (with his assistant) we are indebted for the engagingly lifelike birds which decorate the borders of the Sherborne Abbey Missal (plate 24). But Sifrewast's most famous manuscript is the Lovell Lectionary, commissioned by John, Lord Lovell of Titchmarsh for Salisbury Cathedral. In this he included the famous portrait of himself presenting the volume to his patron – an attractive scene certainly, but the faces look just a little too alike to be true (plate 25).

Sifrewast was really the last in a long tradition of English illuminators. He had no distinguished successors, still less did he found a school. Such achievements as the fifteenth century has to show come not so much in painting as in the revival of outline-drawing. In the 1440s a school of artists had perfected their own form of this, known as the 'tinted outline style' from the shading which was introduced so as to give a fully modelled appearance. A delightful example is the miniature of John Lydgate presenting his book *The Pilgrim* to Thomas Montacute, earl of Salisbury (plate 26). Outline drawing remained popular into the 1470s when John Rous executed his historical pageant roll of the earls of Warwick in this style. Some of the figures – those of the duke of Clarence and his wife, for example – are attractive enough, but hardly rank as artistic masterpieces.

It may well have been the 'tinted outline' technique in manuscript illumination which set the fashion for monochrome wall paintings like those in the chapel of Eton College for which two artists, Gilbert and William Baker, were paid between 1479 and 1488. Despite the impression given by the unmistakeably English names of these two men, the inspiration for their work was clearly Continental. If Flemish painters were not called in, then at least Flemish cartoons must have been used. In fact, the paintings at Eton make an apt commentary on the decline of English art at the end of the middle ages. Even though English artists seem to have been engaged, the style in which they worked was Flemish. This is not surprising when we remember that at this time Jan van Eyck and Roger van der Weyden were making the Low Countries the centre of a new approach to painting based on a sense of perspective and a keen observation of the human figure. Not until after Holbein's visits to the court of Henry VIII in the next century was there any sign of a recovery in English art.

A certain incompatibility between the English and Flemish approaches helps to explain the decline in English art in the fifteenth century. But it is not the whole story. The problem was that methods of production had changed in the course of the middle ages. In the Romanesque period illuminated manuscripts were produced in the monasteries, chiefly at houses like Winchester, Canterbury and Peterborough which had a long tradition of artistic excellence. But during the twelfth and thirteenth centuries, as the demand for service books by private as well as institutional patrons increased, so the place

and mode of production changed. The job moved out of the cloister. What had once been a skill now became a trade. It could be carried on in workshops, like those in Oxford for example, where the 'lymenours' or illuminators are known to have been centred in Catte St. And if a London ordinance of 1403 is to be taken as typical, 'leymenour' and scribe were likely to be two different men, even if they were enrolled in the same guild. Mass production and the division of labour led to a coarsening of the quality of the work.

M. Rickert, *Painting in Britain: The Middle Ages*, Harmondsworth, 1954; W. Oakeshott, *The Artists of the Winchester Bible*, Faber & Faber, 1945.

PARIS, MATTHEW An indication of Matthew's importance in medieval studies is given by the fact that he is the only chronicler to have been made the subject of a modern biography. Most of the information we have about his life Matthew gives us himself. He must have been born in about 1200 because he tells us that he became a monk of St Alban's in 1217. There he was to stay for the rest of his life, except for the odd visit or two to Canterbury or Westminster and for a journey to Norway in 1248.

His enduring fame rests on his historical writings. He took over the St Alban's scriptorium from another monk, Roger of Wendover, in 1236, and remained in charge of it till his death in about 1259. His *magnum opus* was the *Chronica Majorca* (Great Chronicle), the largest and most detailed narrative we have for the middle years of Henry III's reign (q.v., CHRONICLES). Like many medieval chroniclers Matthew aimed to write a universal history embracing everything from the Creation onwards. For the period up to his own day he needed to do no more than transcribe the *Flores Historiarum* (Flowers of History) written by his predecessor Roger of Wendover. But when Matthew took over a pre-existing work, he did not simply fit it into his own narrative. He rewrote it and improved it. Thus many of the most famous stories about wicked King John (q.v.), most of them apocryphal in the first place, were embroidered still further in Matthew's pages. As soon as he moves onto writing about his own times he becomes not only more valuable but also more self-revealing. Sheltered as his life at St Alban's may have been, Matthew knew a great many people who were in a position to provide him with inside information about events at home and abroad. His appetite for news was well-nigh insatiable. And not only that: the intrusion of his own personality into his writings distinguishes him from most other medieval chroniclers. He lambasts the king and the pope; he attacks the friars; he resents taxation and condemns the itinerant justices. Matthew is nothing if not trenchant. But he was not a genius. His views were instinctive rather than well thought out. To suggest, as some writers have done in the past, that he had a theory of constitutional monarchy in which the king would govern with the advice of the barons, his 'natural counsellors', may be according his ideas a dignity they do not deserve. The pro-baronial viewpoint that was to characterize the St Alban's chronicles to their dying day in the fifteenth century is after all found right at the beginning in the work of Wendover.

The highest compliment we can pay Matthew is that he is fascinating to read, and a good artist to boot, as we can see from the delightful drawings that adorn the margins of his manuscripts.

R. Vaughan, *Matthew Paris*, Cambridge, 1958, repr. 1979; V. H. Galbraith, *Roger of Wendover and Matthew Paris*, Univ. of Glasgow, 1944, repr. 1970.

PARLIAMENT In 1236 a case in the Court of King's Bench was adjourned to a session of 'parliament'. That is the earliest occurrence in a documentary source of the word 'parliament'. The earliest reference in a chronicle comes a decade later in 1246 when Matthew Paris (q.v.) tells us that Henry III (q.v.) summoned a parliament of all the English nobility, ecclesiastical as well as secular, to London. What were these parliaments, and what were they supposed to do?

We are given a clue in the Provisions of Oxford (q.v.), 1258, which contained an important clause requiring parliaments to be held three times a year to discuss 'the common needs of the realm'. What was meant by 'the common needs of the realm'? Historians have taken differing views. H. G. Richardson and G. O. Sayles, following a suggestion first made by F. W. Maitland, have argued strongly that the main business was the dispensation of justice. The king assembled with his counsellors in parliament at increasingly regular intervals to hear cases referred to him by the judges and to redress the grievances of subjects who submitted petitions. According to this view parliament was in essence a court. Such an interpretation certainly gains support from the surviving documentation, which is strongly judicial in bias. But other historians, notably J. G. Edwards, have given reasons for doubting whether the king would have convened such important assemblies merely to discuss the grievances of his subjects. Were 'the needs of the realm', which according to the Provisions of Oxford parliaments were to discuss, really confined to judicial matters, he asks? To answer this question properly we would need to know more than we do about what was on the agenda for these meetings; but it does seem likely that the king was seeking the advice of the magnates on a wide range of political and financial as well as judicial business. If, for example, he wished to levy a tax on the property of his subjects, then he needed to obtain 'common consent'. In 1225, 1232 and 1237 Henry III (q.v.) obtained such consent from an assembly of lords. By the 1250s, however, these lords had come to doubt whether they alone had the power to sanction a tax, the incidence of which fell not only on them but on the whole community. Thus, in 1254, when approached once more for a tax, they told the king to summon representatives of the shires and of the clergy as well. It was on this occasion that the knights of the shire, representing the Commons of the realm, were invited to attend a parliament for the first time. They were of course summoned again by Simon de Montfort (q.v.) in 1264 and 1265, when the burgesses came along too, to represent the towns. Rather than portray parliament as an exclusively judicial assembly, it would seem wiser therefore to stress the diversity of the business which it transacted. Pre-eminent among 'the great needs of the realm' was the king's need for financial assistance, and it was accepted by Edward I's reign that whenever sanction was needed for a grant of taxation – usually in the form of the moveables tax – the Commons would have to be present (q.v. TAXATION).

It is important to remember all the same that since the purpose of summoning the representatives of the Commons was normally fiscal, their presence would have been required only at some parliaments and not at others. Of the 19 parliaments held in the early years of Edward I's reign between 1272 and 1289 the knights were present at only four, and the burgesses at only three. On the other hand, of the eight held between 1300 and 1307 the knights and burgesses were present at six. In other words, as the king's need for taxation became greater and more continuous, so the place of the Commons in parliament was bound to become more secure. The last parliament to which the Commons were (probably) not summoned was that of midsummer, 1325.

The lords, spiritual and temporal, received individual summonses to parliament from the king. The representatives of the Commons on the other hand, two knights from each shire and two burgesses from each parliamentary borough or city, were elected – the knights in the county court, the burgesses in the borough court. At times, particularly in the more oligarchical boroughs, the process must have taken the form of selection rather than election, and in the 1330s lack of interest in parliamentary representation is attested by the complaints made against the sheriff of Cambridgeshire that, far from presiding over an election in the county court, he was simply returning his own nominees. By the later fourteenth century, however, the indications certainly in the counties are that election to parliament was regarded as an honour, much sought after by members of the local gentry.

It was the practice by the fourteenth century for a session of parliament to be opened by a speech from a minister of the Crown delivered to both Lords and Commons together in the Painted

Chamber of the Palace of Westminster. The minister, normally the Chancellor by the reign of Richard II, explained the reasons for their meeting, and invited petitions to be submitted. 'Common' petitions went via the clerk of parliament to the king and his council, who used them as the basis for drafting legislation; 'singular' petitions (relating to the grievances of individual persons) went to the receivers, who sorted them and passed them onto the triers. Both assemblies would spend several days discussing the matters or 'points' on which the king and his ministers wanted their advice. One important point would often be a request for taxation, to which it was unlikely that a reply would be given before the Lords and Commons had 'intercommuned' or conferred. Sometimes, as the needs of business required, there would have to be a more formal consultation of king, Lords and Commons assembled together, usually in the White Chamber. On one such occasion, in the Good Parliament of 1376, the Commons all went along together, only to find that some of their number were admitted and the rest excluded. Accordingly, their spokesman, Sir Peter de la Mare, declared that he would not deliver his message till they were all let in. Evidently a forceful man, Sir Peter, a knight of the shire for Herefordshire, is considered to have been the first of the long line of Speakers of the House of Commons. It was also in this parliament (the longest till then held) that the Commons used the process of impeachment (q.v.) for the first time to indict Lord Latimer and other unpopular royal officials before the assembled Lords on charges of corruption.

By the end of Edward III's reign the Commons had acquired all the powers they were to enjoy for the next 200 years,

the most important being control over the supply of funds to the Crown in the form of taxation. The position of the Commons was assured once Edward III had given up bargaining for money independently with the county communities for direct, and with the merchants for indirect, taxation; and it was substantiated in 1407 when it was established that the Lords should merely assent to what had been granted independently by the Commons. Furthermore, the right of announcing the final grant had for some time been the privilege of the Speaker of the Commons.

It is worthwhile in conclusion to contrast the development of the English parliament with its namesake in Paris, which also emerged for the first time in the 1230s. Although initially they were not unlike, the two institutions developed along different lines. The omnicompetence of the English parliament was not paralleled in France, where the *parlement* of Paris remained a purely judicial body, composed of professional lawyers, and the Estates General became the representative assembly. In the fourteenth century a king who needed money might begin by convening a session of the Estates General, but this could do little more than encourage the regional assemblies to make the necessary grants of taxation. Not least among the factors which contributed to the growth of royal absolutism in France was the absence of a national assembly which could set redress of grievance against supply of money.

Historical Studies of the English Parliament, ed. E. B. Fryde & E. Miller, 2 vols., Cambridge, 1970; J. G. Edwards, *The Second Century of the English Parliament*, Oxford, 1979; G.

L. Harriss, *King, Parliament and Public Finance in Medieval England to 1369*, Oxford, 1975.

PASTON LETTERS The Pastons owe their fame to the great collection of letters and papers from which we learn so much about society and politics in fifteenth-century Norfolk. What caused many of the letters to be written was the business association between John Paston I and that irascible old war veteran, Sir John Fastolf (q.v.) of Caister Castle.

John was the eldest son of Judge William Paston, the founder of the family fortunes. Through his wife he had been introduced to Fastolf, whose legal adviser he became. Indeed, so high did he stand in the knight's favour that by the terms of a nuncupative will made two days before his death Fastolf granted him all of his estates in Norfolk and Suffolk except those assigned to the endowment of a college of priests at Caister, the foundation of which he wanted John as a last favour to complete (54*). John was the only one of Fastolf's staff to benefit financially from his years of service to a master renowned for his tight-fistedness. Needless to say, some of the other executors, like William Worcester (q.v.), felt jealous and objected. John therefore had to move quickly, and lost no time in occupying the lands that had come to him. But his responsibilities took him away from home a lot. That is why the letters came to be written. John wanted to keep in touch with his wife Margaret, and she with him. Margaret Paston emerges from the correspondence as a remarkable woman, shrewd and

* References in brackets are to numbers of the letters in *Paston Letters & Papers of the Fifteenth Century*, ed. N. Davis, Oxford, 2 vols., 1971, 1976.

determined, and better than most of the men at looking after the family affairs. She needed to be, because the next 15 years were to be spent in fighting off the attacks of others who staked a claim to the Fastolf inheritance. First off the mark was another executor, the justice Sir William Yelverton, who took the manor of Cotton in Suffolk (644, 645). Then there was John de la Pole, duke of Suffolk, who claimed Hellesdon and Drayton, near Norwich, and sent a raiding party in October 1465 to remind the inhabitants of the two villages of the price they would have to pay for continued loyalty to the Pastons (196). With all this worry it is not surprising that John I died quite young, in 1466 at the age of 45. He had sent his son John II to be brought up at court – a wise decision as it turned out, because the young man was able to use his influence to secure Edward IV's recognition of his title to Caister (896). This counted for something, but not for a lot. The duke of Norfolk had his eyes on Caister too. In 1469 he occupied the castle by force (332, 334). All this took place ten years after Fastolf had died, and still no settlement lay in sight. In 1470, therefore, William Wainfleet, bishop of Winchester, and another of the executors, cut the Gordian knot by relieving Paston of all the estates except for Caister, Hellesdon and Drayton, and transferring the proposed college of priests to his own new foundation of Magdalen College, Oxford (252). Norfolk took no notice. When he did withdraw from Caister, in 1471, it was not out of deference to Wainfleet but because Edward IV (q.v.) had been driven from the throne and replaced, temporarily as it was to happen, by Henry VI. The Pastons moved back into Caister, but only for six months. In June, after Edward IV had recovered the throne, Norfolk took it

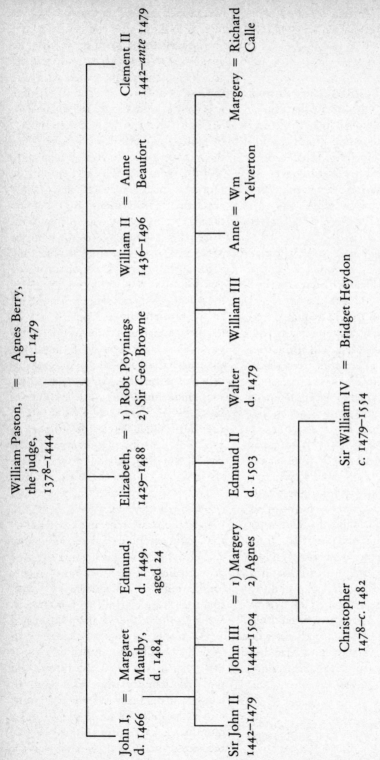

William Paston, = Agnes Berry,
the judge,   d. 1479
1378–1444

John I, = Margaret Mautby, d. 1484
d. 1466

Edmund, d. 1449, aged 24

Elizabeth, = 1) Robt Poynings
1429–1488   2) Sir Geo Browne

William II = Anne Beaufort
1436–1496

Clement II
1442–*ante* 1479

Sir John II
1442–1479

John III = 1) Margery
1444–1504   2) Agnes

Edmund II
d. 1503

Walter
d. 1479

William III

Anne = Wm Yelverton

Margery = Richard Calle

Christopher
1478–c. 1482

Sir William IV = Bridget Heydon
c. 1479–1554

The Pastons in the Fifteenth Century (*simplified*)

again. John Paston II was hardly in a position to do anything about it, because he had fought for the Lancastrians at the battle of Barnet, and though pardoned by Edward IV, obviously no longer enjoyed the favour he once had. The struggle finally came to an end when Norfolk died in 1476. John staked his claim immediately, and the king's council ruled in his favour (268, 299, 300).

John I's widow, Margaret, like many medieval widows, survived her husband for nearly a couple of decades, and lived to see this triumph. It was her fortitude and good advice that had seen her son through many crises. In the early 1470s he was evidently running up debts, and could not even make sure that his late father's memory was properly honoured. 'Yt is a schame', his mother wrote, 'and a thyng that is myche spokyn of in this countre (i.e. county) that your faders grave ston(e) is not mad(e).' (212) Admittedly, however, tombs and brasses (q.v.) did take some time to be delivered, and John had been enquiring only a couple of months earlier how much space was available for the tomb slab in Bromholm Priory (264). It is details of family business like this, not to mention Margaret Paston's concern for her children's love affairs, that make the letters so fascinating to read. The times were turbulent, certainly. The Pastons were trying to hold onto their property while the struggles we know as the Wars of the Roses (q.v.) were being fought. But there was opportunity for leisure too. An inventory of John Paston II's books made shortly after his death in 1479 show that his tastes included Arthurian romances (q.v.), Cicero, heraldry, *The Game and Playe of Chesse*, and a book of statutes, no doubt for reference (316). Favourite outside recreations were hunting and hawking

(269, 270, 354, 574). Marriage in the right social circles was another of Margaret Paston's abiding concerns. She strongly disapproved when her daughter Margery insisted on marrying Richard Calle, the family bailiff (203, 245, 332). On the other hand, prison does not seem to have carried much stigma, for the gentry at least. John Paston I was committed to the Fleet in London no fewer than three times, and was little the worse for it. He could dictate business letters, and amuse himself and his wife by writing doggerel verses (77). His contemporary, Sir Thomas Malory (q.v.), tells us of course that he composed *Le Morte d'Arthur* in Newgate Prison.

PATENT ROLLS Letters issued patent from Chancery were those which were so wrapped that they could be opened and read without breaking the seal. They communicated matters of public business like appointments of justices of the peace, grants of licences and so on. From 1201 copies of these letters were made on parchment sheets stitched head to tail to form rolls.

See also, GOVERNMENT.

PEASANTS REVOLT In several parts of Europe in the later fourteenth century social harmony was shattered by outbreaks of peasant discontent – the Ciompi in 1378 at Florence, the Jacquerie in 1358 and the Maillotins in 1382, both in France, and of course the Peasants Revolt in England in 1381. Each of these rebellions drew on conditions unique to its own time and place. But what contributed in general terms to the instability of this period was the transformation of the economic order caused by the dramatic fall of population. In

England, for example, the Black Death had reduced numbers by between a third and a half from 5–6 million to about 3½ million (q.v. POPULATION). Landowners who before 1348 had been assured a plentiful supply of labour now found themselves in difficulties. Rental income was threatened by the shortage of tenants, and demesne husbandry by rising wage bills. If the landowners were to maintain their standard of living, therefore, they had to cut their costs. This they sought to do by the Ordinance and then the Statute of Labourers, 1351, which pegged wages at pre-plague rates. But they had other weapons in their armoury as well. They could seek to reimpose demesne labour services which had been commuted for money back in the days when in real terms it was as cheap to hire wage labourers. Peasants who held by villein tenure therefore found themselves in the firing line. But, for all the coercive power they had at their disposal, landlords found labour services, particularly ploughing works, difficult to exact in full. If their efforts to enforce them were only partially successful, they had many other powers over their unfree tenants which could be turned to advantage in difficult times. Villeins could be forced to take up vacant holdings. They could be prevented from leaving the manor to seek better conditions elsewhere. They could be held liable not just for entry fines but for such incidental payments as heriot (q.v.) and merchet (q.v.). That landlords were indeed exploiting these potential sources of income to the full is indicated by the fact that, despite the fall in population and everything that followed from that, their incomes in the 1360s were only about 10 per cent lower than they had been before the Black Death. Not surprisingly, the abolition of villeinage was in the forefront of peasant demands

in 1381.

The event that sparked off the Revolt, however, was the collection of the poll taxes. The government was faced with the problem of financing the war with France at a time when it was going badly for England. The yield from the traditional fifteenths and tenths on moveable property had fallen since the Black Death. A new and more lucrative form of taxation was needed. The one that found favour was the poll tax, first levied in 1377 on everyone over 14 at the rate of 4d a head. It was levied again in 1379, at a graduated rate, and in 1380 for a third time, on this occasion at a flat rate of 1s a head, the rich in each village helping out the poor. This was all very well, but what if there was no rich man in the vill? The poor would have to bear the entire burden themselves. Not surprisingly there was widespread evasion. The yield from the tax was less than expected, and in spring 1381 new commissions were appointed in certain counties to investigate corruption and negligence. It was the assault at the end of May on John de Bampton and his fellow commissioners at Brentwood (Essex) that precipitated the uprising.

In Kent it was the activities of another tax collector, the unpopular John Legge, that provoked resistance. On 6 June a band of rebels captured Rochester Castle. On the following day they chose Wat Tyler to be their leader, and marched on Canterbury. From there they moved to Blackheath, overlooking the Thames, a distance they covered in only two days. By now panic had broken out in the capital: Tyler and his followers were opening the Marshalsea prison at Southwark, and the men of Essex were gathering on the eastern outskirts of the City at Mile End. The rebels must have had many sympathizers within the City. Perhaps it was one of them who let the

Kentishmen in on Thursday, 13 June. Later the same day the men of Essex broke in as well, and John of Gaunt's palace of the Savoy was burned to the ground. These events brought about a total collapse of morale in the ruling classes from which only the 13 year old Richard II (q.v.) was exempt. On Friday morning he went out to speak to the rebels at Mile End, where he accepted from them a petition calling for the abolition of villeinage, fair terms of employment and land at 4d an acre. He gave way to their demands and urged them to depart. Depart they did, but not all in the direction he wanted, for the same day there was an assault on the Tower, which resulted in the capture and execution among others of Simon Sudbury, the archbishop of Canterbury. Like most medieval rebels the peasants criticized not the king but those who, they believed, had misled him. The next day (Saturday), therefore, the Kentishmen had no hesitation in responding to Richard's invitation to meet him at Smithfield. Tyler came forward to state their demands, which went further than those made the previous day, and asked for the abolition of lordships and the distribution of the wealth of the Church. This was all too much for one member of the king's retinue who insulted Tyler. A scuffle broke out, in the course of which the rebel leader was stabbed to death by William Walworth, the mayor of London. Richard held his nerve, and rode into the heart of the peasant throng, commanding them to follow him. Now that Tyler was dead, he had little difficulty in persuading them to disperse; and a fortnight later on 2 July he ordered their charters of manumission to be revoked.

How much contact there was between rebels in different parts of the country is difficult to say. But news of the rising in the south-east soon seems to have sparked off disturbances in other localities, even as far north as York, Beverley and Scarborough. In East Anglia the peasant rebels, led by one Geoffrey Litster, enjoyed a brief triumph till they were crushed by Henry Despenser, bishop of Norwich, the only man apart from the youthful king to show any presence of mind that June. At St Alban's the townsfolk led by William Grindcob invaded the precincts of the abbey and extracted a charter from Abbot Thomas de la Mare. At Bury St Edmund's, another Benedictine abbey which had long tried to ignore the town growing up at its gates, events took a more violent turn. John de Cambridge, the prior, was captured and executed. So too was his friend Sir John Cavendish, the Chief Justice, who had a house in the town. Their heads were impaled on spikes next to each other in the pillory, 'and they put the prior's head next to the justice's, now to his ear as if seeking advice, now to his mouth as though showing friendship, wishing in this way to make a mock of the friendship and counsel which had been between them during their lives.'* The antagonism shown towards the king's justices and the legal system in general is a strong theme in the Revolt. The peasants resented the collusion between the lawyers and the great lords, both secular and spiritual, which had the effect of corrupting and distorting the workings of the courts. The unpopularity of the Statute of Labourers was but one element in a much wider dissatisfaction with a legal system in which, as far as the peasants were concerned, the real rulebenders were those who enforced the law.

* Quoted by J. R. Maddicott, *Law & Lordship: Royal Justices as Retainers in Thirteenth & Fourteenth-Century England* (Past & Present Supplement, 4, 1978), 63.

Of the chroniclers who wrote about the Revolt the most perceptive in his analysis of its causes was the famous Froissart, who pointed to the 'ease and riches that the common people were of'. Paradoxically the uprising came not in the early fourteenth century when famine and starvation stalked the land but in the 1380s when prices were falling and wages rising. In the short run the peasants gained nothing from the Revolt. But in the long run the movement of wages and prices worked to their advantage. Large-scale demesne cultivation, as it had been practised in the thirteenth century, offered little hope of profit. By the 1390s most of the big demesnes were being leased, and labour services were no longer needed. At the same time customary tenure was evolving into copyhold tenure, and the distinction between villein and non-villein was one that hardly mattered. The Revolt had a more immediate impact in influencing attitudes than in liberating the peasants. It administered a shock to the lords and gentry. The retaining of justices ceased. The poll taxes were abandoned. Moreover, for the next decade or two the Commons in parliament feared that there might be another uprising. That there was not did not make that fear any the less real.

The Peasants' Revolt of 1381, ed. R. B. Dobson, Macmillan, 1970.

PERPENDICULAR See, ARCHITECTURE, ECCLESIASTICAL.

PILGRIMAGES Like the Crusades (q.v.), pilgrimages were a remarkable manifestation of the strength of popular piety in the middle ages. From all over Europe pilgrim bands, like the one familiar to readers of Chaucer, thronged the well-worn routes to such favoured shrines as those of St Peter at Rome, St Thomas at Canterbury and St James at Santiago de Compostella.

What lay at the root of the pilgrimage ideal was a belief in the potency of saints' relics. This had been shown as early as A.D. 156, when the Christians of Smyrna had taken possession of the bones of their murdered bishop Polycarp, saying they were 'more valuable than refined gold'. Relics, it was believed in the middle ages, brought success in war, conferred protection in times of adversity and restored health to the infirm. A reliquary or shrine was considered to contain not just a collection of bones but the very person of the saint himself. His living presence protected the church where his tomb lay, and it was to him personally that offerings were made. This attitude of mind led to the localization of a saint's cult, even in the case of those like the Virgin Mary whose lives were not associated with a particular sanctuary. Men spoke, for example, of 'Our Lady of Chartres' because what was claimed to be her tunic was preserved in that noble cathedral. There were critics, of course, right from the earliest times, who warned that veneration of relics was in danger of becoming an obstruction to the true understanding of God. But the Church said in reply that people should not worship relics for their own sake, but should look to them to help in the veneration of those who had lived lives of undoubted holiness or had died for the faith.

If that was the official line taken by the Church, it was an exceedingly cautious one, and one moreover that was overtaken by the enthusiasm of the laity. It failed to take account of the miracle-working quality of the relics. Christ in His own mission had resorted to miracles to demonstrate the power of the one true God, His Father. The apostles and the earliest missionaries had likewise performed miracles to prove the superiority of their God to the numerous gods of the pantheistic societies in which they moved. It was believed that in those early and difficult times miracles were necessary to assist in spreading the faith; but once the Conversion was over, they would cease. In fact, of course, they did not, because of the continuing popular demand for miraculous demonstrations of the faith. And the commonest such demonstrations were cases of healing.

How are these to be explained? They could only be accepted in the number that they were – even after spurious ones have been discounted – in an age when medical knowledge was limited. A visit to a shrine was likely to do more good than a visit to a doctor. At least it inspired hope, which was probably more than a visit to a physician would have done in the twelfth century. If the disease was psychological or psycho-somatic, the experience of visiting, say, Canterbury and the shrine of St Thomas might well be enough to do the trick. But there was more to it than that. According to a decree of the Fourth Lateran Council in 1215 illness sprang not from physical ailments but from sin. It followed, then, that the malady was less likely to be cured by the application of medicine than by a visit to the tomb of a saint. Hence the vast crowds of sick and dying who crowded at the gates of a cathedral on the feast day of the blessed martyr contained within its walls.

Not all of those who visited a shrine were at death's door, however. Chaucer's pilgrims, as we know, were fit enough. Another reason for going on pilgrimage was a desire to obtain forgiveness, to perform a penance. By about the eleventh century it had gained acceptance that a man could seek remission for his sins by visiting a shrine, usually one named by his bishop or confessor. Thus the way lay open to using pilgrimages as a form of punishment for particular crimes. We read, for example, that in the twelfth century Scottish convicts were required to visit the shrine of St Cuthbert in Durham Cathedral.

Just as a pilgrimage might enable the penitent to atone for past sins, so it could gain him early remission from the trials of Purgatory. King Robert of France made a tour of nine shrines before his death in 1031 in the hope that he would 'evade the awful sentence of the day of judgement'. But what if a penitent were to resolve on his death-bed to undertake a pilgrimage and then die before having the chance to perform it? In that case the Church would allow him to appoint a vicar to fulfil the obligation. Exploiting that loophole to the full, testators again and again from the fourteenth century onwards took the precaution of leaving a sum of money in their wills for someone – a relative or a clergyman, for example – to make the pilgrimage on their behalf. It could be argued that this was a major step towards debasing the original idea of pilgrimage as an act involving sacrifice or hardship. Once it was accepted that a testator could arrange for someone else to go in his name, then it would not be long before the living made similar arrangements too – hence the so-called vicarious pilgrimages.

Pilgrimages could be to local shrines, or they could be to shrines far away like Rome, Santiago or the Holy Land. The motives that led pilgrims to choose one destination in preference to another remain obscure. Factors of convenience and fashion probably counted for most. Those who could afford it, like Henry of Derby, the future Henry IV (q.v.), in

1393, and some less able to afford it, like Margery Kempe in 1413, went the whole way to the Holy Land. Chaucer's pilgrims, on the other hand, were content to go to Canterbury. Becket's tomb, of course, was the most popular of English shrines, though much less so on the eve of the Dissolution than in the aftermath of the martyr's death. One of the remarkable things about medieval saints' cults is just how short-lived many of them were. Take, for instance, the posthumous reputation of Thomas Cantilupe, bishop of Hereford. After he had died in Italy in 1282 his bones were brought back to his cathedral church at Hereford, which was taking over £178 in offerings by 1290. In 1320 the dean and chapter finally secured his canonization. But by 1336 the saint's cult was already in decline, and by 1388 the annual total of offerings at the shrine only came to £1.6.8. Even at Canterbury trade fell off in the late middle ages. In the later twelfth century offerings averaged £426 *per annum*, and in 1220, the year of the translation of the relics, they totalled no less than £1,142.5.0. But at the Dissolution they averaged a paltry £36 a year. In the late middle ages newer shrines came into being. In the thirteenth century it was Bromholm Priory, sheltering the Holy Rood. A century later it was Walsingham, where the shrine of Our Lady was bringing the canons as much as £260 a year in offerings in 1535.

Before commencing his journey the would-be pilgrim needed to make considerable preparations. First, he would obtain the blessing of his parish priest and confess to all the wrongs that he had committed. Then, if he had property to bequeath, he would make his will. When ready to set off he would don the special garb that symbolized his admission to the pilgrim's order. This consisted of a long, coarse tunic, known as the sclavein, a staff and a broad-brimmed hat turned up at the front on which on the return journey he would sport his pilgrim's badge. For reasons of safety the pilgrims would travel in groups, in early times probably on foot, later more usually on horseback. They would seek hospitality at monasteries or at inns along the road (q.v., ROADS).

Although shrines like Walsingham and Hailes were still pulling in the crowds at the end of the middle ages, the cult of relics and the miracles associated with them were beginning to incur severe criticism, and not just from implacable enemies like Wycliffe and the Lollards (q.v.). The claims of the credulous were treated with more scepticism than ever before, and the authorities conducted full and thorough examination before recognizing any newly proclaimed cult. As Bishop Grandison of Exeter said on one occasion, 'I find these miracles hard to believe and impossible to prove . . . I fear that the people have given themselves over to idolatry.' And yet, as if to belie the allegations of fraud and superstition, shrines like Walsingham and Lourdes still offer as much hope to bands of pilgrims today as the older sanctuaries did years ago.

J. Sumption, *Pilgrimage: an Image of Medieval Religion*, Faber & Faber, 1975.

POITIERS This famous victory, which resulted in the capture of the king of France, was the greatest in the career of Edward, the Black Prince (q.v.). Appointed lieutenant of Gascony by his father, the Prince landed at Bordeaux in September 1355, and used the autumn to lead a chevauchee towards Narbonne and the French Mediterranean coast. The next year he turned northwards, possibly with a view to linking up with Henry of Grosmont, duke of Lancaster in the Loire valley and to their undertaking a joint advance into the French heartland. In the event the destruction of a bridge across the Loire frustrated the plan, and the Prince retreated southwards pursued by an army led by King John. At Maupertuis near Poitiers on 19 September 1356 the English were forced to give battle. Each side employed much the same tactics as at Crecy (q.v.) ten years before, and for much the same reasons. The English adopted a defensive strategy because they were numerically inferior, and the French an offensive one because they were numerically superior. The Prince stationed his archers out in front and his knights and men-at-arms, dismounted, in the rear. King John began by sending in his cavalry, as his father had at Crecy, only to find that they, like their forebears, got mown down by the fire of the English archers. John then ordered the knights to dismount, little realizing that unless they were then combined with the archers there was little point in this manoeuvre. Beyond making such fairly general observations on tactics we can say very little about the ebb and flow of the battle, other than to observe that in its later stages King John himself was taken prisoner. The terms for his release were to be the subject of detailed negotiations between the English and the French for the next four years.

POPULATION Medieval governments in England had no idea how many people they ruled. This was demonstrated in 1371, when Edward III's ministers imposed the villages tax. The Treasurer intended to raise £50,000 by asking each parish for an average of 22s 3d, on the assumption that there were 40,000 parishes in England. Dismayed to find so little money coming in, six months later he had to lift the rate to 116s, on the realization that there were in fact only 8,600 parishes in the country (excluding Cheshire).

Modern historians can do better than that. They can use today's techniques of statistical analysis to overcome the obstacles which prevented medieval governments from making full use of the records they had at their disposal. Of these records the most comprehensive was Domesday Book (q.v.). By 1371 of course it was out of date. And anyway it always did have its limitations. It recorded landholders, not inhabitants; so it said nothing about those who were landless. Moreover, it was not complete. The information that it gave about the towns was notably deficient, and many boroughs were not described in detail at all. Yet, for all its shortcomings, Domesday Book does at least enable a rough calculation to be made of England's population at the end of the eleventh century. That is more than can be done again until the later fourteenth century. Then we have the poll tax returns for 1377, 1379 and 1380–1. Of these the most complete, and arguably the most reliable, are the returns for the tax of 1377, which was levied at an average flat rate of one groat (4d) on each person aged 14 or over. The problem of evasion is still there, but the returns are a start in enabling us to estimate the number of adults in post-Black Death England.

Once we have arrived at a figure for the adult, or male adult, population at any given time, we have to guess the number of dependants. A source like Domesday Book, for example, will give us a figure for the number of adult landholders, but we need a 'multiplier' to convert that into a figure for the total population. In that case we need to know how large was the typical family in the middle ages. Was it nuclear or extended? Did it consist only of the two parents and their children? Or did it consist of grandparents, unmarried adult sons or daughters and perhaps aunts and uncles as well? These questions are all very difficult to answer. Professor J. C. Russell thought that the medieval family was hardly any larger than the modern nucleated family, and suggested a multiplier of no more than 3.5. This figure has been rejected as too low by most other historians who would prefer to settle for a multiplier somewhere in the region of 4.8 to 5.2. Such evidence as there is goes to suggest that in peasant societies adult couples have more children, and support more dependent relatives in their own household, than is common in a modern industrial society.

So if we take a multiplier of about 5, what estimates of population do we arrive at? For 1086 we have 1.6 million, and for 1377 3.5 million, both of which would seem to be about right. But what we would really like to know is the size of England's population on the eve of the Black Death (q.v.) in 1348, and to answer that we need to know the rate of mortality caused by the plague. As usual we have to proceed by means of indirect sources, like manorial account rolls, rentals and so on. For all the attempts that have been made in recent years to minimize its impact, it seems clear from these sources that the Black Death must have carried away between a third and a half of the population. If we work backwards, therefore, from the figure of 3.5 million extracted from the poll tax returns of 1377 we have a pre-plague population of 5–6 million in the 1340s. In other words in the two-and-a-half centuries since the compilation of Domesday Book there had been a three-fold increase in the number of people in England. In the absence of any medical or scientific advances which would have allowed people to live longer, we can only conclude that this increase stemmed from a rise in the birth rate.

How long did it take for population to start growing again after the demographic collapse of 1348–9? The answer depends on the view that is taken of the impact of the later visitations of the plague. It has been argued by some that after the outbreaks of 1361 and 1368 they became fewer in number, and largely confined to the towns. However, the most recent work which has been done in this field tends to support the older and more pessimistic view. According to Dr Hatcher, in little more than a century after 1377 England suffered at least 15 outbreaks of plague or other epidemic diseases of national or near-national proportions. And then there were the many localized visitations in different parts of the country which can be picked up in chronicle references and other sources. The cumulative impact of these visitations, particularly if they hit the young in disproportionately large numbers, could have been enough to prevent the population from replacing itself, let alone increasing. Moreover, the movement of wages and prices provides little support for those who seek to argue that population was beginning to recover in the early- or mid-fifteenth century. The first definite signs of a rise come approximately between 1490 and 1520. The Tudor period then turned out to be one of population explosion, and by 1600, what with the sturdy vagabond problem, contemporaries were loud in complaining that England was an overcrowded isle.

See also, AGRICULTURE.

J. Z. Titow, *English Rural Society*,

1200–1350, Allen & Unwin, 1969; J. Hatcher, *Plague, Population and the English Economy, 1348–1530*, Macmillan, for the Econ. Hist. Soc., 1977.

PREMONSTRATENSIANS The White Canons took their name from the abbey of Premontre near Laon, founded in 1121 by a German, St Norbert of Xanten (*c.* 1080–1134). They came from the same stable, as it were, as the Augustinians or Black Canons (q.v.). In other words, they were one of the new Orders called into being by the renewed spirituality of the twelfth century. Like the Augustinians they tried to offer a semi-monastic way of life to the secular clergy. But unlike them they chose to imitate the simplicity and austerity of the Cistercians (q.v.). This placed them in good stead to benefit from the prohibition on new foundations passed by the General Chapter of the Cistercian Order in 1152: for the piety which had once fed the Cistercians from now on could go to feed the Premonstratensians instead. Between 1170 and 1216 more than 15 of their houses were founded in England, colonized for the most part from the existing houses of Newhouse (Lincs.) or Welbeck (Notts.). The Premonstratensians looked for inspiration to the Cistercians not only in their austere manner of life but also in the centralized constitution they adopted, based on visitations and general chapters. Their abbeys in the British Isles were for the most part of modest size and modest wealth. Few have left extensive remains, but Dryburgh (Scotland) and Bayham (Sussex) are important, and picturesque, exceptions.

D. Knowles, *The Monastic Order in England*, Cambridge, 2nd ed., 1966.

PRISES The Royal right of 'prise' or compulsory purchase bulks prominently in English politics under the three Edwards. The king had long exercised the right of requisitioning the victuals and means of transport he needed for the maintenance of his household on its travels around the realm. No one denied him that right. But its extension and abuse during the Welsh and Scottish wars of the later thirteenth century led to demands for it to be defined more clearly. Goods should never be taken without the owner's consent; they should be paid for; and they should be taken only for the use of the household, not for the whole army. 'Torteous' or unlawful prises were condemned in successive statutes, few of them properly enforced, until the Statute of Purveyors, 1362, brought together earlier legislation and proved to be the definitive statement on the subject for the middle ages. The term 'prises' is often used by historians as if synonymous with 'purveyance'. Until about 1310 it probably was, but by then a distinction had been formulated between purveyance as legitimate purchase in time of emergency and prises as illegal seizure of the subject's property. It was this distinction which the king's critics wanted him to observe.

G. L. Harriss, *King, Parliament & Public Finance in Medieval England to 1369*, Oxford, 1975.

PRIVY SEAL See, GOVERNMENT.

PROVISIONS OF OXFORD The series of two dozen Provisions agreed at Oxford in the spring of 1258 were signficant for giving England a 'constitutional monarchy' for the first time in her history.

The crisis that occasioned their publication arose from Henry III's acceptance from the pope of the Sicilian crown on behalf of his younger son Edmund. What made this such an unattractive proposition was the fact that Sicily was occupied by the pope's enemies, and that Henry was expected to quell them at his own expense. By 1258, even before he had set out, his debts amounted to so much that he had to turn for help to the baronage; and they made financial assistance conditional on the appointment of a committee of 24 to draw up proposals for the reform of the realm. Twelve of its members were to be named by the king and 12 by the baronage.

If Henry expected the balanced membership of this committee to result in mild or innocuous proposals, he was in for a shock. They recommended that a council of 15 should be appointed 'to advise the king in good faith on the government of the kingdom and on all things touching the king and the kingdom.' And as if that were not enough, they went on to revive the old vice-regal office of justiciar (cl. 6) and to subject the other officers of state, the chancellor and treasurer, to the authority of the king and council jointly (cl. 14, 15). Castles were put under the control of new castellans who had strict instructions not to give them up (cl. 8). and finally parliaments were to be held three times a year (cl. 21).

The Provisions of Oxford went so much further than Magna Carta (q.v.) in fettering the king that we must wonder where the reformers got their ideas from. The suggestion that the barons should nominate counsellors to watch over the king had first been floated in 1244, but their appetite for power had been whetted some time before that. Henry III's had been the first royal minority since the Conquest. He had become king at the age of nine, and until he came of age the country was ruled by a council made up of leading barons and royal servants. In 1258 what the reformers set out to do was revive the sort of tutelage they had exercised over the king 40 years before.

Like Magna Carta in 1215 the Provisions of Oxford did not settle matters, but only made them worse. Henry III was determined to recover the authority he had lost, and in 1261 succeeded in obtaining papal absolution from his oath to uphold the reforms. Two years later war broke out between king and barons, and the Provisions were finally buried with Simon de Montfort (q.v.) at the battle of Evesham in August 1265. It was perhaps because they were so revolutionary that they never achieved the lasting fame of Magna Carta, but their importance in the evolution of baronial thinking has assured them of a permanent place in English constitutional history.

Documents of the Baronial Movement of Reform and Rebellion, 1258–1267, ed. R. F. Treharne & I. J. Sanders, Oxford, 1973.

PROVISIONS, PAPAL One of the most regular complaints of the Commons in parliament in the fourteenth century was that the pope was overriding the rights of ordinary 'collators' or patrons by appointing nominees of his own to ecclesiastical benefices in this country. In other words, the pope was using his authority to 'provide' candidates. The first full-blown petition against 'provisions' seems to have been the one submitted to the Carlisle parliament in 1307, but the evils against which it inveighed went back long before that.

Papal intervention in the disposal of

livings was simply one aspect of the centralizing tendencies which concentrated more and more power in the hands of the pope from the twelfth century onwards. The practice had begun under Innocent III, who directed bishops to confer prebends and other benefices on his nominees. In 1245 it was taken further, and legitimized, in Clement IV's decretal *Licet Ecclesiarum* which claimed that the pope alone could fill those benefices vacated in the Roman curia. Under the Avignon popes John XXII and Clement VI the system was carried still further.

Why did the popes gather so much patronage into their own hands? Not, as the English parliament would have us believe, to subvert the Church in these isles by the appointment of disloyal, absentee foreigners. What appears at first sight to have been a papal initiative was in fact a response to the plight of those thousands of well-trained, but under endowed young clerks who came to Rome desperate for preferment. In medieval society it was less what you knew than who you knew that counted. So a clerk of 'Oxenford' or Paris stood little chance of obtaining a benefice unless he had a lordly patron who could give him one. If he was not so fortunate, his only hope lay in asking the pope to overturn the normal patterns of patronage in his favour.

This, of course, was not the way that provisions were seen by the laity who spoke in the English parliament. They objected to the Roman curialists (whose numbers they surely exaggerated), whom they saw appointed to English livings. As Edward III said in 1343, these aliens did not know the faces of their flocks, still less speak their language, and as a result there was a decline in devotion among the people. Reading between the lines, what really bothered Edward III was that *he* would not be able to get *his* nominees appointed to bishoprics if the pope kept filling them. For that reason he was happy to satisfy the Commons by conceding the Statute of Provisors (1351), which allowed clerks appointed by the pope to be imprisoned and held liable to pay compensation. Two years later in 1353 came the first Statute of Praemunire which limited appeals to Rome. A second such Statute followed in 1393. In practice, however, Edward III had no intention of enforcing these laws to the letter. He was prepared to invoke them on occasions when he wanted to extract concessions from the papacy, but once a healthy compromise had been reached, he would relax them again. The kind of arrangement so often agreed was that a vacant see would be filled by provision, and that the candidate provided would be the king's nominee. Such laws existed, therefore, for the king's convenience, and as we well know, they were to prove very convenient indeed in the 1520s when Henry VIII invoked Praemunire against no less a man than Cardinal Wolsey.

G. Barraclough, *Papal Provisions*, Blackwell, 1935; A. Deeley, 'Papal Provision & Royal Rights of Patronage in the early 14th Century', *Eng. Hist. Rev.*, xliii (1928).

R

RICHARD I Richard the Lion Heart became a legend in his own lifetime, and has remained one ever since. For that reason he has never been taken very seriously by serious historians. Bishop Stubbs, the great Victorian constitutional historian, said scathingly that Richard was 'a man of blood, and his crimes were those of one whom long use of warfare had made too familiar with slaughter.' Paradoxically, therefore, Richard remains one of the best known, yet one of the least known of our kings.

He was born on 8 September 1157 at Oxford. His father, Henry II (q.v.), the first Angevin king, ruled an enormous assemblage of territories stretching from Hadrian's Wall to the Pyrenees and including the duchy of Aquitaine which had been brought to him by his formidable wife Eleanor (q.v.). Richard, their second son, was his mother's favourite. Consequently he responded to her influence, and when in 1173 she and Henry, her eldest son, stirred up a rebellion against Henry II, he was happy to join in. It was a major upheaval, known to contemporaries as the 'great war', but by summer 1174 Henry had succeeded in holding his empire together. At Montlouis on 30 September he made peace with his sons.

Reconciled the family might be for the moment, but within a few years the sons were taking up arms again, this time against each other. Henry the son was thirsting to share some of his father's power. Richard had been given Aquitaine to rule, and Geoffrey, the third son, Brittany. Yet the Young Henry had nothing, no lands at all that he could call his own. Idleness bred resentment, and in 1183 he joined those barons in Aquitaine who had risen in rebellion against Richard's heavy-handed rule. What threatened to develop into another major crisis for the Angevin family was averted only by the timely death of the Young King on 11 June.

Richard then found himself in the position his elder brother had once occupied. He was his father's heir, and yet denied any share of power so long as the old man lived. We must try to understand the feelings of frustration he doubtless felt if we are to make sense of the dramatic turn of events that followed. On 18 November 1188 Richard, Henry II and Philip Augustus of France met at Bonmoulins. Richard asked his father to recognize him as his rightful heir. When Henry refused, he turned to the French king, his father's mortal enemy, and did homage to him for all the lands he held on the continent. This ceremony inaugurated the last war that Henry was called upon to fight. He died at Chinon on 6 July 1189.

On hearing of his father's death Richard went to Fontevrault Abbey to pay his last respects. He crossed to England on 13 August, was crowned the following month, and left again on 12 December. Everything now was subordinated to his plan for a joint Anglo-French crusade (q.v.) to recover the cities of Acre and Jerusalem recently taken by Saladin. To oversee the government of the country in his absence he had appointed Hugh Puiset as justiciar and William Longchamp, bishop of Ely, as chancellor; but the two did not get on, and in 1191 Richard, by now in Sicily, had to despatch Walter of

Coutances, archbishop of Rouen, to England to sort things out.

Meanwhile he and King Philip of France were making heavy weather of the journey to the east. Their progress was dogged by interminable disputes which extended even to the terms on which Richard could renounce a pre-contract to Philip's sister in order to marry Berengaria, daughter of the king of Navarre. The marriage finally took place in May 1191, a month before the expedition reached its destination, the port of Acre. Richard's achievements in the east certainly justified his reputation as a great soldier. Five weeks after arriving he had recovered Acre from the Moslems to whom it had fallen four years before. Encouraged by this success his inclination now was to push on to Jerusalem. With the hot eastern sun beating down, he led his troops to within sight of the Holy City; but as he no longer had the manpower or logistical support necessary for undertaking a long siege, he had to settle for a three years' treaty. On 9 October 1192 he set sail for home. On the way he was captured by Leopold, duke of Austria, whom he is supposed to have insulted on the crusade. The duke transferred him to the custody of the Holy Roman Emperor, Henry VI, and by this time the argument over the terms of his release threatened to become bogged down in the vast and intricate web of Anglo-French-German relations. Eventually a ransom of 150,000 marks was agreed.

On 13 March 1194 Richard returned to an England which had been taxed to the hilt to secure his release. But he was away again two months later, off to Normandy to protect his continental dominions from the recurring attacks of the king of France. It was the ambition of King Philip to expel the Angevins from the continent, and, as we know, he was

eventually to be successful. But not in the lifetime of Richard. Not for nothing was he known as Richard, *Coeur de Lion*, the Lion-Heart. He was the greatest soldier of his day, and a fearless campaigner. Castles held to be invincible fell before him. Acre was in Christian hands little more than a month after his arrival there. Moreover, he had a shrewd idea of where the strengths and weaknesses of the Angevin lands lay. He safeguarded the southward approach to Normandy by building the great stronghold of Chateau Gaillard at Les Andelys. And at the end of his life he was concentrating his energies on defending the Limoges area. Here King Philip had forged an alliance with a group of rebel barons with a view to driving a wedge between the northern and southern lands of the Angevin empire. Richard marched south to besiege one of the rebels at Chalus. In the course of the operations he sustained an arrow wound from which he died on 6 April 1199. He was buried alongside his father and mother at Fontevrault Abbey.

See also, MUSIC.

J. Gillingham, *Richard the Lion Heart*, Weidenfeld & Nicolson, 1978.

RICHARD II 'I am Richard II; know ye not that?', Queen Elizabeth is supposed to have said on first seeing Shakespeare's play. It is this comment which has fostered the interpretation of the play as a political allegory, 'intended to warn her of her possible fate if she encouraged flatterers and permitted unjust taxation and monopolies.'* For Bolingbroke read Essex. Whether or not Shakespeare consciously wrote his play as a tract for the times, there is still a

---

* *King Richard the Second*, ed. P. Ure, The Arden Shakespeare, 1956, p. lvii.

strong case for arguing that it brings us nearer to Richard himself than any work written since. Richard wanted to strengthen and exalt kingship in England, and lost his throne for so doing.

Born at Bordeaux on 6 January 1367, the son of the Black Prince (q.v.) and Joan of Kent, he became heir apparent to the English throne on the death of his father in 1376. Twelve months later he succeeded to the throne. For the next three years the country was governed in fact if not in theory by a regency council which continued the policies pursued in Edward III's later years. The cost of maintaining the late king's conquests in France led to the imposition of the famous poll taxes which were to provoke the Peasants' Revolt (q.v.) in 1381. The rebels poured into the capital from Kent and Essex and captured the Tower. Richard rode out to meet them at Smithfield, and promising to accede to their demands persuaded them to disperse. By all accounts he was one of the few members of the ruling class to show any powers of leadership in the crisis.

In the years that followed Richard chose to rely on a small circle of close friends, some of them contemporaries of his like Robert de Vere, others men like Sir Simon Burley who had served his father and from whom he may have picked up his advanced notions of regality. Dissatisfaction with foreign policy, allegations of corruption and criticism of extravagance in the royal household led to the impeachment of the Chancellor, Michael de la Pole, in parliament in October 1386 and to the appointment of a committee of government, resident at Westminster, which was to hold office for one year. Richard avoided its supervision by travelling around England, and sought to clarify the legality of his own position by putting to the judges a series of questions about the nature of the royal prerogative. Their answers afforded the clearest statement of the royal prerogative that Richard could have desired. De Vere, meanwhile, was bringing an army to the king's assistance, but after its defeat at Radcot Bridge (20 December 1387) the king was delivered into the hands of his opponents, the so-called Appellant lords. At the aptly named 'Merciless Parliament' which followed, they 'appealed' Burley and other supporters of Richard and sent them to the executioner's block.

The rule of the Appellants lasted until 3 May 1389, when Richard asserted his full majority for the first time by appointing councillors of his own choice. The next eight years seem a period of deceptive calm in view of the storm that was to follow. Richard's chief intention was to pursue peace with France, and the negotiations led in 1396 to the conclusion of a 28-year truce and the king's marriage to Isabella, daughter of Charles VI of France. It was also agreed, probably in a secret clause, that the French king should aid Richard against his own subjects when requested. So, even if Richard was not necessarily dissimulating in the early 1390s, he was almost certainly contemplating revenge against those who had humiliated him ten years before. In July 1397 he arrested Gloucester, Arundel and Warwick, three of the former Appellant lords. Warwick was imprisoned on the Isle of Man, Arundel was executed and Gloucester died in captivity at Calais. Richard then chose to ratify his triumph by summoning a parliament. In January 1398 he transferred it from Westminster to Shrewsbury, where he persuaded it to take the unprecedented steps of granting him the wool and leather duties *for life* and of delegating to a committee its power to determine all outstanding petitions, including the controversy which had arisen between Henry of Bolingbroke, duke of Hereford, Gaunt's son, and Thomas Mowbray, duke of Norfolk. It was resolved that their quarrel should be settled by trial by battle, but when the duel scheduled for 16 September 1398 was due to begin Richard halted the proceedings and pronounced sentences of exile, on Norfolk for life and on Hereford for ten years. However, just four months later, John of Gaunt (q.v.) died, and Richard had to weigh the advantages to be gained from seizing the Lancastrian inheritance against the fears that would be aroused by so revolutionary a threat to the rights of property. Richard decided to take the risk. In March 1399 he took the Lancastrian lands into royal possession. This act did more than any other to seal his fate. In July 1399, while Richard was in Ireland, Bolingbroke landed on the Yorkshire coast, ostensibly to claim his rightful inheritance. He won the support of the earl of Northumberland, marched south to Bristol and then swung north-westwards to Chester, which he entered on 9 August. Richard, meanwhile, arrived at Conway two days later. Had he remained within the castle, he would at least have been secure, but once persuaded by Northumberland and Archbishop Arundel to give himself up, he became in effect a prisoner. Bolingbroke summoned a parliament to meet in Richard's name. Under duress Richard was persuaded to abdicate, and his supplanter claimed the throne as Henry IV (q.v.). Richard was imprisoned at Pontefract, where he died (or was murdered) in 1400. His remains were interred at King's Langley until they were brought to Westminster Abbey by King Henry V.

The tendency towards megalomania detected by some historians in Richard's character was exaggerated in his last two years, the period described by the chronicler Walsingham as the 'tyranny'. But it is not necessary to condemn Richard as insane to understand what he was doing. His appointment of knights and esquires of the household to such important local offices as that of sheriff (q.v.) indicates that he wanted to place royal government on a more direct and secure basis of power, less dependent for its workings on the goodwill of the magnates. He failed because he inspired fear, and was seen as a threat to the rights of landed property.

A. Tuck, *Richard II and the English Nobility*, Edward Arnold, 1973.

RICHARD III The interest aroused by the character and personality of Richard III is out of all proportion to the duration of his reign, which lasted no more than two years (1483–5). It is all summed up in the question, who killed the princes in the Tower? For centuries regarded as the most villainous king in our history, Richard has more recently been portrayed as the most maligned. His defenders have pointed to the interest which the Tudors had in blackening his reputation. Their own title to the throne depended on denying his. So the picture of the diabolical hunchback familiar to us from Shakespeare was gradually built up. Naturally these early interpretations of Richard's career tell us as much or more about the men who so sedulously fostered them than they do about the king himself. What we need to do now is to see him through the eyes of his contemporaries, not through those of his later detractors. If we do that, what sort of man do we find?

Richard was born on 2 October 1452 at Fotheringhay, the youngest of the surviving children of Richard, duke of York, and his wife Cecily. In 1461 his eldest brother became king as Edward IV, and during the 22 years of his reign Richard, as duke of Gloucester, remained consistently loyal. After 1471 he was entrusted with sweeping powers in the North as Warden of the Western Marches. From his seat at Middleham Castle he held sway over the most lawless part of England with a firmness – and fairness – that won him the respect of the local inhabitants and the favour of the city of York (q.v.). Contrary to Shakespeare's version of events, Richard was not the *eminence grise* behind the execution of his brother, Clarence, in February 1478. The shifty Clarence was charged with treason, and had only himself to blame. If anything, there may well be some truth in the reports that Richard pleaded for his life.

When Edward IV died on 9 April 1483, he left a 13-year old son to succeed him as Edward V. Had the terms of his will been followed, Richard would have become Protector; but the larger grouping on the Council in London, composed of Queen Elizabeth Woodville's relatives, preferred a conciliar form of government which would have reduced Richard to the position of chief councillor. It was apparent that the differences which had built up in Edward IV's lifetime between Richard and his ally Buckingham on the one hand and the Woodville clan on the other were bound to come into the open in a struggle for control over his young heir. When news broke of the king's death, Edward V was at Ludlow, whence the Woodvilles planned to spirit him to London for an early coronation. Richard intercepted the party at Stony Stratford on 30 April, and despatched Earl Rivers and Sir Thomas Vaughan to the north for execution. On hearing of this debacle the queen fled into sanctuary at Westminster, taking her second son Richard with her. The young Edward was placed in the Tower.

So far Richard had acted as the defender of his nephew's interests against the intrigues of the queen and her Woodville relatives. In so doing he had the support of the duke of Buckingham and Lord Hastings. But did Richard intend going any further? Hastings evidently thought so, for Richard found it necessary to remove him. On 13 June he was charged with plotting with the queen and executed. Thereafter events movēd rapidly. On 16 June the queen agreed to hand over her younger son, who joined his brother in the Tower. Then Buckingham made his famous speech at the Guildhall, immortalized by Shakespeare, in which he peddled the story that the children of Edward IV and Elizabeth Woodville were bastards because of a pre-contract between the king and Eleanor Butler, thus making Richard of Gloucester the legitimate heir to the crown. On 25 June the Commons and Lords assented to Richard's succession, and on 6 July he was crowned.

It was destined to be a troubled reign, and contemporaries were not slow to connect the misfortunes that afflicted Richard with the unscrupulous way he had climbed to power. In October 1483, only four months after he had so signally assisted Richard's usurpation, Buckingham rose in rebellion for reasons that can only be guessed at. Could it really have been, as we are sometimes told, to rescue the princes in the Tower? As it happened, Richard had no need to worry, for the torrential rain in the Severn Valley washed away the enthusiasm of Buckingham's supporters. But it was ominous that disaffection spread to Kent and the Home Counties. The duke himself was captured in Shropshire and executed.

To the difficulties of establishing his regime securely were added personal tragedies. In April 1484 the death occurred of his only son Edward (born 1473), followed less than a year later by that of his wife Anne Neville, the Kingmaker's daughter. Inevitably rumours abounded that the usurper was now earning retribution for his evil deeds. Though the country was internally peaceful at the beginning of 1485 Richard in fact could never feel secure so long as the pretender Henry Tudor, earl of Richmond remained at large in Brittany and France. In August 1485 Henry decided to try his luck by landing with a small army at Milford Haven. As he marched across central Wales he picked up enough support to have a respectable army under his command when he met Richard at Bosworth (q.v.) on 22 August. In the battle that followed tactical mistakes and the difficulties encountered in fighting on a constricted site cost Richard the day. He fell in the thick of the fighting. Henry had his body carried naked to Leicester where it was interred at the Greyfriars.

So ended the tragic reign of Richard III. But what of the princes in the Tower? Concern for their safety was voiced even before Richard's coronation. Dominic Mancini, an Italian visitor to England in 1483, tells us that before he left London (in July 1483) they had disappeared from view. In a passage remarkable for the evidence it affords of public sympathy for the princes he goes on to say that men wept when talking of Edward V's disappearance, and that suspicions arose that he had been *sublatum* ('disposed of'). Of course, it is one thing to say that the princes were never seen again after Richard became king and quite another to allege that he was responsible for killing them. But, despite all the work that has been done in recent years to exonerate Richard, there is still enough circumstantial evidence to associate him with the crime. It was clearly in his interest to see them gone, because so long as they lived he would never feel safe on the throne. Moreover, his opponents evidently presumed them dead, or they would not have backed the claims of Henry Tudor. Henry's own Act of Attainder passed against Richard in his first parliament contained the rather vague, but still significant charge of 'shedding infants' blood'. Interestingly, however, the Chancellor of France, Guillaume de Rochefort, had gone very much further in a speech delivered to the Estates General a couple of years earlier in 1484, when he accused Richard of having murdered his nephews. If they had indeed been disposed of by the end of 1483, then it is possible that the skeletons later unearthed in the Tower of two children, one aged about 12, the other about 10, could very likely have been theirs.

The impression left by an examination of the evidence is that Henry VII had no need consciously to blacken Richard's reputation because it was already under cloud of suspicion in his own lifetime. We could defend Richard's actions on the grounds that a royal minority would have led to instability and that he forestalled a Woodville coup; but there is no denying that his association with the disappearance of the princes and the unpopularity he incurred by his usurpation left him so short of support that it was open to so improbable a claimant as Henry Tudor to topple him.

C. Ross, *Richard III*, Eyre Methuen, 1981.

ROADS After the collapse of Roman rule in the fifth century the magnificent road system which had once carried the legions to the furthest corners of Britain fell into decay. Into decay, but not collapse. Even where weeds started sprouting up between the paving stones, the line of the road often survived the passage of time. Late in the eleventh century the law recognized the existence of four great highways on which travellers enjoyed the protection of the king's peace – Watling St, Ermine St, the Fosse Way and Icknield Way. These are still famous names today. And only the Icknield Way has sunk into the obscurity of a country lane.

But what mattered to people in the eleventh century was less the high road which stretched from one end of the country to the other than the lane which led from the village to the local market town. In the course of the Saxon period towns grew up which became the centre of local road systems serving the surrounding countryside. From Oxford and Northampton in the Midlands and Norwich in East Anglia roads radiated in all directions, just as they do today. The same considerations of economic development that served to increase the size and number of the towns served also to extend the network of routes connecting them. In fact, the road system that was to be portrayed on John Ogilby's map published in 1675 was essentially a creation of the middle ages. We can see this if we compare Ogilby's map with the famous one in the Bodleian Library, Oxford, dating from the early fourteenth century and known from the name of a former owner as the Gough Map (Fig. 7). Our anonymous medieval cartographer marked in five principal lines of travel:

1) London, Guildford, Farnham, Winchester, Salisbury, Shaftsbury, Exeter.

2) London to Bristol along the line of the modern A4.

3) London to S. Wales along the line of the present A40 as far as Gloucester, and then via Hereford and Brecon to St David's.

4) London to Carlisle, via St Alban's, Coventry, Lichfield and Lancaster.

5) London to the north again, following the Great North Road for much of the route, but branching westwards across the Pennines so as to reach Carlisle not Berwick.

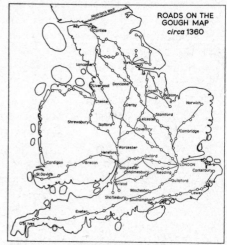

Figure 7 Main roads.

Then as now all the main roads in England radiated from the capital. Travelling north and south was easy. Travelling east and west was more difficult, though not impossible. Worcester was well served by roads. And over in East Anglia Cambridge and Norwich (q.v.) could be reached by turning off the Great North Road at Ware.

What were these medieval roads like? Were they as atrociously bad as we might suppose, impassable in winter and dusty in summer? We can easily exaggerate. The main routes, particularly those stretching northwards to the border, had to be wide enough to allow the passage of armies and to take herds of sheep and cattle. We know that quite early on the king was anxious to lay down the width of a 'royal way', that is, a road always kept open. In 1118 Henry I (q.v.) laid down that two wagons should be able to pass each other, or 16 knights be able to ride abreast. These were not narrow paths cut through the undergrowth; they were wide swathes marching across the countryside.

Most roads of course, would not have been surfaced. We have to imagine a well-trodden path lined by wide grass verges on each side. Only in towns, like Lincoln or Southampton, would the streets have been paved or, as at Winchester, given a flint surface. One of the few public highways to have been paved was the Strand, linking London (q.v.) and Westminster, but by 1353 even its condition had so deteriorated that property-holders along it were ordered to make a footpath seven feet wide on each side of the road. In the towns responsibility for upkeep rested with those whose property fronted onto the road. In the countryside the position was less clear. Sometimes responsibility rested with a local landowner, sometimes not. If the latter, a local benefactor might come to the rescue. In Wiltshire a pedlar woman called Maud Heath encountered so many potholes on the way to Chippenham market that when she died in about 1474 she left money for the erection of a stone causeway 4½ miles long to facilitate passage over the marshy terrain of the Avon valley. If a borough community wanted to undertake repairs or, more ambitiously, to lay down a stone surface, it could obtain permission from the king to impose a toll on travellers – a practice that was, of course, to become very popular in later times.

In the middle ages those who could afford it travelled on horseback, those who could not, on foot. Few added to the discomfort of a journey by using a carriage. Carriages and wagons would be reserved for the luggage. From the considerable body of evidence which has come down to us about the speed of travel in this period, it seems that under normal conditions about 20 or 30 miles could be covered in a day on horseback. Inns at regular intervals along the route offered overnight accommodation.

How did people manage to find their way? As far as we know, there were no signposts, though there may have been milestones. If a group of travellers were undertaking a hazardous or unfamiliar journey, they would probably have hired a guide. We recall in Langland's (q.v.) *Piers Plowman* how Piers spoke up from the crowd and offered to show the Seven Deadly Sins the way to the Shrine of Truth. Langland's employment of this ruse to introduce his hero implies that he expected his readers to have no difficulty in recognizing a character like Piers who would come forward to offer his services to a party of travellers.

If the land route was circuitous or the conditions poor, however, it made better sense to do the journey by water. Thus in 1319, when Edward II invited the scholars of King's Hall, Cambridge, to spend Christmas with him at York (q.v.), the older scholars did the journey on horseback in five days, and their younger colleagues by boat from Cambridge to Spalding, on horseback to Boston, and then the rest of the way by boat again. They arrived three days late. But they very likely had the easier journey.

F. M. Stenton, 'The Road System of Medieval England', *Econ. Hist. Rev.*, vii (1936).

ROBIN HOOD

'If I should die this day', says Sloth in Langland's (q.v.) *Piers Plowman*, 'I'd still not keep awake. I can't sing my Pater Noster properly, as a priest should sing it, but I know the rhymes of Robin Hood and Ranulph, earl of Chester.'

This confession by Sloth, the aptly-named personification of negligent priesthood, is the earliest reference we have to England's most famous medieval outlaw. Langland was writing in about 1377. We can take it, therefore, that the Robin Hood ballads were in circulation by then, even though the oldest surviving manuscript text we have (*Robin Hood and the Monk*) can be dated no earlier than the mid-fifteenth century. The fact that our manuscript sources are so late and so fragmentary makes it very difficult to say just when and how the Robin Hood cycle first became popular. We have only the internal evidence of the ballads themselves. Of these the longest and most instructive is the poem known as the *Gest of Robyn Hode*, which brings together in a single epic cycle a number of separate stories about the outlaw hero.

Its first theme concerns Robin and the knight. Robin declares that he will not eat until he has a guest to join him for dinner. So Little John and his companions detain a knight who, it transpires, is on his way to St Mary's Abbey, York to repay a debt which he has contracted. But the knight is penniless, witness his tatty clothing, and faces the prospect of losing all he possesses. Robin agrees to lend him the necessary sum of £400, and accepts his word that he can offer no better pledge than his faith in the honour of Our Lady. Moreover, he lets Little John accompany him to York. By the time they arrive, the abbot and his friend the justice are looking forward to seizing the knight's lands. Imagine their surprise, then, when he throws the bag of money down onto the table. The knight then takes leave of Little John, and returns to his home in Wyresdale to collect the money to repay Robin.

While the knight is away, the scene returns to the greenwood, where Robin is once again asking Little John to find him a guest for dinner. Who should he find but the cellarer of St Mary's, York. After they have dined, Robin asks his unwilling guest how much money he has on him. The cellarer confesses to carrying only 20 marks, but on examination he is found to have no less than £800. Robin keeps the money and sends the monk packing. When the knight finally arrives to repay the outlaw, he is told that Our Lady has already paid the debt twice over.

The next main theme concerns Little John and the sheriff of Nottingham. The sheriff notices Little John's prowess as an archer and takes him into his service for a year. This is hardly to John's taste, so he picks a quarrel with the sheriff's cook. They come to blows, and the cook fights so well that John persuades him to come and join the outlaws in the forest. With them they take the sheriff's money and plate. A little later the sheriff is decoyed into the forest and forced to eat from his own silverware.

The *Gest* continues with the story of the king's arrival in Nottingham to deal with the outlaws. He disguises himself and sets off on the road through the forest, where predictably he is captured and taken to eat with Robin. Eventually Robin guesses the true identity of his guest, and kneels to beg forgiveness. This the king grants on condition that he enters his service and comes to court. So Robin rides off to start a new life. But he soon grows disenchanted. After little more than a year he returns to his old haunts. The *Gest* closes with a brief account of his death in Kirklees Priory through the treachery of the prioress and her co-conspirator, Sir Roger de Doncaster.

If only we knew a little more about *how* the Robin Hood ballads were composed and circulated, we would be better placed to discover for whom they were composed. As several writers have pointed out, Robin's exploits have a lot in common with those of other outlaws of medieval literature – Fulk Fitzwarin, Eustace the Monk and Gamelyn, for example. Gamelyn, whose career is usually associated with the fourteenth century, was the younger son of a knight who fled to the greenwood and became the head of an outlaw band. He ran into trouble with the sheriff and the justice, but finally, like Robin, was pardoned by the king. It is a case of ringing the changes on the same old well-worn themes. Well-worn they might be, and hardly the stuff of which great literature is made, but their very repetitiveness is significant. It helps to explain their popularity. Take, for instance, the idealization of the outlaw (q.v. OUT-LAWRY). Why was someone placed outside the normal protection of the law, and forced to rob to keep himself and his companions alive, regarded as a hero? Why was the sheriff, the man supposed to uphold the law, regarded as the anti-hero? Surely because the courts of common law were so corrupt that the conventional values of society were inverted. Sympathy was given to those who were the victims of the law not to those who enforced it. So who were the victims of the law? Who were the people whose cause Robin espoused?

In a famous passage in the *Gest* (stanzas 13–15) Robin tells his men whom they should harm and whom they should not:

But loke ye do no husbonde harme
That tylleth with his ploughe.

No more ye shall no gode yeman
That walketh by grene wode shawe;
Ne no knyght ne no squyer
That wol be a gode felawe

These bisshoppes and these archebisshoppes,
Ye shall them bete and bynde;
The hye sherif of Notyingham,
Hym holde ye in your mynde.

Now this does not amount to a straight-forward policy of robbing the rich to give to the poor. Certainly the husbandmen farmers are on the side of the angels. But so too are the knights and esquires – the gentry. It is the mighty bishops and the sheriff who have to be beaten and bound. And interestingly it is an impoverished knight to whose rescue Robin comes in the *Gest*. That immediately suggests that the poet is thinking not of peasant grievances but of the economic problems faced by the knights in the thirteenth century. Again and again in abbey cartularies we come across the piecemeal acquisition of estates belonging to knights who were forced by the inflationary pressures of the day to turn to monastic mortgagees. Is the Robin Hood cycle to be interpreted therefore as an expression of gentry rather than peasant discontent? There are certainly strong grounds for believing so. It was the gentry as much as their inferiors who suffered from the corruption of the legal system. And to judge from the numerous petitions the Commons submitted in parliament, they were no happier than anyone else with the collusion that occurred between sheriffs and wealthy landowners. But, when all that is said, the extraordinary appeal of the legends can only be explained if we suppose that they had a near-universal appeal. Robin transcended 'class'. As Professor Holt has suggested, the stories may have started off in the hall, but they soon went below stairs. And the wider the audience became, the more versions of the story there were put into circulation. *Robin Hood and the Potter* may be a product of the more popular turn that some of the ballads took.

The last question is the most intriguing of all. Did a Robin Hood actually exist? Or was he a figment of popular imagination? If he is to be found anywhere at all, it will have to be in northern England, though just where is open to dispute. The identification with Sherwood Forest in Nottinghamshire rests more on the appearance in the ballads of the notorious sheriff than any references to it by name in the earliest surviving texts. In fact, Sherwood is not mentioned at all in the *Gest*. The area that is mentioned is Barnsdale, Yorkshire, which lies between Doncaster and Pontefract. It was to 'the Sayles' in Barnsdale that Robin Hood despatched Little John to find him a guest for dinner. And significantly this spot is located on a stretch of the Great North Road where robberies are known to have occurred in the middle ages. So did Robin Hood actually exist? The problem is that the unceasing efforts of generations of scholars have yielded so many Robin Hoods that we will never be able to tell which, if any, of them provided the inspiration for the ballads. The candidate with the strongest claim so far is the Robin Hood described as a fugitive in a Yorkshire pipe roll of 1230. But the search for a real Robin Hood, irresistible as it has proved to be, is about as productive as chasing the mirage in the desert.

See also, JUSTICE.

R. B. Dobson & J. Taylor, *Rymes of Robyn Hood: An Introduction to the English Outlaw*, Heinemann, 1976; the articles by J. C. Holt and R. H. Hilton collected in *Peasants, Knights and Heretics*, ed. R. H. Hilton, Cambridge, 1976.

ROMANESQUE See, ARCHITECTURE, ECCLESIASTICAL.

ROSES, WARS OF THE The intermittent struggles lasting from the 1st battle of St Alban's (1455) to the battle of Bosworth (1485) are known as the Wars of the Roses, a term coined not by a contemporary but by Sir Walter Scott in *Anne of Geierstein* (1829). The idea that the two sides adopted the red and the white rose as their respective emblems is of course a much older one, for it was dramatized by Shakespeare in the famous scene in the Temple Garden (*Henry VI Part 1*), where York and his supporters pluck the white rose, and Somerset and his allies the red one. Whether this scene is fact or fiction we cannot say. Certainly the Yorkists were identified with the white rose, but the principal mark of Lancastrian attachment was less likely to have been the red rose than the collar of SS, which had been awarded to the family's retainers ever since the days of John of Gaunt (q.v.), 'time-honoured Lancaster'.

Since the Wars resulted in the replacement of one dynasty by another, Tudor historians not surprisingly jumped to the conclusion that their principal cause was a struggle for the throne. In fact this is doubtful, because the Yorkist lords were remarkably slow to take up arms against King Henry VI (q.v.). It is true that Henry IV's seizure of the crown in 1399 had the unfortunate effect of making the succession an issue in English politics, but the successful kingship of his son Henry V (q.v.), placed the authority of the Lancastrian dynasty beyond all question. What brought it back into question again was the appalling kingship of his successor, Henry VI. By the 1450s Richard, duke of York, had emerged as the principal critic of Queen Margaret and the clique that held sway at Henry's court. The duke had as it happened inherited a claim to the crown, and a good one: he was descended through the female line from Lionel, duke of Clarence, second surviving son of Edward III, whereas the Lancastrians were descended from John of Gaunt, the third son. But it was a claim which would never have been heard had he not found himself excluded from power by the queen. His aim was to force his way back onto King Henry's council, and to do that he needed support. So who could he count on? His brother-in-law, Richard Neville, earl of Salisbury (d. 1460) and his nephew, Richard Neville, earl of Warwick (q.v.) were to be his main allies. The Nevilles were one of the leading families in the north. That made them rivals of the Percy earls of Northumberland. And once the Nevilles lined themselves up behind York, it followed that the Percys would line up behind Queen Margaret and the court.

The outbreak of the Wars of the Roses is usually considered to have come with the 1st battle of St Alban's in 1455. There the bonds of restraint were finally broken. The Yorkists intercepted Henry VI and Somerset who were going to Leicester to attend a Council meeting packed with their supporters. Despite elaborate preliminary negotiations, it came to a battle, and the duke of Somerset and the earl of Northumberland were killed. Though its casualties numbered some of the greatest men in the land, the battle of St Alban's was in fact quite a small-scale affair, and was not immediately followed by any further hostilities. Queen Margaret waited before making her next move. It came in September 1459, when she scattered her enemies at Blore Heath. The Yorkist lords fled for their lives, and from their respective havens of exile – York himself had gone to Ireland, Warwick and Salisbury to Calais (q.v.) – decided that they should launch an invasion of England. In June 1460 Warwick and his party landed at Sandwich. They entered London, and in July marched northwards to Northampton, where they defeated the Lancastrians and captured the king.

On 10 October Duke Richard returned to London, and much to the embarrassment of his supporters laid claim to the throne. The reluctance of the nobility to recognize his title, for they were after all supposed to have been fighting the king's evil advisers and not the king himself, was shown by their equivocal reaction: they allowed Henry to reign for his lifetime, but diverted the succession to York and his heirs. Such a face-saving formula was hardly likely to satisfy Queen Margaret, who was re-assembling her forces in the north. In a change of fortune far from unique in these years of dizzying instability she defeated and killed York at Wakefield (30 December 1460), and marched south, regaining possession of her bemused husband at the 2nd battle of St Alban's (17 February 1461). But she frittered away the fruits of her victory. Her troops went on the rampage on the streets of St Alban's, and the Londoners took fright. On 27 February they opened their gates to the Yorkists. So Queen Margaret had the king, and her opponents the capital. What were they to do? Without a king they could do little. If they wanted to legitimize their actions, they had no alternative but to proclaim one of their own. So they put the new duke of York on the throne as Edward IV (q.v.). On 29 March he gave reality to his title by crushing the Lancastrians at the battle of Towton.

So ended the first phase of the Wars. The Lancastrian partisans were dispersed, and their leaders in exile in Scotland. But the issue was reopened when Warwick and George of Clarence, the king's brother, rebelled in 1469, taking Edward prisoner and executing those Woodville relatives of his to whom they took such violent exception. Complacent though he may have been in the past, Edward now fought back with determination. Warwick wisely fled to France, and there he renewed contact with Queen Margaret and the Lancastrian exiles. In perhaps the most astonishing *volte face* of all in this period he formed an alliance with them with a view to restoring Henry VI. On 13 September 1470 he and Clarence landed near Dartmouth, and Edward was forced to flee. At a time when any English government had difficulty enough in inspiring confidence in its own powers of survival, it is difficult to imagine a less convincing coalition than the one that ruled briefly in 1470–1 under the nominal leadership of the hapless Henry VI. It was brought to an end in the spring with Warwick's death at Barnet (14 April 1471) and Margaret's defeat at Tewkesbury (4 May).

Edward IV passed away peacefully in April 1483; but he had the misfortune to leave a 13-year old son as his heir. The temptation which overcame his uncle Gloucester to seize the crown as King Richard III (q.v.) then undid all the good work that Edward IV had done in restoring political stability in England. His usurpation precipitated the third and final phase of the Wars. Henry Tudor, earl of Richmond, who claimed descent from the Beauforts, chanced his arm against Richard III and emerged victorious at Bosworth (q.v.) on 22 August 1485. He had won the crown, but he was not fully secure until after the battle of Stoke (16 June 1487), when John de la Pole, earl of Lincoln, the Yorkist pretender, was killed. Stoke has better claims than Bosworth to be regarded as the final battle of the Wars of the Roses.

What effect did all this internecine feuding have on the people of England? Compared with, say, the wars of Stephen's reign (1135–54) or the Civil War of the 1640s, remarkably little. The towns escaped lightly. St Alban's was unlucky enough to witness two battles fought in its streets, but on the other hand it was never besieged. This was a war pursued not by long drawn out sieges but by short pitched battles, and even these were largely confined to 1460–1 and 1469–71. The armies moreover were small, composed mostly of the great lords and their retainers. Did the nobles end up destroying each other, then? There were some notable casualties, but whatever period we care to study we will find that the English aristocracy were well-versed in the arts of survival.

See also, BASTARD FEUDALISM.

K. B. McFarlane, 'The Wars of the Roses', *Procs. Brit. Acad.*, L (1964); R. L. Storey, *The End of the House of Lancaster*, Barrie & Rockliff, 1966.

S

SCHOOLS In the middle ages the Church was dependent on education, and education on the Church. Without the clergy there would have been no schools, and without the schools no clergy. It was the needs of organized Christianity which therefore called into being a system of educational provision the size and extent of which we may sometimes underestimate.

At the lowest level there were the 'reading' or 'song' schools, the medieval equivalent of our modern primary schools, to which children were sent from about the age of seven. There they learned to read (probably aloud) and to sing. Elementary establishments of this sort were found not only in the towns, where they were fostered by the liturgical needs of the cathedrals and greater churches, but also in quite a number of country villages. Theobald of Etampes, who was teaching at Oxford in the twelfth century, tells us, admittedly in a polemical tone, that in the villages as well as in the towns there were as many schoolmasters as there were tax-collectors and royal officials. These men were not accomplished scholars; but they were practised enough in letters to be able to offer instruction to any youngsters who could be spared by their parents from labour in the fields.

At about the age of 11 or 12 the more fortunate or more gifted of these children would have been sent to the 'grammar' school – so called because the study of grammar, that is Latin grammar, was the lynchpin of the medieval syllabus. These schools were largely a creation of the twelfth century, when the revival of learning extended the range of edu-

cational opportunities. As several scholars have pointed out, the earliest and most important schools grew up around the cathedrals, and in particular around those served by secular canons as opposed to monks. In due course the schoolmaster became a member of the cathedral chapter and a person of some importance, so that as his duties accumulated he usually appointed a deputy to do the day-to-day teaching. Although we can single out the cathedral schools for special attention, they were only the most notable among many that were called into being at this time.

The standard elementary textbook used to introduce young children to the study of Latin grammar was the *Ars Minor* of Aelius Donatus, a fourth-century writer who had been St Jerome's tutor. After they had mastered Donatus – not an exacting task as his book only extended to a dozen pages – the pupils moved onto the *Doctrinale* of Alexander de Ville Dieu (*c.* 1200), a verse treatise of great popularity which ran through the parts of speech, syntax, metre and so on. At a higher level still, aimed at university students rather than schoolboys, were the books by Priscian, a scholar of Constantinople (*c.* 500), whose lengthy and detailed studies of Latin left no stone unturned. In addition to textbooks the pupils needed dictionaries to enable them to pick up vocabulary. The work which did most to assist them here was the *Elementarium* of Papias, an Italian lexicographer who in 1053 hit on what was then the novel idea of composing a word list in order of initial letter. Obvious though it may be to us today, the concept of alphabetical order was one that took a surprisingly long time to gain acceptance in the middle ages, not least in the archives of the English government which were practically useless without it.

In theory, an education should have cost nothing in the middle ages. The Lateran Council held at Rome in 1179 ordained that each cathedral was to endow a schoolmaster adequately enough to enable him to teach the clerks of his cathedral and other poor scholars free of charge. Cathedrals, as we have seen, had long fulfilled their obligation to maintain a school, but it was the chancellor and not his deputy, the practising teacher, who was the beneficiary of the endowments. In a grammar school, therefore, the only pupils likely to be given a free education were the choristers; the others would have had to pay. That is not to imply that the expense was necessarily going to cripple their parents. For the grammar boys at Merton College, Oxford in 1277 tuition fees were 4d a term or 1s a year. By the fifteenth century the going rate had risen to 8d a term. If the pupils were living away from home, they would also have had to pay for board and lodging, a bill likely to be far higher than that for tuition. At Merton scholars paid 8d a week for board in 1400, and at Winchester commoners 8d to 16d a week in the fifteenth century. As for books we know that a few pupils acquired their own, though they hardly needed to in an age when teaching was for the most part done by reading aloud. More essential was the penner and inkhorn, the sheath-full of pens hung from the belt, which in 1526 could be purchased for as little as 4d.

If schooling were to be provided free, as the Lateran Council of 1179 had envisaged, the schoolmaster would have to be given an adequate benefice to release him from dependence on fees. This the cathedrals rarely succeeded in doing. In the course of the late middle ages, therefore, we often find that the charitable endeavours of founders and benefactors were increasingly directed towards establishing schools adequately endowed to provide free education for the needy and deserving. Sometimes, as at Ottery St Mary in 1338 or Cobham in 1389, these were essentially collegiate or chantry (q.v.) foundations, where the provision of schooling was secondary to the celebration of the divine office. In the 1380s, however, two schools were founded which were important for the novel emphasis which they placed on teaching above religious and devotional observances. The larger was Winchester, founded and endowed on a lavish scale by Bishop William of Wykeham (q.v.) in 1382 for the instruction of 70 scholars, who would spend four or five years there until they qualified for admission to the sister foundation at Oxford (q.v.) later known as New College. The other, perhaps more influential in the long run for being smaller and therefore more compatible with the means at the disposal of most benefactors, was the 'House of Scholars' at Wotton-under-Edge (Gloucs.) founded by Lady Katherine Berkeley in 1384. Like his colleagues at earlier collegiate foundations, the schoolmaster at Wotton had to sing masses for the souls of the foundress and her relatives, but his main duty was to give free instruction in grammar to the two poor scholars who received free board and lodging and to any others who might attend. From then until the Reformation many such endowed schools were to be founded with the aim of providing free schooling to the foundationers and even occasionally, as at Wotton, to all comers. Some of these schools were attached to chantries or hospitals, a few, as at Stratford-on-Avon, to guilds (q.v.). The schoolroom erected at Stratford in 1427 as part of the buildings of the Guild of the Holy Cross is still in use today.

What would life have been like for a schoolboy all those years ago? The implication of the low level of *per capita* tuition fees in the grammar schools is that a master hoping to gain a livelihood would have to teach large classes. In the case of the cathedral schools we are probably talking about 40 or more. If classes were bigger than we would expect today, so too were hours longer. Judging by early Tudor regulations, the day would begin at 6 or 7 in the morning and after lengthy breaks for breakfast and mid-day dinner would culminate in a long haul from one till five in the afternoon. Perhaps to keep his pupils on their toes, the medieval schoolmaster was free in his use of the cane. The schoolboy in Chaucer's *Prioress's Tale* promises to learn the song to the Virgin Mary

Though they should scold me when I cannot say
My primer, though they beat me thrice an hour.*

Chaucer's schoolboy must have been one of many who looked forward to the start of the school holidays. For reasons at which we can only guess holidays were as long in the middle ages as they are today. In the ordinances which she laid down for her school at Wotton-under-Edge Lady Berkeley said they were to last for 2½ weeks at Christmas, a fortnight at Easter, a week at Whitsun and six weeks in the summer.

As for the provision of urinals, to take in conclusion an irreverent but not unimportant aspect of school life, it seems that the boys were supposed to go outside to some recognized spot – too often, according to one Oxford schoolmaster who complained, 'As sone as I am com into the scole, this fellow goith to make water and he goyth oute to the comyn drafte.'

See also, UNIVERSITIES, LANGUAGE AND LITERATURE.

N. Orme, *English Schools in the Middle Ages*, Methuen, 1973.

SCIENCE If technology remained backward in the middle ages, that is not to say that there were no advances in scientific thought. Quite the contrary, some of the theories of motion worked out by medieval scholars anticipate in large measure the theories Galileo was to propose in his *Discourses* in the early seventeenth century. Nor did England herself have any reason to feel ashamed. Oxford could boast of Grosseteste (q.v.) and Bacon (q.v.) in the thirteenth century, and Bradwardine and the Merton mathematicians in the fourteenth. The scrutiny to which these men were subjecting Aristotle's view of the universe was to culminate in its eventual overthrow in the age of the Scientific Revolution.

Since that view was basically the one that the medieval scholastics had of the universe, it would seem best to begin by describing its main outlines. Aristotle's thinking had come to western Europe via the Arab world. One by one his books had been translated into Latin by scholars like the Englishman Adelard of Bath who, in so doing, refined his cosmology and fitted it into a Christian framework. At the centre of the universe, according to Aristotle, lay an immobile Earth, composed of four

---

* Chaucer, *The Canterbury Tales*, ed. N. Coghill, Penguin Classics, 1951, p. 189.

elements – air, water, earth and fire. Around it rotated the moon, the sun, such planets as were then known, and the stars. These were conceived as embedded in a series of concentric spheres, within which they made their orbital motions, preserved and continued by their love of God, who moved them indirectly as the object of that love. The spheres were hidden from the human eye because they were composed of an invisible substance called aether. Outside this universe, in Aristotle's opinion, no matter could exist.

Aristotle's Christian interpreters needed to postulate that it was 'love of God' that made the planets go round, because the master had assumed that anything capable of motion had to be moved by something else. This theory of motion opened up what was to prove one of the most fruitful avenues of scientific investigation in the middle ages, culminating of course at the end of the sixteenth century in the work of Galileo. Aristotle had argued that all terrestrial objects had a natural motion towards the centre of the earth, but that any other motion, contradicting as it would the ordinary tendency of a body to stay in what was regarded as its natural place, was dependent on the operation of a mover distinguishable from the body which it moved. His theory of motion, therefore, unlike the modern one, was a theory of inertia which assumed rest, and asserted that a body would come to rest as soon as the thing imparting motion to it was removed. Aristotle's explanation conformed remarkably well with what direct experience of the world suggested about the nature of motion, but all the same there were two phenomena that gave rise to misgivings. First, why didn't an arrow fall to the ground the moment it left the bow-string? Instead of stopping as soon as it lost contact with the bow

which had given it motion, the arrow continues its motion for another hundred yards or so. Secondly, there was the problem of acceleration. Why did bodies falling to the ground move with an ever accelerating speed?

The answers which were given to these questions at Oxford and Paris in the thirteenth and fourteenth centuries, though adjusting Aristotle's theory in significant respects, were still rooted firmly in his system of physics. They entailed the introduction of the concept of internal resistance. Aristotle had held that in all mixed bodies one of the elements (earth, air, water and fire) would predominate and thus determine the motion of the body, in other words whether it would rise or fall. Not so, it was now argued. Rather, the total power of the light elements should be weighed against the total power of the heavy elements. If the light elements predominated, the body would move upwards, and if the heavy ones did, then it would move down. Consequently, in a falling body, heaviness would be regarded as the motive force and lightness as resistance; in a rising body, lightness would be the motive force and heaviness resistance. Expressed in the language of modern science, motion was therefore determined by the ratio of force to internal resistance. Of course, it was to be left to Galileo to make the vital breakthrough in this field. He was almost certainly familiar with medieval writing on the subject of motion, but whether or not it influenced him in reaching his own conclusions we cannot say. For internal resistance he substituted what we now call specific weight. But for the final formulation of the modern law of inertia we have to wait a little longer, because it required an extra feat of imagination to conceive of that very un-medieval and un-Aristotelian concept, a void. The modern view says that in the absence of any other bodies or external resistance, a body will continue moving to infinity. That is not a conclusion which the medieval thinkers could have reached by direct experience alone.

Motion, naturally enough, led to considerations of velocity. It was in the study and analysis of this problem that the group of mathematicians associated with Merton College, Oxford, made their greatest contribution. As Dr Crombie has written, nearly every important English scientist of the fourteenth century was at some time in his career associated with Merton. Thomas Bradwardine, a distinguished theologian and later archbishop of Canterbury, developed a form of algebra. His contemporaries, John of Dumbleton, William Heytesbury and Richard Swineshead were interested in how long it would take a body to travel a given distance assuming uniform acceleration. The rule which they formulated, known as the mean speed theorem, has been described as the most outstanding single medieval contribution to the history of physics. It states that the distance traversed in a given time by a body uniformly accelerating from rest equals the total time of moving multiplied by the mean of the initial and final velocities ($S=\frac{1}{2}Vft$, where S=distance travelled, Vf=final velocity, and t=time of acceleration). This theory was given a geometric proof in about 1350 by the French mathematician, Nicholas Oresme, and was the precursor of the more detailed laws Newton formulated several centuries later.

For all the intellectual ferment we meet in the thirteenth and fourteenth centuries, medieval science nevertheless failed to break out of its Aristotelian straitjacket. Why? Was it the hold of the Church? Almost certainly the part played by the Church in obstructing scientific research has been exaggerated. For example, Copernicus, who proposed the heliocentric system in a book published in 1543, was a cleric himself and suffered no persecution. On the other hand, it has to be admitted that he did live a long way from Rome. Perhaps the most serious problem lay in the nature of medieval scholastic thought. It became increasingly abstract and divorced from reality. A solution to a scientific problem was seen not as a contribution to the quest for physical reality but as a means of preserving the logical consistency of the Aristotelian system. What distinguishes Copernicus from his medieval forebears, therefore, is that he saw his cosmology not as an artificial construction necessitated by the requirements of logic but as a way of explaining the motions of the real, visible universe. That was a great step forward, but it did build on foundations laid in the middle ages. Sixteenth century thinkers did not achieve this feat of intellectual emancipation without deriving inspiration from the past. This inspiration they found in what, to them, must have been the remarkable discovery that the great Aristotle had not in fact been without critics in earlier times. To take an example relating to the theories of motion we have already discussed, John Philoponus, a Greek commentator of the sixth century A.D., denied that an external medium was always the cause of violent motion. In the 1130s a Spanish Arab, the Latinized form of whose name is Avempace, may have been influenced by Philoponus when he denied Aristotle's claim that the time it took a body to fall was directly proportional to the resistance of the external medium through which it passed. Avempace thought that what we observe as 'ordinary' motion was the difference between hypothetically unobstructed motion and the slowing down due to the medium. The potential of these admittedly still rather vague ideas was never realized in the middle ages, but we are groping towards the theory that natural motion could only occur in a hypothetical vacuum. It is that idea, as we have seen, that lies behind the modern law of inertia. In other words, it was not a failure to experiment or to observe the workings of the universe that held back medieval science but rather a failure to look at things in a new light.

That said, can we point to any technical advances – inventions, as we might say today – that took place in the middle ages? Large scale building construction, of course, made heavy demands on the mathematical and engineering skills of the medieval masons. The need to cover wide spans with stone vaults led to the adoption of the pointed arch, an eastern idea probably brought to the West by the crusaders in about 1100. Industries (q.v.) like glazing and cloth-making also employed complex processes, and ones moreover that demanded some knowledge of chemistry. The introduction of cannons, rudimentary though these instruments were in their early days, represented an advance in the uses to which that knowledge could be put. But the breakthrough in medieval technology that did most to change everyday life was surely the invention of the mechanical clock. The combination of a falling weight which set in motion a series of geared wheels and an escapement mechanism which controlled the rate of motion gave medieval Europe an instrument which at last solved the problem of telling the time of day. The earliest such clock surviving in England is probably the one in Salisbury Cathedral thought to have been made in

about 1386.

See also, BUILDING, STAINED GLASS.

A. C. Crombie, *Augustine to Galileo: the History of Science, A.D. 400–1650*, Falcon, 1952.

SCOTLAND Although it is unnecessary here to dig too deeply into the complexities of Scottish history in the middle ages, some attempt must be made to indicate the main internal developments of the northern kingdom and to show how they influenced events south of the border. It is an important story, and an interesting one too.

In the seventh and eight centuries the border as we know it did not exist. Anglo-Saxon Northumbria stretched from the Humber to the Lothians. The lands of the Picts and the Scots were confined to the present-day Highlands. In about 843, however, the powerful Pictish king Kenneth forced his own people and the Scots together to form a kingdom which, if not united in the modern sense of the word, was at least strong enough to throw the English onto the defensive. In 945 King Edmund ceded Strathclyde (probably including Cumbria) to the Scots, and thirty years later Edgar made over Lothian, bringing the border by the end of the Anglo-Saxon period to just south of Berwick on the east and somewhere by Rere Cross on Stainmore (Yorks.) in the west.

The Scottish king at this time was Malcolm Canmore (1058–92), who had supplanted the infamous Macbeth. His marriage to Margaret, sister of the English pretender, Edgar Athling, had resulted in a number of English refugees coming to the Scottish court. Margaret herself, who was later canonized, used all her considerable influence to undertake the kind of ecclesiastical reforms that Lanfranc (q.v.) was making in England so as to draw the Scottish Church into closer conformity with the new spirit prevailing on the Continent. Malcolm's long reign ended, however, in a crisis. In 1092 William Rufus (q.v.) seized Carlisle and advanced the western border to the line of the Cheviots. Malcolm retaliated by marching south, but before he could achieve anything both he and his son were killed outside Alnwick. Under Donald Bane, Malcolm's brother and successor, there was a reaction against the anglicizing tendencies of the previous reign that lasted until the accession of Margaret's son Edgar (1097–1107). He was succeeded in turn by his two brothers, Alexander (1107–24) and David I (1124–53).

David's reign was one of the most important in Scottish history. Though known in England chiefly for his defeat at the battle of the Standard, 22 August 1138, he was in fact a successful king who did much to place the Scottish monarchy on a firmer footing. Certainly, the Standard put an end to his ambitions in England, but he managed to salvage something from the wreck. King Stephen (q.v.) was too preoccupied by the problems that beset him at home to follow up the victory won in his absence in the north. So when peace was made eight months later David acquired the English earldom of Northumberland for his son Henry. Coupled with his effective occupation of the city of Carlisle, this agreement once more brought the Scottish border down to its limits in the time of Malcolm Canmore. David's involvement in English affairs was taken still further by his tenure of the honour of Huntingdon, which he acquired by his marriage to the daughter of the English earl Waltheof. He was not only a Scottish king but an English tenant-in-chief, and when civil war broke out in England in 1139 he lent his support to the Empress Matilda and her son Henry, the future Henry II (q.v.).

For all his eagerness to extend Scottish influence southwards, it is for his achievement in strengthening royal authority in Scotland itself that David deserves to be remembered. When a reforming influence had last been felt in Scottish affairs, in the reign of Malcolm Canmore, it had been one of English provenance. This time it was Anglo-Norman. With David's encouragement Anglo-Norman families came to settle in Scotland, and feudal tenure took the place of the old Celtic system of land-holding. The new-fangled titles of earl and baron made their appearance alongside the *mormaers* and *toisechs* of Celtic vocabulary. And in central and southern Scotland David began to establish the rudiments of a system of local administration: we hear of the office of sheriff for the first time in 1120.

David died in 1153 leaving an eleven-year-old grandson to succeed him as Malcolm IV. In the years that followed it became painfully apparent that the Scots stood little hope of clinging onto their gains in Northumbria once the English had closed ranks under the strong monarchy of Henry II. Malcolm handed back the northern counties in 1157. His policy was opposed by his brother and successor William the Lion (1165–1214), who took advantage of Henry's misfortunes in 1174 to intervene on the side of the rebels in return for the promise of Northumberland. But his ambitions were thwarted one misty morning when he was captured near Alnwick. He was released the following year on terms that were intended to clarify the relationship between the two kings. William became the vassal of Henry 'for Scotland and all his other lands', and he surrendered the castles of Edinburgh, Roxburgh, Berwick, Jedburgh and Stirling, the five strongest in his kingdom. At first Henry exercized his overlordship to the full, but in later years he relented a little. William's humiliation was finally obliterated in the reign of his successor Richard I (q.v.), who allowed him to redeem his country's independence for a payment of 10,000 marks.

The century that followed was one of the most tranquil in Scotland's history. Skirmishes and raids were still a fact of life along the border, but it gradually became clear that the Scottish kings would be unlikely ever again to push the frontier as far south as the Tees. Instead, they sought to extend their power northwards by subduing the rebellious lords of the Highlands. They even succeeded in making Moray, distant as it was, a shire within the governed area of the kingdom. All the same, this prospect of orderly progress was abruptly terminated one windy March night in 1286 when Alexander III was swept from his horse and killed. It was Scotland's misfortune that he should have died childless. His sole heiress was his three-year-old grand-daughter Margaret of Norway. She set sail for Scotland in 1290, but died while making the passage. As no clearly recognized heir was left, Edward I (q.v.) of England was invited to arbitrate between the two principal claimants, Robert Bruce and John Balliol. He came down in favour of the latter. Once Balliol was installed on the Scottish throne, Edward seized every opportunity to insist on his rights as overlord. He went so far, in fact, that in 1295 the Scots rebelled and placed the government of their country in the

hands of a council of 12. Edward responded by invading the following year.

These sad events ushered in the long period of Anglo-Scottish warfare that was to do so much to shape the respective political destinies of the two nations. Edward seems to have thought that he could deal with the Scots as easily as he had dealt with the Welsh in the 1280s. But the experience of the next few years was to show that a victory in the field was not enough to conquer a country the size of Scotland, and that so far from crushing the spirit of the Scots his campaigns had the contrary effect of awakening Scottish nationalism. Still worse, when the Scots reached an agreement with Philip IV of France he found himself fighting a war on two fronts. This was more than England could bear, and in 1297 discontent boiled over into open opposition to the king's exactions. The Scottish champion, William Wallace, took full opportunity of the crisis to sweep down from the Highlands and defeat the English at Stirling Bridge. By the following year Edward's position at home had recovered sufficiently to allow him to avenge this humiliation at the battle of Falkirk on 22 July. This crushing victory turned the tide of war in favour of the English: Wallace was driven into hiding and eventually captured and executed in 1305, and even magnates like Robert Bruce decided to lay down their arms. If Edward thought that was the end of the war, however, he was in for a rude awakening. In 1306 Bruce murdered his rival John Comyn in the church at Dumfries. The exact motive remains obscure. But it is the sequel that matters. Bruce raised the standard of rebellion once again, and had himself crowned king at Scone. In the following year Edward I died while making his way north, and under his incompetent son Edward II (q.v.) the English conquests in Scotland were whittled away. Feeble though he may have been, not even Edward II was prepared to make an abject surrender. When news reached England in 1314 of the imminent fall of Stirling, he came to its relief with a large and impressive army. Bruce had no option but to fight, but taking advantage of the mistakes made by his opponents he was able to reap one of the most decisive victories of the middle ages (q.v. BANNOCKBURN). Eventually in 1323 Edward decided to agree to a truce, but it took the regime of Isabella and Mortimer, which supplanted his own, to face up to reality and recognize Scottish independence in the Treaty of Northampton, 1328.

Life along the borders in this period of continuous warfare must have been intolerable. Year after year crops were destroyed, and villages burned. Law and order suffered an irreparable breakdown. To protect their respective sides of the border, the English and Scottish kings relied on the services of local magnates, whose power in these disputed areas ultimately exceeded that of the kings whom they nominally served. We think of the Douglases in Scotland, and the Percys and Nevilles in England. Moreover, the success in Scotland of Bruce and the nationalists created a sizeable party of 'disinherited' lords who had forfeited their lands for siding with Balliol and the English. These were the men who incited Edward III (q.v.) – not that he needed much inciting – to reopen the war after Bruce died in 1329 leaving a five-year old son, David II, to succeed him. At Dupplin Moor in 1332 and at Halidon Hill the English succeeded in worsting the Scots, and a puppet king, Edward Balliol, son of John, was put on the

throne. As in the reign of Edward I, however, the Scottish War soon became caught up in a wider conflict with France. David II took refuge with Philip VI in Normandy, and so long as he stayed there it proved impossible for the negotiators to reach agreement on the other matters in dispute between England and France. Fearing that the French might land in England, Edward therefore invaded the Low Countries in 1338, in what proved to be the opening campaign of the Hundred Years War (q.v.). The diversion of the English forces to Flanders had the effect of course of relieving the pressure on Scotland, and in 1341 David returned to his native land.

Like his predecessors he seized every opportunity to create havoc in England when he thought no one was looking. In 1346, with the flower of England's chivalry encamped outside Calais (q.v.), he crossed the border, and was met by a hastily assembled army at Neville's Cross, near Durham, where he was defeated and taken prisoner. The English must hardly have been able to believe their good fortune when they found that for the second time in 200 years they had the Scottish king in their hands. He was finally released in 1357 in return for a ransom of 100,000 marks, a vast sum for a country of only 400,000 people to have to collect. Nevertheless, David made a sincere attempt to honour the terms, and by the time payments ceased in 1383, some 45,000 marks had been handed over.

In the meantime David's unfortunate reign had drawn to a close. He died childless in 1371, and was succeeded by Robert the Steward, the founder of the line of 'Stewart' kings. Robert was the first king for nearly a century who did not have to worry about a threat from the south. The only serious outbreak of hostilities with the English in his reign resulted in a Scottish victory at Otterburn in 1388. But within his realm he was troubled by the increasing unruliness of magnates like the earls of Douglas and of March, on whom the monarchy relied for the defence of the border. Moreover, his son Robert III (1390–1406) faced a serious rival in the duke of Albany, for fear of whom he sent his son and heir James to France for upbringing. Unfortunately, however, James was captured en route by the English a few weeks before his father died. Albany had no wish to see the young king back in Scotland, and consequently took no measures to secure his release. So it was not until 1424 that James I returned from his enforced exile. He proved to be an effective ruler, indeed too effective for the liking of some who found their independence curbed. On the night of 20 February 1437 he was murdered, and the good work he had done in restoring some measure of order was undone during the long minority of his son James II. By the time the new king was reaching maturity it was the turn of England to experience civil strife, and in the manner of his predecessors James took advantage of it to sally forth across the border. It was while he was besieging Roxburgh in 1460 that he had the misfortune to be blown up by one of his own cannons.

By the end of the middle ages both monarchies were to some extent paying the price for the long period of bitter conflict inaugurated by Edward I back in the 1290s. In England the Percys and the Nevilles, whose rivalries contributed to the outbreak of the Wars of the Roses (q.v.) in the 1450s, had built up their mighty concentrations of power under the guise of keeping the Scots at bay. But in course of time these families proved to be an element of instability in the very states they were supposed to protect. So it was in Scotland too. And the Scottish king had to cope not only with the border barons but with the Highland clans who were never properly absorbed into the 'governed area' in the middle ages. Scotland was to remain as divided and turbulent in the sixteenth century as it had been in the fourteenth.

G. W. S. Barrow, *The Anglo-Norman Era in Scottish History*, Oxford, 1980; R. Nicholson, *Scotland: the Later Middle Ages*, Oliver & Boyd, 1974.

SCULPTURE Most of the sculpture we have inherited from the middle ages is to be found in our churches. It was intended both to decorate the building and, so we are told, to instruct the faithful: for those who were illiterate Biblical stories could be imparted visually in sculpture, painting and stained glass (q.v.). But when we actually look at the sculpture, it is surprising to find just how little of it is iconographic in content. In the thirteenth and fourteenth centuries on roof bosses, gargoyles and corbels masons give free play to their imagination by combining Biblical exegesis with light comedy. It is the variety and vitality of medieval sculpture which makes it so enjoyable.

The Normans inherited from the Anglo-Saxons a vigorous sculptural tradition which had drawn on both the barbaric tastes of the North and Christian influences from the Mediterranean to produce some striking works like the crucifixion at Romsey Abbey. At first the Normans had little to contribute. They excelled at architecture (q.v.) not sculpture, and it is remarkable how little their major buildings made use of sculptural adornment. It is when we turn from the cathedrals to small village churches that we find Norman carving at its best – on fonts and tympana for example (the tympanum is the space between the door and the archway of an entrance). We meet dragons and strange beasts and ornamental patterns using the familiar dogtooth and billet-head forms. By the 1130s, however, there was a significant revival in sculpture. From approximately this decade we have the two stone panels at Chichester Cathedral, showing Christ at Bethany and the Raising of Lazarus. The Bethany scene, so memorable for the haunting expression on the faces, has been described as 'one of the outstanding pieces of English medieval sculpture.' The Chichester panels are matched in importance by work which a school over in Herefordshire was producing, in the 1140s of all decades, just when the civil war of Stephen's reign was at its peak. They were less a school than a roving team of sculptors who displayed their skills at the parish churches of Shobdon, Kilpeck and Fownhope. On the south door at Kilpeck we can still see how Viking, Irish and French influences combined to produce lively, sometimes demonic, carvings of dragons, snakes and long trails in which vaguely human figures become engulfed (plates 27a and b). These masons or their successors were responsible for two more masterpieces, the fonts at Castle Frome and Eardisley, which, if we are right in ascribing them to the 1160s, are among the last works of the school (plate 28). The Herefordshire sculptors seem to have retired from the scene as mysteriously as they had arrived.

In the Baptism of Christ on the Castle Frome font Romanesque sculpture attained an eerie intensity that was unsurpassed in England if not in Europe. By the time the Herefordshire school went out of business, however, their style was already being overtaken by the change in taste that marked the evolution of Romanesque into Gothic – a change no less significant in the history of sculpture than in the history of architecture. The wild, semi-abstract scenes that had fascinated the visual taste of the northern barbarians were rejected in favour of life-like figures of the saints portrayed as human beings with whom men and women could identify and sympathize. In France, for example, the entrance portals of cathedrals like Chartres, Rheims and Amiens received figures of saints and angels that are among the most beautiful creations of Christian art. They are the expressions of a more optimistic view of the world – one that had shaken off the associations of the dark, pagan past. In England the nearest we come to the kind of sculpture galleries found in France is the west front of Wells Cathedral (c. 1230–50). Its 176 standing figures, 30 half-size angels and 49 narrative reliefs make up a vast iconographical scheme centred on the Coronation of the Virgin and supported on the south side by Old Testament and on the north side by New Testament scenes.

The assured quality with which this work was carried out was matched inside the cathedral, where stiff-leaf foliage, a characteristic motif of English thirteenth-century sculpture, was employed fully developed for the first time in the nave and transepts. Out of the capitals which crown the pillars grow graceful sprigs of trefoil-shaped leaves. The foliage is not so much stiff as stylized, and it is brought to life by being used as a cover for the many delightful carvings for which Wells is justly famous – the man with toothache and the thieves in the orchard to name but two (plate 3).

By the time Wells was nearing completion developments equally significant for the history of sculpture were taking place at Westminster. In 1245, under King Henry III's (q.v.) patronage, work commenced on rebuilding Edward the Confessor's abbey church. In sculpture no less than in architectural conception the new abbey owed much to French ideas. For example, high up in the transepts are two sets of angels of undeniably French inspiration. They have a gentle smile reminiscent of the celebrated angels of Rheims, but the energetic treatment of the drapery marks them out as definitely English. It is these Westminster figures which very likely provided the inspiration for the famous gallery of angels that fills the triforium of the rebuilt choir of Lincoln Cathedral – the so-called 'Angel Choir'. Less restrained than their forebears at Westminster, these angels – some playing musical instruments, and one even carrying a hawk – were the work of local masons whose style was very different from that practised by the court school.

Another local school of masons, based somewhere in the north, was responsible for the 'leaves of Southwell'. In the 1290s the chapter house of Southwell Minster was rebuilt, and its capitals decorated with foliage of unparalleled realism. Oak, maple, buttercup, hawthorn – we can recognize them all. The canons of Southwell were fortunate not only in employing the sculptors they did but also in choosing to rebuild when they did: in that brief period of the 1290s English botanical sculpture attained a measure of realism never experienced before or since. The vitality we find in the sculpture of that decade is matched of course by the gaiety and inventiveness of ecclesiastical architecture (q.v.) at the same time. Not for nothing is it known as 'Decorated'.

A favourite motif of the period was the undulating ogee curve, used to such good effect for example in the Lady Chapel of Ely Cathedral. The aim was to dissolve surfaces in a sea of decorative ornament. Niche mounted niche, canopy mounted canopy. The finest achievements of this era of superabundant decoration rank among the most daring creations of the middle ages – the Percy tomb at Beverley Minster and the tomb of Edward II at Gloucester – and we find ourselves losing touch with reality as we behold the forest of pinnacles pointing dizzily heavenwards.

Such richness of detail was bound to provoke a contrary movement in favour of simplicity. It came with the arrival of the Perpendicular style, which relied for its effect not on sculptural elaboration but on the simple definition of line. Consequently the later fourteenth and fifteenth centuries show little architectural sculpture to set beside the beautiful work of the thirteenth, and we have to wait for the work undertaken at Westminster Abbey in the early sixteenth to see the last flowering of the sculptor's art before the Reformation. The rows of prophets (c. 1505–15) high up in the triforium of Henry VII's Chapel are obviously the work of a highly accomplished portraitist who knew just which features of the human face needed stressing to bring out the idiosyncracies of personality.

Though the late middle ages can show little figure sculpture of distinction, the abilities of craftsmen found ample outlet in the production of tomb effigies. Many of these were carved in freestone, but an increasingly popular material was alabaster, a form of lime sulphate quarried in Nottinghamshire and Derbyshire. For the most lavish commissions copper-gilt was used. Indeed, the life-size copper effigy of Richard Beauchamp, earl of Warwick (d. 1439) at St Mary's, Warwick, has been described as 'one of the greatest achievements of the English medieval sculptor'.

If figure sculpture by the fifteenth century largely took the form of the production of tomb effigies, was there any form of three-dimensional art which did find favour with late medieval builders and their patrons? We have only to look at King's College Chapel, Cambridge, or the gatehouse of Butley Priory to see that what delighted them was heraldic display. Coats-of-arms and heraldic beasts were carved in profusion on walls both for their undoubted decorative effect and for their value in advertizing genealogical pride and family connections. The Tudor rose and Beaufort portcullis are two well-known motifs that cannot escape the attention of the visitor to any building Henry VII had anything to do with.

See also, BRASSES.

L. Stone, *Sculpture in Britain: the Middle Ages*, Penguin, 2nd ed., 1972.

SEISIN Seisin was a word commonly employed in the twelfth century to describe the possession as opposed to the ownership of land. In a later age, when conveyancing was effected by written instrument, the idea of 'livery of seisin' still survived to describe the ceremony whereby a recipient was led into possession of a piece of land he had acquired. A man who held a free tenement was therefore said to be in seisin. If he was deprived of it, he was said to be disseised. In the 1160s and 1170s Henry II (q.v.) evolved a legal process, known as the Assize of Novel Disseisin, that enabled a person recently disseised of a tenement to recover it. The writ initi-

ating the action instructed the sheriff (q.v.) to summon a jury whose duty it was to ascertain the facts of the case – only the facts, and not any questions of right or wrong that might complicate matters, for the essence of the procedure was its simplicity. Therein too lay the secret of its success.

See also, JUSTICE.

SERMONS Preaching was the principal medium through which the Church communicated its message to the faithful. They could not read the Vulgate Bible for themselves – or at least very few of them could. But they *could* hear its teaching expounded from the pulpit.

The sermons that have come down to us from the middle ages make an important contribution to our knowledge of the social, literary and ecclesiastical history of the period. Most of them date from the fourteenth and fifteenth centuries. Does that mean that more sermons were preached in the fourteenth and fifteenth centuries than ever before, or simply that the earlier ones have been lost? The answer, as so often in history, is probably a combination of both. Ever since the Council of Clovesho in 747 the English hierarchy had been encouraging their clergy to teach the Word of God, but however hard they tried, they could do little to overcome either the reluctance or the inability of so many priests to mount their pulpits. In fact we do not even know whether the churches had pulpits in those far-off days: the oldest surviving ones date from no earlier than the fourteenth century. For all the evidence that points to the rarity of a sermon in church in the eleventh or twelfth centuries, however, there are suggestions as well that those who thirsted for the word could hear it, and hear it from

241

the lips of some very distinguished preachers indeed. Jocelin of Brakelond tells us, for example, that Abbot Samson of Bury St Edmund's, eloquent as he was in French and Latin, was quite happy to preach to the people in English, and even in the local dialect when he was in Norfolk, the county where he was born and bred. That episode, incidentally, gives us a remarkable insight into the linguistic range expected of a twelfth-century preacher, who might find himself called upon to speak in Latin before clerics, French before the nobility and in the vernacular before more humble folk.

What must have led to an increase in the provision of preaching was the coming of the friars (q.v.) in the thirteenth century. The Dominicans (q.v.) or Black Friars significantly enough were known to their contemporaries as the Friars Preachers. In the towns they built vast hall-like churches to accommodate the crowds that came in to listen. Urban society suffered from no shortage of preaching in the late middle ages, because it was chiefly to the towns that the earliest mendicant missions had been directed. But it seems that in the rural parishes too there was an increase in the provision of preaching once the clergy became better educated. Writing in about 1450, the theologian Alexander Carpenter could say that 'now in many places there is greater abundance of preaching of the Word of God than was customary before our time.' In that case how often would a congregation have been treated to a sermon in the late middle ages? Mirk's *Festial*, written in *c.* 1400 for the benefit of a fellow clergyman, contains a cycle of 74 sermons – in other words, one for every Sunday of the year and for a good number of saints' days as well. One recent estimate is that something like 60

sermons a year would have been preached in some of the better-served parishes in England or France.

How did the medieval preacher set about his task? He had to present his message in terms that would be comprehensible to an audience whose education, if any, would rarely have extended beyond the elementary stage (q.v., SCHOOLS). This he did by abandoning generalities in favour of allegorical figures of speech and *exempla*, or moralized anecdotes. Robert Ripon's tale of the bailiff and the devil is a good example. A notoriously oppressive bailiff was riding to his village one day, when en route he met the devil. The bailiff said that he was travelling on his master's business. The devil then enquired if he would freely accept whatever was freely offered to him. The bailiff of course said yes, and likewise enquired of his companion. The devil replied that he would not take whatever men gave to him, but only what they would gladly give with all their heart. 'Quite right', said the bailiff. As they made their way into the village, they met a ploughman angrily commending to the devil his unco-operative plough oxen which kept straying from their course. 'They are yours', said the bailiff. 'No, no', said the devil. 'That man does not give them with all his heart.' They went on, and next they saw a woman wishing her child to the devil because it would not stop crying. 'Now this one is yours', said the bailiff. 'No', replied the devil. 'The woman does not really want to lose her child.' Finally they came to the end of the village where they met a poor old woman whose only cow the bailiff had seized the day before. 'To the devil I commend you', she shrieked with all her heart as she saw the bailiff coming. 'To be sure, this one is mine', said the devil. And then he snatched the bailiff away to the perpetual fires of Hell.

That story of Ripon's illustrates how the preacher had to be a good raconteur. He made sure of retaining the attention of his audience by telling a good story and telling it well. To that end he might employ a number of devices and embellishments. Mirk, who was prior of Lilleshall (Salop), appealed to local tradition by writing homilies for the feasts of the local West Midland saints, Alkmund and Winifred. He also appealed to the legendary and the miraculous; his sermons contained lots of good yarns and lots of stories of miracles and shrines. To that extent he was ultra-traditional in his approach. Not all the pulpit oratory of the late middle ages was so good-humoured, however. Satire – often ruthless satire – poured from the lips of the preachers. In this respect the great Dominican John Bromyard stands in a class of his own. From his pulpit he lambasted the regular clergy for their wealth and avarice; he condemned the rich for their gluttony and extravagance; he attacked the nobility for their oppressiveness and the justices for their corruptibility; and just to be even-handed he complained as well about the slothfulness and idleness of the labouring classes. All that and more is contained within Bromyard's famous homiletic collection, the *Summa Predicantium*.

The richness and variety of medieval sermon literature was demonstrated nearly half a century ago by G. R. Owst in his *Literature and Pulpit in Medieval England*. But if any criticism has to be levelled against this book, which has become a classic in its own right, it must be that Owst takes too static a view of his subject. He recognizes that there was a movement towards a greater realism in sermon literature, but fails to

allow that the content and purpose of sermons may also have changed in the course of the middle ages. In the twelfth and thirteenth centuries preachers, for all the delight they took in the use of satire, kept within the limits of an ecclesiological framework. In the fourteenth and fifteenth centuries, however, preachers were increasingly called on by kings and princes to place their services at the disposal of the State. A sermon would be given at the opening session of a parliament, setting forth the king's case for a grant of taxation. We are told that sermons were given by bishops in favour of the deposition of Edward II. And in 1346 Thomas Bradwardine, the theologian and future archbishop of Canterbury, preached in celebration of Edward III's victories at Neville's Cross and Crecy (q.v.).

The use of the sermon as a medium of secular propaganda, couched in Biblical terms, but accommodated to current political needs, indicates, as Miss Smalley has written, a changed mentality towards interpretation of the Holy Scripture. At the same time, the appreciation by modern scholars that sermons may have been viewed differently as time went on indicates just how far modern sermon studies have advanced since Owst wrote his seminal studies in the 1920s and 1930s. One of Owst's favourite themes was the influence of sermons on the development of English literature. *Piers Plowman*, he claimed, was 'the quintessence of English medieval preaching gathered up into a single metrical piece of unusual charm and vivacity'. Nowadays we know that there was more to it than that. Certainly we can agree with Owst when he said that satirist and allegorist alike were disciples of the pulpit. There are similarities in structure and modes of treatment. But at the same time we must recognize that poet and preacher had differing purposes in mind. The latter placed the emphasis on explaining, on giving a straight, convincing answer to a question about the place of man in God's design for the world. The former, however, placed it on artistry and explanation. To that extent, the dreamer in Langland's (q.v.) masterpiece is a long way indeed from the church pulpit.

G. R. Owst, *Preaching in Medieval England*, Cambridge, 1923; *Literature and Pulpit in Medieval England*, Cambridge, 1933.

SHERIFF The office of sheriff (O.E., *scir gerefa*, shire-reeve) can be traced back as far as the reign of Ethelred the Unready (978–1016), and by the time the Normans arrived, it had emerged as the principal instrument of royal government in the shires. The medieval sheriff was the maid of all work, responsible for collecting the farm (the revenue due to the king from the boroughs and royal demesne lands in the shire), for presiding in the shire court, for making a twice yearly tourn or visitation of the Hundred (q.v.) courts and from the thirteenth century onwards for proclaiming royal statutes at the principal towns in his bailiwick. Under the Norman kings the sheriff attained his greatest power and independence, but by the fourteenth century he was subjected to rigorous Exchequer control and obliged to share his duties with new officials like the coroner (q.v.), the escheator (q.v.), the commissioners of array and the justices of the peace. All the same, if the sheriff became less independent, he evidently did not become any less corrupt, to judge from the evil character accorded him in the Robin Hood (q.v.) legends.

It is apparent from the chorus of criticism voiced in the thirteenth and fourteenth centuries that the king had one conception of the office of sheriff and his subjects quite another. The king, in an effort to maximize his income, wanted to appoint trusty royal servants as sheriffs and to keep them in office for as long as possible. The Commons in parliament, on the other hand, demanded that only well-to-do local gentlemen should be appointed, rich enough not to be tempted by corruption, and that they should hold office for only one year. For a century or more the Crown tried holding its own, but it had given way on most points by 1371. In later times the sheriff lost many of his duties to the lords lieutenant and the justices of the peace, and though his office survives in England to this day, it is of course largely honorific. The modern American sheriff has more in common with his medieval English forebears.

See also, GOVERNMENT.

W. A. Morris, *The Medieval English Sheriff to 1300*, Manchester, 1927, reprinted 1968.

SIGNET See GOVERNMENT.

SPORT A number of modern pastimes were already known in England before 1500, but as we look back at the way people spent their leisure hours in the middle ages, it is the differences rather than the similarities between medieval and modern recreations which stand out most.

William FitzStephen's famous account of London, written in the twelfth century, certainly strikes a familiar note. He tells us that when Moorfields marsh was frozen over the young men would go skating and tobogganing. They would go out into the fields to play ball games; and at Smithfield, he tells us, they could even engage in horse-racing. We might add to this description, the earliest we have of life in London (q.v.), by naming a few ball games that we hear about for the first time later on in the middle ages. Tennis was known by the early fifteenth century, to judge from the tennis-balls episode in Act i, ii of Shakespeare's *Henry V*, which rests on good contemporary authority, and indeed there is a reference in Chaucer's *Troilus and Criseyde* to 'pleyen raket, to and fro'. Cricket is not mentioned by name until the sixteenth century, but it may have developed from an earlier game called 'club-ball' which was banned in a proclamation of 1365. At the foot of the east window in Gloucester Cathedral (c. 1350) is the tiny figure of a man hitting a ball with a club curved at the end. He is usually described as a golfer, and golf was indeed known by the end of the middle ages, but he could equally well be playing hockey or club-ball.

All these were evidently quite popular pursuits, indeed too popular for the government's satisfaction because they were prohibited in 1365. Able-bodied men were told instead to practise archery for the obvious reason that skill in archery was crucial to English success on the battlefields of France. The list of games banned in 1365 – and they weren't just ball games either – provides a good idea of what people liked doing in fourteenth-century England: 'hurling of stones, loggats and quoits, handball, cock-fighting and other vain games of no value' were mentioned.

The prohibition (or attempted prohibition) of cock-fighting reminds us that in the middle ages games involving animals provided idle amusement in a way that would be considered quite improper today. Bear-baiting, for example, is one of the sports illustrated in the margin of a fourteenth-century manuscript of the *Romance of Alexander*. William FitzStephen tells us that on winter mornings in London bears were set to fight each other, or were baited by dogs. And let us not forget as well that hunting was the aristocratic sport *par excellence*. By the early thirteenth century vast tracts of countryside were set aside for the chase, and the deer and the boar within them were protected for the king's enjoyment by the savage code of regulations known as the forest laws. But it was not only the king who enjoyed hunting. So too did the nobility. And so too, according to Chaucer (q.v.), did the pilgrim Monk,

> one of the finest sort
> Who rode the country; hunting was his sport.*

Hunting was the subject of several treatises written in the middle ages, of which the most popular was the one contained in the *Boke of St Alban's*, printed in 1485. This volume also had a chapter on fishing, another popular rural pastime.

If the king and his friends were fond of the chase in day-time, what were they likely to do in the evenings? Since time immemorial they had been listening to minstrels, singing heroic epics, ballads or popular songs. Every nobleman retained his company of minstrels and fools. But at the same time as listening to a background of music and singing, the lord and his friends might play chess, backgammon, cards or dice. All these

---

* Chaucer, *The Canterbury Tales*, ed. N. Coghill, p. 23.

games were known by the late middle ages. Gambling in particular seems to have been a pursuit to which noblemen were addicted. Between September 1413 and March 1414, for part of which time he was staying with Henry V at Eltham, the earl of March lost over £157 at cards, raffle and betting on cock-fighting. The Black Prince is said to have lost as much as £100 on a single day's play with his father.

For the humbler sort there was always drinking. William FitzStephen in his account of London names 'the immoderate drinking of fools' as one of the two plagues from which the city then suffered (q.v., DIET). Most medieval towns (q.v.) were apparently as well supplied with taverns as they were with churches, which means very well indeed. The duty of controlling the quality and price of ale, and the hours at which it could be sold, lay with the local municipal authorities, who then as now made great play of detailed regulations. By the 1530s the rule at Chester was that ale and wine were not to be sold after 9 p.m. on any day or during the hours of divine worship on Sundays. No doubt medieval pubs like their modern counterparts had their 'regulars', and no doubt too there was more than ample drinking-up time.

A. L. Poole, 'Recreations', in *Medieval England*, ed. A. L. Poole, Oxford, 1958.

STAINED GLASS Centuries of neglect have taken a heavy toll of the stained glass that once filled our churches; but what has survived is sufficient in both quality and quantity to emphasize the contrast between the brilliant luminosity of the medieval glass and the insipid sentimentality of the pale substitute for it produced in such abundance by the Victorians.

It is often said that the purpose of stained glass windows was didactic, and no doubt up to a point this is true. In an age when the great majority of church-goers were illiterate, and the Bible was anyway only available in the Latin Vulgate, stained glass windows served to convey the scriptural message through a visual medium. Such an explanation will certainly account for the narrative sequences that were placed at eye-level in windows along the aisles. But what are we to think of the great east window at York Minster, no less than 77ft in height and filled with scene upon scene from the Old Testament at the top and from the Revelation of St John lower down? And what about the glass in the clerestory windows depicting kings and bishops associated with the conversion of northern England? Surely these could not have been 'read', still less understood, by the faithful congregated below. In other words, we are driven to conclude that these lovely windows were there not just to teach, but to create an overall effect, and to inspire a sense of wonder.

The first we hear in England of the glazing of the church windows is in the late seventh century. By then the art of glass manufacture had evidently become extinct here, because Benedict Biscop, abbot of Wearmouth, had to fetch glaziers over from France to work in his churches at Jarrow and Wearmouth. For all intents and purposes, however, the history of glass painting in this country begins in the twelfth century. From c. 1170 we have a panel of a king from a Tree of Jesse at York Minster and from the 1180s the magnificent series of windows in Canterbury Cathedral. The general impression created by this Romanesque glass is one of sombre, intense richness. The very colours that predominated – greens, purples, rubys – served to enhance that atmosphere of awesome mystery that must have pervaded the interior of a church in the age of Becket. If we are to judge from the surviving glass at Canterbury, the subject matter of these early windows included figures of saints, placed high up in the clerestory, and narrative sequences arranged in vertical tiers of medallions in the lancet windows along the aisles. A separate stage of the story was told in each of these medallions, which were formed by bending an iron frame (or 'armature') to whatever shape was required, be it a circle, square or ellipse. Another form of glazing occasionally found in this period is the pattern window, important for the fact that it foreshadows the famous 'grisaille' or grey-patterned glass of the thirteenth century. The popularity of grisaille was probably a response to the desire for better lighting to illuminate the marble shafts and sculptured capitals that characterized early Gothic architecture. Windows were larger of course, but that was not enough. The glass that filled them had to be lighter. Thus the rich colours of the twelfth century gave way to a shimmering greyish-green background on which was painted a foliate pattern that became steadily more naturalistic as time progressed. To appreciate on the grandest scale the kind of effect that could be created we must look at the 'Five Sisters' window in the north transept of York Minster, where five huge lancets, each 53ft high, were all filled with grisaille in the 1250s.

Grisaille glass continued to be used into the following century, but it was the earlier tradition of figures and narrative sequences that proved to be most compatible with the large, multi-opening windows of the 1300s. The characteristic window of this period contained a row of saints, as many as there were openings or 'lights' to be filled, and each one surmounted by an elaborate canopy. Winged angels usually filled the small tracery lights. What considerations influenced the choice of subject-matter in a window? However great the desire of a monastic or cathedral chapter to see all the windows of their church glazed according to a single iconographic scheme, it was usually the wishes of the donor that would have to take precedence. As the Friar tells Lady Fee in *Piers Plowman*, 'We are having a stained glass window made for us, and it's proving rather expensive. If you would care to pay for the glazing yourself, and have your name engraved in the window, you need have no doubts of your eternal salvation.'* As early as the 1290s at Merton College, Oxford, this attitude of mind had led to the inclusion of kneeling figures of the donor, Henry de Mamesfield, in a sequence of no fewer than a dozen windows, with a view no doubt to reminding the onlooker to pray for his soul. In seeking this lavish commemoration of himself in the College Chapel, de Mamesfield may well have been indulging his own sense of vanity; but he set an example that was to be taken up many times over by patrons and donors in the next two centuries (plate 31).

As well as a change in design we must notice a change in the art of painting in the early fourteenth century. This was the discovery of 'silver stain', a method of combining white and yellow on the same piece of glass which was first used in this country, as far as we can now tell, on the 'heraldic widow', at York

* W. Langland, *Piers the Ploughman*, ed. F. Goodridge, Penguin, 1959, p. 46.

Minster (*c.* 1310–20). This had the effect of both tilting the balance in favour of light over dark colours and of reducing the number of separately leaded panels that went to make up a window. Now that the design could be constructed without the need to cut so many pieces of glass, there was more scope for artistic excellence, and what these later windows lost in vividness of colour they gained in architectural conception and originality of design. Some fifteenth-century windows were so vast that they afforded the chance to illustrate a major theme, such as the life of some local saint, by narration in a series of panels beginning at the top left-hand corner and ending at the bottom right (plate 30). How far the onlooker could make sense of what was happening in some of the largest of these windows we have already had reason to question, but the overall effect was superb enough.

Who were the men responsible for these beautiful windows? In the case of the York east window the chance survival till recent times of the contract between patron and glazier has preserved for us the name of John Thornton of Coventry. He was given just three years (1405–8) to complete this vast commission, the implication being that he was the head of a fairly large workshop. Though this important contract at the Minster went to a Coventry firm, York itself was an important centre of glazing, as we can see from the windows that have survived in the city churches. In fact, there were workshops in most major English towns, Norwich, Oxford and London being others worthy of mention.

If we want to learn how stained glass was made in the middle ages, we have to turn to a treatise written in about 1020 by a monk called Theophilus which is still our main authority on the subject.

First of all the master glazier had to sketch a design for his window. Known as the cartoon, this was a full-size drawing, executed in the twelfth century with charcoal on a whitewashed table-top, and in the fifteenth on paper or parchment so that it could be preserved for later use. When the design was ready, and a colour scheme arranged, the glazier took all the different coloured pieces of glass that he needed, laid them on the cartoon and cut them to shape. In the absence of diamond cutters, which were not introduced until the seventeenth century, this no doubt difficult operation was performed with the aid of a red-hot iron. The glass used by the glaziers was known in the trade as 'pot-metal', meaning that it had been coloured throughout by the addition of a metallic oxide of whatever hue was required – cobalt for blue, copper for red, manganese for violet and so on.

When all the pieces of glass were in position, the glazier could begin to paint in details, like faces and drapery folds, taking as his guide the design of the cartoon underneath. The earliest stained glass windows, like those in Canterbury Cathedral, were composed of a vast mosaic of tiny leaded pieces, resplendent in their vivid reds and violets. In the early fourteenth century, however, the art of glass painting was revolutionized, as we have seen by the discovery of 'silver staining'. Someone noticed that a silver salt solution painted on a surface of white glass would turn yellow when fired. The significance of this breakthrough was that it enabled yellow and white areas to be depicted on the same piece of glass, thus reducing the number of separate leaded panes that needed to be used in making a window.

When the painter had finished his job, he could consider the glass ready for firing. This was the method by which the paint was fused onto the surface, so as to prevent it from falling off with the passage of time. The pieces of glass were laid out on a tray covered with quicklime, and fired in a kiln. Once they had cooled, they were brought back to the table, where they were joined together by strips of lead. The window was then ready for delivery to the church.

The richest treasury of stained glass in England is to be found in the Minster and city churches of York. Glass from the Norwich workshops, much of it of the highest quality too, can be seen at East Harling (Norfolk), Long Melford (Suffolk) and in some of the city churches of Norwich itself (plates 29–31).

J. Baker, *English Stained Glass*, Thames & Hudson, 1960.

STEPHEN England in the reign of Stephen (1135–54) was afflicted by a long civil war which has earned notoriety as 'the Anarchy'. Some indication of the measure of suffering it caused is given by a writer at Peterborough Abbey who quoted men as saying openly that Christ and his saints slept.

The war started as a dispute over the succession. After his only legitimate son William had been drowned in 1120 in the wreck of the White Ship, Henry I (q.v.) had made the barons swear to accept his daughter Matilda, wife of the count of Anjou, as heir to the throne. They hardly relished the prospect of a woman ruler, still less the prospect of Geoffrey of Anjou as her consort, but such was the force of the king's personality that they had little choice but to accept. In the event, however, it was not Matilda but Stephen who succeeded to the throne when Henry I died in December 1135. A younger son of the count of Blois,

Stephen was a nephew of the old king, from whom he had received many lands and other marks of favour at the English court. His lightning coup d'etat provided the barons with a convenient excuse to forget the claims of Matilda, and he was crowned on 22 December, and recognized by the pope early the next year.

Despite the oaths which they had sworn to uphold Matilda, the barons supported Stephen almost to a man. By the end of 1139, however, enough people were dissatisfied with his rule to enable Matilda finally to make a bid for the throne. What had gone wrong? The event that triggered off the civil war was the arrest of three leading bishops at Oxford in June 1139 – Roger, bishop of Salisbury, justiciar (q.v.) of England, and his nephews, Nigel, bishop of Ely, and Alexander, bishop of Lincoln. These were the men upon whom Henry I had relied to control the administration of England. Since Bishop Roger and his relatives had obviously grown rich during their years in royal service, Stephen was incited, notably by the count of Meulan, to grab the wealth which it was believed, rightly or wrongly, they had amassed at his and his predecessor's expense. Arriving in England to stake her claim to the throne just three months after the arrest of the bishops, Matilda therefore attracted the support of those former servants of Henry I who now felt insecure under Stephen. The first defector was her half-brother Robert, earl of Gloucester. He was followed by Miles of Gloucester and Brian FitzCount. Both of them honoured the memory of the father by offering their services to the daughter.

Matilda succeeded in attracting enough support to start a war, but not enough to win it. The result was a decade of desultory warfare, known as 'the

Anarchy'. At the beginning of 1141 Matilda seemed like gaining the edge when she captured King Stephen at the battle of Lincoln. She entered the capital in June, but before she could be crowned the Londoners showed their hostility by driving her out. She fled to Winchester, where in the second major battle of the year her half-brother Robert of Gloucester was captured. By November they could do little else but exchange prisoners: so Stephen received his liberty in return for the release of Earl Robert. The remaining years of the war saw no pitched battles of note, and the campaigns pursued by the two sides seem to show few signs of a coherent strategy. It was with some justice that the chronicler, Henry of Huntingdon, observed that Stephen began many things vigorously, but then pursued them slothfully. Much of the warfare was in fact defensive, based on the advantage which castles, erected in great number during the reign, conferred on the defender over the attacker. For example, Stephen held an important castle at Malmesbury (Wilts.), which found itself cut off from his main centres of support in the south-east by a rival fortification of Earl Robert's at Faringdon (Oxon.). To counter the threat to his communications with the West Country, Stephen had therefore to win control of Faringdon. Such was the importance of this castle that its fall and subsequent demolition in 1146 succeeded in tilting the balance of advantage strongly in favour of the king. In the next year Earl Robert died, and at the beginning of 1148 Matilda herself returned to Normandy.

What was the outcome of the war? Although Matilda had given up the fight, Stephen did not emerge triumphant. His greatest misfortune was to lose Normandy (q.v.): the union of England and Normandy, created by William the Conqueror in 1066 had been torn asunder, with Stephen retaining England, and Geoffrey and Matilda winning the duchy. As a result, the great Anglo-Norman families, who held estates on both sides of the Channel, could not recognize Stephen as king of England for fear of forfeiting their lands in Matilda's Normandy. Looking to the future they considered their interests to be best served by promoting the succession to the throne of Matilda's son, Henry of Anjou. Henry crossed to England in 1153, and in August his army came face to face with Stephen's at Wallingford-on-Thames. So far from encouraging the two opposed leaders, the barons actually counselled moderation, for they rightly realized that they stood to lose too much from the forfeitures and confiscations that would follow outright victory by either party. A truce was arranged, and in November it was agreed at Winchester that Stephen would reign for his lifetime, and then be succeeded by Duke Henry, the future Henry II (q.v.). The end came sooner than either side could have expected. Less than a year later, on 25 October 1154, King Stephen died. He was buried in the abbey which he had founded at Faversham in Kent.

For all his faults Stephen seems to have been a more likeable personality than his two Norman predecessors, William II (q.v.) and Henry I. A mild man, soft and good, was how the Peterborough writer described him. He was chivalrous and brave almost to a fault. On the other hand, there may be some truth in William of Malmesbury's charge that he was changeable and untrustworthy, for his actions suggest that he failed to inspire either confidence or trust. But if a greater man than Stephen had become king in 1135, he would have found it difficult to contain the pent-up frustrations that were unleashed within days of Henry I's death. Rival baronial families seized the chance presented by the disputed succession to settle scores under the guise of supporting one or other of the claimants to the throne. Just how extensive was the devastation caused by the war we have no clear means of telling. Even if we discount the worst atrocity stories of castles filled with devils and evil men, we can hardly suppose that rival armies spent season after season campaigning without leaving their mark on the countryside. In the Cambridgeshire Fens, where the notorious Geoffrey de Mandeville had his headquarters in the 1140s, life must have been more than normally intolerable. Indeed, the large number of monastic foundations, one of the most remarkable characteristics of the reign, may reflect the fears of barons and knights who wanted to lay up treasure in heaven to atone for their sins on earth.

R. H. C. Davis, *King Stephen*, Longman, 1967.

T

TAXATION Taxation has become a fashionable subject of historical study in recent years, as much, one feels, because of the concern felt about its burden today as because of its admittedly undoubted importance in the middle ages. What makes it such a worthwhile field of enquiry is the insight it can afford into the evolution of the nation state and the relationships on which it is based. In Anglo-Norman England in the twelfth century the feudal (q.v.) nature of the state was reflected in the heavy reliance of the king on feudal forms of revenue. In later medieval England, on the other hand, the formation of a national political community was reflected in the growth of public taxation granted in parliament (q.v.) for the king to use for the common good.

In the middle ages the king was expected to meet his ordinary expenses from those lands and revenues pertaining to the Crown which we know as the royal demesne (q.v.). In the later parlance of the fourteenth and fifteenth centuries, he was expected 'to live of his own'. Only in times of emergency, when his ordinary revenues might prove inadequate, was he justified in asking his subjects for a grant of extraordinary revenue, i.e. taxation. It is helpful for the purposes of analysis if we divide these sources of extraordinary revenue along the modern lines of direct and indirect taxation, looking first at the former.

When he became king of England in 1066, William the Conqueror inherited the traditional revenues available to the Anglo-Saxon monarchy, the most remarkable of which was the national land tax known as the geld. William and his successors are known to have levied the geld on numerous occasions to pay for their wars, but in the long run its effectiveness as a source of revenue was undermined by the many exemptions granted by Henry I (q.v.) as the price of making it a regular annual exaction. By the 1150s it was raising only £3,000–£4,000 and after 1162 Henry II allowed it to lapse.

With the demise of this one form of national taxation the Angevin kings became more than ever dependent on the landed, feudal and judicial revenues at their command. Indeed, it was these last two sources that proved far and away the most lucrative to exploit. Richard I and John sought to meet the steep increases in their expenditure by using the right of feudal overlordship to exact unprecedented sums from their tenants-in-chief – who by 1215 could stand it no longer, and resorted to rebellion. Magna Carta (q.v.) is concerned as much as anything else to limit the king's right to name whatever figure he liked for wardships, reliefs, scutages and the other so-called 'incidents of feudalism' to which he was entitled.

The main drawback to feudalism as a form of taxation was that, in common with certain modern taxes, it hit the same group of people over and over again, in this case the tenants-in-chief. John (q.v.) knew this. That was why he began to search around for a tax of broader incidence that would produce a yield big enough to meet the needs of government in war-time. He finally achieved his ambition in 1207 with the levy of one-thirteenth on moveable property which raised no less than £60,000. Though collected only once in John's reign because the outcry was so vociferous, the levy on moveables proved to be the lifeline of the English monarchy for the rest of the middle ages, indeed into the sixteenth century. It served medieval governments as income tax serves their modern successors.

Now the king could not of course simply take the property of his subjects without obtaining their consent. As feudal overlord he could take reliefs and other 'incidents' from his tenants-in-chief as an automatic consequence of their feudal relationship. But as king he could not impose a national tax like the moveables levy without showing justification to his subjects. 'What touches all must be approved by all', as the old Roman law adage put it. So where and from whom was he to obtain consent? On several occasions Henry III (q.v.) approached his barons in their capacity as his natural counsellors, but by the 1250s they were coming to doubt whether they alone could speak for the entire community of the realm. In 1254 they told him to summon four knights from each shire to consider his request. A decade later the burgesses from the towns (q.v.) were invited to come along too. The knights and burgesses together were to make up the future House of Commons. National taxation therefore played a crucial part in calling parliament (q.v.) into existence as a national assembly in which the needs of the king could be set against the grievances of his subjects.

When it had been granted, how was the moveables levy collected? By the mid-fourteenth century convention had fixed the rates at one-fifteenth in the countryside and, in an effort to tap the greater urban wealth, one-tenth in the towns. Taxers were appointed in each county and below them sub-taxers who were responsible for the assessment and collection of the tax in the villages. Up to and including 1332 individuals were assessed personally, but after 1334 the government opted to take a fixed global sum from each village or borough community. Apart from a reduction of £4,000 in the proceeds in 1433 to take account of the declining fortunes of towns like Lincoln these sums held good for the next three centuries, despite the obvious shifts in the distribution of wealth. In theory those with moveable wealth worth less than 10s were exempt; but knowing what we do about the corruptibility of medieval tax-collectors we must doubt how far government guidelines were adhered to in practice.

If we turn now to indirect taxes, we find that the most lucrative levies were those imposed on wool exports. The history of the systematic taxation of English medieval trade begins in 1202 when King John, that most inventive of rulers, established customs duties amounting to one-fifteenth of goods imported or exported. These were probably abolished in 1206, but Edward I (q.v.) revived the idea in 1275 when he imposed the so-called Ancient Custom at the rate of half-a-mark on each sack of wool (364 lb.) and 300 wool-fells and a mark on each last of hides. Edward went a stage further in 1294, when on top of this he imposed the 'maltolt' (q.v.) of £3.6.8 on each sack of good wool and £2 on other wool, later standardized at £2 for both. This was so unpopular that it was abolished in 1297, but Edward II (q.v.) brought it back on alien merchants only in 1303. In the course of the next 40 years the maltolt became the object of a bitter struggle between king and parliament, the eventual outcome of which was that the king retained it at the standard rate of 43s 4d, but parliament won the right of granting it. Unfortunately from the point of view of the Exchequer 43s 4d was more than the traffic would bear, and the volume of wool exports fell from over 40,000 sacks in 1304–5 to less than 10,000 in the early sixteenth century. What the government probably did not realize was that the maltolt acted as a protective tariff behind which the domestic cloth industry could grow. Because it was only wool *exports* that were taxed, English cloth producers were able to get their raw material cheaper than their Flemish or Italian competitors. And when they exported their products, they had an edge over their foreign rivals because English broadcloths carried only a light duty of 14d each, equivalent to an *ad valorem* rate of about 3–5%.

With the wool trade in decline and the moveables levy yielding less than before, the government was well aware that the tax system needed reshaping. The poll taxes levied between 1377 and 1381 were one expedient, but in the light of their contribution to the outbreak of the Peasants Revolt (q.v.) the Crown was reluctant to tinker with the system again for some time. In the fifteenth century they experimented with a series of income taxes levied in 1404, 1411, 1431, 1435, 1450, 1472 and 1489, but these hit principally the landowners and evaded those like the clothiers and traders who were of more moderate means.

In the end we are left wondering whether the government in Westminster really had any idea how wealth was distributed across English society, either socially or geographically. What points unmistakably in this direction is the history of the parishes tax of 1371. At the parliament of February 1371 a subsidy of £50,000 was granted, to be levied on each parish at an average rate of 22s 3d. But it was soon apparent that nothing like £50,000 was coming in, and in June a great council was hastily assembled, to persuade the Commons to raise the tax to 116s per village. It had evidently been assumed that there were 40,000 parishes in England, whereas the returns showed that there were only 8,600.

In conclusion, we must say a word or two about the clergy. They were in the unfortunate position of being liable to taxation by both the king and the pope. The increasing frequency of clerical taxation by one or other of these two masters led to the emergence by the reign of Edward III of the twin convocations of York and Canterbury. Though usually summoned by the archbishops to meet at the same time as parliament, the convocations were completely autonomous bodies within which the clergy of the two English provinces could decide how to respond to an appeal to their generosity. The valuation of benefices made in 1291, known as the *Taxation of Pope Nicholas IV*, remained the basis for clerical grants to the Crown for the rest of the middle ages.

G. L. Harriss, *King, Parliament & Public Finance in Medieval England to 1369*, Oxford, 1975; J. R. Maddicott, *The English Peasantry & the Demands of the Crown, 1294–1341 (Past & Present Supplement, 1, 1975).*

TITHES Since before the Norman Conquest the rector of a parish had been entitled to support himself by receiving the tenth part of the agricultural produce of his parishioners. Hence the word tithe. In a wealthy parish this could prove to be a valuable form of endowment. That was why in the twelfth and thirteenth centuries founders of monasteries had often chosen to provide income for their fledgling communities in the form of benefices rather than in the form of land. The new monastery would itself become the corporate rector, and would receive the tithes. Cure of souls would be entrusted to a vicar who would take what later came to be known as the lesser tithes. These might include milk, calves, eggs and young animals. The greater tithes taken by the monastery as corporate rector would include corn, hay and wood.

TOURNAMENTS The highly artificial tilting that took place in the lists in the late middle ages was a far cry from the general melées that tournaments had been a couple of centuries earlier. Tournaments back in the twelfth and thirteenth centuries had little to distinguish them from real battles.

Just how and when the tournament was born we cannot say, but where, we probably can. To go by Ralph of Diss's description of it in his chronicle as the 'conflictus Gallicus', France must have been its birthplace. We can trace the history of these knightly combats as far back as 1130, when they were banned by Pope Innocent II for their danger to life and limb. Nothing daunted, however, the young knights of Europe continued to meet in great tourneying sessions, 40 or 50 of them on each side, fighting from dawn till dusk. These struggles gave young enthusiasts the opportunity to make their name. The *Histoire de Guillaume de Maréchal* tells how William Marshal, a landless knight errant, won such wealth and renown by his exploits that he rose to be lord of Longueville and earl of Pembroke. It was William who introduced young Henry, the son of Henry II (q.v.) to the tournament field – not that he needed much introducing. What was the point of these sometimes lethal melées? For the participants there was evidently the enjoyment of it all. We know that William Marshal fought twice a month in his youth. Tourneying could also be highly profitable for the most successful knight-errants. Marshal was once offered as much as £500 a year each by the count of Flanders and the duke of Burgundy for his services. From the king's point of view practice in arms also served to keep his knights in training for war. It was almost certainly the belief that the French knights were more efficient than his own that led Richard I (q.v.) to legalize tournaments in England in 1194. In practice, however, they must surely have taken place in this country long before that. What Richard did was simply try to encourage the practice.

Richard's enthusiasm was not shared by his two immediate successors on the throne. On the contrary, tournaments were actively discouraged by John and Henry III, and not just because they resulted in so many violent deaths. The main reason was that they served as a cover-up for political opposition. For example, at a tournament held at Dunstable in 1244 the barons agreed on their plans for expelling the papal legate from England. And in 1312 feigned tournaments were used to conceal the rallying of troops to hunt down Edward II's unpopular favourite, Piers Gaveston, who had illicitly returned to England.

The attitude of the Crown began to change in the time of Edward I (1272–1307). In the last years of his reign we still find that tournaments were periodically banned, on the grounds that they distracted knights from the real business of fighting the Scots. But Edward I, unlike his father, actually enjoyed tournaments, and was no mean hand in the lists himself. His policy was therefore to bring the old mass-tournaments under control. What had so often in the past contributed to the turbulence and disorder of these occasions was the behaviour of the esquires who attended on the knights. At Rochester in 1251, for example, they had hammered the fleeing knights with sticks and clubs! Accordingly in 1292 Edward decided to embody in statute form a code of rules that had first been drawn up in 1267.

Knights were limited to three esquires each, and participants were to use only the blunted broad sword for tourneying, not a pointed sword or knife. A committee was set up to enforce the regulations.

By the fourteenth century the nature of the tournament had certainly changed, though less, we may suspect, as a result of Edward I's Statute of Arms than under the influence of chivalric values and Arthurian (q.v.) romance. What had once been a conflict between two massed 'armies' now became a single combat between two champions. Separated by a barrier or tilt, they would charge towards each other with a blunted lance watched by the heralds (q.v.) and by a large crowd of onlookers, ladies included. The tournament had become respectable. It was an entertainment. Nothing demonstrated this more clearly than the so-called Round Tables, in which the actual jousting was just one part, probably only an incidental part of a wider round of social engagements spread over several days. Edward III (q.v.) realized that spending on this kind of pageantry, considerable though it might be, was well worthwhile for the lustre which it conferred on his kingship. In 1343 the expenditure of the royal household rose to as much as £317 a day for the duration of a tournament at Dunstable. Dunstable, incidentally, with Blyth and Brackley was one of the principal tourneying centres in England.

In the fifteenth century the element of display that accompanied a combat in the lists became an end in itself, cultivated to the most fanciful lengths at the court of Burgundy. But it was left to Henry VIII and Francis I of France to set the final seal on the vain posturings of this world of decayed chivalry at the Field of Cloth of Gold in 1520.

N. Denholm-Young, 'The Tournament . . .' in *Studies in Medieval History presented to F. M. Powicke*, eds. Hunt, Pantin & Southern, Oxford, 1948.

TOWNS Although the bulk of England's population lived in the countryside, the towns were vital to the rural economy as centres of exchange and markets for the disposal of produce. Sheltered as they were behind walls and nurtured by the grant of royal privileges and exemptions from tolls, they enjoyed a sense of security which served both to attract traders and to stimulate the growth of non-agrarian occupations. Even so we must remember that the English towns were small. By modern standards many of them would have seemed little better than overgrown villages. London, with a population in the fifteenth century of no more than 40,000–50,000, was the only one that could compare with the great cities of the continent like Ghent and Florence. Even the largest provincial centres in England, such as York or Bristol, would have had difficulty in mustering 10,000 each.

These considerations raise a question that has troubled modern historians probably much more than it did contemporaries; just what was the difference between a town and a village? Size and population hardly constituted a sure guide. For that reason legal definitions have normally been invoked, and the essential characteristic distinguishing an urban settlement has been seen as burgage tenure – in other words, the right to hold land freely for a money rent. So much may well be true, but what really mattered to townsmen was not so much these legal niceties as the desire to have themselves recognized as self-governing communities independent of the surrounding shire. It is this movement towards separateness which formed a major theme in the urban history of the middle ages and which gave the towns their own institutions of government.

When English society was feudalized after the Norman Conquest, the king made sure that he held most of the towns himself 'in chief' (q.v., FEUDALISM) – that entitled him to the profits which were collected for him in each town by the official known as the reeve. Before very long, however, the townsfolk wanted to have a greater say in the running of their own affairs, and at London and Lincoln in 1130 they took the first steps in this direction by winning from Henry I (q.v.) the right of electing the reeve and of themselves collecting and paying over to the king the fixed sum known as the 'farm'. Although this gave them a measure of self-government, the leading citizens still felt that they needed some kind of institution which could express their own interests. This they found in what we know as the 'guild merchant'. Unlike the more familiar craft guilds of the later middle ages, the guild merchant embraced most if not all of the burgesses, whatever their trade. It was the community of burgesses under another name – the guise they assumed to make their demands for more self-government. Just how successful the burgesses were in pressing their demands can be measured in the flood of municipal charters issued by Richard I and John (q.v.). Provided the towns would pay, these two kings were prepared to let them have what they wanted. Constitutionally the result was often anomalous. Towns which had already spawned a 'shadow' government in the shape of the guild merchant now acquired a second and official one in the shape of an elected council with executive officers. These councillors were known interchangeably as jurats, portmen (port = trading centre) or aldermen – borrowing a term used by the guilds (q.v.) – and the executive officers as bailiffs or mayors – borrowing a French word which has survived to this day. Borough community and guild merchant in fact overlapped, and often shared the same officers. They were, if you like, different houses, lived in by the same occupants.

Once the townsfolk had obtained self-government, the guild merchant had served its purpose and faded away. The burgesses had obtained all they wanted from the king. Now they could concentrate on enjoying the higher standard of life that a rising volume of trade brought their way. At the same time many peasants flocked into the towns in search of better conditions than those they found in the countryside. As the towns therefore became more populous, and potentially more difficult to control, so the leading citizens reacted by drawing the reins of power ever more firmly into their own hands. In other words, despite the vague provision in the early charters for officials to be elected, urban government fell into the grip of a charmed elite. By the thirteenth century full citizenship was no longer extended automatically to all those who held by burgage tenure. In London in 1274 the decision was taken to restrict it to those who could obtain it by any of three ways – patrimony, for those born in the city; apprenticeship, which normally lasted three years; and redemption for those with the money to pay.

Not surprisingly, these restrictive tendencies produced a reaction, and in many towns, notably London, the later fourteenth century saw fierce struggles between the oligarchies on the one hand and popular movements led by the craft guilds on the other. It was to give the townsmen a great opportunity to express their views that 'common councils' were grafted onto urban constitutions in the fifteenth century. The way this came about can be illustrated from the history of Norwich (q.v.). In 1417 the old council, which consisted of 24 members, was reconstituted as a committee of aldermen; and a new council of 60, chosen by the four wards of the city, was set up to represent the commons, if we might call them that. 'Outer' or common councils of this kind were established in many towns in the late middle ages in an attempt to satisfy the aspirations of those who had hitherto been denied any say in the affairs of their town. But before long the familiar oligarchical tendencies set in once more. Co-option replaced election, admissions to the freedom were controlled and manipulated, and governing bodies became self-perpetuating elites. In other words, the late middle ages saw the emergence of the notorious 'close corporations' which ran the English towns till their eventual abolition in 1835.

Whether there was any connection between the drift towards oligarchy and the economic difficulties facing the towns in the fifteenth century is hard to say. Did elitist government drive business out? Or was it a response to the fact that business was already going elsewhere? One thing that we can dismiss right away as irrelevent to the argument is the movement towards municipal incorporation that took place at this time. This may well seem more significant to us today than it did to contemporaries. All it did was give the towns the standing at law of corporate personalities. The first such charter of incorporation was granted to Coventry in 1345, and by the end of the middle ages most other towns had acquired them too. What lay behind this enthusiasm for corporate status was the growing acquisition of property by the towns. Of course they had long owned municipal or semi-municipal buildings like guildhalls. But now they were also staking a claim to land that fell vacant within the walls – and after 1348, when countless properties were deprived of their owners by the plague, that could add up to quite a considerable acreage. So the towns became property owners. As they did so, they needed protection at law; and that they obtained by seeking incorporation.

The truth was that many town councils needed all the rental income they could get because the decline in population after the Black Death (q.v.) left them smaller and less prosperous than before. The crowded conditions in the towns enabled the plague to spread quickly, causing a massive drop in numbers. How soon population recovered we can only guess – at Norwich apparently quite quickly, but in many other towns later plague visitations must have prevented an early recovery. As if this were not enough, many of the traditional centres of population, like Winchester and Lincoln, were faced in the late middle ages by a prolonged depression in their staple industry – textiles. To explain this we have to go back a long way, to the twelfth century. The English textile industry (q.v.) had long been run by great merchant employers who treated the weavers and fullers as little better than employees. These two groups, naturally enough, sought to improve their position by forming themselves into guilds through which they could control entry into the

trade and regulate hours and conditions. Faced by this upward pressure on wages at the very time when stiff competition was coming from Flemish products, the merchants retaliated by moving the industry into the countryside where there was already a long tradition of making cloth. Some of the towns, like Lincoln and Beverley, staged a partial recovery in the fourteenth century, but others were less successful, and by 1500 the geographical pattern of textile manufacture looked very different from what it had three centuries before.

The industry had shifted from the old-established towns to areas like East Anglia and the western Cotswolds where swiftly moving streams could turn the wheels of the fulling-mills. The prosperity which textiles brought to the English countryside in the fifteenth and sixteenth centuries is demonstrated today by the noble parish churches of places like Lavenham and Long Melford in Suffolk and Cirencester in Gloucestershire.

It is of course the churches that do most to evoke for us the atmosphere of a medieval town. The division and subdivision of urban parishes in the eleventh and twelfth centuries had left many English towns with a church on almost every street corner. Norwich and Winchester each had as many as 56 churches at the height of the middle ages. Norwich, as James Campbell so aptly puts it, 'was always an over-churched city', and even after demolitions and amalgamations there are still 31 today. But then in medieval London there were over a hundred!

We must remember that in the middle ages parish churches were not places that were visited only on Sundays. They were social centres and meeting places as well. After the citizens of Ipswich had obtained their charter from King John in 1200, it was in the churchyard of St Mary Tower that they met to elect the bailiffs and coroners (q.v.), and again a few months later to hear what these officials had decided. Later on, in the fifteenth century, parish churches became the focus of local loyalties in another way when the religious fraternities under which the guilds (q.v.) so often masqueraded founded chantries and altars in them. Many of these fraternities were modest affairs which could only afford to pay for a candle to burn daily during the celebration of mass. Others, however, were rich enough to pay for the building of a side chapel dedicated to the patron saint of the guild. Sometimes, indeed, the connection was so close that the church became identified with one particular guild or fraternity, as St Helen's, York, was with the glass-painters.

The more substantial guilds and companies had the money not only to endow altars but also to erect halls, like the Merchant Venturers' Hall at York. These of course would be the very grandest civic buildings, and we must not suppose that all urban architecture was on that scale. On the other hand, we would be no more justified in jumping to the opposite conclusion, that every medieval town was squalid and overcrowded. Some no doubt were – Old Sarum, for example, where castle and cathedral were awkward neighbours on a windswept hilltop. That was why Bishop Poore abandoned it in 1221 in favour of a more spacious site a few miles south in the Avon valley. His remarkable idea of transplanting a town from one site to another was imitated three-quarters of a century later by Edward I, who moved the port of Winchelsea from its exposed coastal position to its present location facing Rye. Edward I in fact was keen to promote urban development, not just in England but also in Wales (q.v.) and in the English possessions in France. He was following the example of other lords who had sought to increase their revenues from trade by founding market towns. In all these new settlements the streets were laid out on a straightforward grid plan that says a lot for medieval town planning. Often too the plots – burgage tenements they were called – were quite wide, allowing double-fronted houses to be built. In the course of time these tenements became subdivided, so that tall, jettied houses became the rule, forming such familiar street scenes as the Shambles at York (plate 32). Most town houses were apparently of timber-framed construction, but the evidence suggests that stone, which obviously carried advantages from the point of view of fire prevention, became a more common material in the thirteenth century – for those who could afford it.

And what about the poor? What can we say about their surroundings? We can guess that in the early fourteenth century, when population (q.v.) reached its height, they would have been living in very crowded conditions indeed. But after the Black Death there was at least room for everyone to breathe. There is evidence too that hygiene and sanitation were getting better. We know that from the late thirteenth century tolls were being levied to pay for the paving of streets. One such street, now metal-surfaced but otherwise little changed, is Brasenose Lane in Oxford. Its surface slopes from each side down to the middle, where a gulley carries away the water. It made good sense wherever possible, if these gulleys were not to be open sewers, to run streets vertically up a hillside. The horrors which such planning has created

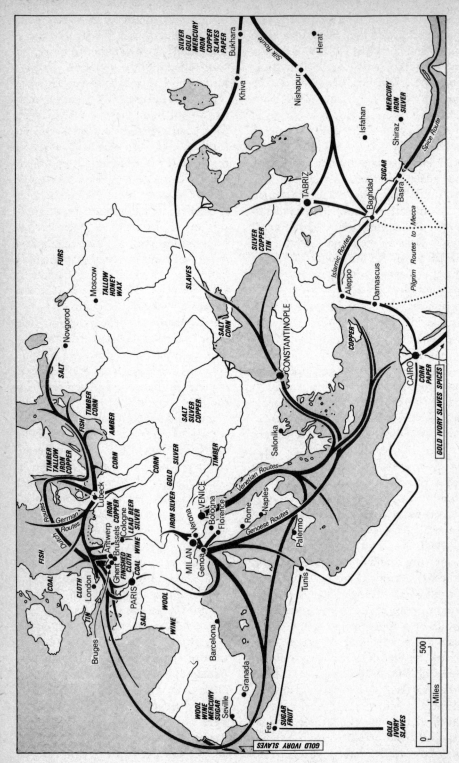

Figure 8 European trade routes in the 1470s.

for the modern motorist can well be seen today at towns like Lincoln and Malmesbury (q.v., ROADS).

Last but not least there would have been the walls – like those which still encircle York and Chester. Just as pavage was levied to pay for improving the streets, so murage was levied to pay for building these fortifications. The walls at Norwich (q.v.) were substantially complete by the 1340s, after half-a-century's labour, but at King's Lynn the circuit proved too much for the citizens and was left unfinished. Thanks to the blessing of a fair measure of internal peace, walls were rarely needed for the primary purpose of defence except in those parts of England along the south coast exposed to the danger of French attacks. Rye, Winchelsea and Southampton immediately spring to mind. Elsewhere they were valued as a kind of glorified customs barrier allowing tolls to be collected with the minimum of evasion. Also, we won't go far wrong in suspecting a strong element of civic pride in the building of walls which symbolized that separation of town from country for which the merchant guilds had struggled back in the twelfth century.

C. Platt, *The English Medieval Town*, Secker & Warburg, 1976.

TROYES, TREATY OF See HUNDRED YEARS WAR

TRADE The map opposite illustrates England's position in the European trading network.

U

UNIVERSITIES The idea of a community of masters licensed to teach at the highest level, in other words a university, is one which we owe entirely to the middle ages.

In the eleventh century there was a revival of learning in Europe which called into existence a number of schools attached to monasteries or cathedrals. Most of them derived such distinction as they had from the presence in their midst of a great teacher, like Lanfranc (q.v.) at Bec. In other words, it was the teacher who made the school. This informality was all very well if the students wanted to get no more than a simple grounding in the arts. But if they wanted to pursue a lengthier course in what were to become the higher faculties of Theology and Law, it would be to their advantage to belong to a more formal and permanent institution that could satisfy the growing professionalization of knowledge of the twelfth century. So the monasteries and cathedral schools were overshadowed as centres of learning by the new schools of Bologna for law and Paris for theology, which were the prototypes of the later universities.

In England no less than on the continent the intellectual renaissance of the twelfth century witnessed the opening of new schools, as for example at Exeter, Northampton and Oxford. With the benefit of hindsight we know that Oxford (q.v.) was to surpass the others in importance, but its early history was not without its ups and downs. The inevitable rivalries between town and gown were liable to lead to violent confrontations, and one of these in the reign of King John ended in the departure of a group of scholars to Cambridge (q.v.). There they stayed, and the sister university was born. The rise of these two universities did not immediately lead to the elimination of the other schools, but it was certainly the aim of Oxford, if not of Cambridge as well, to prevent any rivals from awarding degrees and conferring the licence to teach. In 1264 Oxford used the influence its alumni could exert on Simon de Montfort's administration to suppress the incipient splinter university at Northampton and 70 years later in August 1334 it used similar tactics to thwart a group of secessionist masters at Stamford (Lincs). It was by means of such string-pulling that the 'ancient' universities acquired the joint monopoly of higher education in England which they kept until modern times.

Education in the middle ages was of course a clerical monopoly, its purpose being to train men for a career in the Church. So we have to remember that when undergraduates came up to university at no more than 14 or 15 years of age, they were young clerks in the making. The Liberal Arts course which formed the basis of what we would call their undergraduate years was divided according to ancient usage into the 'trivium' (grammar, rhetoric and logic) lasting three years and the 'quadrivium' (arithmetic, geometry, astronomy and music) lasting another four. By his seventh year a candidate was eligible to supplicate for the degree of Master of Arts for which as for all degrees he was examined orally. Nowadays in Oxbridge, though the exercises and residence requirements it once entailed have long since gone, the M.A. is still taken seven years after matriculation. The more ambitious scholar was then free to begin the exercises leading after about another five years to the degree of Bachelor of Theology and after two more to the doctorate. Interminable as the grind may well have appeared, it was at least shorter than the corresponding course at Paris! In the thirteenth century, in response to the growing demand for well-trained lawyers, Oxford and Cambridge developed two more graduate faculties, namely civil law, involving four year's study for those who had taken their M.A., and canon law, calling for three.

Teaching in medieval Oxford and Cambridge was by a combination of lecturing and disputation. In the schools or lecture rooms the young scholars received a grilling in the works of prescribed authors like Aristotle and Boethius. Once they had familiarized themselves with the texts, and very likely learned them by heart, they were expected to sharpen their wits in that characteristically medieval exercise known as the disputation – where a master or senior pupil would argue a thesis and maintain it against his pupils. Pettyfogging these exercises very likely became, but they certainly encouraged precision of thought and clarity of expression.

Then as now lectures provided by the University were supplemented by instruction given in the colleges and halls. To understand how the system worked, we need at this point to look at the residential side of student life in medieval Oxford and Cambridge. Today we regard them both as collegiate universities. This was not the case in the middle ages. The majority of under-graduates lived not in colleges but in lodging houses known in Oxford as halls and in Cambridge as hostels. These were properties in the town leased on a year-to-year basis by a Principal who took in student lodgers and gave them tuition. St Edmund Hall in Oxford is the one such establishment to have survived to the present day – or rather until 1957, when it became a college in all but name. Having most likely passed their under-graduate years in one of these halls, clerks who wanted to read for a doctorate were then faced with the daunting pros-pect of finding the money they needed to finance the long years of residence that lay ahead. It was to provide the means for them to do this that the earliest colleges were founded in the later thirteenth century. They were corporate insti-tutions endowed with sufficient prop-erty to support a community of fellows and graduates. The first colleges in Oxford were Merton, Balliol and Uni-versity, and in Cambridge, Peterhouse, Michaelhouse and King's Hall, the last two later absorbed into Trinity. The first college to admit undergraduates was Exeter, but then only in the third year of their B.A. course and without any pro-vision for them to be taught. It was William of Wykeham's (q.v.) New College, founded in 1379, which broke new ground in the history of university teaching. According to the statutes, the younger members of the College, all of them of course drawn from the sister foundation at Winchester, were to re-ceive tuition from the older Fellows for a period of three years. It is in this arrangement that the origins of the Oxbridge tutorial system are by tradi-tion sought, though it is fair to add that the originality of the founder's inten-tions are still subject to argument.

Palatial though the buildings of the colleges no doubt were, they housed far fewer students than the halls. In early fifteenth century Oxford the 70-or-so halls were matched by a dozen-and-a-half colleges at the most. For the majority of the undergraduates living accommodation in the halls was likely to be neither spacious nor luxurious. A large-ish hall would have been occupied by between 15 and 20 students, three or four of them to each room. Apart from the Principal only a very well-to-do student, or perhaps a master, would have had a chamber to himself. On the basis of these figures, which admittedly involve a fair amount of conjecture, we can guess that there were something like 1,500 scholars at Oxford in the fifteenth century, rather more than there would have been in contemporary Cambridge.

To say that medieval undergraduates enjoyed few of the comforts of life is in fact only another way of saying that the cost of living was very low. At a time when a single chamber in a college or hall would have fetched 8s or 10s a year in rent, it made good sense for a group of friends to spread the cost by sharing a room or even a bed. Fortunately we have a few figures to show just how cheap it could work out. For John Wood, a student at an Oxford hall in 1424, board and lodging came to 4s 8¾d, or less than 4¾d a week. John Russell, another student in the same hall, paid as little as 3s 4d for seven weeks. Our scholars would have needed some spare cash to spend in the pub or in one or two of the bookshops that then lined Catte St. But by and large life for the under-graduate in medieval Oxford could be economical. It was the length and cost of study in the higher faculties that, as we have seen, moved benefactors like Walter de Merton to found the colleges.

H. Rashdall, *The Universities of Europe in the Middle Ages*, new edn. by F. M. Powicke & A. B. Emden, 3 vols., Oxford, 1936.

VILLEINAGE

VILLEINAGE The origins of villeinage lie back in the Anglo-Saxon period, when peasants were drawn into greater dependence on their lord by accepting from him the gift of a home and some land. They might very likely end up finding themselves tilling his demesne (q.v.) land for several days a week. In the twelfth century, when the king's justices were often asked by lords to determine the legal condition of their tenants, liability to perform labour services was one of the tests they applied. A tenant who did 'week-work' on the demesne was a villein, and one who did not was free. In its heyday in the thirteenth century villeinage was a hereditary condition of personal character. It was not the same as slavery, but it did place severe limitations on freedom. A villein could not leave his village; he had to perform labour services; and he was liable for such payments as merchet (q.v.) and heriot (q.v.). And born a villein, he would always be a villein, and his children after him. What if he were to marry someone of free blood, however? Or acquire land previously held by a free man? Practical considerations like these must have led to a weakening of villeinage in real life. But what did most to bring about its decline was the population (q.v.) fall after 1348, which strengthened the bargaining position of the labouring classes vis-à-vis the lords. The peasants of course demanded freedom when they rebelled in 1381, and for a short while they succeeded in extracting charters of manumission. But in the long run it was the laws of supply and demand which did most to help their cause.

R. H. Hilton, *The Decline of Serfdom in Medieval England*, Economic History Society, 1969.

WALES

WALES Italy, as Metternich once observed, is a geographical expression. The same can be said of medieval Wales. It was a country whose people, united by language, were divided by geography. The very mountain ranges that deterred the English from penetrating too far prevented the Welsh themselves from coming together. At the end of the eleventh century there were three main principalities – Deheubarth in the south and west, Powys in the centre and Gwynedd (or Snowdonia) in the north – and as often as not their rulers would be engaged in either fighting one another or fighting the English. Back in the eighth century Offa had striven to keep out the Welsh in the same way that Hadrian had the Scots – by building a great rampart from one side of the country to the other. Impressive though it was, the Dyke did not prove a lasting solution to the problem of the border; and for as long as the Welsh retained their independence that wide and ill-defined no-man's land west of the Severn known as the March of Wales retained something of the character we associate with the Wild West.

William the Conqueror (q.v.) proposed to defend his newly-won kingdom against the Welsh by appointing three powerful earls along the border, Hugh d'Avranches at Chester, Roger de Montgomery at Shrewsbury and William FitzOsbern at Hereford – rough and determined men whose earlier experiences on the marches of Normandy (q.v.) and Anjou had instructed them in the arts of border warfare. Defence, as so often in history, turned into offence. Before the 1080s were out, Earl Hugh was across the border, fighting at first with considerable success to bring North Wales under Norman rule. However, a major rebellion in 1094 put paid to his early hopes, and the initiative was taken up instead in the south. Robert Fitzhamon, lord of Tewkesbury, advanced into Glamorgan, establishing a castle at Cardiff. After his death in 1107 his successor, Robert, earl of Gloucester, a bastard son of Henry I (q.v.),

continued the offensive, and extended Anglo-Norman lordship into what is now Pembrokeshire. What inspired these early conquistadores was roughly the same combination of motives that had inspired their fathers to follow William of Normandy in 1066: greed, ambition and energy. We must not forget that the Norman conquest and colonization of South Wales was a private enterprise affair, in contrast to Edward I's conquest of Snowdonia in the 1280s, which was state-run. And it was accomplished remarkably quickly too. Why? It was largely a matter of geography. The Glamorgan coastal plain fell to the Normans because it was the kind of flat landscape in which they could practise the tactics of mounted warfare they excelled at. Gwynedd, on the other hand, remained independent for so much longer because its hilly and impenetrable terrain kept out the knights.

Geography therefore enabled upland Wales to preserve its independence and its Celtic identity. What characteristics did that Celtic identity give Welsh society in the middle ages? First of all, it was predominantly a society of freemen Unfree tenants there certainly were, but only in the lowland plains where the manorial system had been imposed did they form a majority of the population. The mountains were peopled by free tenants. Another peculiarity lay in the nature of the seigneurial dues that were imposed. Welsh freemen discharged their obligations by offering a communal render of food and livestock which was less a rent for land than an acknowledgement of lordship, a sort of tribute in other words. The third characteristic of native Welsh society we should notice was its rejection of primogeniture in favour of partible inheritance, i.e. division between coheirs. Inevitably in a country where land was in short supply the result was fragmentation of the open fields. Although the Act of Union brought the English law of primogeniture to Wales in 1536, commentators writing nearly a hundred years later could still notice the effect that partibility had exerted on the pattern of landholding in the Principality.

And above all, of course, there was the tie of language. These, then, were some of the characteristics that gave medieval Welsh society a cultural identity of its own in spite of the all too apparent political disunity. Every so often, however, that disunity would be overcome by the appearance of a leader sufficiently powerful to command the loyalty of all the Welsh peoples. Rhys ap Gruffydd in the later twelfth century was one such prince. Llewellyn the Great of Gwynedd in the early thirteenth was another. Taking advantage of the civil war in England at the end of John's reign, Llewellyn succeeded in extending his rule throughout central and south Wales. But his success, like that of earlier rulers, proved ephemeral. After his death in 1240 Welsh unity crumbled, and with the Treaty of Montgomery in 1247 the English recovered the district between the Dee and the Conway known as the Four Cantrefs. But not for long. In 1256 the Four Cantrefs rebelled and appealed to the new ruler of Gwynedd, Llewellyn ap Gruffydd, who was already striving to restore the dominion exercised by his grandfather. Like his predecessors he was able to take advantage of civil war in England, this time between 1258 and 1265, but after the accession of Edward I (q.v.) in 1272 he had to face a masterful king fully determined to enforce his overlordship in North Wales. Edward was provided with an excuse for intervention when Llewellyn's brother Dafydd took shelter in England following an unsuccessful bid

for power in the Principality. In 1277 what is known rather misleadingly as the first Welsh War broke out, and Edward recovered two of the Four Cantrefs. Five years later with the second Welsh War he ended Welsh independence altogether. When next there was a Prince of Wales, in 1301, it was not a native princeling but the young heir to the English throne.

The conquest of Gwynedd was very different, as we have seen, from the conquest of Glamorgan. It was an act of state. The castles built in the south were privately held. The castles built to encircle Snowdonia were the king's. On the other hand, the techniques used to perpetuate and entrench English rule were much the same. Colonists were established on lands forfeited by the Welsh. New towns were founded. In Wales towns were in fact largely, though not wholly, Anglo-Norman creations. Back in the reign of Henry I the native population had been expelled from Pembroke to make way for Flemish settlers. Again, in the reign of Edward I plantation boroughs were established regardless of the disruption caused to any existing community, be it a Welsh town as at Beaumaris or an abbey as at Conway. At Beaumaris Edward even went so far as to fine a doctor and more than 30 others for unreasonable delay in getting out!

Although there is considerable evidence for what has been termed easy collaboration between English and Welsh in the fourteenth century, the ruthlessness with which the Edwardian settlement was carried out contributed to an under-current of anti-English sentiment. The racial distinction between English and Welsh was one of the most striking characteristics of late-medieval Wales. The new administration recruited most of its senior officials from people of English descent. The lower ranks were staffed by Welshmen certainly; but a Welsh gentleman observing that between 1284 and 1343 not one of the justiciars or chamberlains of North Wales was of his own nationality would be right to conclude that the channels of promotion were well and truly blocked. If there was little outward expression of discontent, apart from attacks on English officials and burgesses in the 1340s, it seems likely that hostility towards English domination was the mainspring of Glendower's rebellion in the early fifteenth century.

Owen Glendower (q.v.) was a well-to-do squire whose estates in North Wales lay close to those of Reginald, Lord Grey of Ruthin. We will probably never know what was the real cause of the feud between them, but a feud there was in 1400, and within a few years it had developed into a full-scale national uprising which it was to take Henry IV's government the best part of a decade to put down. Feelings evidently ran deep, but time was a great healer. Wales was to cause no more problems for English kings in the fifteenth century.

J. E. Lloyd, *History of Wales from the Earliest Times to the Edwardian Conquest*, 2 vols., London, 1911; R. R. Davies, *Lordship and Society in the March of Wales, 1282–1400*, Oxford, 1978, and 'Colonial Wales', *Past & Present*, 65 (1974).

WARDROBE See GOVERNMENT.

WARDSHIP If a feudal tenant died leaving an heir under age, custody of the heir and of his inheritance passed to the lord of whom the lands were held. The lord possessed rights of 'wardship' which lasted until the heir came of age (21 in the case of a man, 14 in the case of a married and 16 an unmarried girl). Wardship was one of the most valuable of all feudal perquisites because it gave a lord temporary possession of an inheritance which he could then either exploit directly or sell to the highest bidder for the duration of the minority. Abuse of the right of wardship in the reign of William II (q.v.) led Henry I (q.v.) to promise that, if granted away, wardships should be given to the widow or next-of-kin of the deceased tenant. Even so both the king and his barons continued to exploit wardships that came into their hands to the full, until the development in the fourteenth century of the form of trust known as the 'enfeoffment to us' provided a legal means whereby this unfortunate consequence of a minority could be avoided.

See also, FEUDALISM.

WHITTINGTON, RICHARD The legend of Dick Whittington and his cat, like a number of other bygone legends, has just enough grounding in historical fact to give it a ring of truth. According to the nursery story, Dick left home to make his fortune in London. He found employment as a kitchen scullion in the house of a merchant whose ships plied the route between England and the Barbary coast. On one occasion the merchant asked his servants if they would each like to contribute some object or possession that would bring good luck to the ship on its passage. Dick gave his cat. When the ship arrived at its destination, the sultan was delighted beyond measure with the cat, because it would rid his palace of its mice and vermin. He showed his gratitude by giving more for it than for anything else on board, and Dick was set on the road to prosperity.

As James Tait once showed, the story of a cat bringing its owner a fortune is a familiar one. We needn't suppose that there is any more truth in this yarn than in any of the others, but the notion of a poor lad made good may not be so far off the mark. Dick's father was Sir William Whittington of Pauntley (Gloucs.). Being the third son, the young lad stood little chance of inheriting the family estates. So he packed his bags and went to London (q.v.), where he accumulated a fortune in the mercery trade. Once he had some capital to spare, he started lending, principally it seems to the king. This was a risky business because a creditor could never be sure of getting his money back, and in financial terms there was little to gain, as loans to the crown did not carry interest. What made lending worthwhile was the access it brought to the corridors of power, as we can see in Whittington's case when he became a member of Henry IV's council in 1400. His links with the court can be traced further back, to the days of Richard II in fact, when the high regard in which he was held carried him to the mayoralty for the first time: Adam Bamme, the mayor of 1397, died during his term of office, and Richard appointed Whittington to take his place until the next election. As it happened, he was then elected for the following year. Whittington served as mayor twice more, in 1406–7 and 1419–20, and as an M.P. in 1416.

The public career of this successful London mercer can therefore be traced in fair detail; it is his personality that proves more elusive. The list of testamentary benefactions in a will often takes us as near to a man as we are ever likely to get when dealing with the middle ages. We can see what it was he had to give away, and who it was that he remembered with gratitude and affection. But in the case of Whittington it is what is omitted from the will that matters. He made no bequests to any of his relatives, friends or servants. His elder brother Robert, now lord of Pauntley, was still alive, but he got nothing. Richard was in touch with him from time to time, but his relationship with his family was evidently not close. Richard had become a Londoner even to the extent, unusual for a merchant, of keeping his fortune in liquid capital rather than choosing to invest it in a country estate. Maybe it was because he had no children. His wife Alice, daughter of Sir Ivo Fitzwaryn, had died before 1414, and he did not marry again. He used much of his fortune to found a college of priests at the church of St Michael, Paternoster Royal, and almshouses for 13 poor men and women. He died in 1423, and was buried in St Michael's.

C. Barron, 'Richard Whittington: the Man behind the Myth', in *Studies in London History presented to P. E. Jones*, ed. A. E. J. Hollaender & W. Kellaway, Hodder & Stoughton, 1969.

WILLIAM I The twin disadvantages of illegitimate birth and the early loss of his father condemned William to an uncertain and unpromising start in life. Yet, despite all the difficulties that lay in his path, he made himself one of the most powerful rulers in the Europe of his day.

William was born at Falaise, probably in 1028, the bastard son of Robert I, duke of Normandy, and Herleve, a tanner's daughter. Though illegitimate, he was allowed to succeed to the duchy in 1035, after his father had died on the way back from the Holy Land. In the middle ages royal minorities were all too often accompanied by a collapse in public order, and this was no exception.

Normandy (q.v.) lapsed into a civil war that was to last the best part of the next ten years. It came to an end in 1047, when William's feudal overlord, King Henry I of France, intervened on his behalf and defeated the rebels at the battle of Val-es-Dunes. But if Henry did not want Normandy to descend into anarchy, neither did he want it to grow into a powerful state overshadowing his own. So once William's authority was restored, he switched his support to Geoffrey, count of Anjou, whom he joined in an attack on Normandy that ended humiliatingly in their joint defeat at Mortemer in February 1054. William was at last free from danger, both internal and external. Indeed, nine years later, after both Henry and Geoffrey had passed from the scene, he was able to carry the war into the enemy camp by occupying Maine, the buffer state which separated Normandy from Anjou. The security which this gave him on his southern border was important in allowing him to depart for England in 1066.

The nature of William's claim to the English throne is a subject which has given rise to much discussion. According to Norman sources, in 1051 he was given a promise of the succession by the childless King Edward the Confessor, whose action seems to have provoked his over-mighty subjects, the Godwin family, into open rebellion. Godwin, earl of Wessex, and his sons, Harold among them, fled from England, but their triumphant return in the following year made Edward's promise to William practically worthless. There matters rested until about 1064, when Harold made his famous visit to Normandy depicted on the Bayeux Tapestry (q.v.). Just why Harold was crossing the Channel we shall never know. The Tapestry simply tells that he was ship-wrecked on the coast of Ponthieu, and that he was transferred to the keeping of Duke William, whose vassal he became in the course of their expedition against the count of Brittany. After returning to Normandy, Harold swore an oath of allegiance to William, which may have included some obligation to uphold the latter's interests at the English court. But after King Edward's death on 5 January 1066 Harold seized the throne, and was crowned the following day. William decided to challenge Harold's possession of the throne, and having obtained papal support assembled a fleet on the Norman coast. He was prevented from sailing as planned in September by the same northerly winds that brought the other claimant, Harold Hardrada, king of Norway, down from Scandinavia to the Yorkshire coast. It was in fact while Harold was in the north, defeating the Norwegians at Stamford Bridge (25 September) that William landed on the Sussex coast, at Pevensey (28 September). Harold marched south again, pausing only at London before he advanced to meet the Normans on a hill, on the edge of the Weald some six miles north of Hastings (q.v.). In the battle that followed (14 October) William emerged as king of England. He was crowned on Christmas Day in Westminster Abbey.

The new king's immediate task was to turn the victory at Hastings into the conquest and settlement of England. Here William was lucky in the support which he received from a tightly-knit, if aggressive, Norman nobility whom he amply rewarded with estates in England, granted in return for the performance of military service. This was the system we know as feudalism (q.v.). The knights whom his tenants-in-chief provided were in constant demand, both in England to crush rebellions in 1068, 1069 and 1070 and across the Channel to recover the city of Le Mans which had rebelled against Norman rule in 1069. Nor was William ever to be entirely free from the fear that another attack might be launched on England from Scandinavia. Cnut of Denmark was planning just such an attempt in 1086 before he was assassinated.

While William was in England, it was his wife Matilda who carried on the government of Normandy, and did it very well. But so far as his sons were concerned, he was hardly any luckier than Henry II (q.v.) was to be a century later. In his final years William was troubled by rebellions led by his eldest son, Robert, which were the more dangerous for bringing together the discontented Norman barons in alliance with Philip I, king of France. It was to cope with the threat from France that William embarked on a campaign in August 1087 that proved to be his last. He was thrown from his horse in the town of Mantes, sustaining injuries from which he died at Rouen on 9 September. His body was interred in the abbey of St Stephen which he had founded at Caen.

William himself was one of the outstanding rulers of his age. His reign coincided with the most creative and expansionist era in the history of the duchy, when Norman ambitions found expression not only in the conquest of England but also in the foundation of the kingdom of Sicily. The battle of Hastings (q.v.) changed the course of English history because it brought about the formation of a cross-Channel dominion over which William ruled as king-duke. England ceased to be an island state, and was not to be one again until the fall of Normandy to the French in 1204.

D. C. Douglas, *William the Conqueror*, Eyre Methuen, 1964; R. A. Brown, *The Normans and the Norman Conquest*, Constable, 1969.

WILLIAM II The second of the Norman kings, known to history as 'Rufus' from his ruddy complexion, was a man whose harsh personality was relieved by none of the good-natured qualities that redeemed his elder brother Robert nor by any of the administrative ability displayed by his younger brother Henry (q.v.). Consequently his reign was remembered chiefly for its oppressiveness.

William the Conqueror died on 9 September 1087. He was succeeded in Normandy (q.v.) by his eldest son Robert and in England by his second son William Rufus. In his youth the new king had been taught by the great Lanfranc (q.v.), but to little advantage. Rufus turned out to be perhaps the most irreligious of our kings, and his efforts to plunder the English Church can be matched only by those of Henry VIII. After Lanfranc died in 1089, he kept the see of Canterbury (q.v.) vacant for four years until 1093 when he lay ill, on the point of death as he thought, and fear compelled him to agree to the appointment of the saintly Anselm (q.v.). He recovered, and no doubt regretted his decision ever afterwards. He and Anselm soon quarrelled. In November 1097 the latter went abroad, where he remained until the accession of Henry I in 1100. The voluntary exile of his archbishop was a slight hindrance for Rufus from the public relations standpoint, but hardly any more, because it provided him with the chance to seize the revenues of Canterbury for the rest of his reign.

He needed all the money he could find to pay for military activity both at home and in Normandy. The problem was that the division of the Conqueror's dominions satisfied no one. William wanted to win Normandy and Robert, rather more half-heartedly, to win England. Thus there was bound to be conflict between the two brothers. Within a year of his coming to the throne Rufus was faced with the first rebellion mounted against him by those who passed as Duke Robert's supporters in England. In fact the prime-mover of this revolt in 1088 was Odo, bishop of Bayeux and earl of Kent, a shifty character who operated more in his own interests than in those of any nominal superior. The rebellion, though failing to win much support from Robert himself, detained Rufus in sieges at Pevensey, Tonbridge and finally at Rochester, where Odo gave himself up. The next uprising came in 1095, when Robert de Mowbray, earl of Northumberland and his supporters tried replacing Rufus. Once again they failed.

That was the last rebellion Rufus faced. Serious though such disaffection may have been, it did not prevent him from taking the offensive against the opposite camp. When he crossed the Channel in 1091, support for Robert melted away, and the duke had to make a settlement granting his brother considerable lands in the duchy. When Rufus finally did have the chance to reunite Normandy with England, however, it came not by force of arms. In 1096 Robert decided to join the First Crusade (q.v.). To equip an army he needed money, and he therefore decided to pawn the duchy to his brother for 10,000 marks of silver. By 1097 Normandy was in Rufus's hands.

William Rufus is today less known for what he did in this life than for the way in which he left it. On 2 August 1100 he was hit by an arrow while engaging in his favourite pursuit – hunting – in the New Forest. Was it an accident? Or was it an assassination? Like the disappearance of the princes in the Tower, it is an interesting historical mystery and one to which we will never know the answer. But there is just the possibility that a plot was hatched involving another of those hunting that day – Rufus's younger brother Henry, who immediately slipped off to be crowned king.

Rufus, it is said, was mourned only by his mercenaries. The body was dumped on a cart and carried to Winchester, where it was buried without any religious ceremony under the central tower of the cathedral. Seven years later the tower fell down, and the monks thought it was God's judgement on them for accepting so notorious an enemy of Christ and his Church. Had they paused to consider the number of other newly-built towers that came tumbling down, the monks might have blamed the foundations instead. But looking at Rufus's career they must have thought that their fears were well-placed. He was irreligious, and ignored spiritual guidance. He treated the temporalities of the Church merely as a supplement to royal revenues. His court had an unsavoury reputation. He never married, and unlike his younger brother Henry he never had any bastard children – shreds of evidence that suggest he may have been a homosexual. Rufus was a king who treated the lands he ruled simply as taxable resources, ripe for exploitation. He was not a bad king in the sense of being ineffective. His subjects must have thought him all too effective. His rule was predatory. He took much and contributed little. For that reason the evil reputation he has left behind him is probably justified.

E. Mason, 'William Rufus: Myth and Reality', *Jnl. of Medieval History*, iii (1977).

WORCESTER, WILLIAM Local antiquarianism and topographical studies are a distinctively English contribution to the sum of historical knowledge, and one which the English gentry made very much their own in the golden age of such amateur scholarship in the eighteenth century. Sir William Dugdale's great volume on Warwickshire, published in 1656, was only the first of a long line of county histories that was to include Atkyns' *Gloucestershire*, Duncomb's *Buckinghamshire* and Nash's *Worcestershire*. But the tradition of topographical and antiquarian writing stretched way back past Dugdale. John Leland, though no longer credited with being Henry VIII's court antiquary – that was a myth thought up later by Camden – was busily jotting down notes as he journeyed round England in the sixteenth century. And long before him William Worcester was doing the same in the more hazardous days of the Wars of the Roses (q.v.).

Worcester in fact was the father of English antiquarian studies. Born at Bristol in about the 1420s, he was educated at Oxford, and probably resided at Hart Hall, now Hertford College. By 1438 he had passed into the service of the distinguished, though by now elderly and irascible, Sir John Fastolf of Caister in Norfolk (q.v.). After Fastolf's death in 1459 he was to complain that he had spent the previous ten years ministering night and day to his invalid master. He also thought himself singularly ill-rewarded for these long years of service. In an earlier age a secretary and amanuensis would have been a cleric supported by the revenues of a church living. Worcester, however, was a layman, and had to support a wife and family on the salary paid by his master. To make matters worse, no provision was made for him in Fastolf's will. Ready as he was to criticise the tight-fistedness of his late employer, Worcester nevertheless fought doggedly for the next 11 or 12 years to see that the terms of his will were carried out when they were challenged by the duke of Norfolk. Only with reluctance did he agree to abandon the struggle in 1470 when he accepted a settlement of the debts still owing to him in return for allowing the archbishop of Canterbury to transfer administration of the estate to Bishop Wainfleet of Winchester.

That left him with more time to pursue his topographical interests. However, we must not suppose that travel was just the way he chose to idle away the years of his leisure. He was first and foremost a man of business, and his journeys around England on Fastolf's behalf had already enabled him to see much of the country. But at last he was free to set out on the long trip to St Michael's Mount on which he had set his heart for years. As usual he took his notebook with him and jotted down details about the places he passed through and the churches he looked at. He may have intended eventually to write them up in a finished version; but when he died in 1482 it was only the notes that he left. Though he is chiefly remembered for his topographical collections, Worcester was a man of wide interests, and astronomy, heraldry and natural history were just some of the subjects that engaged his attention.

See also, PASTON LETTERS.

K. B. McFarlane, 'William Worcester: A Preliminary Survey', *Studies Presented to Sir Hilary Jenkinson*, ed. J. C. Davies, Oxford, 1957.

WINDSOR The present fairy-tale skyline of Windsor Castle, so captivating from afar, was largely the creation of Wyatville in the nineteenth century. Close inspection reveals much of the exterior crenellation to be Gothick rather than Gothic. Even so, the castle which we see today is one of the oldest royal residences in England. In Saxon times the royal palace had been a few miles downstream at Old Windsor, but William the Conqueror chose to erect his new fortification on the steep precipice above the Thames at what is present-day Windsor. Its lay-out, which still governs the plan of the present 13-acre castle, was a variant of the familiar motte-and-bailey scheme: for instead of being defended by a single bailey, the motte was flanked by two, the present Upper and Lower Wards. For the next two centuries there was little to distinguish Windsor from any other royal castle that the king periodically visited. It was not even rebuilt in stone until the reign of that enthusiastic castle builder, Henry II (c. 1165–78). The turning-point in its history came with Edward III's foundation of the Order of the Garter in 1348, when the chapel was reconstituted and dedicated to St George, the patron saint of the Order. Edward III not only inaugurated the long connection between Windsor and the nation's oldest order of chivalry; he also turned the castle into a royal palace, and remodelled the Round Tower and the private apartments in the latest fashions of the day. It was not, however, until the reign of Edward IV that the present magnificent Chapel of St George was begun (1472–1503), to the designs of Henry Janyns and William Vertue. Edward himself was the first king to be interred there, and under his Tudor successors Windsor rivalled Westminster Abbey as a burial place for the royal family.

See also, CASTLES.

WYCLIFFE, JOHN An academic turned controversialist, John Wycliffe was the man from whom the Lollard movement derived its philosophy and inspiration.

He was probably born in Yorkshire in about 1330, but the first we hear of him is at Oxford (q.v.), where he became a Fellow of Merton in 1356. Four years later in 1361 he was elected Master of Balliol. Distinguished though these academic appointments may sound to us today, in the middle ages they were little more than stepping stones to ecclesiastical preferment, and when the Balliol living of Fillingham (Lincs.) came up in 1361, Wycliffe immediately took it. Not that he had any intention of leaving Oxford for good. Within two years he was back, and had taken lodgings at Queen's, a college which had accommodation to spare. His benefice at Fillingham was worth £20 a year, which gave him enough to live on after he had paid a curate to perform the services in his absence. Cash-flow problems forced him to exchange it for the less lucrative living of Ludgershall (Bucks.) in 1368, but that didn't matter too much because by then he had acquired a prebend in the collegiate church of Westbury-on-Trym (Gloucs.). As his critics have not hesitated to point out, Wycliffe like many other medieval scholars was an absentee pluralist. Of course, there was nothing unusual in that. Absenteeism was the price the medieval Church had to pay if its clergy were to be provided with the means to study at a distant university. But it does seem hypocritical of Wycliffe himself to practise the very abuses he was so ready to criticize in others. All we can say is that, judging from his writings, he seems never to have been conscious of this inconsistency.

By the 1370s Wycliffe's intellectual distinction and polemical skills had brought him to the attention of a government seeking somehow to launch an attack on the 'possessioners', the great property-holders in the Church. Ever since the reopening of the Hundred Years War (q.v.) with France in 1369, the English had been thrown onto the defensive. The continued absence of any outstanding victories in the field made the Commons in parliament (q.v.) ever more reluctant to make grants of national taxation (q.v.). If further wealth was to be tapped to pay for the war effort, the Church was the obvious target. In the closing years of Edward III's reign, therefore, the anti-clerical party at court, led by John of Gaunt, duke of Lancaster (q.v.), made use of Wycliffe's pen to launch an attack on papal supremacy and clerical immunity from taxation.

Wycliffe proved only too willing to oblige because the government's policy accorded with his own views. He was asked to justify releasing the secular state from any subordination to the authority of the Church. This he did by a consideration of the related questions of dominion and grace. It was generally agreed by all that 'dominion' or lordship had been instituted over society by God, but beyond that opinions differed. According to the extreme papal theorists, like Giles of Rome, lordship was bestowed by God on secular rulers through the mediation of the Church. No, it was not as simple as that, came the reply. According to the Franciscans, the exercise of lordship was dependent upon being in a state of grace, a quality the Church could never attain until it had divested itself of its vast worldly wealth. With this view Wycliffe was fully in agreement. And he went on to claim that an anointed king had a divine mandate to undertake the reform of the Church within his own realm. All this was just what John of Gaunt wanted to hear – and

predictably it drew a counter-attack from the Church. Wycliffe was summoned to appear before William Courtenay, bishop of London, in St Paul's on 19 February 1377, but the meeting broke up in disorder before his teaching could be condemned.

Had Wycliffe contented himself with scourging the possessioners and attacking papal supremacy, he would have been regarded as an inconvenient polemicist, but no more. After 1379, however, he started to question some of the most fundamental assumptions of the Catholic Church. In the generation before his own the synthesis of reason and faith so painstakingly effected by Aquinas had come under attack from William of Ockham (q.v.), a distinguished Oxford philosopher. Ockham and the nominalists argued that men's knowledge was confined to what they could understand by direct experience. Men could not therefore know God's will and the workings of grace; they were free agents to a greater extent than Catholic theology had ever previously allowed. So radical a departure provoked a strong reply from Thomas Bradwardine, who took the predestinarian position of St Augustine as his point of departure. God, he said, has the capacity of foreknowing everything. Wycliffe went further still: God alone knows who are the elect. He then drew the conclusion that the Church was composed *only* of the elect who might or might not include the priests. In that case there was little point in trusting the clergy, least of all his former allies, the dreadful friars. These arguments supported his own largely instinctive belief that the doctrine of transubstantiation was a trick, perpetrated by the Church, and devoid of any foundation in the Gospels. The sole authority for the Christian religion was the Bible, which he therefore thought should be made available to all in English.

In the last years of his life religious tracts poured forth from his pen in such abundance that they often appear hasty and ill-organized, though never lacking in vigour. Wycliffe was past caring what their consequences were likely to be. In the spring of 1381 he appears to have left Oxford for the safe obscurity of the rectory of Lutterworth, to which he had been presented back in 1374. There he remained until his death on 31 December 1384. Partly because of the exalted patronage he had enjoyed in the past, partly because the beginning of the Great Schism in 1378 had weakened the power of the Church, he escaped excommunication in his life-time. But Courtenay, who was promoted to Canterbury in 1382, lost no time in eradicating the unsound ideas which had grown up in the country's foremost university. Wycliffe's ideas were condemned (though his own name was never mentioned) at a meeting at Blackfriars, London, in May 1382, known from the event which marked its last day as the Earthquake Council. In November 1382 Courtenay took the dramatic step of holding the next meeting of the Canterbury Convocation at Oxford to enforce the Blackfriars decrees and root out the heretics. Henceforth the Lollards (q.v.), as Wycliffe's followers were known, were drawn mainly from the humbler ranks of the clergy and not, as they had been, from the lecture schools of Oxford.

Wycliffe himself was an intellectual, and a dogmatist at that; and though he was interested in politics, he was no politician. He got carried along by the force of his own rather turgid eloquence, far beyond the limits to which his patrons would back him. Yet he never troubled to institutionalize himself. So consistent was he in his opposition to sects that he did little to encourage the one that grew up to propagate his own doctrines.

K. B. McFarlane, *John Wycliffe and the Beginnings of English Nonconformity*, London, 1952.

WYKEHAM, WILLIAM OF   If ever a man benefited from the opportunities for advancement afforded by the medieval Church, that man was William of Wykeham.

He took his name from the village of Wickham (Hants.), where he was born. He was of humble, though not necessarily unfree extraction, and through the generosity of a local benefactor was given an education in Winchester which enabled him to enter the service of the Crown. At what stage he came to the notice of Bishop Edington, the chancellor, we cannot be sure, but it was certainly at Edington's initiative in 1357 that he was put in charge of the king's works at Windsor Castle (q.v.). This appointment gave him control of the building operations at a time when Edward III (q.v.) was transforming the castle into the 'Versailles of its day'. The evident efficiency with which Wykeham discharged his duties marked him out for rapid promotion, and in 1364 he was made keeper of the privy seal, and in 1367 chancellor. 'Everything was done through him, and without him was nothing done', as Froissart so delightfully put it. It goes without saying that Wykeham was well loaded with benefices along the way, the richest of all coming in 1367 when he was promoted to the diocese of Winchester in succession to his former patron Edington.

Like most political bishops, Wykeham was very likely more interested in collecting his revenues than in attending to the finer details of episcopal administration, but it would be wrong to castigate him as the archetypal absentee. Centuries later, when his political involvements have largely been forgotten, it is for the twin foundations of Winchester and New College, Oxford, that he is remembered. In founding a College at Oxford (q.v.) for the education of the secular clergy, Wykeham did no more than follow the example of others before him, like Walter de Merton; but in linking it with a college of scholars in Winchester, he was setting an example which King Henry VI (q.v.) was to follow in the next century when he endowed Eton and King's College, Cambridge.

It took ten years for Wykeham's plans for New College to come to fruition. One reason for the delay was that his political career had run into difficulties. In 1371 complaints about the predominance of churchmen among the king's ministers led to his dismissal from office and replacement by a lay chancellor, Sir Robert Thorp. But Thorp and his colleagues could do no more than Wykeham had to halt the slow erosion of Edward III's conquests in France, and at the Good Parliament of 1376 they in their turn were dismissed, and Wykeham recalled to favour. This was hardly to the liking of John of Gaunt (q.v.), who loathed the clerical party, and as soon as parliament was dissolved he sought to humiliate Wykeham by bringing charges of corruption against him. The timely death of Edward III in June 1377 brought the bishop's suffering to an end, however, and in the reign of Edward's grandson and successor Richard II he was able to resume unhindered his work on the two Colleges.

From 1389 till 1391 he once again held the great seal (q.v., GOVERNMENT), but in his closing years he retired from the fray to initiate, or perhaps more likely to resume, the long task of rebuilding the nave of Winchester Cathedral. His master mason was the ever faithful William Wynford (q.v.), whom he had engaged to design his two Colleges. Wykeham died on 27 September 1404. He was buried at Winchester in the chantry chapel on the south side of the nave which he refers to in his will as 'lately built by me'. At the foot of his effigy are three mischievous-looking clerks kneeling at prayer – one of the most delightful touches in English monumental sculpture.

G. H. Moberley, *Life of William of Wykeham*, 2nd ed., London, 1893.

WYNFORD, WILLIAM In the later fourteenth century England produced several distinguished architects, of whom William Wynford was one of the greatest. He was probably born at Winford (Som't.), though just when we do not know. By 1360 he was employed at Windsor Castle (q.v.) on the ambitious programme of rebuilding which Edward III had commenced there. Since he is referred to by this time as 'master' (i.e., a master mason or architect), we may credit him with conceiving the lay-out of rooms which was to prove so influential in later collegiate architecture: he placed the chapel and hall end-to-end so as to fill up an entire range, an idea he was to use again at Winchester and New College. It was at Windsor that he first worked with William of Wykeham (q.v.), later bishop of Winchester, who was to be his principal patron and employer for the rest of his life. The noble foundations which Wykeham conceived at Winchester and at Oxford offered exciting opportunities for an architect like Wynford, then at the height of his powers. The two Colleges were in process of construction simultaneously and show many similarities, but the plan of Winchester, based as it is on two quadrangles not one, represents an improvement on New College. Incidentially, in the east window of Winchester Chapel Wynford is shown kneeling at prayer alongside Hugh Herland (q.v.), the carpenter, and Simon de Membury, the clerk of the works, both of whom he would have known.

Before these commissions were finished, Wykeham also asked Wynford to undertake the remodelling of the nave of Winchester Cathedral. Rather than demolish the old Norman nave, he chose to preserve it, reshaping the pillars in the latest style and crowning them with a stone vault that seems to leap up into the sky. This composition inevitably begs comparison with the contemporary nave at Canterbury (q.v.), attributed to Henry Yevele (q.v.), and it is hard to judge between them. Each in its own way is a masterpiece, and utterly characteristic of its creator. Wynford died in about 1403, only a few years after Yevele. With them passed an exciting epoch in Perpendicular architecture.

See also, ARCHITECTURE, ECCLESIASTICAL.

Y

YEVELE, HENRY Though regarded for long as England's greatest medieval architect, Yevele has recently suffered the indignity of having his reputation called into question. His place in architectural history derives from his association with such masterpieces as Westminster Hall and the naves of Westminster Abbey and Canterbury Cathedral. From 1360 until his death in 1400 he held the office of 'deviser of the masonry' at Westminster and the Tower – in effect, the king's master mason in southern England – and was evidently so highly regarded that he was invited by ecclesiastical patrons to undertake private commissions, at Canterbury (q.v.) for example, in addition to his official employments.

If Yevele designed all of the buildings attributed to him by his admirers, he must surely have been a very busy man indeed. But did he in fact design them all? In most of the contracts he is found collaborating with other master masons. In this period, long before the professional architect of modern times had made his appearance, the master mason was both an architect-designer and a builder (q.v. BUILDING). It was he who supervised the labourers and contracted for materials. Yevele as a master mason may therefore have been more an entrepreneur than an architect. The reference in his will to 'my marble and latten goods' points as well to an involvement in the production of tombs and brasses (q.v.).

Is it possible, then, to identify Yevele's work on stylistic grounds on occasions when the documentary evidence leaves us in doubt? Mr Harvey has long argued for attributing the Canterbury nave to Yevele on grounds of its similarity to the nave of Westminster Abbey, on which he is known at some stage to have worked. The account rolls show that he was being paid by the abbey in 1387. But was he being paid right at the start in 1375 when work on the nave was first begun? In other words, did Yevele really design it, or was one of the other master masons, John Palterton for example, responsible? In the absence of any further documentary evidence we can only go by the style, and this points unmistakably in Yevele's direction. Palterton's work, which can be seen in the surviving infirmary, was much more old-fashioned.

How does this conclusion affect the argument over who designed Canterbury? A. D. McLees has recently pointed out that Yevele was not in fact retained as a consultant there until 1398, some 19 years after work on the nave had begun. So much may be true, but he is known to have received big payments from the cathedral as far back as 1379–80, which could only have been incurred in connection with work on the new nave. That Yevele was indeed responsible is also suggested by the close similarity between the moulding profiles of the nave piers and west porches at Westminster and Canterbury, indicating that both buildings sprang from the mind of the same mason. At Westminster he followed the basic deisgn of the existing thirteenth century choir (plate 4). At Canterbury he struck out on his own and produced a work of soaring genius, which ranks as one of the greatest achievements of English Gothic. If Yevele's responsibility for this design is accepted, as it seems it

must be, then he stands out as the Christopher Wren of his age.

See also, ARCHITECTURE, ECCLESIASTICAL; WYNFORD, WILLIAM.

J. Harvey, *Henry Yevele*, Batsford, 1944; A. D. McLees, 'Henry Yevele; Disposer of the King's Works of Masonry', *Jnl. Brit. Arch. Assoc.*, 3rd series, xxxvi (1973).

YORK In the narrow winding streets of York we can recapture the spirit of a medieval town better than anywhere else in England. We owe the survival of this remarkable ensemble to the post-medieval decline in the city's prosperity which left it high and dry until the coming of the railway in the nineteenth century. And then the spurt of building which followed affected the suburbs rather than the centre.

The atmosphere of fifteenth century York is best savoured in The Shambles, once the centre of the meat trade, where one irregular storey overhangs another until the two sides of the street almost meet each other at roof level (plate 32). York is fortunate too in that like Chester it retains its circuit of walls. The stretch south of the river, by the railway station, offers one of the best prospects across the city skyline. The view is dominated today, as it was in the middle ages, by the towers of the Minster. The city churches, never as grand or as lofty as those of Norwich, hardly manage to peep above the uneven rooftops. Like the Minster, however, they have been fortunate in retaining a large collection of medieval stained glass (q.v.) windows, those at All Saints, North St., being the best.

The architectural importance of York is matched by the wealth of its historical associations. In the late ninth century it became the centre of a Danish kingdom in the north. To the Danes it was 'Jorvik', from which the present name is derived. Even after this separate kingdom was finally extinguished in 954, the city remained the unacknowledged capital of the north for the rest of the middle ages and beyond, and when Edward III reopened the war against the Scots in the 1330s he made it the seat of his government.

York was also of course the seat of the northern primate of the Church in England. Its archbishops figure less prominently in English history than the archbishops of Canterbury, but all the same they were great public figures who often found themselves drawn away from their province by the demands of government business. The men who were responsible for the day-to-day running of the Minster were the dean and canons. They it was who had to organize and raise money for the long programme of rebuilding between 1220 and 1472 that was to make the Minster the largest surviving medieval church in England. Its spaciousness and its great collection of glass make it one of the great churches of the world.

The Noble City of York, ed. A. Stacpoole, Cerialis Press, York, 1972.

Appendix I

Kings of England, 1066–1485

William I	1066–1087
William II	1087–1100
Henry I	1100–1135
Stephen	1135–1154
Henry II	1154–1189
Richard I	1189–1199
John	1199–1216
Henry III	1216–1272
Edward I	1272–1307
Edward II	1307–1327
Edward III	1327–1377
Richard II	1377–1399
Henry IV	1399–1413
Henry V	1413–1422
Henry VI	1422–1461, 1470–1471
Edward IV	1461–1483
Edward V	April–June, 1483
Richard III	1483–1485

Appendix II

Archbishops of Canterbury, 1070–1500*

Lanfranc	1070–1089
Anselm	1093–1109
Ralph d'Escures	1114–1122
William of Corbeil	1123–1136
Theobald of Bec	1139–1161
Thomas Becket	1162–1170
Richard of Dover	1174–1184
Baldwin	1184–1190
Hubert Walter	1193–1205
Stephen Langton	1207–1228
Richard Grant	1229–1231
Edmund Rich	1234–1240
Boniface of Savoy	1245–1270
Robert Kilwardby	1273–1278
John Pecham	1279–1292
Robert Winchelsey	1294–1313
Walter Reynolds	1313–1327
Simon Meopham	1328–1333
John Stratford	1333–1348
Thomas Bradwardine	1348
Simon Islip	1349–1366
Simon Langham	1366–1368
William Whittlesey	1368–1374
Simon Sudbury	1375–1381
William Courtenay	1381–1396
Thomas Arundel	1396–1397
Roger Walden	1397–1399
Thomas Arundel	1399–1414
Henry Chichele	1414–1443
John Stafford	1443–1452
John Kemp	1452–1454
Thomas Bourchier	1454–1486
John Morton	1486–1500

* The first date given is the year of consecration, not of appointment.

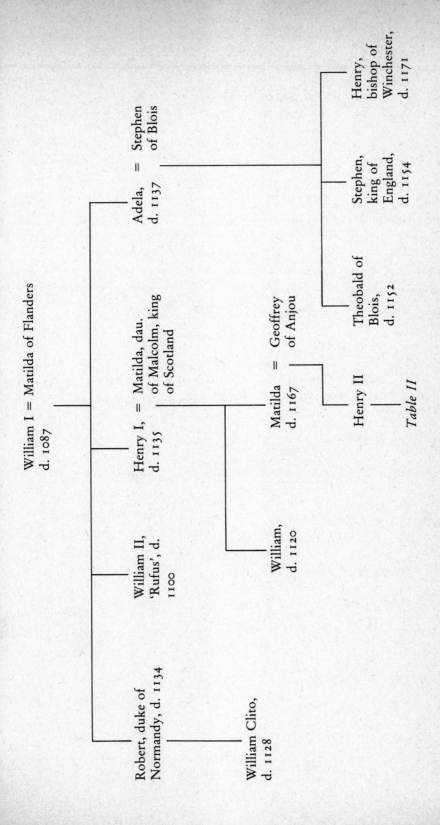

William I = Matilda of Flanders
d. 1087

Robert, duke of Normandy, d. 1134

William Clito, d. 1128

William II, 'Rufus', d. 1100

Henry I, = Matilda, dau. of Malcolm, king
d. 1135   of Scotland

William, d. 1120

Matilda = Geoffrey
d. 1167   of Anjou

Henry II

Table II

Adela, = Stephen
d. 1137   of Blois

Theobald of Blois, d. 1152

Stephen, king of England, d. 1154

Henry, bishop of Winchester, d. 1171

Table I: **William the Conqueror and his Children**

281

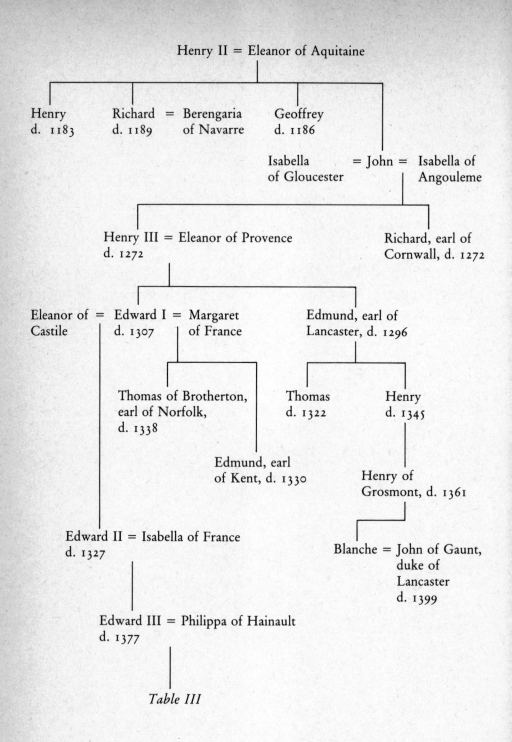

Table II **Henry II and his Descendants** *(simplified)*

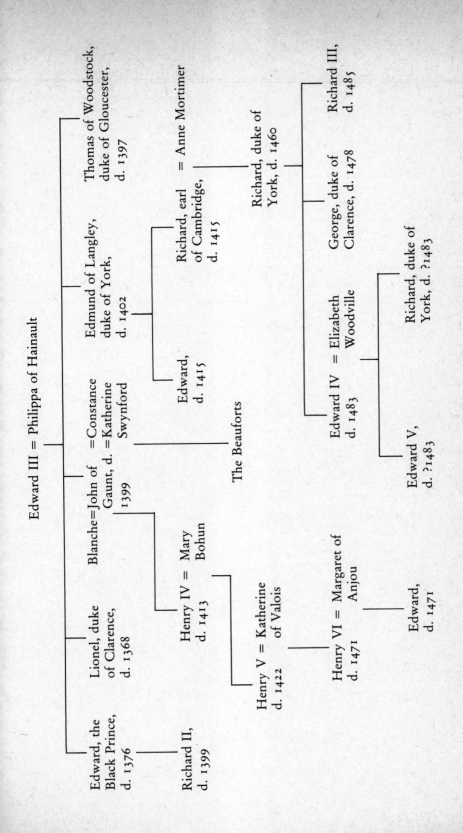

Table III: **Edward III and his Descendants** (*simplified*)